SPINOZA'S MODERNITY

Studies in German Jewish Cultural History and Literature

PAUL MENDES-FLOHR, SERIES EDITOR

SPINOZA'S MODERNITY

Mendelssohn, Lessing, and Heine

WILLI GOETSCHEL

THE UNIVERSITY OF WISCONSIN PRESS

The University of Wisconsin Press
1930 Monroe Street
Madison, Wisconsin 53711

www.wisc.edu/wisconsinpress/

3 Henrietta Street
London WC2E 8LU, England

5 4 3 2 1

Printed in the United States of America

Library of Congress Cataloging-in-Publication Data
Goetschel, Willi, 1958–
Spinoza's modernity : Mendelssohn, Lessing, and Heine / Willi Goetschel.
p. cm. — (Studies in German Jewish cultural history and literature)
Includes bibliographical references and index.
ISBN 0-299-19080-3 (hc)
1. Spinoza, Benedictus de, 1632–1677. 2. Spinoza, Benedictus de, 1632–1677—Influence. 3. Mendelssohn, Moses, 1729–1786. 4. Lessing, Gotthold Ephraim, 1729–1781. 5. Heine, Heinrich, 1797–1856. 6. Enlightenment. 7. Philosophy, Jewish. I. Title. II. Series.
B3998.G63 2003
199'.492—dc21 2003007693

CONTENTS

ACKNOWLEDGMENTS

This book has been part of a long journey. Hermann Levin Goldschmidt was the first to introduce me to Spinoza and the universe of his philosophy, to Jewish thought and the profoundly critical importance Spinoza represents for modernity. His work, thought, and friendship taught me to revisit intellectual history in my own critical terms. Without his unflagging encouragement and support this book would never have been written. When Raymond Geuss suggested I write a book on Spinoza, it took me a while to realize that he pointed out what I had already begun.

Chapter 6 draws on "Moses Mendelssohn und das Projekt der Aufklärung," *The Germanic Review* 71 (1996): 163–75. Chapter 16, "Negotiating Truth: On Nathan's Business," is a revision of an article that appeared in *Lessing Yearbook* 28 (1997): 105–23. Chapter 17 is a revised version of an article published in German in *Aufklärung und Skepsis: Internationaler Heine-Kongreß 1997 zum 200. Geburtstag,* ed. Joseph A. Kruse, Bernd Witte, and Karin Füllner (Stuttgart: J. B. Metzlersche Verlagsbuchhandlung and Carl Ernst Poeschel Verlag GmbH, 1999), 571–85. Chapter 18 is a revision of an article that appeared in *The Germanic Review* 74 (1999): 271–82. I would like to thank the Helen Dwight Reid Educational Foundation, the *Lessing Yearbook,* and J. B. Metzlersche Verlagsbuchhandlung and Carl Ernst Poeschel Verlag GmbH in Stuttgart for granting me permission to reprint revised versions of these articles. All translations without reference, including quotes from non-English literature, are mine unless indicated otherwise.

In the early stages, Ursula Goldenbaum was most helpful in making the Forschungsschwerpunkt Aufklärung in Potsdam a congenial place to start work on this book. During my year as Alexander von Humboldt fellow, Manfred Walther became an invaluable source of support. His expertise and enthusiasm have been a continuing encouragement. The continuing dialogue with David Suchoff has provided an inspiring source of support in developing, formulating, and clarifying much of what went into this book. The comments of Haskell Block, a generous and attentive reader and interlocutor, have been most welcome and helpful throughout. The section on Heine's "Hebrew Melodies" is much indebted to discussions with Nils Roemer. Robert Gibbs was instrumental in helping me decide how best to frame my argument on Spinoza. Martin Yaffe generously provided early versions of his translation of Spinoza's *Theological-Political Treatise*. My special thanks go to Samira and Daniel who both in their own way have helped me in seeing this book to its completion.

ABBREVIATIONS

B Heine. *Sämtliche Schriften.* Ed. Klaus Briegleb. 2nd ed. Munich: Hanser, 1975–85, and Munich: Deutscher Taschenbuchverlag, 1997.

C Selections from "Lessing's Philosophical/Theological Writings." Trans. Henry Chadwick, Lessing. *Nathan the Wise, Minna von Barnhelm, and Other Plays and Writings.* Ed. Peter Demetz. New York: Continuum 1991, 309–335.

CW *The Collected Works of Spinoza.* Ed. and trans. Edwin Curley. Vol. 1. Princeton: Princeton University Press, 1985.

D Mendelssohn. *Philosophical Writings.* Ed. and trans. Daniel O. Dahlstrom. Cambridge: Cambridge University Press, 1997.

E Spinoza. *Ethics* (following number refers to books 1–5, e.g., E2)

P	Proposition
Def	Definition
Dem	Demonstration
Corol	Corollary
Schol	Scholium

HD *The Complete Poems of Heinrich Heine: A Modern English Version.* Trans. Hal Draper. Boston: Suhrkamp/Insel, 1982.

J Mendelssohn. *Jerusalem, or On Religious Power and Judaism.* Trans. Allan Arkush, intro. and commentary by

Alexander Altmann. Hanover, N.H.: University Press of New England, 1983.

Jub A Mendelssohn. *Gesammelte Schriften. Jubiläumsausgabe.* Berlin, 1929–32; Breslau, 1938; Stuttgart–Bad Cannstatt: Friedrich Frommann-Günther Holzboog, 1974–98.

L Lessing. *Werke.* Ed. Herbert G. Göpfert. Munich: Hanser, 1979.

M "Nathan the Wise." Trans. Bayard Quincy Morgan, Lessing. *Nathan the Wise, Minna von Barnhelm, and Other Plays and Writings.* Ed. Peter Demetz. New York: Continuum, 1991, 173–275.

R Heine. *On the History of Religion and Philosophy in Germany.* In Heine, *Selected Prose,* trans. and ed. Ritchie Robertson. London: Penguin, 1993.

Shirley Spinoza. *Political Treatise.* Trans. Samuel Shirley. Introduction and Notes by Steven Barbone and Lee Rice. Indianapolis and Cambridge: Hackett, 2000.

TIE Spinoza. *Tractatus de intellectus emendatione.*

TP Spinoza. *Tractatus politicus.*

TTP Spinoza. *Tractatus theologico-politicus/Theologisch-Politischer Traktat.* Ed. Günter Gawlick and Friedrich Niewöhner. Darmstadt: Wissenschaftliche Buchgesellschaft, 1979.

Y Spinoza. *Theologico-Political Treatise.* Trans. Martin D. Yaffe. Focus Philosophical Library. Newburyport, Mass.: Pullins, 2004.

Z "Ernst and Falk. Conversations for the Freemasons." Trans. William L. Zwiebel, Lessing. *Nathan the Wise, Minna von Barnhelm, and Other Plays and Writings.* Ed. Peter Demetz. New York: Continuum, 1991.

SPINOZA'S MODERNITY

INTRODUCTION

The Scandal of Spinoza's Jewishness

THIS BOOK ARGUES THAT SPINOZA'S THOUGHT represents an untold story of the Enlightenment and yields new insights about the critical impulse that shaped early conceptions of modernity. Although the innovative spirit of pioneers of modernity such as Mendelssohn, Lessing, and Heine has been largely downplayed if not ignored, reading these writers through Spinoza recovers a trajectory whose significance has been marginalized but whose theoretical potential makes it a key moment in the formation of modern critical thought. Although the notion that the reception of Spinoza presents a formative moment in the emergence of modern critical thought has, in the last decades, gained some acceptance, the study of the specificity of the filiations of Spinozist thought in modern German and Jewish thought has not received the attention it deserves. A curious side effect of this development is that Spinoza has been allowed to become a kind of absent presence. A blanket concession of his importance often accompanies sustained disinterest in the particulars of its genealogy, transforming him into an almost invisible figure in the current discourse on modernity. The logic behind this erasure is far from being accidental and helps to explain the similarly neglected reception history of some of Spinoza's most original readers—Mendelssohn, Lessing, and Heine. This book attempts to recover the traces of this historical line and to reconstruct its trajectory as central to the critical tradition that informs modern philosophy, despite its own apparent forgetfulness.

Spinoza's rethinking of the practice of critique, his redefinition of autonomy and independence as self-determination and self-realization, and his argument that the psychodynamic play of the affects represents a crucial form of self-liberation are all grounded in a consistent nominalist and philosophically refined materialist position that makes Spinoza and his reception crucially important to our critical evaluation of the Enlightenment project. The interest of this study, however, goes far beyond a critical recovery of a reception history marked by an unusual degree of extreme historical contingencies, for full justice can be done to the projects of both Mendelssohn and Lessing only when Spinoza comes into focus as the elucidating background. Equally, the poetic and philosophical force of Heine's project regains fuller scope once it is read with regard to its resolutely Spinozist impulse. Spinoza is, at crucial moments in both Mendelssohn and Lessing, the single most important author to inform, support, and define each writer's intellectual trajectory. In both Mendelssohn and Lessing, a radically critical impulse asserts itself against the potential closure of metaphysical thought produced by compromise formations such as precariously secularized notions of the divine in human nature, the immortality of the soul, morality, civility, and tolerance. Spinoza helped motivate and inform the persistent commitment to critique characteristic of Mendelssohn, Lessing, and Heine: the project of articulating, exposing, and examining what cannot be settled a priori. In turn, this new look at the history of Spinoza reception allows us to see the consequence of the marginalization of the "Jewish" reception as a failure to grasp the Jewish dimension in Spinoza's thought as a key to understanding his philosophical project in critical terms.

Whether openly or hidden, Spinoza's Jewishness stands at the center of any discussion of his work. There is no way to avoid Spinoza's Jewishness, as it, in overt or covert form, has come to inform any appropriation, reception, or rejection of his radical modernity. Indeed, Spinoza's Jewishness has been a topic as old as the reception of Spinoza's thought itself. Its discussion can be seen as a reliable indicator of how the process of emancipation, secularization, and liberalization plays itself out on both Jewish and non-Jewish fronts. From early association of Spinoza with Kabbalist thought to the association of his Jewishness with Zionism and assimilation, Spinoza has stood in the cross fire of the debate on the question of the role of Judaism and Jewish identity in modernity.[1]

This is no coincidence, for Spinoza's rethinking of the relationship between the particular and the universal stands at the center of his thought. Resolutely universal, Spinoza's philosophy proposes a theoretical framework that enables one to address the particular no longer as simply opposed to the universal but as linked to and determining it. For Spinoza, the particular thus assumes a constitutive role in the construction of the universal. He formulates a mode of thinking that comprehends the particular and local as configurations of the universal in its concrete, historical, social, and cultural individuation. Behind the scandal of Spinoza's Jewishness stands the scandal of the fundamentally new way he conceives the particular and the universal, which is directly opposed to the logic of most forms of universalism. And the scandal of such a conception of the particular and the universal is the scandal of Spinoza's Jewishness.

Spinoza's Jewishness presents a scandal for philosophy because his approach articulates a profoundly and unreservedly universal outlook that forces philosophy to rethink the claim to universality. In critical contrast with much of modern European thought, Spinoza is so unabashedly provocative because his universalism is founded in his particularity, his Jewishness. The link between Spinoza's Judaism and his universalism has been and remains an irritant for histories of philosophy that—whether secularized or not—ignore the deeply hidden but nonetheless powerful messianic moment of his thought. The endless debates addressing Spinoza either as renegade and traitor to Judaism or as Judaism's finest and most advanced modern representative respond to the challenge presented by his reconception of the particular and the universal, a challenge so radical that it seems to render any discussion of his own specificity impossible.[2] In turn, such a perceived impossibility has given rise to an image of Spinoza oscillating between a conventionally understood particularist and an equally conventionally understood universalist angle. Spinoza has thus been surrounded by an aura of incomprehension and mystery that has relegated him to the regions of an unspecificity difficult to reconcile with his insistently nominalist stance and keen sense of historical specificity. Too universal for some and too particular when historicized uncritically, Spinoza too often is presented as bereft of any specificity. The attempt to enrich the picture with a fuller and more complete historical context counters the efforts of a philosophical historiography that tries to win over even its most outspoken critics to the view of Spinoza as outsider whose own history and specificity presents an underexposed but ultimately negligible past of a self-invented champion on the universal path of philosophy, a path considered as unproblematically always already existent. As a result, Spinoza has disappeared in the twilight of the night, in which—in the eye of the Hegelian owl of Minerva—all, indeed, does appear gray in gray.

While most discussions concerning Spinoza and his relationship to or significance for Judaism are limited to explicitly "Jewish" themes, particularly to an examination of the *Theological-Political Treatise*,[3] I argue that Spinoza's Jewishness, if it has any theoretical import, plays itself out at the central nodal points of his philosophy. As a consequence, sample identifications of Jewish "doctrines" to which Spinoza would or would not subscribe—such as his resolutely anti-anthropomorphic conception of God, whose omnipresence points to rationalist as well as mystical strands in Jewish tradition, and his views on the mortality of the soul, the mind-body relationship, and the position of man in the universe—provide little support for a satisfactory answer. Against such approaches, I propose to examine how Spinoza's philosophical project engages his Jewishness as a challenge that carries great theoretical potential and marks his thought as radically modern.

Spinoza's radically modern universalist thrust rests on a notion of the significance of the particular that figures the particular/universal no longer as disjunctive pair that excludes the possibility of thinking the particular as connected to the universal, that can only posit a universal as devoid of any particularity. For Spinoza, the particular and the universal are imagined in a framework that exceeds an exclusionary mode. Spinoza allows them to be thought together, connected in a continuous chain of being that neither descends nor ascends but connects all that exists "geometrically" in nonhierarchical fashion. Furthermore, Spinoza not only brings such an alternative approach into view but carries out its implications. His political theory, his theory of man, nature, culture, and history, and his hermeneutic theory all share a single critical concern: to reimagine the interdependence of the particular and the universal in a new way.

Yet, Spinoza's Jewishness is a scandal, and one that does not come to an end easily. Or so at least the endless discussions that drive his reception seem to suggest. It is a scandal that with every revival of the debate about his Jewishness testifies to the virulence of the conflict at hand: the scandal that Spinoza is or is not universal enough, is or is not particular enough to satisfy the various philosophical, cultural, religious, and ideological expectations and sensitivities. As long as it seems possible to celebrate Spinoza only as a philosopher detached from his tradition, imagined in a decontextualized environment as an avant-garde universalist, or, alternatively, to figure him reductively as the result of one or another kind of particularism (i.e., Judaism), the critical trajectory of his thought awaits its full realization.

SPINOZA'S MODERNITY

Taking the scandal of Spinoza's Jewishness as an index for the challenge his thought represents as a reconception of the universal and the particular allows us to open the case of Spinoza's modernity in a new way. If we pay critical attention to Spinoza's recasting of the notions of the particular and the universal in a fundamentally new fashion, his modernity will receive historically sharper contours. This will allow us not only to better understand his intervention in the context of his time but also to understand him as a theorist who still provokes and stimulates contemporary critical theory.

If Spinoza's ontology, as I argue in chapter 1, defines the particular and the universal within a nonhierarchical order, the full significance of this new view unfolds only once its epistemological, anthropological, social, cultural, and religious implications gain specificity. The particular drive behind Spinoza's conception of God as Nature or Being reveals its critical impetus when seen as a direct challenge to the theological and metaphysical assumptions of modern European thought.

In Spinoza, this move to a change of how to think the particular and the universal also finds expression in his rethinking of epistemological theory, as chapter 2 illustrates. Spinoza no longer imagines the process of cognition in terms of the classical philosophical tradition as transition or even ascension from a particular to a universal notion of the object under consideration. Instead, he formulates an epistemology that no longer posits any universal as given but starts with the singular object of knowledge from which it proceeds in a nonteleological manner. With the rejection of the classic hierarchical concept of the universal, the particular is no longer cast as epistemological embarrassment but assumes a positive meaning. In other words, the upshot of Spinoza's epistemological theory is that any universal at which we might arrive is always a universal notion based on the particular and only as good and valid as reason's chain of concatenation is grounded in the particulars from which it constructs its universal. As a result, the universal no longer appears as criterion of truth, as measure of the validity to which every particular must submit. Rather, the truth is the criterion of itself and of untruth (*veritas index sui et falsitas*). The circular movement does not indicate a flaw in Spinoza's argument but is intended. It expresses the difference his epistemology introduces into the truth concept that stresses the distinction between the idea and the thing of which we form an idea we call truth.

Spinoza's revision of the relationship of the particular and the universal thus points beyond his own unease with a philosophical structure that determines a key category of thought. His revision is carried out with systematic consistency and has an impact on crucial aspects of both metaphysics and practical philosophy that call for reevaluation of key philosophical assumptions. Spinoza's epistemology suggests that what he argues in detail for ontology, anthropology, and his theory of politics, religion, and culture holds true even for the concept of truth itself. While sharing the critical concerns of modern philosophies of nature from Gassendi to Hobbes, Spinoza's materialist impulse moves in close vicinity but also in distinct difference to this tradition of materialism. If Spinoza responds to the need for a more comprehensive accommodation of the fundamental role of nature for human nature, society, and culture, he does so by inscribing into the concept of nature a notion that differs from the seventeenth-century European naturalism whose roots of persistent dualism inform even those of his contemporaries who consider themselves no longer dependent on Christian thought.

His new conception of affect as the determining force in human nature redefines the relationship of body, mind, and soul as one that is no longer cast in a mind-body dualism as it breaks ground for an innovative insight into the affective economy as the determining moment in the dynamics of human nature. This approach introduces the possibility of conceptualizing individuality as the site where the universal forces of nature cause—that is, give rise to—a particular, infinitely variable configuration of what we perceive as body and mind, a configuration that, as a consequence, represents the universal in the shape of its ever differently constituted specificity.

Although the affects are the determining factor in shaping each and every human in terms of body and mind, they are not conceived as states of psychological consciousness, as chapter 3 shows. Instead, the subconscious, of which they are both representations, points beyond a mind-body dualism to what connects and governs both mind and body but is not completely accessible to rationality. Affects can be physical and psychological, and Spinoza's point is that they are always inseparably both. The central place the theory of affects assumes in Spinoza's thought can only be fully appreciated when the pointedly materialist moment in his notion of the affects is fully understood. It is the materialist moment of the theory of the affects that provides Spinoza with the theoretical framework for a notion of individuality that moves beyond a psychologistic understanding of the individual and provides a strong notion of human nature. Aspiring to ever higher differentiation, Spinoza anchors human nature firmly in a spatiotemporal specificity. The theory of affects thus redefines the question of the relationship of the particular and the universal by relocating the universal within the particularity of every human being, just as Spinoza's ontology does this for everything that exists.

The fundamental importance of the affects for Spinoza is most fully expressed in his theory of politics, as a reading of the *Political Treatise* illustrates in chapter 5. Thanks to his dynamic concept of how the affective economy plays itself out in social and political arrangements, Spinoza is able to formulate a notion of the mass as multitude that presages the modern insight, advanced by Freud, that the individual functions continuously with the mass. By acknowledging the affects as the crucial force at the center of the political sphere, Spinoza moves the focus of his political theory away from the site of conflict between the universal and the particular (between "society" and the "individual"), which was the focus of decisive opposition of classic political philosophy from Plato to Hobbes, to a level where the universal and particular emerge as mutually constitutive forces of the political sphere. The question of the affects thus stands beyond or beneath the conflict between the individual and society, at the center of both the issue of political power and impotence and of the question of socially and politically viable constructions. Just as the affects fundamentally change the way the particular and the universal are thought with respect to human nature, their role, properly understood, redefines how the space of the political is imagined.

This paradigmatic shift achieved by Spinoza's political theory has for some been suspect for its bold departure from what seemed to be philosophically secure notions of the individual's autonomy as mind in a body and of the distinction between individual and society. But the critical point of Spinoza's intervention is precisely to question the self-evidence of constructs such as "individual" and "society." His alternative approach not only exposes the hidden assumptions behind such constructs but also makes it possible to reach beyond their theoretical impasse. What seems like a total erasure of the categories of the particular and the universal—and such a view provoked no small degree of concern and anxiety—is rather an innovative reconfiguration of these categories. As a consequence, the anxiety that drives the traditional view of the particular and the universal as an oppositional pair can be understood as the desire for a security that is refused by the sort of critical look at the constitutive myths of the political that Spinoza suggests.

According to Spinoza, religion serves politics as a myth with a fundamental legitimizing function. Moreover, he argues that religion, genetically and historically understood and in its self-definition, points to a political dimension that constitutes, defines, and shapes it. But this also implies that religion as a function of social and political life does have a positive, constructive significance for how the political is theorized. As a consequence, the problem of religion in modernity emerges as a theological-political complex. This complex, however, seems to resist any critical examination as long as the underlying assumptions on which theology's claims rest remain unexamined. In reexamining the claims of theology, Spinoza brings out the autonomous spheres of philosophy and religion. This allows him, as I show in chapter 4, to differentiate between the universal claims of philosophy and the claims of theology, which he portrays as theorizable only as particular, historically contingent, and therefore nonuniversalizable. For Spinoza, theological claims are thus of little use for normative application outside a specific cultural framework. Although the *Theological-Political Treatise* is on the surface cautiously conciliatory but noncommittal toward Christianity (but still offensive enough to many Jewish critics), it rejects all the universalist pretenses of historical religions on the grounds of a thorough reexamination of theology's claims on its own terms. The hermeneutic exercise of the *Theological-Political Treatise* aims at expounding theology as a noncognitive but distinctly cultural and political practice of securing social control. This hermeneutic thus makes it possible to direct attention to the intrinsically nonuniversal nature of religion and theology. Theological claims thus appear, according to their own hermeneutics, to be intrinsically particularist.

The *Theological-Political Treatise* has traditionally been read as a relentless attack on Judaism and its institutions, and consequently as a blanket rejection of theological claims to power and authority. However, for Spinoza, the theocracy of the state of the Hebrews serves as the only historical model of true democracy, a fact that adds an interesting complication to the *Treatise*'s argument. Its critical approaches to theology and politics call for a different conception of the distinction of the particular and the universal than the one that theology and politics themselves presuppose—and this on the very grounds of the hermeneutics that Spinoza develops through a reading of Scripture. Far from offering a simple reversal of the relationship between theology and politics that would hand the reins of power, previously held by theology, to politics, Spinoza unhinges the fixed alternative of elevating either politics or theology as authority on the distinction of the universal from the particular as he exposes the constitutive particular moments in both politics and theology.

The issue of Jewishness thus returns as a central aspect in Spinoza as it manifests itself through the critical attitude with regard to how he tackles the fundamental categories of the particular and the universal. Although it cannot be stressed enough that the recognition of Spinoza's Jewish background, his family's and community's Marrano culture, and the historical juncture of Sephardic Jews in the seventeenth century is necessary and long overdue, to address the question of Spinoza's Jewishness requires more than historical study. It calls for a reading that realizes the significance of Spinoza's Jewishness not simply in biographical terms as looming before, behind, and around his work but as present at the heart of his writing. Spinoza has long been classified as an heir to Descartes and Hobbes, but his biography, as José Faur rightly emphasizes, clearly points to the formative role that Jewish—orthodox and heretic, even converso—tradition played in the development of his philosophy.[4] Spinoza was certainly not the Oriental that Hegel liked to see in him. Rather, he is a Jewish philosopher who endeavors to write philosophy in which he himself, as legitimate representative of the whole of human society, would no longer be stamped as Jew—as outsider, menace, or "state within a state," as was the Jewish legal status in the Diaspora—or just as a question mark but instead as a free agent on equal standing with everyone else. Deeply inscribed in Spinoza's philosophy, this concern springing from his Jewishness defines the radical nature of his modernity.

SPINOZA IN GERMANY

The traditional view of the significance of Spinoza's impact on eighteenth- and nineteenth-century German culture and philosophy has long been defined by a reading that would identify the metaphysics and ontology of Spinoza as the exclusive points of reference for tracing the stages of his reception. In addition, consideration has traditionally been given to the theological implications of Spinoza's thought as far as they were seen to follow logically from his metaphysics. This view has been largely determined by prominence ascribed to the pantheism dispute (or Spinoza dispute) that Jacobi had so effectively sparked in the 1780s. Jacobi's striking intervention determined how generations of German philosophers would come to see, interpret, and comment on Spinoza and his philosophy. But the biased manner in which Jacobi would fashion his reading of Spinoza as representative of a metaphysical position also led to the eclipse of interpretations of Spinoza that not only preceded Jacobi but made his own reading possible. Through Jacobi, the carefully balanced, differentiated understanding of Spinoza's import for the development of modern philosophy—a development both Mendelssohn and Lessing championed—was virtually eclipsed in a single stroke.

The fact that only traces of this reception have survived in the memory of the historiography of philosophy owes much to the way in which Jacobi launched and pursued the pantheism dispute, creating a sensational stir in the 1780s. In a series of open letters to Mendelssohn, Jacobi claimed that the late Lessing's conversations proved him to be a Spinozist and, therefore, in Jacobi's eyes, a fatalist. Such an allegation posed a severe challenge to Enlightenment thought, for by pigeonholing Spinoza as the fatal example of rationalism's dire consequences, Jacobi forged Lessing's alleged admission of his Spinozism into an indictment of the Enlightenment as a whole. While couched as a sophisticated and profound philosophical challenge, the tactical maneuvering that surrounds Jacobi's charge involves more than simply academic or purely theoretical concerns. Jacobi's pointed insistence on the priority of the practical interest of reason over its theoretical use in addressing the great metaphysical questions, buttressed by the peculiar claims of his interpretation of Kantian criticism, questions the distinction between philosophical and religious categories central to Enlightenment thought. Yet while this subversive approach poses a profound theoretical challenge to one of the crucial tenets of the Enlightenment, it lends itself also to blurring the delicate line separating philosophical argumentation from the personal. Jacobi's charged and highly convoluted argumentation thus did not only disorient Mendelssohn in his attempt at figuring out Jacobi's hidden theoretical claims—claims that Jacobi's rhetorical fireworks made difficult to identify amidst the irritating smoke screen of personal innuendo. Jacobi's unabating obsession with the exposure of Spinozism as the ultimate consequence of rationalism and, therefore, a menace to humanity came to haunt him until the end of his life. As the controversy around Spinoza became Jacobi's platform for the development of his own philosophy, the revisiting of the scene of this controversy with Mendelssohn at the end of his life led him to reveal his agenda in a less inhibited way. While the early letters *Über die Lehre des Spinoza* (1785) presented Lessing in the warmest lights of congeniality, producing a young Jacobi who, though critical of Spinoza, nevertheless played the enthusiastic philosophical ally of Lessing, the old Jacobi—dropping, if only for an instance, all pretense—notes at the end of his life in 1819, "how Lessing had been a Spinozist and how I am none" ("wie Lessing ein Spinozist gewesen, und wie ich selber keiner sey").[5]

And certainly Jacobi's 1819 preface to the third edition of his Spinoza letters left no doubt how deep the disagreement between him and Mendelssohn really runs. Here, Jacobi no longer glossed over the profound theological implications of his earlier intervention, going so far as to advance a principal opposition between Christianity on the one hand and paganism and Islam on the other—an opposition whose implications clearly enough signal on which side Judaism would fall.[6] The increasingly theologically charged tropes of this preface do not shy away from directly invoking Luther and Paulus, and even enlisting Socrates for his cause against Spinoza (351). Indicting in unequivocal terms all that is not Christian, Jacobi's claim for the priority and unchallenged truth of belief resting on religious feeling as the fundament of humanity (350) carries him to a new and bold conception of a battle of God's children against the Titans, a portrayal of disturbingly Manichaean proportions:

> Philosophy of light stands against philosophy of night, anthropomorphism against pantheism, the true rationalism against the inverted mirror image of understanding, Christianity against paganism . . . paganism is cosmotheistic. . . . The faith of the children and the people contains therefore more that is sublime and better than the bare knowledge of the philosopher *without faith*.

> Lichtphilosophie steht gegen Nachtphilosophie, Anthropomorphismus gegen Pantheismus, der wahre Rationalismus gegen ein verkehrtes Spiegelbild des Verstandes, Christenthum gegen Heydenthum . . . das Heydenthum ist

> cosmotheistisch. . . . Der Kinder- und Volkglaube enthält darum Höheres und Besseres als das bloße Wissen des Philosophen *ohne Glauben.* (351)

But already in 1786, as soon as Mendelssohn had died, Jacobi felt free to shed off the smooth but secretive tone for a less charitable one. Now certain to remain the last to speak, Jacobi not only does not feel any longer obliged to stick to honoring the tact of granting peace to the deceased ("De mortuis nil nisi bene") but also seems unwilling to display much of his otherwise so fervently extolled Christian love. Only months after Mendelssohn left the scene, Jacobi's *Wider Mendelssohns Beschuldigungen betreffend die Briefe über die Lehre des Spinoza* accuses Mendelssohn of "pious fraud" that would protect him from catching a cold from the rough wind of truth or the draft of history (278). But Mendelssohn is not only a "sly Socrates" (289) but also dishonest (303–4), charged not only with "conscious untruth" ("wissentliche Unwahrheit") but "intentional fraud" ("vorsetzlicher Betrug" [326]), a man from whose "philosophical synagogue" Jacobi chooses gladly to be banned (324). But Jacobi does not spare rhetorical effects in order to "demask" or rather crush an opponent who is no more. By extensively citing Lessing, Jacobi creates a narrative of a successful enlisting of the great and undisputed authority for his cause. Through the medium of Jacobi, Lessing's voice appears to have been summoned just to quarrel with his old friend Mendelssohn—far beyond their graves. Enlisting passages from Lessing's writings for his crusade against a self-defined form of Spinozism, Jacobi's rhetorical method of cut and paste stages an effective opposition as if Lessing's passages were originally written in order to be hurled at Mendelssohn. And in order to preclude any legitimacy of Mendelssohn's own recourse to Lessing, Jacobi launches out to sever the last and most celebrated link that would connect Lessing with Mendelssohn, *Nathan the Wise.* Already soon after its publication in 1779, *Nathan the Wise* came to play a crucial role in the context of German Jewish emancipation discourse. This drama, in whose protagonist, Nathan, many saw the idealized portrayal of Mendelssohn, served as pièce de résistance for demonstrating the deep affinity between Lessing and Mendelssohn, and by extension as a powerful plea for the emancipation of the Jews.

In his effort to reject such an understanding in a manner that leaves no room for any possibility of enlisting *Nathan the Wise* in Mendelssohn's defense, Jacobi risks throwing the baby out with the bathwater. For he claims that *Nathan the Wise* serves the simple purpose of denouncing all religion:

> The intention of this poem is so obvious that it presents itself to every reader; the intention to put the spirit of all revelation under suspicion and to present every system of religion without distinction as system in a hateful light.
>
> Die Absicht dieses Gedichts liegt ja so klar zu Tage, daß sie jedem Leser von selbst entgegen kommt; die Absicht, den Geist aller Offenbarung verdächtig zu machen, und jedes System von Religion, ohne Unterschied, *als System,* in einem gehäßigen Lichte darzustellen. (310)

The only religiosity left, Jacobi suggests not without guile, is precisely the piety and wisdom recommended by Spinoza. In the face of Jacobi's single-minded manner of ascribing Spinoza an atheist position, Lessing's position is stretched to an interpretation that threatens to undo Jacobi's entire strategy of using Lessing as undisputable authority for his case.

But it is only after Mendelssohn's death that Jacobi shares the most damaging verdict with his audience. While Jacobi had originally simply reported Lessing's apology of Mendelssohn, he now produced a Lessing who regretted that though Mendelssohn was bright, accurate, and extraordinary, he was no metaphysical mind (296).[7] For the reception of Mendelssohn, such a statement proved to be devastating.[8]

It came as no surprise that this dispute, where both sides did not withhold personal insinuations, was linked with calamity, for according to Mendelssohn's friends, his early death was due in part to Jacobi's provocation. This dispute, however, has eclipsed the achievements of the preceding reception of Spinoza, which had created a philosophical climate that allowed Jacobi and his contemporaries to grasp Spinoza's modernity in the first place. Jacobi's campaign sparked and defined the Spinoza dispute, and it shaped the discussion for a long time to come by advancing a particular reading of Spinoza—one that, ironically, ignored precisely those aspects of Spinoza's philosophy that had been the most fertile and productive ones for Mendelssohn and Lessing. As a result, the recognition of Spinoza's significance for the reconstitution of epistemology, political theory, psychology, and aesthetics fell by the wayside.

As a result, Spinoza's signal contributions to the discussion of the theological-political nexus and to political theory, and his key innovative reformulation of the theory of affects, with its refined concept of the psychodynamic economy regulating human nature, have been ignored. But it is precisely in these areas that crucial impulses of Spinozist thought have informed both Mendelssohn and Lessing and have through their work entered German literary, philosophical, and theological discourse.[9]

Recognizing this multifaceted import of Spinoza for the reconstitution of the post-Cartesian agenda makes it possible to read the pantheism dispute in a critical way. Opening the scope of the debate in this fashion allows us to register the multilayered but often coded reception behind the conventional icon of Spinoza as the most vilified and, at the same time, most deified philosopher in modern times. Behind the alleged atheist, excommunicated Jew, and outsider thus emerges a significant source for key theoretical impulses that helped shape modern thought.

Mendelssohn's, Lessing's, and Heine's creative and critical appropriations of Spinozist thought thus give us a better appreciation for the provocation that Spinoza's modernity presents. The recovery of the largely forgotten and obscured Spinoza connection of eighteenth-century thought allows us to recontextualize three key figures at the crossroads of philosophy and literature whose canonical reputations have unjustly overshadowed their significance—an erasure, ironically, brought about by the stature accorded them in conventional historiography. The accepted narrative of the Spinoza reception as a defeat of narrow, rationalist Enlightenment accomplished by a heroic German idealism now warrants revision. Under the iconographic patina the pantheism dispute has created, sedimented over in the historiography of the last two centuries, a fresh, radical, and surprisingly modern Mendelssohn, Lessing, and Heine await us: a Mendelssohn, Lessing, and Heine with a Spinozist edge.

With the emergence of new readings in the last few decades, it is now possible to assess Spinoza's significance for the formation of modern literature and philosophy in Germany in a more differentiated manner. New readings of Spinoza, often inspired by an Althusserian perspective (Balibar, Macherey, Moreau, Montag), but also the work of Deleuze as well as the most recent studies by Steven Nadler, Jonathan Israel, and others,[10] complicate and enrich the Spinoza reception in a productive way. Manfred Walther has convincingly argued for a more sophisticated model of reception history that no longer reduces the reception to instances of wholesale adoption of Spinoza's metaphysics and ontology along with a particular set of theological convictions but, instead, traces the historical impact in different, singular aspects of his philosophy beyond and beneath the limited surface impression of his metaphysics and ontology. Attention to such partial reception of Spinoza's thought, Walther points out, will produce a richer and more accurate picture of a reception of Spinoza's thought.[11]

Reading Mendelssohn, Lessing, and Heine anew thus promises to break the spell cast by the Leibniz-Wolff school and the equally distorting optics of Jacobi's ontological-metaphysical screen. Critical evaluation of Spinoza's presence in Mendelssohn, Lessing, and Heine provides us with an unrestrictedly modern view of authors who are still predominantly treated, in the case of Mendelssohn and Lessing, as doctrinaire Enlightenment rationalists and, in Lessing's case, occasionally also as a post-rationalist of a mystic stripe and in the case of Heine as a post-romantic modernist more by instinct and persuasion than by theoretically informed conviction.

SPINOZA THROUGH MENDELSSOHN

With the completion of the new scholarly edition of the complete works of Moses Mendelssohn, and the new scholarship that has been published in the last few years,[12] Mendelssohn is no longer an elusive figure whose contribution has been hard to pin down in intellectual history. With his writings on literary criticism (most of which originally were published anonymously and sometimes ascribed to other writers), aesthetics, political philosophy, theory of culture, religion, and philosophy now gathered under his name, Mendelssohn's specific project demands a new assessment.

In Spinoza, his Jewish forerunner in the philosophical tradition, Mendelssohn faced an inevitable model for identification, but the comparison was also imposed on him in a limiting way by his contemporaries. For a Jewish philosopher simply "was" a Spinoza, albeit, as Lessing's helpful prognosis for his friend put it, a new Spinoza without his predecessor's faults. Mendelssohn faces this challenge head-on in his first publication as he mounts what in Lessing's terms might be called a rescue of Spinoza. Mendelssohn's aesthetic theory and its constitutive nexus between emotion and cognition reformulates the importance of the aesthetic for the project of enlightenment and emancipation. The results were far reaching: in his contribution to the exchange on tragedy with Nicolai and Lessing, Mendelssohn formulates a dramatic theory that, with the help of his Spinozist aesthetics, proposes a significant (if currently unrecognized) argument for the autonomy of the aesthetic.

In similarly critical fashion, Mendelssohn's political philosophy, his philosophy of religion, his modern concept of Judaism, his theories of culture and tradition, and his approach to the questions of history, assimilation, and emancipation all take their cue from Spinoza. Mendelssohn's introduction to Manasseh Ben Israel's *Vindication of the Jews* and his *Jerusalem, or On Religious Power and Judaism* both illustrate how Spinoza allows Mendelssohn to develop his own position on the relation of church and state and on the legal and political status of minority groups like the Jews.

In his final work, the *Morgenstunden,* Mendelssohn not only defends his friend Lessing as a representative figure for the project of enlightenment, under attack by Jacobi, but also sorts out the politics of Jacobi's agenda. Read as a coded refutation of Jacobi's political and cultural stance, *Morgenstunden* presents a carefully worded endorsement of Spinoza, offered in the guise of a "purification."

SPINOZA THROUGH LESSING

Even if Lessing had read Spinoza before he met Mendelssohn, it was the discussion with Mendelssohn that led to an intensified engagement with Spinoza's thought. Lessing's "Spinozist exercises" document the degree to which Lessing immersed himself in Spinoza early on. Lessing's proto-pragmatist concept of truth bears a remarkable family resemblance to Spinoza's. If not directly derived from Spinoza, Lessing's enlightenment pragmatism attests to the deep affinity between the epistemological projects of the two thinkers. Essays like *Über die Evidenz der Beweise für die Wahrheit der Christlichen Religion* and *Das Testament Johannis* echo Spinoza's *Theological-Political Treatise* and highlight his decisive import for the formation of Lessing's critical thought.

The dialogues on Freemasonry, *Ernst and Falk,* address key notions of Spinoza's political theory. In addition, Lessing's discussion of the relation between secrecy and the idea of the public—a crucial contribution to modern democratic theory—can be fully appreciated only when the Spinozist framework of Lessing's political theory is acknowledged.

If we read Lessing's *Education of Mankind* with the *Theological-Political Treatise* in mind, it soon becomes clear that the former is not, as is often claimed, speculative theological reflection but rather a thought experiment along the lines laid out in the *Theological-Political Treatise.* Here Lessing probes and exposes the limits of theology with a critical intent. Moving beyond the speculative claims of a philosophy of history, Lessing thinks through the conditions for a fully secularized concept of enlightenment. Taking its cue from Spinoza's *Ethics* and *Theological-Political Treatise,* Lessing's text signals its critical distance from theology, naive teleological thinking, and a flat concept of rationalism.

A critical rereading of Lessing's *Nathan the Wise* fleshes out Spinoza's crucial role for the conception of religious freedom that the play explores. Along with an artful use of the miracle discourse taken from Spinoza, Lessing employs Spinoza's theory of the affects, his ethics, and his theory of religion. In addition, the structure of the play follows Spinoza's distinction between three levels of cognition, a model that allows Lessing to distinguish instrumental from intuitive reason. While conventional interpretations stress the play's plea for tolerance, reading it in the context of Spinoza's more challenging call for freedom of religion demonstrates that applying the concept of tolerance to the play produces a hermeneutic screen that ignores the drama's more radical argument for unrestricted freedom of religion and religious difference.

SPINOZA'S NEW PLACE

But it is Heine who first argues for a full recognition of the profound import of Spinoza for German culture. In *On the History of Religion and Philosophy in Germany,* Heine introduces Spinoza as the critical axis for his version of a counterhistory of German philosophy. In this work, Heine presents a counternarrative that challenges Hegel's account of Spinoza, thus taking issue with the grand scheme of the development of philosophy. Heine's daring rewriting of the history of pantheism replaces Jacobi's conventional framing of the question and the historiography of philosophy that follows in his tracks. With Heine's provocative advocacy for Spinoza as the paradigmatic figure in modern German progressive thought, Mendelssohn's and Lessing's projects of critically embracing Spinoza are brought to their triumphant conclusion. Heine's ebullient celebration of Spinoza as the philosopher of pantheist liberation also prepares the ground for a new understanding of culture, tradition, and historiography.

A "pantheist of the joyful sort,"[13] Heine takes his cue for his profoundly modern notion of tradition and history from the striking interpretation of Spinoza that appears in Mendelssohn and Lessing. "Jehuda ben Halevy," the central poem in Heine's "Hebrew Melodies," demonstrates how liberating Spinoza's critical spirit provides a theoretical framework for conceiving culture, tradition, and history anew: not as merely determining factors of human existence but rather as social constructions available for renegotiation in the interest of emancipation. Spinoza's innovative place in intellectual history is fully affirmed both in Heine's counterhistory of philosophy and in his literary practice that carries on Spinoza's critical project. Heine thus represents the crucial link connecting the Spinoza reception of the eighteenth century with the revolutionary force of nineteenth-century thought.

PART I

SPINOZA'S MODERNITY

CHAPTER I

THE NEW METAPHYSICAL FRAMEWORK OF ONTOLOGY

SPINOZA HAS COME TO REPRESENT A persistent provocation for modern European thought. The author of a work notable for the stone-hewn objectivity of its geometrical design has, over the course of the centuries, become the single most attacked, vilified, and, at the same time, the most saintly, even at times deified, figure inspiring strands of the Enlightenment as well as of romanticism and idealism. It is no coincidence that such a powerful resonance has had, in turn, a formative impact on the course of the reception of his thought. The name of Spinoza invokes a reception whose affective overcharge still influences today's understanding more profoundly than is often realized. If there is one common theme running through the reception, it is the continuous testimony to the enduring force of the critical challenge Spinoza's modernity represents.

This modernity articulates itself in the critique it brings to bear on central issues of metaphysics and social and political philosophy as well as hermeneutics and epistemology. The political and metatheoretical impulse behind Spinoza's interventions makes itself felt in the unique way his philosophy, in the eyes of many critics nothing more than another innocuous metaphysical system on its surface, launches a radical critique of traditional thought underneath.[1] As a result, Spinoza's thought prompts a revision of the very idea of philosophy, proposing nothing less than a radically modern type of philosophical praxis.

One of the difficulties in discussing the specificity of Spinoza's philosophy is the question of where and how to start: how to locate his philosophy's beginning, center, or end. Is it the theory of knowledge that lays the ground for his ethics, or is it the ontological framework that precedes and, as it were, foregrounds his thought, or is it his ethics, or, possibly, the critique of religion that provides the ground from which his philosophy proceeds? Attempts to resolve these questions lead to an interpretative circle, reminding us that privileging any one aspect of Spinoza's philosophy would mean ignoring the constellative effect his philosophy produces. Spinoza's metaphysics seems to disorient—or reorient—the reader who looks for a hierarchically structured ontological order.

His metaphysics is a project committed to exposing the lacunae that limit the discursive order of rationalist and empiricist constructions. The systematic interconnection and interdependence of all parts signal Spinoza's radically democratic impulse that challenges the traditional concept of order and hierarchy at its core.[2] The idea of the all-inclusive connection of everything with everything else is grounded in a conception of immanence that Spinoza works out in a systematically consistent fashion. In the perspective of Spinoza's groundbreaking view, nothing can be regarded any longer as a transcendent "beyond," set apart from or granted extraterritorial status in relation to his system of thought itself. Everything has become part of the system's "inside." This use of immanence as a means of conceptual integration considers everything—and therefore every thinking thing as well—as part of a comprehensive metaphysical system.[3] In such a model there is simply no longer any point in locating an outside from which observation or ratiocination would be conceivable as an activity detached from other systemic activities.

The entry of the term "pantheism" early on in Spinoza's reception and the raging battle over how to interpret such pantheism did little to clarify, and even blurred, the issue it claimed to define. Critics scarcely seemed to notice that Spinoza himself, cautious to a wearying degree in his terminology, never employed the term to describe his philosophy.[4] Yet the argument over Spinoza's pantheism, erupting in the pantheism debate of the 1780s, was quick to register the critical impulse that underlay Spinoza's thought. By assimilating that impulse into their various philosophical agendas, participants in the debate used pantheism as a kind of screen that allowed each to steer the discussion in a way that served his own interests. However, the identification of Spinoza's thought with pantheism led to an emphasis of the onto-theological aspects, obscuring the significance of the metaphysical-critical shift that would call for a changed perspective in which Spinoza's thought would present itself.[5] One consequence of the pantheism debate was that Spinoza came to be read backwards, as a metaphysician with his own onto-theology, when his philosophy—quite hostile to any such interpretation—would argue for a discourse free of unexamined theological or metaphysical assumptions and would stress the functional and systemic aspect in his considerations.[6]

Categorizing Spinoza as a pantheist—a position that was instrumental in the rise of German idealism—requires us, however, to overlook aspects that are central to his thought. For, rather than taking the cue from key oppositional pairs such as God/Nature and immanence/transcendence and reconfirming them, Spinoza proposes a fundamental change in the way these dichotomies are thought to play themselves out. Spinoza's reinterpretation of philosophy is part and parcel of a comprehensive critical enterprise intent on revising the classic topoi of metaphysics. Spinoza moves toward a reconstruction of philosophy as he revises its architecture from the bottom up, a project that necessitates the redesigning of philosophical concepts as he seeks to adapt them to the criteria of theoretical consistency.

Although attention to Spinoza's reinscription of key concepts will illustrate the radical break his thought initiates, the significance of his thought as a whole becomes apparent only if the constellative force and comprehensive scope of his overall theoretical shift is fully appreciated. Spinoza does away with ranking concepts hierarchically and instead introduces a conception of equality grounded in ontology itself. He thus argues for a dignity of all that exists that accompanies the onto-theological status of all thought and matter on every ontological level of existence.

As lapidary as the style of the *Ethics* might seem,[7] its basic ontological foundation deploys a circular movement that aims at reconstructing philosophy from a perspective grounded in but critical of the Jewish tradition as well as Descartes and Hobbes. In a paradigmatic way, the *Ethics*' opening definition—that of the *causa sui*—introduces the notion of an ontologically self-sufficient, dynamic substance of everything that exists, thereby announcing Spinoza's signal departure from traditional ontology.

The notion that Spinoza's ontology is nothing but an anachronistic variant of traditional ontology has served to distract readers, however, from the critical effect of the *Ethics*' ontological framework. Though epistemological reflection appears to follow ontology's lead, since the theory of knowledge—embedded in the framework of the *Ethics*—seems to depend on ontology, Spinoza refuses to privilege ontology over epistemology. Instead, the architecture of the *Ethics* suggests that the epistemological project can never fully abstract and isolate itself from the context that conditions it. Consequently, the epistemological project always remains to a certain extent outside the grasp of full comprehension.

For Spinoza, ontology is a way of opening up a critical perspective. His terminological notation highlights the underlying connections that link everything with everything else in an all-inclusive ontological nexus. This pointedly anti-hierarchical bent carries revolutionizing implications for the way in which the idea of the great chain of being is recast. This ontological order no longer imagines the world hierarchically. Rather, emphasis on the functional aspect frees from the perspective of a preordained hierarchy and allows for a view from which phenomena can be interpreted in the light of the new science, but—and this is the turn Spinoza's ontology adds—without losing sight of the fact that individual data need always to be interpreted in the light of the whole. According to Spinoza, all of our discursive knowledge remains necessarily partial and gains its meaning only in connection with the whole, which, however, can never be fully determined in itself but instead is a dynamic concept fueled by the expansion of the knowledge of particulars. The dynamic moment that defines the relationship between the universal and the particular is a constitutive element, endowing Spinoza's nominalism with its critical force.

According to Spinoza's metaphysics, everything that exists is a part, and therefore an expression, of God, that is, Nature or Substance. Substance is the ground from which all being originates. But we cannot perceive this underlying primary Substance directly. It manifests itself only through its attributes, two of which are perceptible by us, as human nature is a part of them as well: res cogitans and res extensa, the thinking thing and the extended (i.e., corporeal or bodily) thing.

Everything we perceive manifests itself to us through the aspects of body and mind. This metaphysical ontology argues that our knowledge is structured somewhat like the following: while ontology establishes the possibility that we might grasp something in its particularity, that same ontological ground secures the ontological status of every particular as an expression of Substance and thus as representing the universal. That Substance as a whole, however, appearing as it does under the aspect of body and mind, remains beyond any totalizable discursive grasp. As understanding garners knowledge through the aspect in which a particular object manifests itself, it can also grasp things in their dual aspect: as individual entities on the one hand and as partial manifestations of the interconnected yet unfathomable ground of being on the other. In this way, the relationship between the particular and the universal is expressed ontologically as both difference and identity.

Like the ontological model, reason appears in a discursive form, defined by its instrumental character, or as intuitive reason, whose nondiscursive nature allows it to connect with God or Nature in a quasi-mystical fashion based on the knowledge discursive reason provides. This unique double move preserves both the distinctness of the individual thing as entity and the idea of an irreducible whole that cannot be broken down into particular constituents. Spinoza's ontological conception plays out this tension in a dialogical rather than dialectical fashion.

Moving beyond the dichotomy of immanence and transcendence, Spinoza's system resolves this bipolar opposition by exposing it as the hidden assumption of conventional metaphysical thought. Refusing to accord any privilege to either side of the mind-body divide, he instead addresses both simply as aspects of that one and only Substance that undergirds all its forms of expressions. Positing a single universal Substance argues, therefore, neither simply for immanence or transcendence as authentic truths but proves such privileging itself as inadequate. Spinoza's uncompromisingly consistent stand insists that a reductionist view of immanence or transcendence would miss the complexly intertwined, constitutive relationship between Substance and its modifications, that is, between the universal and its particular expressions. The *Ethics*' perspicacious attention to the ontological construction of the particular and universal makes it, as Husserl expressed it, "the *first universal ontology*."[8]

Spinoza's approach sets off an unrestricted examination of everything under the aspect of the attributes of mind and body and recognizes the importance of marking the limits of knowledge. This epistemologico-critical moment is already deeply inscribed in Spinoza's metaphysics, whose structure itself represents a critical reflection on the conditions that make knowledge possible. Knowledge thus emerges as a bidirectional process and human endeavor. While the more we know about particulars the more we know of God and of the whole, our knowledge of the particular itself depends from the start on a grasp of the whole that, in turn, structures the process of knowledge. The particular ontological framework of Spinoza's metaphysics prefigures the production of knowledge as a process where knowledge is produced through a constant interconnection of the whole and its parts in an open-ended manner. Knowledge for Spinoza is the incessant activity of discursive reason spurring the mind on to the higher stage of intuitive reason, which transcends the merely introspective, contemplative, and instrumental uses of reason.

Descartes, Hobbes, and the new science had provided methods that allowed them to focus on particulars without needing to heed the larger scheme of the universe and the interdependence of all things. But the cost of their approach was that they lacked a critical consideration of the ultimate limits of discursive reason. Critical of such philosophical closure but taking full advantage of the groundbreaking innovation of the new science, Spinoza proposes an ontological framework that critically reflects on the metaphysical assumptions underlying the new concept of Nature. The systemic structure of his ontology is designed to accommodate a sophisticated notion of immanence capable of theorizing the limits of discursive knowledge.

This systematic openness takes the modern conception of Nature to a new level by combining a mechanistic, atomistic understanding of nature with a comprehensive vision of nature as Substance. Spinoza's concept of Nature accommodates both the analytic and discursive aspect on the one hand and the intuitive and holistic aspect on the other. While Spinoza's distinction of Nature as *natura naturata* and *natura naturans* casts Nature on the one hand as causally determinable, it allows us, on the other hand, to comprehend its spontaneous and self-generating side, which is only partially accessible to discursive reason. This dynamic that inhabits the heart of Spinoza's concept of nature inscribes its irreducibility, as it were, within ontology itself.

This Spinozist shift has profound consequences for epistemology, as the ontological difference blocks any immediate discursive access that would lead to direct knowledge of nature as a whole, an insight reserved for another kind of knowledge—*scientia intuitiva,* as Spinoza calls it, or intuitive knowledge.

Rather than consolidating the scope of traditional metaphysics, the *Ethics*' ontology breaks down the hierarchical structures of the scholastic philosophical tradition which the philosophers of the new science (e.g., Bacon, Descartes, and Hobbes) had challenged. But unlike these new philosophers, Spinoza dismantles traditional ontological preferences on their own terms from within. The latinizing cast of his ontology has been charged with philosophical and historical anachronism, seen as either some sort of ill-conceived metaphysical revisionism or an unfortunate redux of Cartesianism. One result has been that the critical thrust behind Spinoza's ontology often went unrecognized. This has allowed his metaphysics to be viewed as nothing more than a transitional placeholder marking the divide between old and new ways of doing philosophy.

But what makes Spinoza—unlike Descartes and Hobbes—seem stuck at the threshold of modern philosophy rather than part of its breakthrough to modernity is that Spinoza, unlike Descartes and Hobbes, aims at more than simply replacing an obsolete form of philosophy with a new one. Spinoza's metaphysics engages the project of transforming traditional philosophical thought by critically rethinking its inherited status. Those elements of Spinoza's thought that seem to be building on the obsolete structure of traditional metaphysics are actually Spinoza's way of developing a new approach without losing sight of problematic elements inhabiting both the old and the new philosophy. The particular shape Spinoza gives his philosophy remains unusually sensitive to the dialectical play between the philosophical tradition and the new science. What thus appears to be obsolete in the form of Spinoza's thought can instead be understood as a critical reflection on the conditions of philosophical innovation.

At the core of the *Ethics* lies Spinoza's categorical rejection of any kind of teleological thinking, which he exposes as the fundamental fault of traditional philosophy. To Spinoza, teleological thinking reveals not so much the nature of things as the way imagination caters to our wishful thinking. The unswervingly anti-teleological thrust of his philosophy singles out teleological thinking as the source of all prejudices. The claim that "all final causes are nothing but human fictions" (CW 442) ("omnes causas finales nihil nisi humana esse figmenta" [E1 Appendix]) carries radical consequences for adequately evaluating any ontological framework, and it bears fundamental implications for epistemology, anthropology, and religious and political philosophy as well. Spinoza's anti-teleological critique not only denounces the Aristotelian and teleological view of the scholastic philosophical tradition as illusory and false but also stakes out a position that bears all the earmarks of radical modernity.[9]

But Spinoza's interest consists of more than a critique of an obsolete form of philosophical thought that has hobbled the proper use of reason and hemmed in its liberating potential. His philosophical stance also enables him to expose traces of teleological thinking present within modern philosophy itself. Although staunchly anti-teleological thinkers like Descartes and Hobbes certainly shared this desire to abandon the constraints of Aristotelian metaphysics once and for all, the comforts of teleological thinking and its suasive power exert their pull beneath the surface of their thought. For neither Descartes nor Hobbes succeeded in freeing themselves completely from teleological patterns of thought. Although the principles of Descartes's philosophy appear resolutely free of all teleological assumptions, the Cartesian universe lacks a consistently nonteleological metaphysical framework. And although Hobbes, as stubborn materialist, seems to be free of teleological aspirations, his practical philosophy relies on concepts often operating according to teleological assumptions—residues that, while running counter to Hobbes's explicit claims, nonetheless inform his social and political philosophy in a way Spinoza would reject.[10]

At the center of his ontological framework Spinoza places the *conatus,* which he defines as the force through which each thing strives to remain or persevere in its being as the actual essence of that thing: "The striving by which each thing strives to persevere in its being is nothing but the actual essence of the thing" (CW 499) ("Conatus, quo unaquaeque res in suo esse perseverare conatur, nihil est praeter ipsius rei actualem essentiam" [E3P7]). He calls this conatus will (*voluntas*) if it is related to the mind, but he calls it striving or drive (*appetitus*) if it is related at the same time to the mind and the body. In this case the conatus expresses the essence of human nature (E3P9 Schol). "In suo esse perseverare" (E3P6ff.), the nature of the conatus, is for Spinoza the striving that is ontologically universal. It differs from the Aristotelian *entelecheia,* with its teleologically encoded end, in that the conatus has no preprogrammed final cause. The conatus is conceived as a purely immanent cause that is ontologically linked to Substance as its particular form of expression.

This resolutely anti-teleological concept of self-preservation allows Spinoza to formulate a new view of human nature and, as a consequence, a new principle ordering individual and social life. While Hobbes signals a move toward this new view, Spinoza provides the metaphysically consistent grounds for this new conception. In this context, Spinoza's conatus marks a crucial step in the development of what Dieter Henrich has called the "basic structure of modern philosophy."[11] Although Henrich defines the ascendancy of this Stoic principle that all things possess a divine spark, making them essentially equal, as the distinguishing characteristic of modern metaphysics, Blumenberg has cautioned against following this lead from Dilthey, whose attempts at reducing Spinoza to Stoic thought seem problematic at best.[12]

If self-preservation is one of the distinguishing characteristics of modern philosophy, Spinoza gives its ontological formulation its classic expression.[13] In defining the conatus as the universal ontological principle that informs and defines all being, Spinoza identifies the basic principle of the new rationality.[14] His signal contribution consists in grounding rationality in a metaphysics that fully attends to its material basis.

The fact that Spinoza's *mos geometricus* has been criticized as a method out of step with the course of modern philosophy does not lack irony. For the *Ethics*' use of the *mos geometricus* was intended to infuse the argumentation with a sense of clarity and transparency that would help rather than obstruct understanding. Ironically, the Euclidean model of geometric demonstration has made readers less comfortable with a design more significant for its form of expression than for its method.[15] The geometric order—Spinoza does not speak of method but of *mos*—emphasizes the constructivist aspect of metaphysics. The Latin term *mos*, often mistranslated "method," suggests custom, habit, manner, mores, law, prescription, order. While "method" implies metatheoretical reflection, the semantic field of *mos* points to ethical and moral connotations. What the geometric order then implies is not the privileging of a scientific paradigm of method but the pedagogical design of philosophy as an outline, reflecting on its own discourse in a compelling fashion.[16] Just as geometry determines the rules of relations and proportions of things regardless of their quality, so Spinoza's geometrical order stresses the functional, systemic aspects of the construction of knowledge. In this way, knowledge is presented as an objective construction whose objective validity nonetheless depends on the adequacy of its intellectual construction, not on the thing itself. This view of knowledge as the adequate construction of a perception that is itself a modification of one or another attribute of Substance emphasizes the didactic intent of Spinoza's geometric method. The form of the geometric proof in Spinoza's presentation highlights a constructivist rather than an objectivist concern.

The manual-like style of the *Ethics* models a philosophy that is autodidactic in the precise meaning of the term. This is not the least reason why laymen and -women felt attracted to the *Ethics*, for the autodidactic form gives rise to a uniquely auto-emancipative experience. This aspect is central to Spinoza's philosophy. What might appear to some readers as the formidable imposition of philosophical authority comes into view as Spinoza's articulation of a metaphysical discourse that foregrounds the possibility for autonomy, philosophical self-sufficiency, and empowerment.

CHAPTER 2

UNDERSTANDING UNDERSTANDING

Spinoza's Epistemology

ABOUT THE TIME SPINOZA DRAFTED the outline for his epistemological theory in his treatise *On the Improvement of the Understanding* (*Tractatus de intellectus emendatione et de via qua in veram rerum cognitionem dirigitur*), Johannes Vermeer, his peer in age, painted *The Art of Painting* or *Artist's Studio* (1665/66).[1] Staging the paradoxical situation of representing the act of self-reflection, Vermeer paints himself painting, but with a twist. Painting himself from the back, an angle of vision that remains otherwise inaccessible, Vermeer inverts the conventional form of the artist's self-representation facing the viewer.

The scene visualizes the theme of spatial arrangement. The viewer's gaze is allowed a look into an otherwise closed space, set off by a heavy curtain pulled back for the viewer's convenience. The artist faces the canvas, paying full attention to the model, a woman dressed as an allegory and/or muse. Fanfare, book, and the blue color of her dress and hat all convey a wealth of possible meaning. The model's eyes, half closed, take up the theme, the problem of inside/outside, of margins, borders, and boundaries. A huge map, dominating the back wall, representing the demarcation of frontiers, continues the theme of borders and margins.

The formulaic, sparsely furnished room nevertheless appears well equipped, as if to illustrate the painting's theme of traveling the borders between the finite and the infinite. Here, everything represents a transitional point and part of an infinite continuum. The mood is introspective,

Johannes Vermeer van Delft, Artist's Studio (Kunsthistorisches Museum, Wien)

tranquil, contemplative. The canvas in the picture shows the painter's first brushstrokes depicting the model's blue hat. From there the viewer's eye wanders to the "original," if it can be called that. The difference in color and shape between the posing model and her hat's representation makes one wonder. The colors of the model's hat (which the artist is in the process of painting) are less intense and the shape is different, even though the viewer's angle of vision follows the painter's line of sight. Rather than merely reproducing from "nature," the artist's very first brushstrokes mark the difference between the object and its representation. The portrait, the picture intimates, will not be the representation of the model. The model only serves as stand-in for the artist's imagination, which leads his hand and uses the staged scene to assist his inspiration. The scene thus suggests a reversal of the relationship between model and artist: it is no longer the artist who is inspired by the muse but rather he who inspires the model to represent a muse.[2] Vermeer's self-portrait addresses the problem of representation in a manner that visualizes Spinoza's concerns. For, according to Spinoza, imagining and representing truth is not simply a part of an anamnetic method of recovering what already exists "out there" but a process of constructing knowledge by deploying the mind's capacities to form, associate, and examine ideas.

Just as painting the allegory/muse of art or history[3] amounts to reinventing and reconstructing the subject on canvas, so Spinoza conceives of the production of knowledge as dependent solely on the consistency of its constituent ideas. The scene's staging of the embedded, enveloped existence (curtain, map, the character of light) and the meditative yet creative mood, concentrated and full of potential, staging the artist's aura of creativity, visualizes Spinoza's epistemological project. Vermeer's painting produces its enchanting force by staging the paradox of truth and representation in a contemplative manner.[4]

Whether or not *On the Improvement of the Understanding* is indeed the inaugurating work of Spinoza's philosophy (as some scholars have suggested),[5] Spinoza certainly views the question of the relation between epistemology and metaphysics, between ethics and politics, as a central concern. This poses the question of the place of the epistemological treatise with regard to the "philosophy proper," the "Principia philosophiae," as Spinoza first had planned to call the *Ethics*.[6] Is *On the Improvement of the Understanding* a propaedeutic introduction to philosophy as it finds its final shape in the *Ethics*, or does it already present, as it initiates the search for truth, an element of that philosophy itself? The fact that no final answer can be given may be seen as a cue, for the treatise argues for a way of life which in turn points to a theory of knowledge that cannot be isolated from the existential project that serves at its basis.[7] Significantly, Spinoza does not ground these epistemological considerations in a moment of origin. Instead, the opening words of the treatise stress the crucial importance of experience: "After experience had taught me that all the things which regularly occur in ordinary life are empty and futile" (CW 3) ("Postquam me Experientia docuit, omnia, quae in communi vita frequenter occurrunt, vana, et futilia esse" [TIE§ 1]). Yet, Spinoza conceives experience to comprise more than what empiricist and rationalist views would admit. Experience does not just teach facts but also prepares the path to wisdom.

Whereas Descartes's *Meditations* stage an autobiographical scene whose specific point in space and time is supposed to produce a break with the existential condition of finitude as it promises to open up a window to the absolute, Spinoza's narrative projects a different trajectory. It presents an ego that is no longer cast as a purely cognitive function placed on a cold winter's day behind a pipe in a comfortably heated room in Germany. In clear contrast to such a stylization, Spinoza's narrative ego moves in a distinctly different sphere as it runs through the moments of decisions in the narrator's life—albeit in an equally stylized manner that appears strangely removed from the world of experience it sums up. Yet it is precisely this kind of narrative that forces the ego to pay full attention to the fact that it is firmly entrenched within the limits that define the conditions of human existence. To Descartes's carefully staged revelatory story, which has knowledge start at a distinct point in space and time, Spinoza responds with one that reiterates the process of knowledge as an experience that, instead of being traced back to one specific moment, consists in the total effect of a person's life praxis.[8] Moving on a plain that seems strictly classical—the three ways of life, the resignation from honor, riches, and power, and so forth[9]—Spinoza inscribes a critical difference in what, on the surface, appears as formulaic account. For Spinoza's is not an unreflected kind of classicism but a creative appropriation of classical forms through which he advances his new, differentiated concept of the self.

Spinoza's approach suggests a reflective attitude toward what the procedure of the production of knowledge involves. His postulate to consider things "sub quadam specie aeternitatis" requires thought to remain within the limits of the human condition it wishes to transcend.[10] This heuristic postulate acknowledges the problematic structure of the epistemological aporia in which the Spinozan narrator finds himself caught. The impossibility of ever reaching an ideal vantage point that would secure limitless access to knowledge "sub quadam specie aeternitatis" is already contemplated in the ontological framework. By consistently rejecting any hierarchical structure, Spinoza consequently rules out any privileged position of an epistemological vantage point, as it were, self-contained as a "state in a state."[11] The cautionary reservation expressed in the consequent use of *quadam* ("as it were") signals a crucial difference from the Cartesian concept of the ego. With the idea of understanding operating "under the aspect, as it were, of eternity," Spinoza articulates a sense of reflexivity that allows him to theorize the epistemological function itself as emerging from an ontological situation that remains constitutive. In contrast to Descartes, the ego represents for Spinoza an always already precarious epistemological vehicle.

On the Improvement of the Understanding does not give a definition of what understanding is but rather of how it can be improved. The definitions given are pragmatic in nature. They describe the rules of operations but do not mistake them for their essence. The title of the treatise could not be more explicit about what is, after all, at stake if an epistemology is to be introduced: *Tractatus de intellectus emendatione et de via qua in veram rerum cognitionem dirigitur.* This *Treatise on the Improvement of Understanding and the Way in Which It Has to Be Directed to Attain True Knowledge* intimates that such an enterprise reaches beyond the province of epistemological competence in the narrow sense. The program, announced in the opening paragraphs, formulates a whole vision of life. The understanding of understanding, it now becomes clear, is intricately connected to how we conceive life in general, and our lives in particular.

Method assumes in Spinoza a new meaning as it transcends the technical, scientistic definition it had for Hobbes and redefines the meaning Descartes had ascribed to this term. For an approach that reduces method to just an epistemological device, the treatise suggests, creates more problems than it can ultimately solve. The clear-cut distinction between truth and its standard, which Descartes had hoped to establish with recourse to a doubt-free *fundamentum inconcussum* ("irreversible foundation") with his concept of the ego, leads, as the treatise shows, into a spiral of infinite regress. The moment a criterion for certainty is introduced, the epistemological problem simply shifts to the question of the grounds for legitimation of the criterion itself. As a result, an infinite regress is initiated that can only be brought to an arbitrary halt. To illustrate this point, Spinoza uses the example of a speculative history of the production of a basic tool. In order to produce a hammer, iron needs to be forged. However, to do this, we, in turn, need a hammer. As a result, one could argue, it is impossible to forge iron and therefore produce a hammer. The production of the cognitive tools that Spinoza calls *instrumenta intellectualia*, necessary for knowledge, is not very different. They emerge over time by themselves free of any outside assistance, by virtue of their intrinsic development alone. Such a view also provides the possibility for a historical understanding of knowledge as a slowly emerging process, a process whose result can nevertheless be described in terms of a self-determined praxis. It also addresses the question of the existence of innate ideas. Although we certainly have innate ideas, Spinoza admits, they are originally in a latent or undeveloped stage. It is only by way of their unfolding, refinement, and clarification that they become adequate ideas.

As a consequence, Spinoza conceives certainty in the context of determining what an adequate idea is, which is defined by the "objective essence of a thing" (§35). This means that truth has no need of a sign other than itself (§36). Method is thus recast as reflexive knowledge (*cognitio reflexiva*), that is, as the idea of an idea (*idea ideae* [§38]). The Cartesian and Hobbesian models of episteme are in this way replaced by one that introduces a gradual or continuous rather then a discrete or principal quality into the process of knowledge production. It is a model that emphasizes the continuous nature of knowledge, whose reflexive character does not permit a closure caused by extrinsic reasons. Truth is thus conceived in terms of a process.[12] The dynamic and processual aspect is what defines the crucial moment of this new understanding of method: "the more the mind knows, the better it understands its own powers and the order of Nature. . . . In these things . . . the whole of Method consists" (CW 20–21) ("quo plura mens novit, eo melius et suas vires, et ordinem Naturae intelligit. . . . in quibus tota consistit Methodus" [§40]). Spinoza thus moves away from the empirical approach of, for instance, Bacon, whose inductive method lacks an epistemological meta-reflection and whose fixation on the imperative to stock up data mortgages the empiricist agenda with metaphysical baggage. Likewise, Spinoza distances himself from a Cartesian philosophy of mind, whose exclusive privileging of a rationalist constructivism betrays an equally problematic metaphysical option. What in Spinoza is often taken for just another obsolete rationalist attempt at constructivism[13] is to be understood as Spinoza's careful navigating between the problems that Cartesian, Baconian, and Hobbesian epistemological theories present.[14]

If it is true that Spinoza's treatise appears to be performing a somewhat circular movement, its critical significance emerges only in comparison with the epistemological models it challenges.[15] For it critically exposes the hidden metaphysical implications of their claims. Although the treatise outlines an alternative model of epistemology, the explicit grounding in metaphysics is not introduced until the *Ethics* to which the treatise points. The circular movement of the epistemological argument highlights that any theory of knowledge rests, in the final analysis, on a larger philosophical conception of the nature of things from which the epistemological argument cannot be detached.[16]

The treatise opens with a narrative that serves more than a merely ornamental purpose. A conscious attempt at refashioning the Cartesian narrative in order to accommodate an epistemological method that avoids Descartes's systemic problems, it projects a theoretical trajectory that grasps the question of the nexus between the foundation of reason and its application—that is, theory and praxis—as the central problem of philosophy. Yet in identifying this as its key concern, the narrative assumes at the same time an existential and to some degree even quasi-religious note, for it broaches the question of truth as one that is intimately connected to the larger ethical issue of how to lead a life of reason.

What might appear as a reverting to some kind of concept realism or an ultimately ineffective variety of nominalism[17] emerges as a carefully targeted critique of seventeenth-century theories of knowledge. The treatise staunchly resists the truncation and compartmentalization of thought into units abstracted and separated from their objects. This critical opposition to granting movements of the thinking process the status of ultimate knowledge secures Spinoza's position against skepticism.

Spinoza thus opens his approach to a metatheoretical reflection. As a result, the critical impulse of his narrative suggests that the "purity" of one's thought is the "purity" of one's life, or, less theologically, that the function of knowledge is always a function of the specificity of the life that produces the conditions for its respective particular form of knowledge. The epistemological interests that guide the cognitive process thus cannot be done away with, or so the treatise argues. While

Spinoza's precursors propose concepts of truth that rely either on an empiricist (Bacon), convention-based (Hobbes), or rationalist (Descartes) foundation, Spinoza suggests that they hinge on the kind of metaphysical assumptions implied in their respective methods.

In its obstinate refusal to grant easy exit from the maze of epistemological aporias, Spinoza's epistemology indicates that there is no easy way out. The recurrence of questions that remain unanswered brings home the point that the process of knowledge does not take place in a space different from the one we inhabit. It is right here, where we live our lives, as part of our praxis that cognition arises as the other, reflective process of this life.

Although the treatise eventually leads to the point where the *Ethics* will pick up the argument, it would be misleading to impose a teleological structure on this critique of epistemology.[18] For the point of Spinoza's epistemology is not to arrive at the knowledge of God or his metaphysical names but to remind us that our knowledge rests on a foundation that determines the course our reasoning will take. For Spinoza's critical point is that this foundation lies beyond the grasp of any epistemological conjecture. As a result, the process of knowledge remains necessarily interminable.

The mind's map as it is charted in the treatise takes new shape. The process of knowledge becomes a dynamic exchange between two faculties: imagination (*fictio*) and understanding (*intellectio*). They both share the sphere of ideas. But the *potentia intelligendi* finds itself pitched against the *potentia fingendi,* which lives off the lack of the intellect's influence (§58). The fine line of distinguishing between the two faculties constitutes for Spinoza the foundation of knowledge, a point so strikingly visualized in Vermeer's painting. The first part of the treatise ends thus with the conclusion that the true idea (*idea vera*) must be the idea of the most perfect being (*ens perfectissima* [§49]). Only now has it become possible to distinguish the true idea from fictitious ideas (*ideae fictae*), false ideas (*ideae falsae*), and dubious ideas (*ideae dubiae*). Ideas, this shows, are not always a product of knowledge. They are distinguished with regard to their origin and defined by whether they are produced by imagination, reasoning, or a mixture of both.

Although it has been argued that Spinoza entertains realist notions,[19] his universalism is shot through with a consistently nominalist tendency.[20] His theory of general notions (*notiones communes*) deserves special attention, as it is here that his position emerges most clearly. The particular point of Spinoza's theory of general notions is that it bases their universal validity not in an independent, fixed sphere of intellectual knowledge but rather in what they have in common with other bodies (E2P38 Corol). From this it follows "that the Mind is the more capable of perceiving many things adequately as its Body has meanings in common with other bodies" (CW 475) ("quod Mens eo aptior est ad plura adaequate percipiendum, quo ejus Corpus plura habet cum aliis corporibus communia" [E2P39 Corol]). In this way, Spinoza's "realism" is firmly grounded in a distinctly nonrealist standpoint. To further complicate matters, Spinoza points out that

> these notions are not formed by all [Nagelate Schriften: men] in the same way, but vary from one to another, in accordance with what the body has more often been affected by, and what the Mind imagines or recollects more easily. (CW 477)

> has notiones non ab omnibus eodem modo formari; sed apud unumquemque variare pro ratione rei, a qua corpus affectum saepius fuit, quamque facilius Mens imaginatur, vel recordatur. (E2P40 Schol 1)

In *On the Improvement of the Understanding,* Spinoza introduces four different modes of perceptions: (1) hearsay, (2) mere experience, (3) conclusions through reasoning, and (4) knowledge of a thing through its essence or proximate cause (TIE §19). In the *Ethics,* he expands the distinction of the four different modes of perception into a theory of universals. According to the *Ethics* (E2P40 Schol 2), universals are formed from:

1) singular things which have been represented to us through the senses in a way that is mutilated, confused, and without order for the intellect (random experience), and
2) signs.

These two kinds form the first mode of knowledge that is constructed through opinion or imagination;

3) common notions and adequate ideas of the properties of things.

In this consists the second mode of knowledge or reason;[21]

4) The third kind of knowledge, intuitive knowledge (scientia intuitiva) proceeds from the adequate idea of the formal essence of some attributes of God to the adequate knowledge of the essence of things. (CW 477–78)

As a result, the status of universals depends on the class of knowledge from which a particular notion originates. The different genealogies of universals that Spinoza outlines give the classic debate of nominalism versus realism a new turn. Although Spinoza allows for some kind of conceptual realism, he does so only in a manner that conceives universals as grounded in concrete knowledge of individuals. In underlining the material base necessary for the formation of general notions, he encodes reason with a notion of difference that resists dissolution into abstract universalism.[22]

Intuitive knowledge remains the only candidate to qualify for the claim of universal validity. But—and this is the crucial distinction—intuitive knowledge is conceived as a nondiscursive mode of knowledge. Although Spinoza's epistemological theory may betray some of the surface traits of conceptual realism, closer examination shows that Spinoza formulates a position that conceives universals as always qualified. This is a nominalism of singularity.[23]

The more general the idea we have of something is, the more confused it will be, but the more specific such an idea is, the more it will follow the order of nature. While imagination is thus associated with abstraction and generalization, knowledge is defined by singularity and specificity of the idea of its objects. Imagination, moreover, does not create new knowledge but only reshuffles the memory in new ways. However, it does not create knowledge in this way. False ideas (*ideae falsae*) add to the fictitious ideas simply the affirmation of the existence of what they represent. Doubtful ideas (*ideae dubiae*) are ideas that lack clear and distinct quality due to confusion caused by deception of the senses. Such doubt is easily removed by way of recourse to what we really know in terms of true ideas.

As all knowledge is predicated on the distinction between imagination and reason or understanding, the forging of chimeras as well as of words is the work of imagination. Words are thus nothing but signs of things as our imagination fashions them: "[W]ords are part of the imagination . . . they are only signs of things as they are in the imagination, but not as they are in the intellect" (CW 38) ("[V]erba sint pars imaginationis . . . non sint nisi signa rerum, prout sint in imaginatione, non autem prout sunt in intellectu" [§§88–89]).[24] Pressing this point to its conclusion, Spinoza leaves no doubt about his skepticism with regard to the limits of language:

> We affirm and deny many things because the nature of words—not the nature of things—allows us to affirm them. And in our ignorance of this, we easily take something false to be true. (CW 38)

> Multa affirmamus et negamus, quia natura verborum id affirmare et negare patitur, non vero rerum natura; adeoque hac ignorata facile aliquid falsum pro vero sumeremus. (§89)

As a consequence, there are no linguistic criteria that can guarantee the truth of knowledge.[25] This leads to a notion of definition that is no longer conceived as a real definition that would express the essence of a thing. Instead, and based on Hobbes's genetic definition, Spinoza proposes a different approach.

What at first sight appears to be a rather essentialist claim that a definition has to express the innermost nature of a thing ("intima essentia rei" [§95]) in fact anticipates proto-pragmatist ideas, an aspect for which Peirce has felt such affinity.[26] For the "intima essentia rei" is no metaphysical entity but denotes in Spinoza the ensemble of all the properties of an object that we can observe. The opposite of an abstract and general notion, such a definition provides the means to generate the idea of a thing in our mind as far as the operative parameters of its effects are concerned.

While Hobbes's theory of definition assumes that according to his—however refined—mechanistic model of nature all objects can be grasped in their full and innermost being, Spinoza opposes, or at least contradicts, a complete congruence of things and thoughts. Instead, he argues for a parallelism of the order of things and thought. But this casts nature, unlike Hobbes's completely mechanistic view, as a discursively inaccessible substratum. This view stands in close affinity with the pragmatism of Peirce, whose description of definition resonates with Spinoza's.[27] Moving between the Cartesian, Hobbesian, and Baconian models and with a strategy no less convincing than the one Leibniz introduced,[28] Spinoza's stand critically reflects the problematic of seventeenth-century epistemology.

Reconfiguring the particular and universal, Spinoza's theory of knowledge advances a view that places the recognition of the constitutive moment of particularity for the production of knowledge at its center. Universalism, it suggests, rests necessarily on the particularity of experience. As a result, knowledge and truth cannot be arrived at by a way of reasoning proceeding along universals that exclude the particular. Instead, Spinoza describes knowledge and truth as a process enabled by the undiminished recognition of the constitutive role of the particular. This universalism no longer hinges on an exclusionary kind of reasoning but acknowledges the recognition of the particular as a key moment for its construction.

The treatise breaks off at the point of transition to the *Ethics*. The epistemological argument, it turns out, cannot be contained as a purely epistemological one even within the limits of the treatise. It calls for a larger philosophical framework, and this is what the *Ethics* provides. The critical result of the treatise consists, then, in the recognition that an epistemology, in order to be self-sufficient, requires an approach whose concept of method comprises, beyond a restrictive understanding as a sort of logics of knowledge, the meaning of method as a way of life. Only such a comprehensive understanding of method provides full autonomy for the production of knowledge. With this argument, Spinoza reformulates the strategies of epistemology in Bacon, Hobbes, and Descartes and grounds the project of epistemology in a framework of self-sufficiency. For only a firm anchoring within the framework of metaphysics guarantees epistemology its own autonomy. Whereas Bacon, Hobbes, and Descartes saw epistemology as a free and independent enterprise, they in fact applied it as an instrument to legitimize their claims, claims which Spinoza, on the other hand, recognized to be heterogeneous to their epistemologies if they were to be considered as genuinely autonomous and self-regulating tools. Critical of the instrumental understanding of reason their epistemologies seemed to imply, Spinoza moves toward a conception of reason that stresses its dynamic aspect as a self-constituent faculty.

CHAPTER 3

A PSYCHODYNAMIC THEORY OF AFFECTS

SPINOZA'S THEORY OF AFFECTS represents one of the most innovative parts of his philosophy. It prefigures in a crucial way what Freud called the drama of the narcissist blow meted out to the ego.[1] Although the theory of affects presents a radical and consistent attack against conventional conceptions of self, mind, body, and soul, it seems that this challenge has gone largely unnoticed in the historiography of philosophy.[2] Nevertheless, Spinoza's systematic examination of the role and functioning of the affects has profoundly informed modern theorizing in moral philosophy, psychology, and aesthetics.

Philosophy has traditionally viewed emotions and passions as some sort of disturbance if not nuisance to the project of understanding the mind and achieving ethical perfection.[3] This has not only been true for Plato, Aristotle, and the classic philosophical tradition they engendered. Even the age of new science, which—following the cue of Epicureanism—was eager to mark its radical break with classic philosophy, did not bring about much change in this respect. While Machiavelli, Montaigne, and Hobbes gave attention, for the first time, to the importance of the emotions and passions as an issue central for a sound comprehension of human nature, their philosophies did not provide a sufficient explanation of the operative nexus between the emotions, the passions, and the mind. But if this nexus did indeed exist, as these philosophers claimed, adequate examination of it seemed warranted.

The classic dichotomy dividing human soul into the higher faculty of the active mind and the passive animal drive associated with the body made it impossible to theorize how emotions and passions would affect the mind in more than coincidental ways. In the classic Platonic image of cage and prisoner,[4] the mind's autonomy was conceptually locked in the idea of human nature divided into mind on the one hand and body on the other. This view, however, skewed the determining role that the stirring dynamics of the emotions and passions played in guiding if not controlling human life.

Spinoza not only recognized the need to address this problem but realized that philosophical anthropology had to be grounded in an understanding of human nature that would no longer seek to separate the psychological aspects from the ontological substratum that undergirds them. This departure from the traditional mind-body dichotomy allowed Spinoza to address emotions and passions in the face of their unmitigated ontological significance. As a consequence, emotions and passions are seen as natural forces and no longer to be feared as irrational. Determining human actions in a natural way, they can now be understood to follow a logic of their own. As a result, affects present for Spinoza a natural part in the constitution of rationality.[5] To control them requires not only a better psychological grasp of their functioning but an ontologically consistent conception of the mechanics, or more precisely, the psychodynamic economy, that regulates mind and body. This emphasis on the embeddedness of the mind within an ontological framework makes it possible to consider emotions and passions as more than merely by-products of our material existence.

Based on the first two parts of the *Ethics*—a universal ontology and a theory of knowledge production—the second half develops a theory of the passions that reconfigures the traditional view of action and agency from the bottom up. While the conventional distinction between action and passion rests on a particular conception of autonomy and heteronomy, Spinoza questions the very assumptions on which these distinctions are based. In reformulating the concepts of freedom and necessity on the grounds of a reconstructed metaphysics, Spinoza pushes the discussion to the point of almost complete reversal of the traditional meaning of these two concepts. Acknowledging the degree to which human agency is steeped in the realm of passions, Spinoza's project of the liberation from dependence on, and even servitude to, the passions marks a critical turn.[6]

Theories of human nature, from Plato to Descartes and Hobbes, have always assumed a clear and distinct difference between autonomy and heteronomy. But this was only possible by presupposing a preexistent, indestructible, unchangeable inner core of a self or ego, however this might be defined. Exposing the problematic assumptions of this presupposition, the *Ethics* refutes such positing of the ego as a firm and invariable point of reference. Despite all their radical differences, both Hobbes's mechanistic form of materialism and Descartes's rationalism rest—if only, as in Hobbes's case, without recognizing it—on the assumption of a construction of the self that, if nothing else, nevertheless implies some sort of existence of freedom of will. Although Hobbes and other philosophers may have problematized the idea of free will at great length in theory, the political and social outlook of their philosophies suggests otherwise, for their underlying theories of political authority admit the notion of a strong voluntarism through the back door.

Against such conflicting prospects, Spinoza formulates a metaphysics whose conception of freedom reflects the implications of psychophysical parallelism.[7] For Spinoza, the parallelism between mind and body is conceived as ontologically inscribed in the double aspect under which we are able to conceive what exists: "The Mind and the Body are one and the same Individual, which is conceived now under the attribute of Thought, now under the attribute of Extension" (CW 467) ("Mentem, & Corpus unum, & idem esse Individuum, quod jam sub Cogitationis, jam sub Extensionis attributo concipitur" [E2P21 Schol]). As a result, there is no longer room for a causal relationship between body and mind. Instead, Spinoza's strict parallelism, conceiving body and mind as modifications of one and the same underlying cause, calls for a revision of the mind-body problematic. This provides the platform for a new understanding of the psychosomatic condition of human nature: "The Body cannot determine the Mind to thinking, and the Mind cannot determine the Body to motion, to rest or anything else (if there is anything else)" (CW 494) ("Nec Corpus Mentem ad cogitandum, nec Mens Corpus ad motum, neque quietem, nec ad aliquid [si quid est] aliud determinare potest" [E3P2]). As a consequence, the individual emerges as the site where the forces of nature collide and negotiate an equilibrium. Yet Spinoza's conception of the dynamic nature of the individual does not disempower it entirely. On the contrary, this account of the precarious nature of the individual's constitutive forces provides the basis for a psychophysical dynamic that enables the reconception of self-determination in a groundbreaking way, for it advances a theory of self-realization through empowerment as therapy. The implications of Spinoza's ontology-based metaphysics appear thus in their critical intent to formulate a dynamically understood concept of the self. This leads to a radical redefinition of freedom and necessity.

The proposition of the parallelism between the order of the body and the order of the mind helps to address phenomena that otherwise would remain unaccounted for. In this context, the point

> that the order, *or* connection, of things is one, whether nature is conceived under this attribute or that; hence the order of actions and passions of our Body is, by nature, at one with the order of actions and passions of the Mind (CW 494)

> ut ordo, sive rerum concatenatio una sit, sive natura, sub hoc, sive sub illo attributo concipiatur, consequenter ut ordo actionum, & passionum Corporis nostri simul sit natura cum ordine actionum, & passionum Mentis (E3P2 Schol)

helps theorize the following proposition: what appears under the attribute of thought as decision or free will or under the aspect of extension as determination or compulsion are one and the same, that is, the result of the play of affects. Genevieve Lloyd has expressed this most succinctly: "[T]o think Spinozistically of mind and body together is not to think of an intermingling of two kinds of things that are in principle separable. It is to think of the same reality in two distinct ways."[8]

In order to understand the critical significance of Spinoza's theory of affects, one must recognize the importance of his contribution in formulating a differentiated understanding of the psychophysical condition of human nature. Although the term "affect" has been in use since antiquity, it basically gained currency to signify "passion." The equation of affect and passion had been in place until the seventeenth century.[9] While Spinoza draws occasionally from the Stoics' classic theory of affects,[10] his own definition and use of the term marks a fundamental departure from the traditional view.

At the beginning of part 3 of the *Ethics*, Spinoza introduces his definition of *affect* in no ambiguous terms:

> By affect I understand affections of the Body by which the Body's power of acting is increased or diminished, aided or restrained, and at the same time, the ideas of these affections.
>
> *Therefore, if we can be the adequate cause of any of these affections, I understand by the Affect an action; otherwise, a passion.* (CW 493)[11]

> Per *Affectum* intelligo Corporis affectiones, quibus ipsius Corporis agendi potentia augetur, vel minuitur, juvatur, vel coercetur, & simul harum affectionum affectionum ideas.
>
> Si itaque alicujus harum affectionum adaequata possimus esse causa, tum per Affectum *actionem* intelligo, alias *passionem.* (E3 Def 3)

As the notion of affects comes to include anything that affects the mind or body, be it in a passive or active manner, Spinoza's extensive use illustrates the key role the affects assume in reformulating the relation between mind and body. With Spinoza, it is now possible to account for the undiminished specificity of the psychophysical condition of human nature as the basis for ethics. In this light, Spinoza's assertion that "no one, to my knowledge, has determined the nature and powers of the Affects, nor what, on the other hand, the Mind can do to moderate them" (CW 491) ("Affectuum naturam, & vires, & quid contra Mens in iisdem moderandis possit, nemo, quod sciam, determinavit" [E3 Praefatio]) is no exaggeration. For his examination of the nature and function of the affects broaches yet-uncharted territory. What appears to conventional wisdom as freedom of actions or compulsion of passions, as free will or determination, is the result of a voluntarist model of human nature that still rests on the assumption of a dualism of mind and body along with the conception of a causal relation that posits, consciously or not, the mind as being in charge of the body. Replacing this dualistic, hierarchical model with one that attends to the centrality of the psychosomatic whole, Spinoza's notion of the affects addresses the psychophysical nexus that constitutes human nature. As a notion that reconnects what philosophic tradition had separated—mind and body—the affects occupy a peculiar intermediary position. While the dynamics of the affects reflect the vital life of the emotions and passions, affects represent for Spinoza more than merely external and contingent factors. They highlight the constitutive interface of mind and body that is grounded in the underlying substance that causes their correspondence and produces the individual in its individuality.

In refusing to reduce the affects to either soul or body, Spinoza criticizes Descartes and proposes a solution to the gridlock of the post-Cartesian mind-body dichotomy. At the same time, Spinoza's view on the irreducibility of mind and body signals an advance over Hobbes's naturalistic model, afflicted by mechanistic reductionism. Spinoza's introduction of a concept hinging on function rather than essence announces a paradigm shift that carries critical implications. But this functional approach does not lose sight of the materiality of the affects. On the contrary, it is precisely a functional understanding of the affects that allows Spinoza to appreciate the individuality of each human being in its irreducible psychophysical entity. For Spinoza, every individual affective experience is singular, because each individual's psychophysical constitution is composed of an infinite array of differences that give everyone a different psychodynamic potential (E3P57). The affects allow us therefore to conceive individuality in a way that credits the infinite possibility defining human existence.[12]

By treating human actions and desire (*appetitus*) as if they were lines, surfaces, or bodies (E3 Praefatio, last sentence), Spinoza is able to account for the infinite possibilities in which human nature finds expression. The geometric order makes it possible to represent the infinite variations in which human complexity manifests itself and to theorize individuality in a new way. The geometric order also illustrates how the quantitative intensity of the affects can overwrite their quality. It is therefore the intensity that determines the struggle between conflicting affects, as the more powerful affects suppress or cancel out the weaker ones. This way, the dynamics of the affects produce the equilibrium that defines the individual in its particular specificity (E4P7).

The *Ethics* defines joy, sadness, and desire (*laetitia, tristitia, cupiditas*) as the three primitive or primary affects from which all others spring (E3P11 Schol; E3 Def 4 Explicatio). Joy is potentially the strongest affect, outlasting all others, as it is conceived as overall enhancement of the individual's psychophysical state.[13] Joy or the transition to a more perfect psychophysical state thus becomes the affect that—compared to all others—emerges as the most powerful one in the balance of the play of affects. As the process of knowledge represents precisely such a transition from a less to a more perfect state, knowledge understood as a combination of epistemological and affective aspects emerges as the strongest affect altogether. As a passive affect (a "passion" in the literal sense) ceases to be passive once we form a clear and distinct idea of it

(E5P3), adequate knowledge of the affects becomes the strongest antidote to affectual passivity (E5P4 Schol). The strongest affect is therefore the one produced by adequate knowledge. In this manner, Spinoza's epistemology is part and parcel of a theory of affects that remains solidly rooted in his ontology.

The geometric model enables Spinoza to conceptualize the way in which the affects determine human actions and desires, permitting him to explain the role of the affects without the need to account for the specific qualities of their makeup. For Spinoza, the affects are not just an internal affair but account for interactions with the external world undertaken in the interest of self-preservation.[14] As both physical and psychological entities, the affects are value-determined and at the same time determinants of value, for they always carry a positive or negative value. Considered as physical entities, they represent a change in the individual's somatic state, whether an increase or decrease; considered as a psychosomatic unity, an affect relates to the external world in a positive or negative way.[15]

Spinoza's geometric presentation permits his discussion to examine in purely descriptive, value-free terms how the cathexis of value occurs in the first place. The dual character of individual affective states and their dynamics determine, on the one hand, the nature of the individual, and on the other, how the individual acts upon and interacts with the external world. Spinoza's treatment of the affects represents thus a circumspect argument that reflects an unusual awareness of the descriptive, therapeutic, and ethical dimensions simultaneously at play in affectual experience. This grounds Spinoza's ethics in a psychosomatically sophisticated conception of self-determination.

Spinoza's *Ethics* can in this way be understood as a philosophy of self-empowerment in the precise meaning of the term. His metaphysics rests upon a strong conception of individuality, which in turn is firmly grounded in an ontology that affirms the constitutive role of the interplay of identity and difference for constructing the individual. Although Spinoza redefines the concept of autonomy and freedom in a way that has led to the dismissal of his philosophy as reductive and determinist, his reformulation of human freedom and autonomy in terms of self-determination and self-preservation, understood as self-realization, breaks new ground for a dynamic conception of individuality that takes the psychosomatic constitution of human nature as the basis for the individual's open-ended potential for self-realization. This has profound consequences for the social, political, and legal conception of the subject as a genuinely modern construction at the intersection of post-Cartesian and post-Hobbesian philosophy.

The imagination's role in the theory of affects casts cognition as the interplay of forces that occurs within the affectual economy and has important implications for aesthetics. The double character of imagination as both the faculty for representing objects and ideas and the crucial agent in the economy of affects makes the aesthetic the crucial sociocultural site for the play of the affects. Mendelssohn will define affectual play as the linchpin of his aesthetic theory, an affectual experience whose aesthetic importance was first described by Spinoza. While creating images of what is absent, imagination simultaneously requires a discharge or release of affective energy as part of the imaginative process. To the extent that imagination is crucial to the cognitive process, the aesthetic sphere plays a central role in the production of our knowledge of the world. Spinoza's revalorization of imagination accords the aesthetic a new ontological significance. The theory of the affects thus prepares the way for theorizing the transformative power of aesthetics. By challenging traditional definitions of the beautiful and sublime, an affect-based aesthetics like Mendelssohn's will lead to a rethinking of traditional aesthetic categories. After Spinoza, imagination can no longer be viewed as a merely receptive and passive faculty but rather as the site where an affective charge finds its form of expression, one that represents as much as it transforms.

We can now understand to what extent the geometric presentation of the *Ethics* itself has an aesthetic function. The particular form of the *Ethics* produces an aesthetic effect that encourages a dynamic play with and within the reader. Its design aims at releasing the liberating process of knowledge that transforms self-determination into the self-realization of the free human being.

CHAPTER 4

SPINOZA'S THEORY OF RELIGION, HERMENEUTIC, AND TRADITION

SPINOZA IS THE FIRST MODERN THINKER who attempts not only to detach the political sphere from theology—a project both Machiavelli and Hobbes had already pioneered—but also to formulate a hermeneutic theory legitimating the separation of what he argues represent two intrinsically different spheres.[1] The *Theological-Political Treatise*'s central concern, the claim for "libertas philosophandi," requires a principal reflection on the status, role, and competence of philosophy if this claim is to do more than simply reiterate a well-meaning plea for freedom of thought and speech. In order to legitimate this call, the *Theological-Political Treatise* grounds its argumentation in a hermeneutic.

However, Spinoza reception has been partially oblivious to the fact that the *Theological-Political Treatise* articulates the first modern hermeneutic. But the task of differentiating theology from philosophy places this hermeneutic at the crossroads between and before philosophy and theology, breaking ground for a modern conception of hermeneutic. Spinoza's project to separate theology and philosophy advances a new hermeneutic that demarcates the two spheres as it delimits the claims of each. Spinoza is aware that a viable separation is possible only if both theology and philosophy reach a self-understanding that accords with their own sphere of competence. Unless this is realized, the separation between philosophy and theology lacks firm theoretical grounding and thus remains specious.

This situation accounts for the dual structure of the argument the *Theological-Political Treatise* presents. On the one hand, Spinoza requires a form of reason that is self-sufficient and autonomous. On the other hand, and equally crucial, is the presentation of religion as a domain in its own right defined by its own concerns. By differentiating the two spheres as areas with their own specific and legitimate scope, Spinoza delineates a demarcation that assigns the competence, range, and function of philosophy and religion in accordance with their respective aims and concerns. This means that as the *Theological-Political Treatise* produces a differentiation of the two spheres, it is forced to address the issue of how to motivate and ground the divide it lays out. Such a move thus presupposes a turn to a self-reflexive mode if it is to avoid falling back into an infinite regress.

In this way, the argument of the *Theological-Political Treatise* proceeds by way of a differentiation that aims at doing full justice to the specificity of both sides, the concerns and nature of both theology and philosophy. A distinctive feature of the *Theological-Political Treatise* is that it reflects this issue in a way both implicit and yet formative for the shaping of the argument. As a consequence, the treatise formulates its interpretation of the nature of religion and its theory of political philosophy in terms of a theory of hermeneutic. With this move Spinoza articulates an early reflection on discourse differentiation that casts the problem of constructing theory in a way that will gain paradigmatic importance for theorists such as Mendelssohn, Lessing, and Kant.

In the *Theological-Political Treatise* this hermeneutic takes shape in two ways: first, in a theory of interpretation, and second, through the interpretation of Scripture that, in turn, grounds and reconfirms the theoretical framework in which a hermeneutic is developed as a study of Scripture's own hermeneutic features. The theory and practice of interpretation combine in a systematic reflection on hermeneutics based on a fresh look at the text of Scripture.

The *Theological-Political Treatise* addresses the hermeneutic circle by pointing out that most interpreters start with the hermeneutic principle that Scripture as a whole is, by definition, both infallible and divine throughout. Such a view creates a vicious circle of interpretation, but its more serious consequence, ironically, is to deprive interpretation of the scriptural text of any claim to authenticity, for this way the result of interpretation is already posited from the start. Interpretation thus would be reduced to the reiteration of its own assumptions, with such circular reference undermining any title to validity which scriptural interpretation might claim:

> Namely, the very thing that ultimately has to be established from an understanding of it and by strict examination, and which we are taught far better from what does not need human fantasies in the least, they state at the very outset as a rule for its interpretation.[2]

> [I]d nempe ipsum, quod ex ejusdem intellectione et severo examine demum deberet constare, et quod ex ipsa, quae humanis figmentis minime indiget, longe melius edoceremur, in primo limine pro regula ipsius interpretationis statuunt.[3]

As a result, an interpretation that operates under the guiding assumption of unquestioned divinity undermines the idea of interpretation itself—and as a consequence of divinity. Against the contention that the text is only allowed to say what it is allowed to say, only a principal reflection on the nature of interpretation guarantees the end to such tautological circling. In addition, the *Theological-Political Treatise* argues that the hermeneutic of interpretation has to correspond to the nature of the text it explicates. This means that any interpretation has to attend to the cultural, historical, and spiritual specificity of a text and its context in order to make interpretation possible. What is thus needed is an impartial examination of Scripture as a prerequisite of the project of the *Theological-Political Treatise:*

> I painstakingly set about to examine Scripture anew in a full and free spirit and to affirm nothing about it and admit nothing as its teaching which I was not taught by it very clearly. (Y Preface 5.1)

> [S]edulo statui Scripturam de novo integro et libero animo examinare, et nihil de eadem affirmare nihilque tanquem ejus doctrinam admittere, quod ab eadem clarissime non edocerer. (TTP 16)

Revisiting the debate on whether revelation or reason should be accorded primacy in interpreting Scripture, Spinoza gives this problem a new turn. Rather than opting for one or the other, he confronts reason and revelation in a way that forces the conventional contentions and conflicting claims advanced by both sides to a new solution. Just as the *Theological-Political Treatise* argues the issue to call for a consistent practice of hermeneutic, so it demonstrates that such a hermeneutic must respect the integrity of the text. Spinoza's argument prefigures in an interesting way the considerations Hermann Cohen devotes in his *Religion of Reason* to a similar paradox: while religion for Cohen is unquestionably independent of reason, the faculty of reason is nonetheless required in order to construct the concepts that are necessary to grasp religious ideas, which in turn make the interpretation of Scripture's religious message possible.[4]

While it may seem ironic that Cohen—who vehemently scorned Spinoza for what he considered his unforgivable betrayal of Judaism—takes up Spinoza's argument, albeit with a different, almost opposite theoretical trajectory in mind, Cohen's deliberations shed an elucidating light on Spinoza's view of the complex, mutually constitutive correlation of revelation and reason. Spinoza's view is all the more telling as it maintains at the same time that both religion and reason must avoid any encroachment on each other: "that Scripture leaves reason absolutely free and has nothing in common with Philosophy; but the latter as well as the former stands on its own proper footing" (Y Preface 5.7) ("Scripturam rationem absolute liberam relinquere et nihil cum philosophia commune habere, sed tam hanc quam illam proprio suo tali niti" [TTP 18]). It is only the insistence on the autonomy of each sphere that allows for the kind of methodological reflection that remains impossible as long as an examination of the nature and competence of each sphere is missing. Although polemic undertones are never far away, the *Theological-Political Treatise*'s pointed manner nevertheless reflects a critical awareness of the methodological problems involved. As Spinoza notes:

> I painstakingly set about to examine Scripture anew in a full and free spirit and to affirm nothing about it and to admit nothing as its teaching which I was not taught by it very clearly. With this caution, I therefore contrived a Method of interpreting the Sacred scrolls and, instructed in this, began before everything to question what Prophecy was, and for what reason God revealed himself to Prophets, and why they were accepted by God. (Y Preface 5.1–2)

> [S]edulo statui Scripturam de novo integro et libero animo examinare, et nihil de eadem affirmare nihilque tanquem ejus doctrinam admittere, quod

> ab eadem clarissime non edocerer. Hac igitur cautione methodum sacra volumina interpretandi concinnavi, et hac instructus quaerere ante omnia incepi, quid esset prophetia? et qua ratione Deus sese prophetis revelaverit? et cur Deo accepti fuerint? (TTP 16)

But rather than remain in the abstract, Spinoza approaches the question of the nature of revelation by considering how Scripture itself introduces the concept of revelation. Such a direct confrontation with Scripture guarantees an approach that stays close to the text at the same time it provides the needed cover to protect the *Theological-Political Treatise*'s argumentation against charges of infidelity. This procedure carries the added advantage of mining Scripture itself for direct support while enabling Spinoza to challenge the uncritical understanding of the sacred texts.

In addressing the issue of prophecy, Spinoza joins the classic Jewish controversy over whether religion is to be understood as a rational or irrational phenomenon. But instead of taking sides, Spinoza transforms the discussion of the nature, status, and role of prophecy into a question of hermeneutics. This emphasis on the hermeneutic aspects of prophecy shifts the focus from the event of revelation and the supposedly privileged access of prophets to the divine to the point that mediation hinges on an act of hermeneutics. Prophecy thus comes into focus as a form of translation of the visions, voices, and other messages the prophet receives from God. Insofar as the moment of mediation, that is, the translation of the divine experience into human language, is concerned, prophecy itself—not only its articulation but, more importantly, its function as medium between the divine and the human—emerges as an eminently hermeneutic activity. The prophet is thus not someone who reveals the divine in person but rather a person who—through the medium of human nature and the body—*interprets* revelation.[5]

In Hebrew, the word for "prophet," as Spinoza points out, is the word for speaker and interpreter: "For among the Hebrews, a Prophet is called נביא, navi, that is, orator and interpreter" (Y 1.1.3) ("Propheta enim apud Hebraeos vocatur נביא nabi, id est orator et interpres" [TTP 30]).[6] With this emphasis on the mediating role of the prophet as translator and interpreter of the divine, Spinoza couches prophecy in terms of human activity rather than as a heavenly mission. In identifying the hermeneutic mission as prophecy's central task, he argues that prophecy and natural cognition are principally the same, for the prophet's effort at translation produces, as translation, natural knowledge. In direct opposition to the traditional view that prophecy stands out as a special kind of knowledge, Spinoza argues that natural knowledge is a form of prophecy, or rather that prophecy presents the general form of all knowledge in the first place.

This might at first glance look like a trick of sophistry, but behind the polemical note of this bold reversal lies a theoretical concern that proves decisive for the clarification of the hermeneutic character of prophecy. It is in this context no coincidence that Spinoza has the first chapter of the *Theological-Political Treatise* open with the definition: "Prophecy, or Revelation, is certain knowledge of some matter revealed by God to human beings" (Y 1.1.1) ("Prophetia sive relevatio est rei alicujus certa cognitio a Deo hominibus revelata" [TTP 30]). As Spinoza argues, this definition implies that with equal right natural knowledge can be called prophecy: "For the things we know by the natural light depend solely on knowledge of God and his eternal decrees" (Y 1.2.2) ("Nam ea, quae lumine naturali cognoscimus, a sola Dei cognitione ejusque aeternis decretis dependent" [TTP 30/32]). As a consequence, natural knowledge can be called divine. With this move, Spinoza opens up the possibility of understanding prophecy as an inner-worldly practice. Consequently, prophecy cannot be detached from the limitation faced by all hermeneutic activity. Acknowledged as a universal power whose potential all human beings possess (Y 1.2.3; TTP 33), prophecy, like cognition in general, emerges as an inherent capacity of human nature. As a result, prophecy requires no supernatural explanation. Prophets are human translators of a specific form of natural cognition rather than exponents of divine truths only accessible to them or to others in equally privileged positions.

Because prophecy functions through the mediation effected by words and images—be they true or imagined—the faculty that performs this mediating function is the imagination. For Spinoza, imagination becomes the criterion for differentiating religion from philosophy. Whereas relegating prophecy to the sphere of imagination might suggest polemical and anti-religious undertones, it also paves the way for a conception of religion that will grant religiosity a legitimate place of its own. For imagination plays a crucial role in the economy of affectual life.

One of the most striking implications of Spinoza's discussion of prophecy is that Scripture itself represents a translation and interpretation. This point is exemplified in the discussion the *Theological-Political Treatise* devotes to the question of the nature of miracles. The miracle, far from presenting objective evidence, marks the point at which human hermeneutic competence has been surpassed. For Spinoza, "miracle" is a designation for the breakdown in rational explanation and the taking of refuge in the realm of the unexplainable—the "asylum ignorantiae." But if the miracle serves as a figure for expressing the shortcomings of rational explanation, it cannot serve as an explanation itself. Rather, the miracle is a placeholder for what transcends the capacity of human understanding. However, the attempt to infer knowledge from what exceeds our grasp undermines its own premises. In other words, to attempt to explain what evades any rational explanation produces a hermeneutic short circuit that creates the impression of the miraculous. But this effect, the *Theological-Political Treatise* insists, does not produce any kind of evidence by itself.[7]

In addition, Spinoza raises the issue of miracles performed by false prophets. Insidiously, tradition tells us that true miracles have been performed by false prophets, posing a challenge to the hermeneutic of miracle interpretation (Y 6.1.37; TTP 205). Pointedly, the chapter on miracles concludes with a quote from Josephus describing Alexander the Great's exploiting such a miracle and marching his army through water that had parted for a shortcut (Y 6.1.100; TTP 227). The hermeneutic vortex that results is unlikely to support any claims that miracles produce meaning in and of themselves. For Spinoza, miracles serve thus as a way to compensate for the lack or breakdown of rational explanation. This means

> that the noun "miracle" cannot be understood except with respect to the opinions of human beings, and signifies nothing else but a work whose natural cause we cannot explain on the model of some other, usual thing; or, at least, that the one who writes or narrates the miracle cannot so explain it. (Y 6.1.17)

> nomen miraculi non nisi respective ad hominum opiniones posse intelligi et nihil aliud significare quam opus, cujus causam naturalem exemplo alterius rei solitae explicare non possumus, vel saltem ipse non potest, qui miraculum scribit aut narrat. (TTP 194)

Many reports of miracles can be explained naturally if attention is given to the particular use of expressions and figurative speech, while others may simply remain obscure. In this case it has to be assumed that the text has been tampered with, for "we absolutely conclude here that everything that is narrated in Scripture as having happened in reality has necessarily happened in accordance with the laws of nature, as everything does" (Y 6.1.67; TTP 214). While common use of the term "miracle" imagines it to take place when the laws of nature have been suspended, outside, as it were, the natural order, Spinoza's point is quite the contrary—that the authentically miraculous is part of the continuous and permanent texture of the laws of nature themselves.

> To interpret the miracles of Scripture and to understand on the basis of their narratives how they really happened, therefore, it is necessary to know the opinions of those who first narrated them and left them to us in writing [. . .] (Y 6.1.75)

> Igitur ad miracula Scripturae interpretandum et ex eorum narrationibus intelligendum, quomodo ipsa revera contigerint, necesse est opiniones eorum scire, qui ipsa primi narraverunt et qui nobis ea scripto reliquerunt. (TTP 216)

As a result, miracles do not speak—that is, they do not explain, justify, or articulate by themselves any religious idea, doctrine of belief, or truth for that matter. Instead, the *Theological-Political Treatise* argues, miracles require an effort at interpretation in order to be identified as miracles, that is, in order to be assigned the status of having exceeded discursive interpretability. In order to identify, understand, and retrieve its appellative meaning, that is, to "read" a miracle, a hermeneutic framework has to be in place. For the transcendent character of miracles shows them to be a construction based on a hermeneutic intervention. Exposing the miracle's precarious factual status, the *Theological-Political Treatise* shows it to be the product of discursive reasoning, that is, of interpretation. Consequently, the discourse on miracles is always already constituted by reason. In other words, for a claim to the miraculous to be made, the miracle must become part of discursive reason. But to the degree it becomes part of discursive reasoning, it exposes itself to the criteria and the judgment of reason, which it cannot escape as long as it is supposed to express claims or discursively applicable meaning.

Chapter 7, "De interpretatione Scripturae," takes this conclusion a step further as it formulates the "true method of interpreting Scripture"

(Y 7.1.8; TTP 230). In short, Spinoza notes, "the method of interpreting Scripture scarcely differs from the method of interpreting nature, but agrees with it completely" (Y 7.1.9; TTP 230). Interpretation thus comes into focus as a rational procedure (independent of the nature of its subject). Removed from the exclusive jurisdiction of theology, interpretation is a practice whose secular character makes it part of philosophy and therefore fully independent of the claims of theology. The classic metaphor of the book of nature that had gained wide currency since the Renaissance receives here its radical, anti-theological twist:

> For just as the method of interpreting nature consists mainly in laying out a history of nature on the basis of which, as on the basis of certain data, we conclude the definitions of natural things, so too it is necessary for interpreting Scripture to furnish its straightforward history and conclude on the basis of it by legitimate inferences, as on the basis of certain data and principles, the mind of the authors of Scripture. (Y 7.1.10)

> Nam sicuti methodus interpretandi naturam in hoc potissimum consistit, in concinnanda scilicet historia naturae, ex qua, utpote ex certis datis, rerum naturalium definitiones concludimus; sic etiam ad Scripturam interpretandam necesse est ejus sinceram historiam adornare, et ex ea tanquam ex certis dati et principiis mentem authorum Scripturae legitimis consequentiis concludere. (TTP 230/232)

As we rely on natural history to provide the basis to arrive at certain data and the definitions of things, we need an "authentic history" for the interpretation of Scripture ("sincera historia Scripturam interpretandam" [TTP 230]) in order to reach conclusions from certain data and principles derived from the understanding of the intention of the authors of Scripture ("mens authorum Scriptorum" [TTP 230/232]). The consequence of such an approach is that interpretation has firmly to be based on Scripture itself (*sola scriptura*) in the same way that the cognition of nature depends exclusively on nature as the sole source (Y 7.1.12; TTP 230).

As Scripture and history become the sole sources for interpretation, interpretation has as its only guidelines the hermeneutic rules provided by a critical grasp of the history of Scripture itself. As a result, no meaning can be derived from Scripture that cannot clearly be inferred from its history (Y 7.1.23; TTP 234). Historical understanding thus stakes out the hermeneutic parameters that define the grounds for interpretation. Setting the task for a detailed examination of the historical nature and the linguistic particularities of Scripture, the *Theological-Political Treatise* formulates the agenda of modern critical Bible research, including the need for a history of Hebrew necessary not only in order to read the Old Testament but equally necessary, as Spinoza pointedly observes, for interpreting the New Testament.

Spinoza holds an extensive notion of the history of language that comprises its culture and society, a context crucial for understanding the meaning of Scripture. In addition, the *Theological-Political Treatise* calls for a critical examination of the history of transmission and tradition of the sources, including the study of the various versions and emendations that exist of the texts transmitted. While the *Theological-Political Treatise* thus formulates a comprehensive modern research program, Spinoza insists at the same time that although one is better able to interpret the words of an author when one is better acquainted with the author's mind and mentality ("genius et ingenium" [TTP 238]), we as readers are nevertheless

> not permitted to twist the mind of Scripture to the dictates of our own reason and to our preconceived opinions; but the whole knowledge of the Bible is to be sought solely from itself. (Y 7.3.13)

> nobis non licet ad dictamina nostrae rationis et ad nostras praeconceptas opiniones mentem Scripturae torquere, sed tota Bibliorum cognitio ab iisdem solis est petenda. (TTP 238)

Meaning thus gains its own significance over and against the sound dictate of reason. Berel Lang astutely sums up the "modernist" turn that is announced in Spinoza's emphasis on the distinction between meaning and truth: "The interpretation of a text, Spinoza insists—even of the Bible, and all the more so for other texts—depends not on the truth of the meaning disclosed by that process, but only on the recovery of meaning itself, irrespective of whether that meaning conforms to doctrine. Interpretation, in other words, need not—cannot—answer authority."[8] With the distinction between meaning and truth, history and tradition gain a new role for hermeneutics. Tradition represents the medium that provides the grounds for interpretation. But rather than viewing it to be static, Spinoza stresses the sociohistorical dynamics that determine the role of tradition. Instead of the sedimentation of the status quo, tradition emerges as the effect of historical development. As a consequence, tradition loses its normative grip as it represents for Spinoza the historical frame of reference in which interpretation becomes possible in the first place. Devoid of any normative content, tradition represents no longer a deontological given but, rather, functions as the agent by and through which identity—that is, the contingent construction of particularity—is produced. Tradition thus provides the grounds for interpretation, but by way of an exclusively non-normative hermeneutic. Seeing tradition as a product of culture, manufactured like all other human artifacts, Spinoza casts it as an agent of change, correction, and reinvention.

Consequently, Spinoza sees traditions as always partial. They are the product of social and political developments and as such neither sacred nor taboo. Nor do they have to represent a nuisance. They are formations that emerge not monolithically but as the effect of the synergy of a plurality of traditions. Spinoza emphasizes the plural meaning of traditions when he introduces a distinct use of the term in the plural. This takes place in the context of the explanation of the emergence of traditions as the foundation of the canon of Scripture by rabbinic scholars whom Spinoza, idiosyncratically enough, simply calls Pharisees. Spinoza calls the decisions at which they arrive "decrees, which they call traditions" (annotation 25 to Y 10.2.54; "decreta, quae traditiones vocant" [TTP 368]). Nevertheless, Spinoza is aware that in order to criticize traditions one has to be able to argue from within their framework. Otherwise there would be no access whatsoever to the interpretation of traditions at all.

While traditions of organized forms of religion raise questions with regard to the possible adulteration of the meaning of Scripture's authors (Y 7.25.40; TTP 248), the *Theological-Political Treatise* stresses, on the other hand, the need for reliability of the tradition of the meaning of words and phrases. Exegesis thus necessarily hinges on tradition. The distinction between tradition of particular types of exegesis (e.g., orthodox, catholic, etc.) and the philological tradition of the Massorah produces less a clear-cut divide than it exposes the dialectical relationship between tradition and interpretation.

Spinoza's insistence upon restricting the interpretation of Scripture to the resources of Scripture itself presses for a sharper conceptualization of tradition as an intricate weave of religious, social, and political constructions. Although interpretation operates within the hermeneutic scope of such weaves, it produces its meaning by the creative appropriation of traditions. As a consequence, tradition is no longer conceived as having sprung from pristine and immutable origins but rather as the product of a hermeneutic praxis. In distinction to a hermeneutic posing as a self-regulating process of interpretation, Spinoza's concept of tradition highlights the constitutive nexus of tradition and its critique. For it is the critique of tradition that provides the grounds for the hermeneutic framework required for the possibility of interpretation.

Theorizing tradition in this way gives rise to a heightened awareness of the historicity not only of religious but also of social and political institutions. The hermeneutic praxis of the *Theological-Political Treatise* articulates a sensitivity for the historical that anticipates the critical concerns of modern historicism.[9] Although a concept of history will emerge only later, Spinoza's keen sense for contingency allows him to formulate a "critical theory of fortune" that addresses the issue of historicity in an uncompromising manner.[10]

While tradition represents the historical basis required for any interpretation, recourse to tradition alone does not yet provide all that is needed. Another element is at work in the act of interpretation, and it is connected to the issue of political authority. This point is intimately linked with the history of the tradition of Scripture, or so the *Theological-Political Treatise* presents it. The history of the political institutions of the state of the Hebrews identifies in the struggle for political authority the place where all interpretation eventually is arbitrated. Yet rather than simply following the order of the political power arrangements of the ancient Hebrews, the *Theological-Political Treatise* suggests with its outline of the political order just how intricately tied the theological-political knot really is. It becomes increasingly clear that interpretations are conditioned by sociopolitical processes contingent on the political order in which they are played out. The case of the state of the Hebrews illustrates that although privileging theological over political authority defies the very essence of the message of Scripture, a simple inversion would present an equally unviable response. For political authority, when it participates in interpretation, remains implicated in theological reasoning. In both cases, the integrity of the other sphere is jeopardized. As a consequence, the concept of political authority has to be reworked, and this is precisely what the remainder of the *Theological-Political Treatise* proceeds to do.

Thus the separation of theology from philosophy is warranted not only to establish a secure demarcation to limit the claims of theology but also to formulate a secularized concept of political authority. Tied to the problem of interpretation, any conception of the political that does not address this separation remains vulnerable to subjection to theological claims. In hyphenating the theological and the political, Spinoza's *Theological-Political Treatise* presses the point of the problem of their interpenetration and the need for the separation and recognition of the respective independence of each from the other. But it also signals that the separation of the two is a project that awaits realization. The hyphenation brings home the difficult relationship of the two spheres as they stand over and against each other in unmediated manner: coupled together in incompatible pairing, their hyphenation brings out their continuing conflict that informs the paradox of modernity as its fundamental challenge.

CHAPTER 5

A NONCONTRACTUAL THEORY OF THE POLITICAL ORDER

THE RADICAL NATURE OF THE CHALLENGE Spinoza presents emerges most clearly in the way he theorizes power, state, and government. But Spinoza does not actually mount a frontal attack on traditional forms of political legitimation. Rather, his analysis of political institutions proposes a different approach to theorizing the concept of power itself. His choice of the term *imperium* for the state—in contrast to *res publica,* his term for the state's concerns—marks a distinction crucial to the exercise of power in the civil state, a distinction that informs whatever political structure might ground the exercise of power in a given polity.[1]

Critical of the analyses of Machiavelli and Hobbes, Spinoza proposes a new understanding of the nature and function of the political.[2] His innovative move consists not so much in introducing an alternative view but rather in pressing for a reconceptualization of the political that follows the reconfiguration of metaphysics carried out in the *Ethics.* Based on the radical ontology of the *Ethics,* this means the reconstitution of political theory from the bottom up. The methodological reflection underlying this move plays an important role. The distinctive character of Spinoza's political theory consists in his attempt to ground it in a philosophical framework capable of answering the critical concerns of his metaphysical reflections. Although Spinoza's political thought may raise more questions than it can answer, it exposes the teleological implications of the normative content of the presuppositions underpinning classic political theory.

Whereas Machiavelli and Hobbes operate under the ultimately teleological assumption that state power—given the powers that be—requires a legitimation that can pacify and dominate the naturally anarchic state of things in a more or less effective form, Spinoza is preoccupied by an altogether different concern. Following the lead provided by his ontology, he argues that as long as political theory relies on problematic constructs such as contract, power transfer, representation (in the Baroque sense), government, and the state, such reasoning lends itself to the dictate of a teleological reason that only reinforces, if not legitimates, the status quo.

For Spinoza, however, the fait accompli of the status quo in no way justifies philosophy's underwriting the rules of the game that allow the imperium's power calculus to function. Spinoza is in this regard more wary than Hobbes, who in the end seems more preoccupied with dismantling the regnant theory of patriarchy and setting up possessive individualism in its place than with charting the full complexity and complicity that the process of legitimating authority involves.[3] Spinoza's point, however, lies in his theory's built-in resistance to instrumentalization. The pointedly non-instrumental character of his argumentation militates against any exploitation of theory for political gain. His examination of the theoretical commitments of key concepts of political thought leads to a revolutionary shift toward a reorientation and redefinition of political philosophy as a critical project.

The opening word of the *Political Treatise*—"affects"—names the grounds on which Spinoza's political theory is based.[4] Rather than power, force, state, law, rights, or government, the crux of political life consists for Spinoza in what undergirds all these concepts and what determines human behavior: the affects. To the degree that they not only represent manifestations of inner life but function as the motor for human motivations, the affects drive behavior, attitudes, and actions. The concept of the affects thus informs and shapes Spinoza's political theory in two crucial ways. Pointing forward to Spinoza's reconception of political theory, the introduction of the affects at the beginning of the *Political Treatise* marks his theory of politics as one built on his *Ethics*' theory of the affects. Acknowledging the fundamental import of affects allows Spinoza to theorize the link between the ethical and the political without having to subscribe to tacit norms or implications that might impose unforeseen consequences that could jeopardize if not undo the project of a theory of politics based on autonomy and self-determination.

The reasons and natural foundations for government ("imperii causae et fundamenta naturalia") can be found in the common nature that is the condition, or constitution, of human beings ("ex hominum communi natura seu conditione" [TP I§7]). The operative term here is *communi.* Starting with Plato, human nature had always been seen as the foundation on which political philosophy would rest. Aristotle no less than Machiavelli or Hobbes claimed the same. Yet while the recognition of human nature as the basis for political philosophy had become a convention, the problem was how to theorize it so that it would adequately accommodate the imperative to accord this insight its proper attention. For the moment of transition from philosophical anthropology to political philosophy is characterized by a glitch that would, in a peculiar move of erasure, overwrite the ethical with an extra-ethical impulse. Spinoza seems to direct his critique precisely against such a supplementation. In opposition to such tendencies, the *Political Treatise*'s insertion of the affects at the beginning inscribes the importance of human affectivity in unmistakable terms at the heart of ethics, politics, and the economy of knowledge production.

Spinoza's understanding of the affective contingency of human nature also aims at that originary layer preceding distinctions such as egotist/altruist or natural/civil, which are based on derivative notions of human nature. The recognition of the fundamental role of the affects by political theory combines thus with a dynamic grasp of nature in general. This connection conceives human nature as part and parcel of a comprehensive concept of nature, which in turn resists pressing human nature into a fixed mold or pattern. Quite the contrary, emphasis on the central importance of affectivity enables Spinoza to theorize human behavior in a manner that remains free from the snares of normative thinking. It is precisely such a "naturalistic," anti-moralistic approach that enables Spinoza to pursue the philosophical project spelled out in the *Ethics.* As a result, the *Political Treatise* avoids the typical snare of reasoning about politics, the import of vested moral or political interests into political theory. This recognition of the constitutive role of human affectivity serves as Spinoza's critical lever to dislodge the repressive hold of paternalist and absolutist political discourse.

Arguing for a substantially different definition of natural rights than did his predecessors, Spinoza offers a radicalized conception of nature that critically informs the way he frames his theory of politics. If nature assumes a dynamic meaning, so do, by implication, natural rights and the laws of nature, albeit in a critical way. Spinoza's definition, with its equation of right with might, or more precisely, "powerpotential" (*potentia*), introduces a line of argument that, while seemingly taking Machiavelli and Hobbes to their logical conclusion, provides instead the grounds for a new stage of a critical theory of politics. Spinoza phrases his answer to the question of how to define natural right ("quid jus naturae sit") in the following way: "that every natural thing has as much right from Nature as it has power to exist and to act" (Shirley 38) ("unamquamque rem naturalem tantum juris ex natura habere, quantum potentiae habet ad existendum et operandum" [TP II§3]). As a consequence, natural rights are identical with the laws of nature, *jus naturae* is equated with *potentia naturae* (II§4).[5] But Spinoza's formula of right = power (*jus* = *potentia*) carries subversive significance.[6] Whereas Hobbes would expect natural law to guarantee the state's legitimacy, Spinoza simply realizes the full rational potential inherent in Hobbes's theory of power. He defines natural right as the result of what is possible. The potentiality of the possible is, in turn, determined by the natural *potentia*. The way Spinoza brings the concept *potentia* into play revokes the normative implications that inform Hobbes's concept. In Spinoza, *potentia* denotes the form of power in its strong, constructive sense. Fashioning it in this manner opens the way for an understanding that, for example, allows him to address force and violence less as *potentia* than as its lack.

The difference between Hobbes's mechanistic theory of physics and Spinoza's dynamic understanding accounts for a subtle yet decisive difference in their concepts of *potentia*. While Spinoza seems—to the outrage of his contemporaries—simply to follow Machiavelli's and Hobbes's view on natural right, he transforms their discourse of power politics into an emancipatory philosophy of nature. The equation of *potentia* with right becomes Spinoza's formula for the transformation of political theory into a theory of the political.

Conceiving natural rights as those claims backed by *potentia*, the content of natural rights remains open to and is defined by the actual *potentia*. As *potentia* denotes a reality that is intrinsically dynamic, in flux, and resistant to formalization, natural rights are no longer imagined as written in stone. A change of *potentia* results in a change in the way they may be articulated. Although natural rights thus become in some sense negotiable, the parameters of such negotiations are strictly determined by the radius of *potentia*. In this way, Spinoza combines the possibility of casting natural rights as an evolving project that can be adapted to any kind of sociopolitical development with a solid core notion of their inalienability. Spinoza introduces this view, as it were, in analogy with divine right, properly understood. In this context, Spinoza's key formula *Deus sive Natura* gains new meaning as an expression of his interest in grounding political rights. For he defines divine right in tandem with his conception of natural rights (TP II§3). Not unlike negative theology, the idea of "natural rights" allows us to move to a functional definition that remains principally open, about which it is possible to affirm any assertions only with reference to a concept of *potentia* that remains to some degree inexhaustible. Consequently, the concept of freedom takes its systematic place at the heart of the architectonics of his metaphysics.

What at first seems to be a quasi-cynical undertone and has often enough been decried as such turns out to be the critical point of a political theory that faces the tempting reductionism of rationalism's power calculus head-on. By exposing the heart of what is falsely conceived as the rationality of power plays, Spinoza challenges the normative—and normatively dubious—core of realpolitik on its own terms.

Together with the right = might equation, the emphasis on the role of affectivity provides the platform for arguing that natural power—that is, natural rights ("naturalis potentia sive jus")—are not to be understood as grounded in the rationality of human nature but, instead, in whatever drive determines people to act and preserve their existence ("sed quocunque appetitu, quo ad agendum determinantur quoque se conservare conantur" [TP II§5]). But whereas Spinoza maintains that conventionally understood forms of rationality play no role for a theoretically consistent definition of natural rights, he comprehends the nonrational side of human nature quite differently from Machiavelli and Hobbes. For Spinoza, human desire is firmly tied to the instinct of self-preservation. But this instinct does not imply irrational behavior. The theory of affects allows Spinoza to distinguish his view from one that casts human nature in terms of the opposition between rational and irrational. Such a dualistic perspective would severely limit the possibility of accounting for the specific conditionality of human nature, which, in Spinoza's view, resists such a quick and easy, yet rather consequential, distinction. While traditional political philosophy leads, sooner or later, to the identification of reason as the exclusive basis on which to build a political structure and its institutions, be it in the name of paternalist or contractual responsibility, Spinoza stresses the sheer inadequacy of such a line of argumentation. For, ironically—his underlying argument runs—such a view ultimately jeopardizes the power that reason possesses.

Embedded in nature, human nature obeys the laws of nature. To argue otherwise would mean, as Spinoza points out, to claim it to operate independently, as if it were a state within a state (TP II§6). As a part of nature, human beings derive the same rights from their existence as anything else. And like anything else, human beings are in no way in need of justification or legitimation, nor are they in any state of grace or sinful fall.

With the instinct for preserving one's existence, however, the issue of self-determination is introduced at the ontological level. For according to Spinoza's understanding of the dynamics of nature, the preservation of one's existence does not denote an activity of merely conserving what already exists, a sort of decay prevention or simple continuation of the status quo. Rather, and more significantly, preservation of one's existence involves the dynamics of self-determination. Affectivity, it is important to bear in mind, does not impose restrictions alone but also plays the role of the facilitator, motor, and reservoir of energy for every human action.

In taking a philosophically differentiated stand on affectivity as the point of departure for grounding political theory, Spinoza initiates a double move. His insertion of affectivity as the underlying material foundation of political theory marks his difference from empiricist and rationalist theories, which lack the necessary framework to account for the specific way in which affects shape and define political reality and its institutions. In contrast, Spinoza's departure from the conventional distinction between the rational and the irrational projects a different picture of rationality and its limitations. At the same time, this move represents an intervention that takes the redefinition of affects—fully developed in the *Ethics*—to its political conclusions. Not only do the affects determine people's actions, but their complex economy is evaluated in its crucial significance for the construction of the theory of politics. Once the model of the dichotomous pattern active/passive is replaced by a model of the economy of affects, it becomes possible for political theory to address them as more than just mechanistic, exterior factors. Instead, the adequate understanding of their dynamics provides the grounds for the kind of political practice of self-determination and autonomy the *Ethics* envisions: a state of freedom where the power of affects is transformed into the self-emancipatory power of the mind, a mind which for

Spinoza remains inseparably connected to the body. As the headings of the final two parts of the *Ethics* signal, Spinoza imagines the development as that of a long, winding road to freedom, from human servitude subject to control by the affects to the power of the mind that prepares the way for human freedom: that is, "De Servitude Humana, seu de Affectuum Viribus" to the promise of "De Potentia Intellectus, seu de Libertate Humana."

Only after Spinoza has established affectivity as the material base for human action does he proceed to address the dialectics of reason. He describes reason as the tenuous, negotiated balance achieved between antagonistic affects. Liberated from its rationalist Cartesian framework and its underpinnings, reason no longer appears as an invariable given of human nature but rather as the product of affectual countercurrents. Constituting itself in the process of working through the claims and counterclaims produced by the clashing of opposing affects, reason emerges as the culminating moment in the balancing of the affectual economy—as a regulative idea, as it were. This view does away with the kind of foundational fantasies otherwise predominant in classic seventeenth-century political theory. It serves as a safeguard against theories that want to reduce human actions to a preconceived form of rationality, theories whose view on social and political regimes runs counter to a critical concept of rationality. Replacing voluntaristic free will with a psychodynamic theory of affects, Spinoza opens up the way for a dynamic understanding of human interaction.

As a consequence, the model of the social contract appears increasingly problematic. In its place, Spinoza introduces an accumulation or fusion model. As the *Political Treatise* succinctly puts it: "If two men come together and join forces, they have more power over Nature, and consequently more right, than either one alone" (Shirley 43)[7] ("Si duo simul conveniant et vires jungant, plus simul possunt et consequenter plus juris in naturam simul habent, quam uterque solus" [TP II§13]). The rejection of the contract model is not incidental but a crucial feature in the design of Spinoza's political theory.[8] According the affects proper attention leads thus to a counterargument against the contract model as its rationalistic assumptions become problematic in the light of the economy of the affects. By describing the process of instituting political order in terms of fusion of power (*potentia*) rather than the transfer of power to a yet-to-be-imagined, yet-to-be-constructed state power—an explanation leaning heavily on hidden teleological reasoning—Spinoza avoids the fallacy at the heart of the social contract theory. Instead, he replaces its fictional moment with a theoretical model free of speculative assumptions ultimately relying on pre- or extralegal legitimation. While this model of fusion may have problems of its own, its critical force consists in exposing the contract model's hidden presuppositions.[9]

To this end, Spinoza introduces a notion of sovereignty that opposes the idea of a full or even partial surrender of power to the government or state (*imperium*). Against Hobbes, Spinoza argues that it is not the transaction of power that establishes rights—that is, the transfer of rights from a people to their chief—but rather through the transfer among the people that right is constituted. This definition of the state reformulates Hobbes's views from the bottom up. In the state of nature that precedes but also determines the civil state, Hobbes imagines an anarchic absence of structure and order (in accordance with his ontology of corporeal mechanics) that could found order only through a transformative act. Such transformation, he maintains, can only occur through a complete transfer of all claims to sovereignty to a new authority, the king.[10] The blind spot in this argument lies in assuming that such a transaction of rights would necessarily lead to the constitution of sovereignty. Hobbes, however, fails to account for how the transfer of any rights could of itself bring about the surplus needed to found contractual sovereignty. His model stands or falls with the assumption that sovereignty is already in place prior to and independently of such a transfer or that sovereignty is simply established by force of the symbolic act of this transfer.

Spinoza develops a methodologically critical and differentiated way of addressing this asymmetry at the heart of the contract model's transaction formula. His discussion alerts us to the fact that explanations of the transition from a quasi-mythical state of nature to the institution of a civil state turn on presuppositions that, in the final analysis, prove to rest on shifty grounds. For these accounts operate under the assumption that imagining a transformation of the state of nature on the grounds of a concept of the civil state already in place would not mean to beg the question. Spinoza goes on to suggest that contract models are oblivious to the importance of organic political structures and modes of exercising power that may resist the imposition of the contract model and its transaction formula. In short, Spinoza suggests that the asymmetry inherent in such a transformation belies the claims on which the very idea of the contract is based.

The brevity and simplicity of Spinoza's definition of sovereignty does away with such a misguided approach and sets a new concept of the masses in its place: "This right, which is defined by the power of a people, is usually called sovereignty" (Shirley 44) ("Hoc jus, quod multitudinis potentia definitur, imperium appellari solet" [TP II§17]). *Multitudo* denotes the common basis that both the state of nature and the civil state share. As a common denominator, this concept of the masses offers a different account of the constitution of sovereignty. For Spinoza, sovereignty's constitution occurs crucially before the transition to the civil state takes place. Unlike his predecessors, Spinoza grounds the legitimacy of political authority wholly in the power of the masses, defining government as an office inherent in the people themselves and guaranteed by their natural rights. Spinoza's political theory bases itself in the rights of the masses (*multitudo*), and it does so in a forceful way.[11]

One result is that Spinoza's conception of the civil state differs substantially from that of the contract models. After Spinoza deals with natural right in chapter 2 of the *Political Treatise*, the opening of chapter 3 starts with the discussion of the right of civil state: "The order maintained by any state is called civil" (Shirley 48) ("Imperii cujuscunque status dicitur civilis" [TP III§1]). Like the right of the individual in the state of nature, Spinoza judges the authority of the civil state to extend as far as its power may reach (TP III§2). Again, the equation turns on what *potentia* means in this context, for the equation works both ways. Rights can be claimed, but only as far as the powerpotential may reach. In other words, the state is bound by its own constitutive condition, which in turn is determined by the role played by the masses (*multitudo*). The state qua state does not create or constitute new rights. Its prerogatives are strictly delimited by the state's constituting authority, that is to say, by the masses. "For every man's natural right (if we consider the matter correctly) does not cease in a civil order" (Shirley 49) ("nam jus naturae uniuscujusque [si recte rem perpendamus] in statu civili non cessat" [TP III§3]). As a consequence, the foundation of the civil state effects no transformation of the nature and status of natural rights. Its task, instead, is to establish a framework in which those rights can be expressed and realized. Spinoza in this way ensures that political philosophy will not lose sight of the crucial aspect of natural rights that allows the foundation of the civil state to take place and remains present as its constitutive factor—a point that will play an important role in Mendelssohn's theory of the state. What links the natural and civil state is the functional parallelism expressed in the as-if structure Spinoza employs to characterize the bond cementing the state into one body. His formula "una veluti mente" stresses the fictional and constructivist but crucial element involved in the construction of the state. In introducing this formula as early as chapter 2 of the *Political Treatise,* which discusses the natural state, Spinoza underscores the fact that the basis for this conception is rooted in nature. Here, the as-if construction "omnes una veluti mente ducuntur" (TP II§16) is introduced to address the question of why and how laws function in general, a figure of speech that highlights the constructivist aspect of the legislative function itself.

Like the anti-teleological thrust of Spinoza's metaphysics as a whole, the expression "una veluti mente ducuntur" contains no organic or pseudo-Platonic connotations. Implying both the potential strength and weakness of the ever precarious status of the civil order, the ambiguity of this formula points to the problematic inherent in any form the state may take.[12]

Only here does Spinoza introduce reason as the means of optimizing the life of the individual and the state, but not by postulating or positing reason as a fixed property. Taking the cue from his central trope for imagining how the ideal state might function, Spinoza develops his argument in precise correspondence with the theory of human nature and natural rights. For just as the individual is seen to be all the more powerful the more he or she follows the voice of reason, so the legitimate authority of the state and its government increases to the extent that they are informed by reason. For Spinoza, reason and powerpotential are interrelated. Unlike the Cartesian rationalist or the Hobbesian mechanist, Spinoza comprehends reason as a function that correlates to or results from nature, not as a force detached from or even opposed to it. The *conatus,* nature's tendency toward self-preservation, obeys the same natural laws as the laws that constitute thought. This parallelism informs Spinoza's metaphysical framework deeply enough to make it constitutive for his conception of political theory. But it does not supply a prescription as to how political ideals must look, for such prescriptions remain for Spinoza strictly dependent on the reality of political arrangements in place. Reason cannot dictate in absolute terms what is right. The "reason of state" is always the reason of the multitude constituting that state, which in turn is determined by the individuals who make up that multitude. The expression "una veluti mente" does not so much establish a norm as simply highlight the intricate constitution that makes the civil state. This makes the formula resistant to instrumentalization.

There is no other way, it suggests, to conceive of such *una mens* or "state spirit" other than as the democratically perfected realization of the political power of the multitude. Spinoza unfolds this dynamic conception of the state in subsequent chapters of the *Political Treatise* that discuss the three main forms of political order: monarchy, aristocracy, and democracy.

The formulation that *potestas* is determined by *potentia* (TP IV§1 and earlier) signals Spinoza's key critical distinction between political power as institutionalized claim and actual powerpotential. Analogous to the distinction between *natura naturans* and *natura naturata*, *potentia* comprises *potestas* as part which, however, is never identical with it. This distinction allows Spinoza to combine a Machiavellian approach to politics with the view that the source of power lies ultimately with the people. Spinoza highlights the critical difference between power understood as *potentia* as the legitimizing ground (the people as sovereign) on the one hand and *potestas* or executive power on the other. While *potestas* follows its own logic, it lasts only as long as *potentia* underwrites it. For Spinoza, understanding this law of political power constitutes reason in the political context. To act against it is tantamount to "sinning," a word Spinoza had previously emptied of any theological meaning and redefined as something possible only in the civil state (TP II§§18–19), an act whose primary meaning denotes self-harm. To break the rules of reason thus means to go against the interests of self-preservation of the body that constitutes the state, that is, the individual: "and it is in this sense we can say that a commonwealth does wrong [literally: commits a sin], when it does something contrary to the dictates of reason" (Shirley 58) ("et hoc sensu dicere possumus, civitatem peccare, quando contra rationis dictamen aliquid agit" [TP IV§4]). As a result, Spinoza's concern of how to construct political legitimacy devoid of unintended normative implications is rephrased as the question of what form of state constitution is preferable to others—in other words, what is the best form of government? Spinoza preempts the normative implications that usually govern such discussions by couching it in different terms, as if he were willing to admit a teleological view into his argument after all: "The best way to organize a state is easily discovered by considering the purpose of civil order, which is nothing other than peace and security of life" (Shirley 61) ("Qualis autem optimus cujusqunque imperii sit status facile ex fine status civilis cognoscitur: qui scilicet nullus alius est quam pax vitaeque securitas" [TP V§2]). But what follows is an argument that no state will last unless it is founded on principles that guarantee peace and security. The distinction between *potestas* and *potentia* suggests that if civil rights are grounded in natural rights the latter provide the foundation for the legitimation of civil rights and cannot therefore be replaced by them. For key notions like peace, security, law, obedience, and citizenship (*civitas*) this means that the juxtaposition of civil versus natural rights no longer implies the possibility of natural rights' being overwritten by civil rights. At this point the *Ethics*' dynamic understanding of nature buttresses the argument in a crucial way. For Spinoza, the formula "peace and security of life" points beyond a political solution in the conventional sense to one that embraces what today is called social and cultural life. It is Spinoza's "materialist" stand that gives this passage a crucial turn. The parallelism between thought (*res cogitans*) and the physical world (*res extensa*) renders it impossible to sever one from the other or reduce body to mind or vice versa. As a result, it becomes impossible to define peace negatively and declare it, with Hobbes, to be the absence of war. Spinoza takes great care to make this clear:

> For peace is not just the absence of war, but a virtue which comes from strength of mind: for obedience (section 19, chapter 2) is the steadfast will to carry out orders enjoined by the general decree of the commonwealth. (Shirley 62)

> Pax enim non belli privatio, sed virtus est, quae ex animi fortitudine oritur: est namque obsequium (per art. 19. cap. II) constans voluntas id exequendi, quod ex communi civitatis decret fieri debet. (TP V§4)

What makes a state a state are those moments that create an environment conducive to the free development of the powerpotential of every member of society in a manner optimal for society as a whole. No longer conceived as tools of domination and control, law and order are transformed into instruments for self-preservation qua self-realization that provide the grounding for a structure constituted "from the bottom up." "Pax enim non belli privatio" ("For peace is not mere absence of war") announces a fundamental paradigm shift in political theory. For the notion of peace as absence of war is predicated on the notion of war, which in turn is based on the derivative concept of *potestas* rather than *potentia,* the primary concept that constitutes political power in the first place. However, to ground political theory in the derivative function of *potestas* instead of *potentia* leads to the categorical mistake of investing executive power with the authority of ultimate legitimation, a power exclusively held by those who represent the unrestricted entirety of *potentia,* that is, the multitude. Spinoza's concept of peace, on the other hand, replaces Hobbes's bleak perspective with the idea of self-determination.[13] In Spinoza, peace serves as guarantor that no outside consideration alien to the political sphere alters the conception of *civitas* based on autonomous self-determination. This reversal of the Hobbesian definition of peace as the absence of war highlights the radically different approach Spinoza takes: "a commonwealth whose peace depends on the sluggish spirit of its subjects who are led like sheep to learn simply to be slaves can more properly be called a desert than a commonwealth" (Shirley 62) ("Illa praeterea civitas, cujus pax a subditorum inertia pendet, qui scilicet veluti pecora ducuntur ut tantum servire discant, rectius solitudo quam civitas dici potest" [TP V§4]). Spinoza's biting sarcasm exposes the problematic nature of the paradigm of the self-sufficient and lonely individual at the center of modern political philosophy.[14] Illustrating his point with another image, this time drawn from the world of physiology, Spinoza continues:

> So when we say that the best state is one where men pass their lives in harmony, I am speaking of human life, which is characterized not just by the circulation of the blood and other features common to all animals, but especially by reason, the true virtue and life of the mind. (Shirley 62)

> Cum ergo dicimus, illud imperium optimum esse, ubi homines concorditer vitam transigunt, vitam humanam intelligo, quae non sola sanguinis circulatione et aliis, quae omnibus animalibus sunt communia, sed quae maxime ratione, vera mentis virtute et vita, definitur. (TP V§5)

However, Spinoza's pointed refusal of a physical or, for that matter, a physiological model does not give way to any kind of reductive rationalism. The Spinozist concept of reason carefully mediates between these extremes on the basis of the ontological parallelism developed in his metaphysics. Reason thus does not simply replace war or any other "reality" as point of reference; rather, it delineates the complex ensemble of conditions that define life in all its irreducibility. To define human life according to reason in the Spinozist sense means according the issue of self-determination center stage. Rather than viewing the relationship between reason and the irrationality of the masses in terms of opposition or conflict, Spinoza comprehends them as two aspects under which human life manifests itself. This allows him to imagine a state of harmony that might be established between them, a state he calls the free multitude (*multitudo libera*).

In a radical move, Spinoza, then, advances the paradigm of the free multitude as the subject and agent that constitutes the civil state and thus from the outset as the only legitimate sovereign. Guided by hope rather than fear, the free multitude is independent, autonomous, peaceful, and governed by reason, that is, by itself (TP V§6). On this note and with the recourse to Machiavelli as the political thinker who warned against the surrender of all power to any one individual, Spinoza brings the discussion of the key concepts of political philosophy in the first half of the *Tractatus politicus* to its conclusion.

The concept of the free multitude thus assumes a paradigmatic role. The discussion of the three forms of government in the second half of the *Tractatus politicus* formulates an indirect yet systematic critique of political theory and practice. For Spinoza, there is clearly no single, ideal form of government and political state, for every state is ultimately the result of the social and historical conditions that determine its form. Spinoza nonetheless follows a consistent strategy that seeks to maximize opportunities for self-determination within political structures. Even monarchy and aristocracy emerge in this light as radically democratized forms of political organizations. The *Political Treatise*'s mode of argument effectively reconstitutes the power conventionally associated with a specific individual or polity and decentralizes the decision-making processes in a way that reimagines the state as a self-determining body politic. It seems rather striking, as Balibar has pointed out, that the consequence of this radically democratic conception eventually threatens to undermine Spinoza's construction of democracy as such. That the treatise breaks off at this point and its crowning conclusion remained unwritten may, after all, be no coincidence, Balibar suggests, for it is here that the aporia of democracy surfaces in a radicalized form as rupture or impossibility.[15]

Yet whatever difficulties a political theory of democracy may pose, Spinoza's concept of the free multitude exposes and reformulates this problem in a critical manner. His stress on the body politic's continual need to deliberate and consult with itself envisions the political state as intrinsically public in nature, that is, literally a *res publica*.[16] Like

Machiavelli, Spinoza utilizes the history of the Roman republic less out of nostalgia than as a platform for his own ideas:

> For if "while the Romans debate, Saguntum is lost," on the other hand, when all decisions are made by a few men who have only themselves to please, freedom and the common good are lost. The fact is that men's wits are too obtuse to get straight to the heart of every question, but by discussing, listening to others, and debating, their wits are sharpened, and by exploring every avenue, they eventually discover what they are seeking, something that meets with general approval and that no one had previously thought of. (Shirley 126)

> Nam si, dum Romani deliberant, perit Saguntus, dum contra pauci ex solo suo affectu omnia decernerunt, perit libertas communeque bonum. Sunt namque humana ingenia hebetiora, quam ut omnia statim penetrare possint; sed consulendo, audiendo et disputando acuuntur, et dum omnia tentant media, ea, quae volunt, tandem inveniunt, quae omnes probant et de quibus nemo antea cogitasset. (TP IX§14)

Here, reason takes on a new role in political theory. The epistemological project Spinoza had formulated in his theory of the improvement of the intellect (*Tractatus de intellectus emendatione*) begins to show its political significance. Reason and autonomy are theorized as linked in a manner that prefigures Rousseau[17] yet avoids falling under the spell of his organic quasi-mythical model of community. Instead, Spinoza's conception of political autonomy and self-determination invests reason with an emancipatory dynamic. Reason assumes a constructive role in the process of constituting the political arena, but it remains free from normative impositions. In this manner, Spinoza forcefully places reason as emancipated form of self-determination at the center of the political sphere.

This concept of reason is no longer Cartesian or Hobbesian but distinctly Spinozist. Originating from human affectivity, reason as its most evolved stage leads the way to the lasting institution of freedom and self-determination. The activist implications reason projects are thus not coincidental but spring directly from the political intent inscribed in Spinoza's political theory, a theory whose metatheoretical reflection on power and powerpotential reaffirms the legitimacy of the concern for the individual as a key issue for a critical theory of politics.

Spinoza is particularly concerned with the checks and balances that control political power, in the notion that a complex weave of political competencies and tasks is crucial to consensus building in a well-functioning state. Addressing the problem of power and political interests as an intrinsically philosophical one, the treatise poses the question of institutionalization in a radicalized way.[18] The profoundly anarchist streak that informs Spinoza's argument is closely connected to his particular nominalism. If Spinoza's innovative point in his radical account of natural rights was apparent enough in his uncompromising treatment of social contract theory and his notion of the multitude, the significance of the treatise points beyond this to the problematic status of all legitimations of institutional power as such. Breaking off at this point, the *Political Treatise* does not necessarily signal a failure in the argument. Instead, this interruption suggests a critical resistance to a premature closure. By keeping this project open-ended, Spinoza stakes out a theoretical space that only the realization of a practice of reason will be able to formulate that remains yet to emerge.

PART II

SPINOZA THROUGH MENDELSSOHN

CHAPTER 6

FROM THE MARGINS OF PHILOSOPHY

Mendelssohn's Aesthetic Theory of Mixed Sentiments

AT THE HEART OF MOSES MENDELSSOHN'S THOUGHT seems to lie a paradox that imposes itself in the way his work is discussed. Whereas for the eighteenth century the preeminence of his pivotal role for the foundation of modern German literature and philosophy remained undisputed and required no special explanation, it is, ironically, the seamless absorption of Mendelssohn's contribution to a new conception of aesthetic theory that seems to have obscured the signal import of his thought for the formation of eighteenth-century aesthetic and literary discourse. As Mendelssohn's subtle shifts and innovations were subsequently taken up by his contemporaries, from Goethe to Kant, they became a fixture in the discursive inventory of his time. In short, Mendelssohn's notions turned into paradigms. What had thus originally been introduced as change and innovation was increasingly simply taken as the consequent expression of the consensus Mendelssohn's theorizing had created in the first place—as "popular philosophy" at its best and the revival of the classic art of conversing at its worst. Mistaken for theoretical currency of the period, embellished with some incidental refinement here and there, Mendelssohn's contributions to philosophy and modern cultural criticism went, therefore, mostly underappreciated if not ignored in their specific, critical significance.

If historians of eighteenth-century literature and philosophy thus paid Mendelssohn little attention, there has emerged on the other hand a continual stream of Mendelssohn studies. However, this branch of scholarship, mainly grouped around the celebration of Mendelssohn anniversaries, has had, with the exception of some occasional benevolent acknowledgments, no further consequences. In the meantime, quietly and unassumingly, the publication of the new edition of Mendelssohn's works has come to its completion. Along with Alexander Altmann's painstakingly detailed contextualization of the philosopher's writing within his contemporaneous environment, Mendelssohn's position as metaphysician, aesthetician, political thinker, and Enlightenment figure has been firmly established.[1]

In its scope, however, the field of Mendelssohn study has remained somewhat asymmetrical. On the one hand, and mainly centering around the event of Mendelssohn anniversaries, Mendelssohn's role as champion of Jewish emancipation has been given full attention. On the other hand, monographs of the more scholarly areas of his work have produced a series of philological studies. Over time, these two sides have largely ignored each other, producing a popular image on the one hand and a scholarly image on the other. Thus the two disparate sides that have emerged of Mendelssohn—as both the popular, political figure and the subtle-minded, attentive critic of aesthetic detail—have created a peculiarly split view of the Jewish philosopher inhabiting two separate and, as it were, divided worlds. Only recent efforts have opened up an approach challenging this kind of interpretative division of labor whose hermeneutic fatality has been to classify Mendelssohn according to the research arrangements of the contemporary organization of academic disciplines rather than to examine his thought in terms of his project as a whole. This new interest points beyond the narrow scope of reception history to a new appreciation of the significance accorded to Mendelssohn today, especially, but not exclusively, with regard to the signal contribution of his theory and conception of Judaism.[2]

However, there are several reasons for the fact that a more fully rounded picture of Mendelssohn has yet to emerge. There is, after all, very little that could be called "canonical writing" in the conventional sense to which an interpretation could turn in order to secure Mendelssohn as a classic. Work-oriented philological research has only recently attended to the fact that works-in-progress—minor works such as reviews, epistolary genres, correspondence, and short fragments of notes and individual interventions—may represent important if not decisive instances of theoretical statements and must therefore not be neglected.

To be sure, Mendelssohn did not perceive himself in the first place as an author of an independent, coherent body of text. Rather, his self-understanding was that of an insistent interrogator, critic, examiner, and commentator.[3] Starting out with his philosophical dialogues, the *Philosophische Gespräche* and *Über die Empfindung* (both published anonymously in 1755)—the latter an epistolary dialogue that itself introduces a great measure of dialogues as the fictive correspondents enjoy reporting their conversations on philosophical topics word for word—Mendelssohn sets tone and method quite subtly. Although Mendelssohn is usually considered a disciple and follower of Leibniz and Wolff, in whose school of thought he had trained himself once he was given the opportunity to expand his education beyond his original training in classic medieval Jewish philosophy, it is no coincidence that, in his own writing, he practices a style quite different from the assertive, rather doctrinaire, and often self-congratulatory style of Wolff. Opening up his discourse to a dialogic form of presentation, Mendelssohn brings new air to philosophy, not only in dialogues but also in a form that reflects a new dialogical way of thinking that is wary of the pitfalls of the monolithic construction of systems. In this fashion, Mendelssohn introduces not only a lighter touch to metaphysics but, more importantly, creates an opportunity to delimit the discursive practice and to air concerns and views otherwise excluded from philosophical discourse.[4]

If Mendelssohn's writing was predicated by the limits and restrictions he encountered as a Jew who wished to join the republic of letters, he forged these restraints into his own discursive virtue. Transfixed by the status of the repressed and muted, just "tolerated," Mendelssohn turned his own experience of exclusion from the center of discourse into the project of emancipation and participation. His own form of writing critically reflects the problematic nature of his marginalized position. By staging his philosophical conversations in an underhanded manner, Mendelssohn artfully broaches the question of the rules and stipulations of the discursive play in which he strives to participate.

Mendelssohn's choice of subject matter is then not accidental. His interest in the foundation of aesthetics receives a deeper meaning when seen in the context of his own need for legitimating his self-positioning. In Mendelssohn's mission to free aesthetics from the tutelage of moral philosophy and to establish aesthetics as an independent discipline, traces of his attempt to address the problem of Leibniz's and Wolff's grounding of metaphysics in a Christian-based framework become discernible.

Mendelssohn research has divided its appraisal according to the disciplines to which it has assigned the subjects addressed by Mendelssohn. This has created the impression of a distinct differentiation of the disciplines, a differentiation that, however, was only just about to constitute itself. Whereas Mendelssohn and his contemporaries found themselves developing theories to institute the differentiation between philosophy and literature, morals and aesthetics, and politics and religion as they argued for the independence for each of these subject areas, this process of differentiation was only just about to begin in Mendelssohn's time. What we might call, anachronistically, the interdisciplinary—or more precisely, the predisciplinary—mode of thinking best describes the critical concern of Mendelssohn's theoretical interests. These interests implicitly share the tacit yet central urgency for a Jew to reflect on the conditions, costs, and stipulations that need to be met in order to enter, participate in, and contribute to contemporary culture and philosophy. Whether it concerns the nature of contingency, Rousseau's second discourse, the role of Spinoza, or the nature of reason or evil, Mendelssohn's interest is thus never just an academic one but one that stresses the concern for what he calls at some point "the connection of all things" ("Zusammenhang aller Dinge"). This attention to "the connection of all things" allows Mendelssohn to address what most critics claim to be his deep-seated predicament: the alleged separation of the philosopher from the engaged Jew. To Mendelssohn, the emancipatory moment of his philosophical practice consists in that, as far as he is concerned, such a split does not only not occur but that it is exactly his perspicaciously couched philosophical trajectory that exposes the perception of such a split as an imaginary, problematic assumption of a flawed rationalism.

For Mendelssohn, the connection is always there. The issue of Jewish identity is never far away or simply suspended, and by no means is it cordoned off from his philosophical and aesthetic interests. Instead, the specifically critical impulse of Mendelssohn's thinking thrives on the recognition of the intimate connection of all of his concerns—theoretical, practical, intellectual, and political. The unique form in which Mendelssohn sustains this link highlights the self-reflective turn that characterizes his thought. An example of how his concerns interfere in a critical way with his readings can be found in his comment on a remark in Rousseau's second discourse. There Rousseau observes that the offense of somebody's rights is equivalent to war. Mendelssohn notes that this is applicable to the plight of the Jews, whose situation can, consequently, be described as war, too:

> Whose rights are illicitly injured is made war upon; Jews are therefore incessantly made war upon. If one has more power than the part that is made war upon this one may make use of cunning.
>
> Wessen Rechte auf eine unerlaubte Weise gekränkt werden, der wird bekriegt; daher werden die Juden unaufhörlich bekriegt. Wenn man dem bekriegten Theil an Macht überlegen ist, so mag er sich der List bedienen. (Jub A 2, 8)[5]

Prompted by Rousseau's conclusions, which do not speak to the particular situation of disenfranchised Jews in Europe, Mendelssohn voices his critical concern early on. Mindful of Mendelssohn's own precarious position, this note illustrates how he engages the predicament of his Jewishness directly as a critical force to rethink the views and opinions of his contemporaries.

The view that Mendelssohn never seems to have left the grounds of Leibniz-Wolffian principles[6] has created the impression of him as a somewhat old-fashioned, antiquated figure caught between the "two worlds," the medieval ghetto and modern Europe of the Enlightenment.[7] If the Leibniz-Wolffian framework certainly defines the methodological and theoretical platform on which Mendelssohn formulates his thought, it is important to note that the attraction of such a systematic framework lies in its potential to serve as the kind of secure base necessary in order to express the needs of an outsider like Mendelssohn. The fact that this system proved sufficiently comprehensive to address concerns of modernity in a systematic and critical fashion made it a promising vehicle for a philosopher who looked for reliability. Its logical stringency seemed to provide the kind of coherence and consistency other alternatives at the time did not offer. Taken in the pragmatic way in which Wolffian philosophy lent itself to application, this system carried, despite its antiquated rigidity, the promise of genuine philosophical solidity. For Mendelssohn at least, its framework presented a methodical way of thinking whose logical transparency would safeguard against the flaws and errors of other systems of metaphysics.

Given the prominent family resemblance with Leibniz's and Wolff's metaphysical framework, it seems only natural to read Mendelssohn in the light of the context of their philosophical systems. But this family resemblance points back to a deeper affinity with Spinoza as Leibniz and Wolff remain defined by the desire to break away from his metaphysics that poses a formative challenge to their thought. Especially when in the case of some applications of Leibniz-Wolffian principles Mendelssohn proves to be an independent interpreter of their philosophies, it is interesting to note that his reading often suggests a turn to what seems to denote an implicit agreement with a Spinoza-inspired view. However, it is not so much a question of influence or dependence but rather the occurrence of such correspondence that calls for attention. For it is due to some concerns shared by both Mendelssohn and Spinoza that a particular constellation emerges that leads Mendelssohn to arguments and formulations similar to those we find in Spinoza, even though direct influence may quite often seem out of the question. Beyond the issue of influence, whose methodological quandaries would pose more questions than it could answer, the crucial point consists in the fact that the shared concern in responding to the challenge of modernity—which in both Mendelssohn and Spinoza is key to their projects—produces responses with a remarkable family resemblance. Seen in this way, the edifice of Leibniz-Wolffian philosophy can be understood as the structure of thought standing between the two philosophers through which Mendelssohn, as it were, communicates with Spinoza. In this way, Wolffian philosophy serves as a screen that allows Mendelssohn to formulate his critique in a methodologically reflected fashion, in a manner that, at the same time, provides the necessary protection against the unwarranted and perilous consequences that an open association with Spinozism would entail. As Leibniz and Wolff can, in a way, both be viewed as representing to some degree a variation of the basic model of metaphysics introduced by Spinoza, the innovative aspects of Mendelssohn's reading of Leibniz and Wolff present in a cautiously reflected fashion some Spinozist elements that the philosophies of Leibniz and Wolff had dropped, reconstructed, or transformed.[8] Acknowledging this point allows us to register the implicit dynamics of a mode of expression that, at first sight, carries the appearance of just moving along conventional lines of a preset metaphysical discourse but which, upon closer inspection, brings these very lines to exposure.

The self-conscious manner in which Mendelssohn employs Leibniz as the most feasible philosophical position changes the ontological status of Leibnizian metaphysics from indisputably true to an understanding that privileges one form of metaphysics over another simply in terms of which one provides the more probable and plausible form of theoretical reasoning. This methodologically critical attitude indicates a decisive shift from a traditional position distinguishing between true and false to a position that pragmatically distinguishes between a more or less convincing degree of evidence. Such an understanding of the heuristic value of metaphysics implies no longer the validity of unquestioned truths but simply illustrates Mendelssohn's option to operate within a logically sound structure. Mendelssohn introduces his changes as inconspicuous, subtle differentiations, but his revisions prove to be more than just minor corrections, for these differentiations represent a constant critical reminder of the problematic nature of the conditions of philosophical discourse, its contingent character, and, as a consequence, the impossibility for closure and final determination in philosophical reflection, whose very element is defined by fluidity and constant motion.

As a budding philosopher, Mendelssohn, as a Jew unwilling to forsake his particularity, quite naturally faced some of the same problems Spinoza had had to come to terms with a century earlier. Both found themselves confronted with the fact that philosophy was defined by metaphysical assumptions steeped in a Christian understanding of philosophy, a philosophy that even in its secularized varieties had a distinct Christian foundation. In the case of Leibniz, for example, strong undercurrents of Lutheran theology informed his philosophy strongly enough to pose a problem for a non-Christian like Mendelssohn.

On the other hand, Spinoza—perceived as the alien if not exotic, "oriental" philosopher[9]—had established a full-fledged metaphysics along with a complete, "universal ontology"[10] that presented a challenging alternative to the Christian-based metaphysics of his time. In this context, Spinoza stood out as a philosopher who succeeded in replacing an implicitly Christian-defined framework of metaphysics with a fully self-sufficient philosophical system that would no longer hinge on any particular religious creed. Mendelssohn would thus find himself in the same corner Spinoza occupied. They shared some of the same questions, concerns, and reservations that a Jewish philosopher would harbor when confronted with modern European thought.

Spinoza's endeavor to rethink, by way of an ontology grounded in a dynamic conception of nature, the mind-body problem and the theory of affects—both announcing the project of a resolute liberation of body and soul—intensely reverberates in Mendelssohn. There are many instances where Mendelssohn formulates positions that might be construed as Wolffian or responding to contemporary issues, or some refinement of a Leibnizian view, yet the deviations and slight adjustments inscribed in his position remind us that his thought cannot be reduced to one or another position. Instead, the inscription of these corrections, variations, and differentiations critically points beyond the scope of these metaphysical systems. Mendelssohn's stress on the importance of the physical and material aspects of human nature and culture, the determining role that the affects play, and the comprehensive and consequential notion of perfection as the calling and determination of man and the concept of nature all propose a metaphysical framework that responds to the Leibniz-Wolffian frame of reference with interpretations and revisions leaning toward a Spinozist point of view. Even where one might argue for a consistent Leibnizian position in Mendelssohn, the underlying tenor voices a pointedly Spinozist reading of Leibniz. No wonder that in the eyes of Lessing, Mendelssohn had the promise to become a second Spinoza, one, however, without the faults of the first one.[11]

At the latest by 1754, it is possible to document Mendelssohn's study of Spinoza's *Ethics*. The recurrent surfacing of the name and ideas of Spinoza in conversations and in the correspondence with Lessing reveals how intense the discussion about him must have been during this early period when Spinoza played a formative role in the shaping of their ideas. Consequently, it is with a bold and provocative rescue of Spinoza that Mendelssohn inaugurates his publishing career. Anonymously published in 1755, the *Philosophical Dialogues* (*Philosophische Gespräche*) open with an unlikely move for a student of Leibniz and Wolff. It has been only thanks to the radical thought of Spinoza, the author argues, that philosophy has been able to reach the heights of Leibniz's vantage point. Leibniz, in short, would not have been possible without Spinoza's errors. Much like Lessing's "rescues," Mendelssohn fashions his argument strategically. While granting that Spinoza's philosophy is flawed, Mendelssohn at the same time maintains that it is in Spinoza that Leibniz's idea of preestablished harmony was prefigured in its basic outline.[12] Through the attempt to rehabilitate Spinoza, Mendelssohn broaches the question of exclusion from and acceptance in the discourse of philosophy. As a result, the *Philosophical Dialogues* indirectly address the question of how the discourse of philosophy functions and how it is constituted. For if philosophy develops in a different way than the histories of philosophy portray it, the dialogues suggest, the need for proper assessment of the role of the individual philosopher emerges with new urgency. Mechanisms of exclusion and inclusion thus call for critical investigation because they determine the parameters that define philosophy itself.

With this figure of rescue, Mendelssohn responds to the formidable challenge of joining a project from which he, as a Jew, is excluded. Reclaiming a place for Spinoza enables Mendelssohn to open up the limited hermeneutic horizon of Christian theology that defines the scope of philosophy. By injecting Spinoza into the discourse, Mendelssohn thus is able to project himself into philosophy. More than simply adding a correction to the record of the historiography of philosophy, the *Philosophical Dialogues* perform the opening of a space for Mendelssohn to enter philosophy. In this way, they touch on a central issue in modern philosophy: the question of the philosopher's self-reflection with regard to the pragmatic conditions of the discursive constitution of philosophy.

But Spinoza comes to symbolize the starting point from which Mendelssohn and Lessing launch their debates not only with regard to questions concerning metaphysics and theology but also concerning drama, the functions of tragedy, the staging of emotions, and other questions related to aesthetics.[13] For an adequate understanding of the dynamics that are released onstage requires a more refined theory of sentiments and emotions than those current in aesthetic and moral theories of the time. Only in Spinoza, however, could they find a refined analysis of the functions of emotions and passions that offered a consistent explanation of the powerful dynamics at work in human nature.

Über die Empfindungen (1755), published shortly after *Philosophische Gespräche*, treats topics such as the sentiments, beauty, and perfection, including, in a fictional exchange of letters, a long digression on the moral acceptability of suicide. The correspondents, Palemon and Euphranor,[14] are, by courtesy of the anonymous editor/author, imagined to continue the conversations they—or their fictional alter egos—had begun in Shaftesbury.

The 1761 preface to the *Philosophische Schriften* introduces the "Rhapsodie, oder Zusätze zu den Briefen über die Empfindungen" as "some observations about the nature of mixed sentiments that are composed of pleasure and displeasure and about the astonishing power of their effect on the soul" (D 3).[15] In Spinoza's terms, this represents nothing less than a collection of elements toward a theory of affects. For according to Spinoza, affects result not only from the mixture of pleasure and displeasure but also from desire. Spinoza calls these sources of all affects *laetitia, tristitia,* and *cupiditas* (joy, sadness, desire). What, in the context of the discussions of the 1750s, makes for such a strikingly different role in Mendelssohn compared to the one accorded to the affects by contemporaneous theorists is his interest in advancing an analysis of aesthetics in the framework of a dynamic model of human nature that is grounded in a coherent and consistent ontology. Conscious of the insufficiencies of the current theories of sentiments, Mendelssohn advocates a concept of nature that acknowledges the full range of the dynamics and the divinity of nature as creative force. To Mendelssohn, feeling, sentiments, and affects are not detached, disconnected occurrences of individual subjectivity. Rather, their nature can only be properly understood if they are recognized as integrated and constitutive elements of human nature.

In a programmatic way, Euphranor summarizes the enlightenment project of the theory of affects in *Über die Empfindungen.* The meteorological metaphor for enlightenment adds here a new aspect. Contrary to the understanding of the Enlightenment as a reductionist enterprise of rationalism gone astray, this passage articulates Mendelssohn's critical awareness of the function of affects in the process of the search for truth. The decisive role Mendelssohn ascribes to the economy of affects, not only in terms of the problem of knowledge but also with regard to the liberation from the domination by the passions, is expressed in a telling enlightenment metaphor: "If we want to quell the storm of an unpleasant passion, reason commands us to reflect on the causes of our displeasure and to clarify the concepts. Only out of these clouds does the violent storm arise, and the furor of the passions vanishes as soon as it becomes sunny in our soul" (D 12).[16] As Mendelssohn sums up this movement of enlightenment: "The emotion vanishes as soon as concepts are elucidated" (D 12).[17] In 1755 this was worded slightly differently: "The emotion vanishes when all concepts are distinct" ("Der Affect verschwindet; sobald die Begriffe deutlich werden").[18] In commenting on this passage, Altmann points out that this insight can be traced to Spinoza (E5P3): "An affect, which is a passion, ceases to be a passion, as soon as we form a clear and distinct idea thereof." Altmann suggests that Mendelssohn may well have had this proposition in mind when he wrote the passage just quoted.[19] This passage may lend itself to a rationalist interpretation, but the last clause—"the furor of the passions vanishes as soon as it becomes sunny in our soul" ("und so bald es in unsrer Seele heiter wird, so verschwindet das Toben der Leidenschaft")—emphasizes that it is only after the emotional turmoil has cleared up, once the soul becomes sunny (*heiter* signifies the serene state of the psyche as well as a cleared sky), that the storm of passions recedes. Unless the power of passions is kept in check (Mendelssohn uses for this the word *Gewalt*)—and this means the recognition of the whole force and impact of the affects on the progress of knowledge—there will be no enlightenment.

If we follow most interpreters—as well as Theokles, who expresses his deeply felt thanks to his heroes Locke, Wolff, and Leibniz—Spinoza seems curiously absent from this list of credits. Yet this is a list of one of the characters, not of Mendelssohn himself. At the other end of the correspondence stands Euphranor, whose enthusiasm for nature resonates more with some sort of Shaftesbury's enthusiasm with a distinct Spinozist ring. It is, however, Theokles whose intellectual leadership makes him the mentor for young Euphranor and who expresses ideas that display a striking resemblance to those of Spinoza. Not only does Theokles view nature as the most dignified subject for observation to instantiate his thoughts (D 15–16; Jub A 1, 244), but what makes nature so noble is its divine origin (D 16–17; Jub A 1, 245). The parallelism between mind and body and the central role of the senses for the affects—and, as a consequence, for the sentiments—point beyond the metaphysical framework of Leibniz and Wolff and toward the unique way in which Spinoza grasps these issues. The reflections on miracles, which stress the argument that it is ultimately the causality of the laws of nature that is truly wonderful and admirable, as well as the idea that the more we understand the parts of nature the more we will eventually comprehend nature as a whole and, therefore, God (D 16–17; Jub A 1, 244), go beyond the aesthetic enthusiasm of Shaftesbury. Their theoretical implications bear a distinctly Spinozist note.[20]

But Mendelssohn's most important difference from traditional metaphysics is the way he redefines perfection. Leibniz and Wolff had defined perfection as the harmonious development of all forces in nature or in man. Mendelssohn takes this idea a step further as he connects perfection with self-preservation, which, for Mendelssohn as for Spinoza, is tantamount to self-realization. In Mendelssohn's use, the term "perfection" thus gains a richer sense, indicating, instead of stasis, a continual, pulsating dynamic in the nature of the universe. Mendelssohn imagines perfection no longer as a classicist pruning and smoothing off the edges but rather as the realization of the full potential of the affective economy.[21] From the idea that perfection implies the imitation of an absolute, exterior standard, perfection shifts now to denote self-determination: "Regarded as a determination of the mind and cut off from its fleshy companion, from sensual rapture, the pure gratification of the soul must be grounded in the positive powers of our soul and not in its incapacity, not in the limitation of these original powers" (D 19).[22] This is also precisely the project as Spinoza formulates it in the headings of parts 4 and 5 of the *Ethics,* where he juxtaposes "human bondage or the power of the affects" against "the power of reason or human freedom."

In "Rhapsodie," Mendelssohn further clarifies the concept of perfection. He ties it closely to the idea of the equality of the senses and of reason (D 139–40; Jub A 1, 392–93). The dynamic nature of the concept becomes obvious when he goes on to explain that isolation, abstraction, and stasis are the very opposite of what he has in mind: "But true perfection is a living flame, constantly fanning out and becoming stronger and stronger the more it is able to fan out. The inclination to communicate itself and to reproduce the good that one enjoys is implanted in the soul as much as the instinct to preserve oneself. We become more perfect, if everything that surrounds us is perfect; we become happier if we are able to make everything around us happy" (D 152).[23] The almost cosmological quality of the concept of perfection, its status as a natural law, is expressed in a proposition that reaches such poetic density that it reminds one of Werther's enthusiasm for the divine character of nature as *natura naturans:* "This universal law, this nerve of happiness, runs through all parts of creation, blooms in the rose, stirs in the worm, and thinks, wills, and feels blissfully in the human being" (D 154).[24]

Mendelssohn formulates the connection between his pedagogical project and its anchoring within a philosophical framework in a systematic manner in "Von der Herrschaft über die Neigungen." He has used the systematic content of this piece of 1757 for the concluding parts of "Rhapsodie" four years later. But it is in this short draft that Mendelssohn links aesthetics and ethics in a principal and programmatic way:

> If we are supposed to be encouraged to live virtuously one must not be satisfied to have demonstrated with all rigor the laudability of virtue but one also has to have made us familiar with a great number of motivating reasons and we must learn to think over this number of motives quickly.

> Sollen wir zu einem tugendhaften Wandel aufgemuntert werden, so muß man sich nicht begnügen, uns die Löblichkeit der Tugend nach aller Strenge demonstrirt zu haben; sondern man muß uns mit einer großen Menge von Bewegungsgründen bekannt machen, und wir müssen lernen, diese Menge von Motiven schnell zu überdenken. (Jub A 2, 150–51)

Mendelssohn's project is, thus, to "transform the symbolic [i.e., discursive] conclusion of practical morals into intuitive cognition" ("symbolische Schlüsse der practischen Sittenlehre in eine anschauende Erkenntniß verwandeln" (Jub A 2, 152). For this transformation leads to an increase of power over the control of the will. This is possible because the abstract notions are reduced to singular events placed in nature. In this way, we are enabled to observe them more closely. To connect the symbolic cognition of the value of virtue with intuitive cognition, Mendelssohn argues, brings the lower faculties of the soul in harmony with the higher faculties and makes one, as a consequence, perfectly virtuous ("vollkommen tugendhaft" [Jub A 2, 153]).

Intuitive cognition assumes a central role for the achievement of perfection, yet it alone does not suffice. Rather, Mendelssohn suggests that perfection can only be achieved by way of harmonious correspondence between symbolic and intuitive cognition. Each form of cognition in isolation lacks the capacity to gain control over the power of the feelings and passions. It is only through the combination of both forms of cognition that "moral sensitiveness" *(sittliche Empfindsamkeit)* is established as its synthesis (Jub A 2, 153). What is decisive is thus the combination of the rational and the intuitive components, judgment and sensitivity (*Empfindlichkeit*). As a result, the state of perfection does not represent stasis but a complex balance whose play of equilibrium resists fixation and arrestation. "Moral sensitiveness" without support of judgment remains indifferent toward virtue or vice, and sensitivity by itself does not make a person virtuous. It is only when judgment is also improved, and both judgment and sensitivity combine, that a person becomes virtuous. Temperament taken alone remains neutral, too, for it is capable only of increasing or decreasing innate "moral sensitiveness" (Jub A 2, 154).

Two aspects of this systematic grounding of aesthetics on the foundation of ethics seem to be of particular relevance. First is the complex way in which Mendelssohn formulates aesthetic experience as a sort of a catalyst for self-improvement and, as a result, emancipation of human nature from the internal powers of repression. Here, the central significance of aesthetics for the project of enlightenment, particularly the emphasis on autonomy and independence, receives its critical motivation. Second is the differentiated role that a developed awareness of the power of affects and feelings can assume: this heightened awareness illustrates that beyond a rationalist attitude, Mendelssohn possesses a highly developed sensitivity for the affects' constitutive role in the formation of reason and the will.

Mendelssohn's goal of formalizing the impact of the affects and feelings for cognition carries a distinctly Spinozist note. As in Spinoza's theory of affective economy, the maximizing of the power of the affects serves the emancipatory goal of transforming affects into reason. Bamberger notes in this context Mendelssohn's remarkably counter-conventional turn that underlines the innovative character of his view of the aesthetic function of the senses as he parts company, at this point, with Leibniz and Baumgarten.[25] This turn illustrates the need to revise the view that Mendelssohn moved along the tracks of the Leibniz-Wolff school. While seventeenth-century materialists like Gassendi and Hobbes clearly break ground for a revalorization of the sensual and its material base, it is not until Spinoza provides a balanced, metaphysically coherent framework that an ontologically differentiated approach to the sensual is formulated.

In "Rhapsodie," Mendelssohn takes the consequences a step further. There he concludes that while it is correct to call virtue a science (*Wissenschaft*), it must be remembered that realizing virtue requires more than scientific conviction (*wissenschaftliche Ueberzeugung*). Artful practice and proficiency (*kunstmässige Uebung und Fertigkeit*) are necessary to attain complete virtue (D 166; Jub A 1, 421). It is important to note that this theory of a kind of virtuoso virtue that stresses its temporal dimension transcends the mere aspects of technicality. The crucial importance of art and aesthetic exercise has direct implications for the conception of virtue itself. Recognizing the role of temporality as constitutive for the development of a well-trained and coordinated proficiency to exercise virtue redefines the way ethics is theorized. For ethics is now no longer conceived as an exclusively rationality- and intellect-based doctrine. Moreover, Mendelssohn directly links this problem to the imperative to acknowledge the dignity of human nature: "One must become acquainted with the true dignity of the human being and consider the sublimity of the human being's ethical nature in the proper light" (D 165).[26] Virtue thus also depends on the positive image we are able to project onto ourselves: "As an ancient philosopher put it, if someone has the appropriate respect for himself, then he will be all the more inclined to obey the voice of virtue. The shortest path to ethical depravity is to have a low estimation of human nature" (D 165).[27] What Mendelssohn has in mind here takes on a sharper edge when he continues:

> Initially this estimation presents itself in the form of self-knowledge, humility; but it is false as soon as it is applied more to the human race than to the individual and more to what we are as human beings than to what is peculiar to each of us on our own. Then it produces misanthropy rather than self-knowledge, pusillanimity rather than humility, demoralizing the powers of the mind far too much and making us almost indifferent towards good and evil.[28]

Against this ultimately immoral view and its paralyzing consequences, which the rational understanding of the nature of virtue seems to prescribe, Mendelssohn offers a different solution: "With true humility in his heart, a person may be proud of the human being's dignity and of the rank which humanity occupies in creation. We must be something important in our own eyes, and what we do and refrain from doing must be of some significance, if we are to espouse the cause of the good with zeal and energy" (D 165).[29]

But this can only happen either by constant practice (*anhaltende Uebung*) or by intuitive knowledge (D 165; Jub A 1, 421). In this way, a "wholesome enthusiasm" (*heilsamer Enthusiasmus* [D 165; Jub A 1, 421]) awakens in us for the call of virtue. In this fashion, Mendelssohn's aesthetic program serves to propose a conception of enlightenment that is conceived as a project of self-emancipation.

CHAPTER 7

THE EXCHANGE ON TRAGEDY

IN THE EXCHANGE ON TRAGEDY instigated by Nicolai and conducted by himself, Mendelssohn, and Lessing in epistolary form, Mendelssohn carries his theory of the affects to a new level. While the three friends agree that *Mitleid* (pity, compassion, but also sympathy) represents one of the central affects that tragedy is supposed to activate, Mendelssohn insists that *Mitleid* is not the only affect to play a role in tragedy.[1]

Prior to this exchange, *Mitleid* had played an important role in Mendelssohn's moral reasoning, and to some degree it seemed as if Lessing was simply reiterating Mendelssohn's view when he assigned special significance to *Mitleid* on the stage. In *Über die Empfindungen,* Mendelssohn had equated *Mitleid* with the *Schrecken* (fright, terror) experienced in tragedy, which, he argues, is nothing but pity that takes us by surprise ("nichts als ein Mitleiden, das uns schnell überrascht" [Jub A 1, 307, and 110 for the text of the 1755 edition]). There he calls *Mitleid* a mix of agreeable and disagreeable sentiments ("eine Vermischung von angenehmen und unangenehmen Empfindungen" [307]). But already earlier, he had Palemon declare:

> The stage has its own ethos. In life nothing is ethically good that is not grounded in our perfection. On the stage, on the other hand, everything that is grounded in powerful passions is good. The purpose of the tragedy is to arouse passion. (D 58)[2]

> Die Schaubühne hat ihre besondere Sittlichkeit. Im Leben ist nichts sittlich gut, das nicht in unsrer Vollkommenheit gegründet ist; auf der Schaubühne hingegen ist es alles, was in der heftigen Leidenschaft seinen Grund hat. Der Zweck des Trauerspiels ist Leidenschaften zu erregen. (Jub A 1, 94)

In his *Abhandlung vom Trauerspiele,* Nicolai repeats this view and makes it the centerpiece of his program for the modern German stage play.[3] But while Mendelssohn urges us to consider the import of *Mitleid* in the context of a general theory of affects, Lessing wishes to isolate his focus on the role of *Mitleid* alone.

For Lessing, *Mitleid* is the crucial affect that links the aesthetics of the stage with the ethics of our cognitive faculties. Nicolai and Mendelssohn, however, wish to hold *Mitleid* back from dominating center stage all alone. The debate becomes a difficult one because the concerns advanced by both sides are ultimately incongruous. For while both parties may eventually arrive at quite similar and compatible views, the difference driving their discussion overdetermines the discourse in a way that rules out any sort of terminological simplicity. The function ascribed to *Mitleid* by each side is so different that the efforts to clarify its nature provide no grounds that would make it possible to settle the matter satisfactorily.

For Lessing, *Mitleid* represents the conceptual and dramaturgic link connecting the stage with life. It is the key emotion that sets off the dynamics of both recognition and identification while at the same time reconstituting morality. For *Mitleid* critically redefines the social and political conceptions that determine the parameters of society's morals. As the central affect experienced, *Mitleid* points beyond morals as they stand to their extra-moral, originary, and, as it were, natural source. Understood in this way, *Mitleid* expands and transforms the socially determined limits of morals in a critical movement that transforms it into the aesthetic and affective, emotive response to dramatic conflicts and their tragic outcome on the stage. In reducing tragedy to the singular function of producing *Mitleid,* Lessing frees the stage from excessive rules and identifies *Mitleid*'s specific ethical/aesthetic source as the drama's culminating point. This allows him to define drama anew: with *Mitleid* as its center, the drama's sociopolitical impulse is revealed as its genuine, unifying theme. Arguing for a functional continuity from Aristotle to modernity, Lessing develops a conception of *Mitleid* that emphasizes the transformative and emancipatory power of the drama's dynamic. By stressing the function of *Mitleid* to be com-passion (*Mit-Leiden*), Lessing speaks to drama's materially aesthetic force. The spectator is thus conceived not as a detached observer this side of the spectacle's power but as an involved agent connected with the stage performance by *Mitleid*'s emotional force.

Lessing's vision of drama aims at overcoming the rationality based and rule-determined dramatic theory of the French and German theater of his time. The energy released in Lessing's own plays gestures toward the kind of affect that defines *Mitleid* for him: an experience of identificatory involvement that would lead to a reassessment of one's own morals.[4] But for Nicolai and Mendelssohn, any advantage gained by such a view would be eclipsed by the problems such a solution would imply. For them, *Mitleid* cannot be singled out from the multitude of other affects as a primary or particularly crucial form of affect. Instead, *Mitleid* represents a mixed sentiment. This means *Mitleid* cannot be conceived as an independent element in the play of affects. Because it is a composite state, made up of other affects, the dynamics of *Mitleid* points to the affective dynamic in general.[5] It is these affects that constitute, along with other sentiments, the mixed emotional feeling that produces *Mitleid*.

Mendelssohn's theory of affects, as *Über die Empfindungen* shows, was already developed to some degree at the outset of the exchange on tragedy. Rather than isolating the function of specific affects, *Über die Empfindungen* argued the economy of affects in general to be the crucial constitutive force that promotes moral development. According to Mendelssohn, the issue was not so much which sentiment would play which role but rather the effect produced by the economy of dramatic sentiments as a whole. His understanding of the economy of the energy and thus power of the affects stresses the quantitative rather than qualitative aspect of the issue, for the latter would, after all, be determined by the former's impact. This approach allows Mendelssohn to focus on the autonomy of the stage and aesthetic representation in general, for the release of affects called forth by drama had no direct, unmediated connection with the constitution of morality. For Mendelssohn, morality was grounded in an altogether different sphere. Affects such as *Mitleid* possess the ability to reshuffle energy and its cathexes and thus to trigger a change in the dynamic and its balance that might eventually lead to a new affective equilibrium. This affective process, he argues, gives them a central role in the formation of morality. But affects cannot themselves produce moral behavior, nor can they ground or change morality itself.

However, to Mendelssohn, the autonomy of the stage is not an end in itself but rather the consequence of a more general consideration. For him, the autonomy of the stage—which possesses a morality of its own—becomes the complement to his conception of the economy of affects. Only the free play of the affects, a full and untrammeled release of their dynamic potential, can produce a firm and sound grounding for morality. Such a solid foundation can only be secured, paradoxically, by the unlimited, uncensured play of the affects, which in turn is possible only if the stage is guaranteed comprehensive, unrestricted autonomy.

In a way, then, the two sides differed in the manner in which they conceived morality to be constituted. Lessing recognized *Mitleid* as the lead idea in tragedy, whereas Mendelssohn and Nicolai viewed the economy of the affects as the key to understanding the dramatic process as a catalyst for morality's formation. So, while *Mitleid* in Lessing often seems to challenge moral patterns and preconceptions in order to reconceive an existing moral framework in universal and liberal terms, the play of affects that drama can set free, according to Mendelssohn and Nicolai, would increase the release of the dynamics of affects to such an extent that reason could, as the strongest and most permanent affect, take charge in precisely the fashion Spinoza had described in the *Ethics*.

Reason could be arrived at, to be sure, by both routes. And this common ground both sides share makes the discussion all the more confusing as their differences appear to be merely technical and terminological in nature and, ultimately, easy to reconcile. But this disagreement on the role of *Mitleid* allows a systematic difference on the function of reason to find dramatic expression. Like Rousseau, Lessing understands *Mitleid* as the particular, individually experienced sentiment that leads to a universalist and open moral practice.[6] Concrete and human, the human sentiment per se, *Mitleid*—the primary feeling of and for humanity—is imagined to open the way to a conception of humanity free of socially and historically contingent control and repression. *Mitleid,* the most personal and intimate feeling, is thus acknowledged as the universal bond linking all of humanity. This most visceral and basic emotion constitutes reason from the bottom up rather than as a rationalist preconceived fixture. Reason thus remains open to redefinition because, and as long as, it is based on the living fundament of actual, experienced *Mitleid.* So long as reason and morality maintain this connection with *Mitleid* as their source, they appear securely grounded in the experience of reality and life.

Mendelssohn, on the other hand, follows a line of reasoning closer, in this respect, to Spinoza. For him the question is not so much how to define morals from the bottom up but rather how to arrive at the cognitive stage that will set one's sight free to recognize reason's dictates and demands. For Mendelssohn, the role and function of the affects in general is fundamental to the constitution of reason. However, unlike Lessing and Rousseau, he does not view the affects themselves as integral to the process of moral reasoning. Rather—and here he follows Spinoza—affects do not, by themselves, lead to the establishment of a moral code, but they are the very vehicle through which the affect of reason emerges in a complicated process of self-constitution. But the content of reasoning itself remains independent from the concrete experience of this or that instance of *Mitleid.* According to this view, the privileging of one particular sentiment over another threatens an unwarranted fettering of the free play of the affects' dynamics. Instead, Mendelssohn argues that the affectual dynamic, open-ended as it might be, creates a free and critical space in which moral reasoning, autonomously determining itself, emerges in an act of self-constitution.

For Mendelssohn (and Spinoza), this aspect of self-determination is of central importance. As progressive—even subversive—as Lessing's (and Rousseau's) theory of *Mitleid* might be, its particularistic rooting in specific socially conditioned, and therefore contingent, experiences betrays traces of its dependence on a source that has its origin in contingency and therefore remains subject to heteronomy.

Although these differences are not explicitly addressed in the exchange on tragedy or elsewhere in the discussions between Mendelssohn and Lessing, they nevertheless frame the interests both sides articulate. Looming in the background, they define the context and account for the impossibility of resolving the difference of opinions. Because the surface of the debate is defined by the discussion on tragedy and stage play in general, the critical literature has ignored the larger, more general issue at stake here. In the debate on *Mitleid,* these deeper differences between Lessing and Mendelssohn are brought out in a productive way. And although these foundational philosophical disagreements are never spelled out, or at least never brought to full exposure, the contention itself forces both sides to a clarification of their positions. Analysis of the exchange thus provides us with a differentiated assessment only if these overarching, principal differences between the two sides are kept in mind.[7]

Critically responding to Nicolai's treatise on tragedy, Lessing signals his opposition from the very start: "The human being with the greatest sympathy is the best human being" ("Der mitleidigste Mensch ist der beste Mensch" [Jub A 11, 67]). In a statement that he introduces to Nicolai in the letter addressed to both friends with reference to the other addressee, Mendelssohn, Lessing declares: "And now I refer to a proposition which Mr. Moses may in the meantime demonstrate to you if you wish to doubt it despite your own feeling" ("Und nun berufe ich mich auf einen Satz, den Ihnen Herr Moses vorläufig demonstriren mag, wenn Sie, Ihrem eignen Gefühl zum Trotz, daran zweifeln wollen" [Jub A 11, 67]).[8] But it is also Mendelssohn who argues that if the discussion on tragedy is not to be reduced to direct moral rules and expectations, a general theory of the dynamics of the affects is required. For *Mitleid* in itself does not necessarily constitute a sufficient condition for morality's achievement: "Also pity can lead us to vice if it is not governed by reason, by cold symbolical reason which one has to ban entirely from the theater if one wants to please" ("Auch das Mitleiden kann uns zu Untugenden bringen, wenn es nicht von der Vernunft regiert wird, von der kalten symbolischen Vernunft, die man gänzlich von dem Theater verbannen muß, wenn man gefallen will" [Jub A 11, 86]). To this, Lessing replies with a more precise formulation of the role of *Mitleid* in his definition of tragedy: "Tragedy is supposed to exercise pity in general and not to make us feel pity in this or that case" ("Das Trauerspiel soll das Mitleiden nur überhaupt *üben*, und nicht uns in diesem oder jenem Falle zum Mitleiden bestimmen" [Jub A 11, 93]). As a result, Lessing revises his earlier assertion that the most sympathetic human being is also the best one. His new formulation appears to meet Mendelssohn's concerns more appropriately when he now writes: "this is the best human being who has the greatest mastery for pity" ("derjenige [ist] der beste Mensch, der die größte Fertigkeit im Mitleiden hat" [Jub A 11, 93]). And he continues, in the same letter: "I am myself opposed to Aristotle who seems to me to have everywhere departed from a wrong explanation of pity. And if I miss the truth less I owe this alone to your better concept of pity" ("Ich bin selbst wider Aristoteles, welcher mir überall eine falsche Erklärung des Mitleids zum Grunde gelegt zu haben scheint. Und wenn ich die Wahrheit weniger verfehle, so habe ich es allein *Ihrem* bessern Begriffe von Mitleiden zu danken" [Jub A 11, 95]). But with the next letter, a few weeks later, Mendelssohn again presses his point, explaining in more detail that *Mitleid* only plays a supporting role in providing the affective energy in the pursuit of the desired goods. As far as he is concerned, the nature of the affects themselves can be ignored. What counts is the power they exert.

> That even mastery to bemitleiden [pity] (allow me this Swiss word) does not always have a good effect becomes clear thanks to my thoughts on moral sensitivity which without the assistance of judgment makes our feeling only more tender and spurs us to chase both true and illusory goods with greater desire.
>
> Daß aber selbst die Fertigkeit zu *bemitleiden* (erlauben Sie mir dieses schweizerische Wort) nicht immer gute Wirkung thut, erhellet aus meinen Gedanken von der sittlichen Empfindlichkeit, die ohne Hülfe der Urtheilskraft unser Gefühl nur zärtlicher macht, und uns antreibt, sowohl wahren als scheinbaren Gütern mit größerer Begierde nachzujagen. (Jub A 11, 102)

But it is Lessing's distinction between affects and the imitation or reenactment of the affects (letter 42) that allows Mendelssohn to take his next and crucial step in developing his theory of mixed feelings (letter 43). Mendelssohn now is able to distinguish conceptually between affects and the representation of affects onstage. As a result, the problem of why the performance of bad moral behavior can be aesthetically pleasing can be addressed without recourse to moral explanations. It now becomes possible to discuss this point within an exclusively aesthetic framework whose dynamic outlook is based on the acknowledgment of the power of the affects. This allows Mendelssohn to forego the classic Aristotelian requirement that tragedy must have a cleansing effect. Catharsis is therefore no longer tied to the traditional moralistic and utilitarian conception of tragedy as an institution introduced to maintain the moral order of society. Rather, tragedy now comes into focus as art in its purely aesthetic aspect, free of any normative program, which is to say, independent of any social or political restrictions. The crucial paragraph in this respect is the "document of capitulation," as Mendelssohn playfully calls his attempt at clarifying their positions—a different kind of peace agreement, he underhandedly seems to suggest, than the one Frederick the Great needed six more years to reach in order to end the Seven Years War: "Yes, nothing but affects are capable to exercise this moral taste. The tragedy must thus produce affects but not *cleanse* them" ("Ja, nichts als Affekten sind vermögend, diesen moralischen Geschmack zu üben.

Das Trauerspiel muß also Affekten erregen, aber nicht *reinigen*" [Jub A 11, 129]).[9] Tragedy can now be conceived as the space where the energies of the affects are released. Free of moral undertones or presuppositions which at this stage would only blur the picture, the laws of dramatic performance can be examined in their very own dynamics. Once the affects receive their own space in which they can unfold, the natural interplay of the affects leads to its own establishment of order. The release and realization of the affects contained in the individual triggers a release of energy that, in turn, expands the potential for the cognitive faculties to assume their power. Freed from the supposition of direct causal nexus between the affects represented and the affects evoked by such representations, tragedy is no longer expected to program specific types of behavior by lifting its didactic finger. Rather, tragedy is now set free to engage and, thus, to train the affective capability in an unrestricted way; drama is now conceived as fully self-determined, seeking the best manner to effectively represent the affects onstage.

Against Lessing's reservations, Mendelssohn and Nicolai maintain in their "capitulation" that it is not a question of which affect—pity (*Mitleid)* or admiration (*Bewunderung*), or any other affect, for that matter—should rule or dominate in tragedy. To them, the decisive aspect consists, instead, in activating the potential of the power of the affects in general (Jub A 11, 129).

But the demand for clarification, it seems, sent Mendelssohn back to Spinoza's theory of affects, for three months later he adds as a postscript to a letter to Lessing a discussion of a passage from the *Ethics,* "which I had copied for you a while ago" (Jub A 11, 148). At the end of these excerpts, Mendelssohn stresses the value of Spinoza's theory of the affects for their discussion and for contemporary thought in general:

> In general, I find in Spinoza's theory of the affects so much profundity that I am wondering how the modern philosophers have been able to pass over this matter so fast. Wolff, Reusch and Baumgarten have barely more of this than the mere explanation of the term.

> Ueberhaupt finde ich in Spinozens Theorie von den Affekten so viel Gründliches, daß ich mich verwundere, wie die neuern Weltweisen über diese Materie so haben hinweg eilen können. Kaum hat Wolf, Reusch und Baumgarten mehr davon, als die bloße Worterklärung. (Jub A 11, 149)

Mendelssohn had obviously closely studied the ontological passages of part 1 of the *Ethics* three years earlier while constructing his rescue of Spinoza's thought. But this is the first time he cites Spinoza's theory of the affects (of the later parts of the *Ethics*) *expressis verbis*. If Mendelssohn's understanding of the functioning of the affects in *Über die Empfindungen* and possibly at the early stage of the letter exchange on tragedy appears more often than not to echo Spinoza's position on the dynamic nature of affects, Mendelssohn is now faced with the challenge of developing his conception of affects in his essays of 1757–58 and the "Rhapsodie," following 1761, and it is here that Spinoza resurfaces at the center of his thought.

To Mendelssohn, the affinity between Spinoza's thought and his own is striking, so much so that he remarks the significant agreement between Spinoza's metaphysics and his own. In a parenthetical aside in his letter to Lessing, Mendelssohn's comment on the concept critical to his moral and aesthetic considerations, the concept of perfection, invokes Spinoza's theory of the *conatus*, the driving force of self-preservation which, in Spinoza's terms, is tantamount to self-realization and self-determination: "I don't think it necessary to have to tell you that suum esse, suam perfectionem, and suam realitatem conservare mean all the same" ("Ihnen werde ich wohl nicht zu sagen nöthig haben, daß suum esse, suam perfectionem, suam realitatem conservare, einerley bedeuten" [Jub A 11, 149]). The conclusion that neither Wolff nor Baumgarten would provide an adequate understanding of the nature and functioning of affects demonstrates the extent to which Mendelssohn becomes aware of both: the need for independent critical investigation that rejected the restrictions of the Leibniz-Wolff school of thought, and the critical potential of Spinoza's philosophy, which promises to avoid or overcome some of the difficulties inherent to the Leibniz-Wolffian framework. Indeed, the way in which Mendelssohn places the discussion of the affects at the center of his aesthetic and moral investigations, the dynamic power and cognitive functions he ascribes to them, and their decidedly nonhierarchical view bring the projects of Mendelssohn and Spinoza into close vicinity.

When he raises an objection against Lessing's ascribing specific literary genres to specific kinds of affects, Mendelssohn refers to the new philosophy of nature from which art should takes its cue:

> With regard to the works of nature one has determined in the last century that they are not divided by their master [i.e., nature] into particular

and separated classes. Why should we not have art imitate nature in this respect?

In Ansehung der Werke der Natur hat man in dem letzten Jahrhundert ausgemacht, daß sie von ihrer Meisterinn in keine besondern und getrennten Klassen eingetheilt sind. Warum wollen wir die Kunst nicht auch hierinn eine Nachahmerin der Natur werden lassen? (Jub A 11, 99)

Clearly, this idea is not found in Leibniz or the Wolffian school, whose understanding of nature is rather instrumentally restricted to a narrow sort of ratiocentrist view of nature. Instead, it points to the naturalist philosophies of Bacon and Hobbes. But it is none other than Spinoza who provides the ontologically adequate metaphysics for this view.

Against Lessing's efforts to determine *Mitleid* as the specific tragic affect, Mendelssohn points out that no affect is to be excluded from the stage for other than dramatically motivated reasons:

Do not therefore exclude any passion from the theater. As soon as the imitated passion is able by intuition to convince us of the excellence of imitation it deserves to be performed onstage. Hatred and disgust, too, can despite Aristotle and his followers please on the stage because it suffices if the imitated passion can convince that the imitation is similar to the original.

Schließen Sie also keine einzige Leidenschaft vom Theater aus. So bald die nachgeahmte Leidenschaft uns anschauend von der Vortrefflichkeit der Nachahmung überzeugen kann, so verdient sie auf der Bühne aufgeführt zu werden. Auch der Haß und der Abscheu können, trotz dem Aristoteles und allen seinen Anhängern, auf der Schaubühne gefallen, weil es genug ist, wenn die nachgeahmte Leidenschaft überzeugen kann, daß die Nachahmung dem Urbilde ähnlich sey. (Jub A 11, 99)

In this context, Mendelssohn refers Lessing to his sketch "Von der Illusion" (Jub A 2, 154–55), the last section of the draft "Von der Herrschaft über die Neigungen" which accompanies the letter. Continuing his argument, Mendelssohn then turns to a summary of the theoretical underpinnings of his thoughts on stage performance:

From my thoughts on the domination over the inclinations you will see how beneficial it is for virtue if the general, abstract concepts are reduced

> to individual cases. This reduction can take place by way of experience, by examples or by invention. Our symbolical knowledge is always transformed to intuitive knowledge which animates the power of the motives, and its quantity becomes larger than the quantity of sensual pleasure that opposes it.
>
> Aus meinen Gedanken *von der Herrschaft über die Neigungen* werden Sie ersehen, wie zuträglich es der Tugend sey, wenn die allgemeinen abstrakten Begriffe auf einzelne Fälle reducirt werden. Diese Reduktion kann durch die Erfahrung, durch Beyspiele oder auch durch Erdichtung geschehen. Unsere symbolische Erkenntniß wird allemahl in eine anschauende verwandelt, die Gewalt der Motive wird belebt, und ihre Quantität wird größer, als die Quantität der sinnlichen Lust, die sich ihnen widersetzt. (Jub A 11, 102)

This terminological shorthand describes the potential of the emancipatory project Mendelssohn recognizes in the stage play, and it also describes the implications of his enlightenment project for practical philosophy in general. The practical philosopher connects the abstract ideas of ethics to the concrete actions of everyday life, as Mendelssohn had explained half a year earlier in a letter to Resewitz:

> By this we reach a mastery to determine ourselves according to this recognized truth; our choice of the good becomes a kind of instinct and if, then, the passions storm in us, this moral truth is no longer just a speculative abstraction that is positioned in our soul alone for defense but it presents itself in our mind in association with innumerable other truths, with innumerable small actions which we exercise on the grounds of being caused by this truth.
>
> Hierdurch erlangen wir eine Fertigkeit, uns nach dieser erkannten Wahrheit zu bestimmen; unsere Wahl des Guten wird zu einer Art von Instinct, und wenn alsdenn die Leidenschaften in uns stürmen; so ist diese moralische Wahrheit nicht mehr blos abstracte Speculation, die in unserer Seele einzeln zur Gegenwehr dahin gestellt ist; sondern sie stellet sich unserem Gemüthe in Verknüpfung mit unzähllichen andern Wahrheiten, mit unzähllichen kleinen Handlungen vor, die wir nach ihrer Veranlaßung ausgeübt haben. (Jub A 11, 44)

Such a procedure, Mendelssohn continues, creates a synergetic effect, a constellation in which the good that has been recognized is transformed into the affect of the good, which thus counterbalances the negative passions:

> All these representations taken together transform themselves into an affect; sensations rise up against sensations: and if the passion is not too strong it can be weakened by the counter-effect of the good affect to such a degree that it possesses no more activity than any other speculation.

> Alle diese Vorstellungen zusammen verwandeln sich in einen Affect; es stehen Empfindungen wider Empfindungen auf: und wenn die Leidenschaft nicht allzuheftig ist; so kann sie so sehr durch die Gegenwürkung des guten Affects geschwächt werden, daß ihr nicht mehr Thätigkeit bleibet, als sonst einer bloßen Speculation. (Jub A 11, 44)

The self-regulating system of the affects works the same way in everyday life as it does onstage. In tragedy, however, the affects are mediated through the aesthetic rules governing a process of representation that, in turn, takes on its own specific affective qualities. Like a catalyst, the aesthetic sphere intensifies the play of the affects and, consequently, speeds up the process of cognition. The relationship between ethics and aesthetics stands out all the more clearly for their intricate connection. Precisely because of the nature of the affects, the sphere of aesthetic production is now set free from the dictate of reasoning, for such a dictate, the dynamics of the affects proves, must remain impotent in the face of the power of the passions. The latter can be controlled solely by intervention that takes place in the passions' own terms. And it is tragedy, or stage play in general, followed by other art, which provides the scene that is particularly useful for acting out the drama of the affects.

In "Observations on the Sources and Connections of the Fine Arts and the Sciences" ("Betrachtungen über die Quellen und die Verbindungen der schönen Künste und Wissenschaften" [1757]), Mendelssohn develops his aesthetics more systematically. I follow the text of the revised version of this essay which Mendelssohn inserts a few years later in his *Philosophische Schriften* (1761/1771). In this edition, the essay, now renamed "On the Main Principles of the Fine Arts and Sciences" ("Ueber die Hauptgrundsätze der schönen Künste und Wissenschaften"), follows the "Rhapsodie," as its sequel as it were. The essay moves toward a more resolute approach to the theory of aesthetics, formulating an argument in which the theoretical and moral implications of Mendelssohn's epistemological interests emerge more distinctly. The opening paragraph addresses the larger theoretical framework in which these aesthetic investigations are placed as a particularly appropriate method to examine the question about the nature and functioning of the soul in general: "The human soul is as inexhaustible as nature; mere reflection cannot possibly establish everything about it, and everyday experience is rarely decisive" (D 169) ("Die menschliche Seele ist so unerschöpflich als die Natur; das bloße Nachdenken kann unmöglich alles ergründen, was ihr zukömmt, und die alltägliche Erfahrung pflegt selten entscheidend zu seyn" [Jub A 1, 427]). As a result, the question of where the philosopher must turn to find the proper material for his investigations arises with clarity. The answer comes as a rhetorical question: "Yet are there any phenomena that move every impulse of the human soul more than the effects of the fine arts do?" (D 169) ("Bey welchen Erscheinungen sind aber wohl alle Triebfedern der menschlichen Seele mehr in Bewegung, als bey den Wirkungen der schönen Künste?" [Jub A 1, 427]). To be sure, in the course of his argument Mendelssohn adds more precision to this question by limiting its scope to an inquiry into aesthetics. Rephrased, the question now becomes: "what do the beauties of nature and of art have in common, what relation do they have to the human soul, such that they are so pleasing to it?" (D 171) ("was haben die Schönheiten der Natur und der Kunst gemein, welche Beziehung haben sie auf die menschliche Seele, dadurch sie ihr so wohlgefallen?" [highlighted by spaced type, Jub A 1, 429]). But the decisive moment of this reformulation remains that the soul as a whole is understood to represent the central subject for investigation, not just a certain aspect or isolated faculty of it. The pursuit of aesthetic theory, then, is never detached from the larger, comprehensive philosophical concerns that frame these aesthetics. And it is for this reason that Mendelssohn's revalorization of sensate cognition assumes a significance that transcends the limits of aesthetics alone.

As he moves away from conceiving the criterion for the arts to be mimetic imitation of nature—he criticizes Batteux precisely for such a reduction of the function of art (D 170–71; Jub A 1, 429)—Mendelssohn directs his attention to the intrapsychic effects that different art forms can possess. This shift has often been seen as signifying a move from an objectivist understanding toward a more subjectivist, more advanced aesthetic position. Wellbery, for one, has rightly questioned such a classification. But the cost of overemphasizing the semiotic aspect is paid in turn by the resulting oversight of the deeper metaphysical implications that motivate this shift.[10] However, a look at the framing of Mendelssohn's discussion reveals that he aims—in an almost transcendental move[11]—beyond an aesthetics that still operates along the lines of the distinction "objective versus subjective." For his interests do not lie primarily in formulating an aesthetics but rather in reaching, through a better understanding of how artistic representation works, a better grasp of how the soul actually functions. To categorize this interest as simply an example of the subjective turn might shed some light on Mendelssohn's role in eighteenth-century German aesthetics as far as his instrumental role for the transition from an objective to a subjective conception is concerned, but such an assessment may at the same time prevent a critical appreciation of the deeper reasons for Mendelssohn's primary interest in aesthetics.

Now, the decisive moment when feelings and passions are released or triggered happens when, in Leibniz-Wolffian parlance, sensate cognition, clear but not distinct, takes place. It is, so to speak, the linkage between the so-called lower and higher faculties of the soul that presents the special point of epistemological interest. As Bamberger points out, it is here that Mendelssohn gives new meaning to the sensual (*Sinnlichkeit* [Jub A 1, xxxvi]). The question behind Mendelssohn's interest in aesthetics consists, thus, in how to assess and understand the forces that constitute virtue, that is, independence and autonomy; and, as a consequence, how these forces can be controlled and guided to gain the power over one's self in order to constitute autonomy. Seen in this light, the efforts at reformulating the definitions of sensate representation receive their precise practical philosophical significance.

> An instant of knowledge is called "sensuous," however, not simply if it is felt by the external senses, but in general whenever we perceive a large array of an object's features all at once without being able to separate them distinctly from each other. (D 172)

> Man nennet aber eine Erkenntniß *sinnlich,* nicht blos wenn sie von den äußern Sinnen empfunden wird; sondern überhaupt, so oft wir von einem Gegenstande eine große Menge von Merkmalen auf einmal wahrnehmen, ohne sie deutlich auseinander setzen zu können. (Jub A 1, 430)

The nature of arts and letters consists exactly in such sensate-perfect representations, that is, more precisely, in such sensate perfections represented and staged by art: "[T]he essence of the fine arts and sciences consists in an artful, sensuously perfect representation or in a sensuous perfection represented by art" (D 172–73) ("Das Wesen der schönen Künste und Wissenschaften besteht in einer *künstlichen sinnlich-vollkommenen* Vorstellung, oder in einer *durch die Kunst vorgestellten sinnlichen Vollkommenheit*" [Jub A 1, 431]). It is because of this insight that art can present an especially elucidating case study for an analysis of how the soul functions, that is, the point of interface between the emotional and cognitive faculties. For art, through its representations, stages moments of crystallization of their linkage in which feelings and passions enable the "higher faculties" of the mind to assume their role and act in the first place.

In determining the constitutive role of the affects in the process of cognition—for knowledge and the striving for the good are in his view identical—Mendelssohn reaches a differentiated conception of enlightenment. Enlightenment is now no longer conceived as a ratiocentric enterprise but as a project reflecting the affective dimension of human nature in full, the influence it exerts on cognition, imagination, and, as a consequence, on the process of decision making and its execution. Mendelssohn does not formulate a full-fledged aesthetics but instead turns his investigation in a different direction. Once the exact connection between ethics and aesthetics has been determined, he brings his findings to bear on his larger, practical philosophical project. A look at his aesthetic writings reveals their central concern as the quest to define the relation between the different faculties of the soul and senses more precisely. In principle, then, Mendelssohn—as Altmann has argued—is more of a metaphysician of aesthetics than an aesthetician.[12] The specific aspect of his interest in aesthetics concerns the interface, reciprocal interaction, and boundaries between psychology—understood in the manner of his time as ancillary to moral philosophy—and aesthetics. The primary interest of his investigations consists therefore in the particular conditions of the interplay between cognition and imagination. In this respect, aesthetics as an autonomous discipline demonstrates that the soul—which Mendelssohn identifies with the total of the cognitive and representational faculties—has a dynamic nature with the potential to develop in any direction of perfection. And perfection Mendelssohn defines in a resolutely comprehensive manner as self-realization, the unfolding of all productive latent capabilities. As pointed out earlier, this idea of perfection carries for Mendelssohn a distinct Spinozist undertone.[13]

Two years after the publication of "Rhapsodie," Mendelssohn's *On Evidence in Metaphysical Sciences* (*Abhandlung über die Evidenz*) won the 1763 competition of the Berlin Royal Academy.[14] In this work's concluding section, which treats the role of evidence in the foundation of ethics, Mendelssohn names four means by which the lower faculties of the soul can be harmonized through the use of reason: (1) accumulation of motives (*Häufung der Bewegungsgründe*), (2) practice, (3) agreeable sentiment (*angenehme Empfindung*), and (4) intuitive cognition (*anschauende Erkenntnis*).[15] The aesthetic element of moral actions as addressed in the "Rhapsodie" now resurfaces in a more systematic context. Practice, speed, agreeable sentiment, and intuitive cognition all play an important role in the description of the aesthetic experience in "Rhapsodie." Now, in the treatise on evidence, the same capabilities appear in the context of a metaphysical and epistemological discussion that takes up their meaning for ethics. Agreeable sentiment and intuitive cognition here receive a new examination that expands on the discussion of these terms in the earlier work.

The agreeable sentiment is what determines imagination, which, in turn, mediates between reason and desire:

> If rational grounds are supported by beauty and grace, then the imagination is easily lured into agreement. Perfection is the mainspring of reason, and pleasant sentiment the bait of imagination. [. . .] The former make it honorable, the latter pleasant. The former show the way to happiness while the latter strew the path with flowers. (D 305–6)

> Wenn die Vernunftgründe von Schönheit und Anmuth unterstützt werden; so wird die Einbildungskraft leicht zu Uebereinstimmung gereizt. Die Vollkommenheit ist die Triebfeder der Vernunft und die angenehme Empfindung, die Lockspeise der Einbildungskraft. [. . .] Jene machen sie verehrungswerth, diese angenehm. Jene zeigen den Weg zur Glückseligkeit, und diese bestreuen ihn mit Blumen. (Jub A 2, 327)

In the fragment "Über das Erkenntnis-, das Empfindungs- und das Begehrungsvermögen" ("On the faculty of cognition, sensation, and desire,"

1776), the faculty of sensation is placed directly between reason and desire (Jub A 3.1, 276). Imagination assumes a role that comes close to the one this faculty soon will receive in Kant.

Here it is important to stress that if Mendelssohn may sound playful and unassuming in this text, giving sensation, as it were, its playground, the argument is an altogether more principal one. The affective, emotional sphere is defined as a constitutive moment in the process of achieving harmony between the faculties of the soul, and it is this harmony alone that allows the soul to achieve the state of perfection in its freedom and autonomy. As a result, reason only points out the road to happiness, whereas it is the agreeable sentiments of imagination that strew its path with flowers. But it is only the joining of the two faculties that allows the road pointed out by reason to actually be taken. The picture Mendelssohn paints here highlights how the emotive aspect of imagination works to mark out those grounds, or road, by "strewing it with flowers." It is thus beauty and grace that possess the necessary motive force that enables necessary motivation to actually follow reason—hence their systematic significance to the framework of Mendelssohn's theory of motivation.

Intuitive cognition is the fourth means to bring imagination and reason to agreement. By means of examples, general reasons can be transformed, as it were, into "sensate concepts" (*sinnliche Begriffe*). For according to Mendelssohn, examples work in practice better than maxims: "It [the example] has a stronger influence on the mind's approval because it stirs the senses and jostles the imagination" (D 306) ("Es hat einen stärkern Einfluß in den Beyfall des Gemüths, weil es die Sinne rühret, die Einbildungskraft erschüttert" [Jub A 2, 328]). This is why history, according to this view,[16] like the Aesopian fable, is so useful to the moral faculties. Both can serve as didactic pictorializations of abstract maxims that, by themselves, lack the power to motivate imagination. Evidence in ethics is, then, "conviction of the heart" (*Ueberzeugung des Herzens*). It is achieved through the harmonious interplay of the ensemble of the forces that determine imagination. Principles therefore

> must be enlivened by *examples,* supported by the force of *pleasant sentiment,* kept constantly effective by *practice,* and finally transformed into a *proficiency.* Then there emerges the conviction of the heart that is our ultimate and most eminent purpose in the ethics. (D 306)

müssen durch *Beyspiele* belebt von der Gewalt der *angenehmen Empfindung* unterstützt, durch die *Uebung* in beständiger Würksamkeit erhalten, und endlich in *Fertigkeit* verwandelt werden. Alsdenn entstehet die *Ueberzeugung des Herzens,* die in der Sittenlehre unser vornehmster Endzweck ist. (Jub A 2, 328)

This is why "each kind of knowledge has its value" (D 306).[17] The system of ethical truths thus assumes its power not through abstract ratiocination alone but through the "fire and strength of the mind" (Jub A 2, 329). But the place where the "fire and strength of the mind" are generated is the place where the play of the affects is made possible, free of any restrictions. This is the sphere of aesthetics. There the forces of the soul interact in such a way that the economy of the affects triggers the dynamic that creates the framework in which equilibrium of the cognitive forces becomes possible. The liberating effect of this process is emphasized, once more, in the conclusion of the treatise on evidence as if to stress the practical aspect of this epistemological investigation:

Who is capable of such a sublime enthusiasm is able to become master of his inclinations under guidance of the most rigorous reason, to govern the wild storm of the passions according to the cue of wisdom and to found the most lovely harmony between heart and mind which neither fear nor hope, neither pain nor pleasure will be able to disturb.

Wer einer so erhabenen Begeisterung fähig ist, kann unter Anführung der strengesten Vernunft, Herr über seine Neigungen werden, den wilden Sturm der Leidenschaften nach dem Winke der Weisheit regieren, und zwischen Herz und Geist die holdseligste Eintracht stiften, die weder Furcht noch Hofnung, weder Schmerz noch Wollust zu stöhren vermag. (Jub A 2, 329)

The end of the exchange on tragedy did not mean that the discussion itself came to an end. In his *Hamburgische Dramaturgie,* Lessing not only picks up where the correspondence had left off a decade earlier but also integrates some of the criticism Mendelssohn had voiced. Revisiting the question of the nature of tragedy, Lessing this time grafts his discussion onto an interpretation of Aristotle's theory of tragedy. This allows him to move away from his earlier position that made pity the exclusively defining character of tragedy.

Quoting extensively from Mendelssohn's *On Sentiments,* Lessing now takes Mendelssohn's conception of pity as mixed feeling into account.[18] Reading pity with Mendelssohn, Lessing redefines its role anew. Pity appears now—in his particular interpretation of the Aristotelian scheme—in a necessary conjunction with fear (*phobos*). Rather than the exclusive agent, pity is now considered a necessary but no longer exclusive defining component of tragedy. Pity is no longer understood as the aim of tragic drama but as what triggers the "probable fear" in us which, in turn, will turn into a continuing passion in our own lives, once the performance is over, assisting us in the purification of our own passions.[19] To some extent, then, Lessing's revisiting of the debate on tragedy in his *Hamburgische Dramaturgie* strikes a peculiar compromise in which Lessing gets to keep pity as a key defining element of tragedy. But now, pity's exclusive status is moderated by the equal standing of the role that is now assigned to fear.[20]

But more telling than Lessing's rather particular interpretation of Aristotle are his own dramas. In the context of his drama production, the *Hamburgische Dramaturgie* takes an intermediate position whose theoretical claims represent an experimental stage for self-clarification that are counterbalanced by his dramas.[21] This reorientation takes place in two ways. First, pity is reconstituted as it emerges more clearly as a category of drama and reception aesthetics and loses, in this reconstructive effort, the original and distinct moral note Lessing had given it at the start, a result far from unaffected by Mendelssohn's argument. Second, the actual economy of affects at play in Lessing's dramas from *Minna von Barnhelm* to *Emilia Galotti* and *Nathan der Weise* resists a simple reduction to the Aristotelian framework. Instead, Lessing's mature dramas accommodate a conception of the free and unrestricted play of affects. This conception becomes the basis for a dramatic affect that corresponds to the Spinozist understanding of dramatic affect that Mendelssohn has so forcefully proposed. Lessing's reformulations of drama in theory and his actual playwriting practice can thus be read as a productive response to the challenge posed by Mendelssohn's criticism. This response does not cave in and stray from its own determination, but neither does it shy away from exposing its conception to crucial modifications. The deep affinity of Mendelssohn's and Lessing's project appears in its full significance only when critical attention is paid to their crucial differences. In this light, Lessing, who remains more conventional in his theory than in his practice, emerges as creatively challenged by the more radical trajectory of the thinking of Mendelssohn, the allegedly more conventional figure.[22]

CHAPTER 8

STAKING OUT GROUNDS FOR PUBLIC REASON

Lavater's Challenge

WITH THE SUCCESS OF *Phädon oder über die Unsterblichkeit der Seele,* Mendelssohn's fame was established throughout Europe.[1] Inspired by Plato's *Phaedo,* Mendelssohn's dialogues on the immortality of the soul present a powerful plea for the recognition of human individuality as grounded in every person's inalienable right to particularity. Celebrated for its clarity and stylistic elegance, *Phädon* addresses through the figure of Socrates the difficulty Mendelssohn faces as a philosophical outsider. While Mendelssohn's donning of Socratic style, method, and persona led critics to salute him as the new German Socrates, Mendelssohn employs the figure of Socrates—a pagan rather than a Christian—to illustrate his own situation. In describing the character of Socrates, Mendelssohn portrays not so much Socrates' personality as the cultural constellation in which his character's life and thought are embedded, an environment whose description highlights in a more than coincidental manner Mendelssohn's own predicament:

> He had on the one hand to conquer the prejudices of his own education, to enlighten the ignorance of others, to refute sophistry and calumny of his adversaries, to bear poverty, to contend against established power, and, what was still more hard than either, to dissipate the dark terrors of superstition. On the other hand, the feeble understandings of his fellow citizens required to be managed with great tenderness, that he might draw no

reproaches upon himself, or lessen the influence which the poorest religion has on the morals of weak minds.[2]

> Er hatte, von der einen Seite, seine eigenen Vorurtheile der Erziehung zu besiegen, die Unwissenheit anderer zu beleuchten, Sophisterey zu bestreiten, Bosheit, Neid, Verleumdung und Beschimpfung von Seiten seiner Gegner auszuhalten, Armuth zu ertragen, festgesetzte Macht zu bekämpfen, und, was das schwerste war, die finstern Schrecknisse des Aberglaubens zu vereiteln. Von der andern Seite waren die schwachen Gemüter seiner Mitbürger zu schonen, Ärgernisse zu vermeiden, und der gute Einfluß, den selbst die albernste Religion auf die Sitten der Einfältigen hat, nicht zu verscherzen. (Jub A 3.1, 15–16)

In advancing a strictly philosophical argument for the immortality of the soul, the dialogues claim that such reasoning must take place completely independently from the demands of religions. Mendelssohn's Socrates lives in a time that does not share the crippling theological assumptions of Mendelssohn's time, a time that, in any case, has been instrumental in shaping modern European culture as Mendelssohn argues in his appendix to the third edition of the dialogue. Mendelssohn's argument proceeds in a cautiously indirect manner to make this point:

> With regard to truths of reason, one can agree with someone and still find several things unauthenticated which he accepts on account of his belief. Since brotherly toleration is so strongly recommended to the political world, friends of truth have first of all to cultivate it among themselves. What lies in the competence of belief we will leave to the individual's conscience without imposing us as their judges.

> Man kann in Absicht auf Vernunftwahrheiten mit jemanden übereinstimmen, und dennoch verschiedenes unglaubwürdig finden, das er auf Glauben annimmt. Da die brüderliche Duldung der politischen Welt so sehr empfohlen wird; so müssen sie Freunde der Wahrheit billig zuerst unter sich hegen. Was des Glaubens ist, wollen wir dem Gewissen und der Beruhigung eines jeden überlassen, ohne uns zu Richtern darüber aufzuwerfen. (Jub A 3.1, 151)

What Mendelssohn demands here is, ironically, not tolerance from the world but tolerance from his fellow philosophers. The concern to argue for a discursive space in which speculative thought can be articulated free of association to one or another religious party is, in the eyes of this Mendelssohnian Socrates, intimately linked to the project of philosophical investigation. Through Socrates, Mendelssohn thus gives voice to a problem he himself faces even when writing such a seemingly innocuous text like a reworking of Plato.

> Wisdom knows a universal fatherland, a universal religion, and if it tolerates divisions, it does not tolerate the unkindness, misanthropy of such divisions which you have made the foundation of your political institutions.—This is how, I think, a man like Socrates would think in our days and seen from this angle, the mantle of modern philosophy, which I have given him, would not seem entirely unfitting.

> Die Weisheit kennet ein allgemeines Vaterland, eine allgemeine Religion, und wenn sie gleich Abtheilungen duldet; so billiget sie doch das Unholde, Menschenfeindliche derselben nicht, das ihr zum Grunde eurer politischen Einrichtungen gelegt habet.—So würde, dünkt mich, ein Mann wie Sokrates in unsern Tagen denken und aus diesem Gesichtspunkte angesehen, dürfte ihm der Mantel der neuern Weltweisheit, den ich ihm umgehangen, so unschicklich nicht lassen. (Jub A 3.1, 151–52)

The striking point of this "Socratic" statement is the acknowledgment of the intimate linkage between intellectual freedom and philosophy on the one hand and political order on the other. The narrative frame of *Phädon* thus introduces in the shadow of the conventional nature of its philosophical subject a critical view of the restrictions that, in Mendelssohn's own experience, haunt the philosopher and philosophy. What distinguishes Mendelssohn from the historical Socrates is thus the importance given to hope as the driving motivation for assuming that the soul does not disappear with the demise of the body. Citing "the hope of a better future" (Jub A 3.1, 115) as an argument motivating the idea of the immortality of the soul does thus not lead to an anachronistic projecting of Mendelssohn's own desires onto Greek philosophy but presents his strategy to propose the conception of immortality as a notion to formulate a new understanding of individuality embracing an undeniably messianic vision. In Mendelssohn's *Phädon,* the argument of immortality serves as the discursive frame for theorizing individuality in terms of a radically secularized conception of the individual as self-determining principle independent of any kind of theological hold. The metaphysical garb provides for Mendelssohn the platform to formulate the claim to individuality as a genuinely philosophical concern. Grounding the concept of individuality in a philosophical speculation free from theological constraints constitutes the particularity of all individuals as metaphysically equal.

The overwhelming international success of *Phädon* might have owed not the least of its impact to this bold metaphysical move precisely because it was so elegantly and persuasively wrapped in the guise of a historical figure representing the "universally" shared point of origin and reference of Western philosophy. But just as it seemed as if Mendelssohn had established himself as a literary critic and philosopher warmly welcomed as renowned voice in the republic of letters, he found himself confronted with a charge that appeared to challenge all his achievements at once. Lavater's public bid had a shattering effect on Mendelssohn's life, one from which he never fully recovered. Along with his translation of Bonnet's *La palingénésie philosophique ou Idées sur l'état passé et sur l'état futur des êtres vivans,* Lavater had published a dedicatory epistle addressed to Mendelssohn, inviting him to examine the arguments of Bonnet's demonstration of the truth of Christianity, asking Mendelssohn to either refute Bonnet or else do what reason would demand, namely, to convert to the religion of truth.[3] This initiative brought home to both Mendelssohn and the reading public just how tenuous the position of a Jewish philosopher still was. Although Mendelssohn was deeply offended by being publicly provoked to do what he so carefully had refused, that is, to take a public stand with regard to Judaism, the public, too, was put at unease by the prospect of seeing Mendelssohn engage in a religious dispute worthy of neither his stature nor the level of Enlightenment discourse most contemporaries had hoped to have achieved. For in invoking Mendelssohn's Jewish difference, Lavater threatened to efface the free spirit of the public sphere in the most insidious way, creating a situation in which Mendelssohn found himself in a position defined by the precariously asymmetric terms on which such a dispute, if it were to take place, was to be fought, terms that would severely curtail the chance for free speech, thus undermining the openness and fairness of free public exchange. The outbreak of Mendelssohn's illness following this incident, which forced him to abandon his much-beloved application to speculative philosophy, was early on attributed to the unwarranted surprise attack by the Swiss theologian Lavater, whose zealous enthusiasm was shunned with embarrassment by most contemporaries. For Mendelssohn, however, the consequence of Lavater's provocation was to redirect his energies from metaphysics to the practical work of explaining and legitimizing Judaism as a culture that was fully qualified to participate in the project of enlightenment and modernity.

Forced to reconsider the grounds for legitimation, Mendelssohn found himself thrown into a debate beset by a minefield of theological-political implications he so long had successfully averted. To Lavater's call for public explanation—an act of tactless importunity—Mendelssohn responds with the examination of the theological-political implications informing Lavater's missionary zeal. Mendelssohn answers Lavater's theological proposition with a philosophical examination of Bonnet's reasons. This strategy counters Lavater's peculiar strategy of using publicity to control, rather than enable, a debate on religion.

Mendelssohn's notes jotted down in defense against Lavater's provocation—the "Gegenbetrachtungen," or "Counter-Observations"—carry beneath their dignified sobriety and objectivity a tone of utter disappointment in the face of the incomprehension and intolerance that Lavater displays in the very name of tolerance. Despondently, Mendelssohn notes: "Where the most loving tolerance rules it is practiced the least with respect to us" ("Wo die liebreichste Toleranz herrschet, da wird sie in Ansehung unser am wenigsten ausgeübt" [Jub A 7, 104]. These notes formulate much of the central points on which Mendelssohn will expand a decade later in his introduction to Manasseh Ben Israel's *Vindication of the Jews* (1782) and *Jerusalem, or On Religious Power and Judaism* (1783). Written primarily for the purpose of self-clarification, the "Gegenbetrachtungen" are more explicit than Mendelssohn's published statements with regard to the religious difference that makes it impossible and inconceivable for him to embrace Christianity as Lavater seemed to have hoped so naively. These notes present an outline for Mendelssohn's conception of philosophy of religion as one that is firmly grounded in reason as the ultimate criterion and point of reference for philosophical discussion. According to Mendelssohn, reason and religion do not contradict but rather complement each other as two ways that lead, in the last analysis, to the same result, that is, the recognition of truth under whatever guise it might appear. Mendelssohn's uncompromising stand on the intrinsically reasonable nature of religion combines a radical version of natural religion with the idea that the covenant of Judaism is based on revelation as legislation. In an original turn, Mendelssohn thus combines an advanced position of natural religion with Spinoza's interpretation of the covenant as legislation exclusively devised for constituting a theocratic state at a particular moment in the history of the Hebrews. Mendelssohn's application of Spinoza casts religion in Enlightenment fashion but without forsaking the cultural and historical specificity of Judaism, which, on the very grounds of reason itself, Mendelssohn envisions as a religion that wholeheartedly embraces modernity. Even more radically, Mendelssohn's argument for Judaism as a religion of reason stresses the potential for the intrinsically progressive and trailblazing significance of Judaism for modernity. A comparison with Christianity, Mendelssohn signals, would in this regard, were it to be carried out, turn out to the latter's disadvantage.

Embedding his discussion within the framework of a theory of natural religion that conceives all the truths relevant for life to be equally accessible to all of humanity, Mendelssohn reveals a conception of the nature of revelation and religion that is different from Christian notions. Although he notes that accepting Christian doctrines would impose severe limitations on reason—"What fetters for my reason!" ("Welche Fessel für meine Vernunfft!" [Jub A 7, 91])—making it for him impossible to accept any single one of them, he asserts reason as the only conceivable universal authority through which it might become possible to unite humanity as a whole. As he formulates his rejection of the universal validity of Christian doctrines:

> that I cannot accept any single one of the propositions cited here, that I believe to have to abandon *my* reason, and to deny all that I know of the first principles of human knowledge if I were supposed to hold these propositions to be true.
>
> daß ich keinen einzigen von diesen angeführten Sätzen annehmen kan, daß ich glaube *meine* Vernunft abschwöhren, und alles, was *mir* von den ersten Grundsätzen der menschl. Erkentnis bekant ist, verleugnen zu müssen, wenn ich diese Sätze für wahr halten sollte. (Jub A 7, 94–95)

Mendelssohn consistently objects to any claims that the content of specific revelations, time- and spacebound as they are by necessity, has universal validity, that is, any significance beyond the specific meaning they have with regard to the particular addressee to which they are revealed.

> I have always held proofs for the necessity of revelation to be very dangerous that are more general than the revelation itself. If the human race were to be miserable without revelation why, then, does the greatest part of the human race live without *true revelation*? Why have both Indias to wait until it pleases the Europeans to send them some priests to bring them the tidings without which they can neither live virtuously nor happily? To bring them tidings that they can neither understand nor use according to their circumstances and knowledge?

> Ich habe jederzeit die Beweise für die Nothwendigkeit einer Offenbarung für sehr gefährlich gehalten, die allgemeiner sind, als die Offenb. selbst. Wenn denn das menschliche Geschlecht, ohne Off. verderbt und elend seyn müsse, warum lebt denn der größte Teil des menschlichen Geschlechts ohne *wahre Offenbarung*? Warum müssen beide Indien warten, bis es den Europäern gefällt, ihnen einige Pfaffen zu zuschiken, die ihnen Bothschafft bringen, ohne welche sie weder tugendhaft noch glückseelig haben leben können? Ihnen Botschafft bringen, die sie nach ihren Umständen und nach der Lage ihrer Erkentnis, weder verstehen, noch gebrauchen können. (Jub A 7, 73)[4]

Instead of belatedly sending missionaries to all corners of the world, providence has chosen another avenue. As Mendelssohn points out, society, as it emerges, produces everywhere notions and moral conviction of the truth of natural religion necessary for its very formation. Starting out with rough yet indispensable prejudices, the process of civilization and refinement replaces in the course of history these prejudices with more reasonable ideas. Revelation as such, Mendelssohn observes, is therefore not necessary for those nations that have not received any revelation on their own, for they are in any case already in possession of the truths of natural religion, which provides them with the necessary moral and religious knowledge to enjoy complete spiritual happiness (Jub A 7, 74–75). This distinctly particularist approach to revelation, coupled with a resolute conviction of radical religious universalism of natural religion, has far-reaching consequences for the conception of history. Any Eurocentric or other kind of limited view of history is therefore principally challenged and shown to be opposed to both true religion and reason.

Insisting that man is born to achieve happiness through virtue alone (Jub A 7, 76) and that revelation is merely dispensed for a particular people to divulge to them the specific intentions divine providence may have for them, Mendelssohn sees religion firmly established as a sociopolitical reality. On the other hand, however, the substance of religion is defined in its universal form as natural religion, understood in a strictly minimalist sense stripped of any revelatory or esoteric meaning. This move leads to a redefinition of religion that is both intrinsically religious and rational, for this conception grants natural religion unrestricted universality in terms of its common core. Revelation, rightfully understood, thus does not exclude but fully affirms the universal claim to self-determination with regard to religion. On the other hand, this conception also grants historical forms of religions new importance, as their historicity is recognized as the key to a proper understanding of culture and society. Now, having addressed religion as an indispensable and necessary component of culture and society, its key function in social and political theory comes into sharper focus. But precisely because Mendelssohn recognizes the full significance of religion, he is able to formulate a theory that rejects any claims for control that religious institutions have become accustomed to view as their guaranteed and inalienable prerogative. Instead, this view immunizes against any such arrogation of power in the guise of piety.

Whether or not Mendelssohn is aware of how closely he follows Spinoza, his argumentation resonates with Spinoza's view of religious claims as a theological-political issue rather than merely a theological one. Attending to the theological-political implications of the conflict between reason and religion enables Mendelssohn, like Spinoza, to recognize the claims of religion as legitimate as long as they are understood as claims to particularity, and to resist them when they are inadequately universalized.

Drafted for private self-clarification, the notes of Mendelssohn's "Gegenbetrachtungen" do not expand any further on the topic of the specifics of natural religion. But the crucial point is that, unlike other conceptions of natural religion, they emphasize the evolutionary rather than some particular doctrinary aspect. Untrammeled by historical, contingent forms, the basic meaning of morality and happiness retains thus, conceived in terms of natural religion, its universal character. As its precondition and constitutive element, natural religion informs the regulation of every society. Mendelssohn states the paradox of an evolutionary scheme—which nevertheless appears as the only way to account for this phenomenon, given the limitations of reason itself—clearly when he notes:

> It is due to superstition that the common people is convinced of very important truths without which it cannot be happy when living in sociable interaction. Hopefully, none will pose the question whether superstition is powerful enough to produce moral conviction and the question: whether it behooves the Highest Being to have indispensable truths ground in prejudices refutes itself. It must by all means have behooved it for experience teaches that this has really been the case with the greatest part of the human race.
>
> Das gemeine Volk ist aus Aberglauben von sehr wichtigen Wahrheiten überzeugt, ohne welche es im Zustande des geselligen Lebens nicht glücklich seyn kan. Niemand wird hoffentlich die Frage aufwerfen, ob der Aberglauben mächtig genug sey, moralische Ueberzeugung zu würken, und die Frage: ob es dem höchsten W. anständig sey, unentbehrliche Wahrheiten auf Vorutheile gründen zu lassen, widerlegt sich von selbst. Es muß allerdings seiner anständig gewesen seyn, da die Erfahrung lehret, daß es bey dem größten Theil des menschl. Gesch. würklich geschehen ist. (Jub A 7, 74–75)

Reaching the limits of reasoning's competence, this paradox is answered, as Mendelssohn expresses it, by the facts. In any case, as this process of civilization unfolds, natural religion is, in the course of the emergence of reason, at no point superseded by revelation:

> As a people becomes gradually moral and enlightened, sound reasons will replace the prejudices. The free spirit who overturns a prejudice on which a useful truth rests commits a worthless action. However, often a worthless action gives occasion that in place of a frail superstition more lasting pillars are placed. If the degree of enlightenment of a people allows it, all indispensable truths necessary for the happiness of humanity can be built on rational knowledge.
>
> So wie ein Volk nach u. nach gesittet und erleuchtet wird, so treten vernünftige Gründe an die Stelle der Vorurtheile. Der Freygeist, der ein Vorurtheil umstößt, auf welches sich eine nützliche Wahrheit stützet, begehet eine nichts würdige Handlung, allein oft giebt diese nichtswürdige Handlung Gelegenheit, daß an die Stelle des morschen Aberglaubens, dauerhaftere Pfeiler untergestützt werden. Wenn der Grad der Erleuchtung eines Volks es zuläßt; so können am Ende alle zur Glückseligkeit des M.G. [Menschengeschlechts] unentbehrliche Wahrheiten auf vernünftige Erkentnis gebauet werden. (Jub A 7, 75)

Rather than rendering religion superfluous, this disclaimer opens the way to a critical understanding of religion beyond an obsolete monopoly for truth claims with regard to metaphysics or salvation. For this disclaimer also frees religion from its subjection to serve as a default system for reason. Although, ignoring this insight, theologians may continue to mistake metaphysics for theology and, as a consequence, jeopardize the integrity of both disciplines, it is the liberation of natural religion from the constraints of traditional theology that foregrounds the possibility for a modern sense of religiosity. This new kind of religiosity signals a deepened awareness of the dialectically complex relationship between reason and religion, the equally complex relationship between the universal and the particular, and the paradox of historicism. Reason, Mendelssohn indicates, never is the last, or for that matter first, answer—such a view being the prerogative of a fundamentalist attitude—but it is strong enough to provide the necessary framework for securing the necessary notions of morality and happiness in terms of natural religion.

A central moment of the challenge in Bonnet's argumentation represents his use of miracles as indisputable authority. For the generation of young sentimentalists born around the mid-eighteenth century, miracles represent the ultimate sublime.[5] According to them, it is not so much an interruption in the order of nature—traditionally taken as the sign of divine intervention—that makes the miracle. More significantly, it is now the glimpse of the divine as it presents itself through the working of miracles thus sending forth its mild beam of providence. As a consequence, the ability to recognize a miracle becomes a sign of the right religious refinement more than of anything else. And to deny miracles the significance underlaid by Christian theologians becomes the explicit refusal of divinity's claims altogether, or so the argument suggests.

In order to expose the problematic assumptions defining the hermeneutic setup of the discourse on miracles, Mendelssohn first has to examine the discourse on miracles itself. His discussion hammers home the point that miracles themselves do not carry any messages. Although they might occur as a sign of divine assurance endorsing the messenger and his message—a claim that, however, can never be excepted from last doubts, as Mendelssohn argues—miracles do not, in themselves, present any evidence for the veracity and truth of the message itself. For the establishment of such a claim requires the hermeneutic activity of constructing a meaning of the message, which, after all, is but a sign, and as such requires an act of interpretation that—given the nature of hermeneutics necessarily presupposing some use of reason—cannot be conceived to be incompatible with reason or with Scripture (Jub A 7, 89–90). The distinction between miracles and revelation proper—or more specifically, between the content of revelation and the accompanying circumstances under which revelation takes place—effectively pulverizes the theological hold on miracles. If Mendelssohn does not consciously follow the cue of Spinoza, his approach certainly resonates with Spinoza's analysis.

While miracles may or may not indicate divine intervention, they carry only complementary, moral evidence. They do not provide any legitimation in and for themselves. Read as signs, miracles, Mendelssohn's argument suggests, have thus only secondary meaning created through hermeneutic activity. Although they may or may not represent (though they always stage) divine intervention—a question that, in the final analysis, can only be answered retrospectively and tentatively—they do not by themselves enunciate any message or doctrine. Instead, miracles are always silent and, therefore, in need of interpretation. And interpretation, in order to be capable of consensus, is subject to the standards of reason.[6] As Mendelssohn sums up:

> If the alleged translator of the language of divine miracles has, at the same time, given doctrines that contradict these certain truths of reason, all miraculous facts which he cites to give credence to his mission lack force; it is not necessary that I more closely examine his actions that appear to be extraordinary. For one incontrovertible proof of the contrary defeats all possible moral certainty.

> Hat der vorgegebene Dolmetsch der göttlichen Wunder Sprache auch zugleich Lehren gegeben, die diesen ausgemachten Vernunftwahrheiten zu wider sind; so sind alle wunderhafte Thatsachen, die er zum Creditif seiner Gesandtschafft anführet, ohne Kraft; so ist es unnöthig, daß ich seine ausserordentlich scheinende Handlungen, oder seinen moralischen Charakter näher untersuche, denn *ein* unumstößlicher Beweis vom Gegentheil überwiegt alle mögliche moralische Gewißheit. (Jub A 7, 83)[7]

Although Moses performed his miracles only as a matter of necessity (*Nothdurft, Jub A 7,* 86) in order to respond to the demands and expectations of his time, Mendelssohn makes the exception with one miracle that by its sheer dimensions sets it aside as a singular case. The revelation at

Mount Sinai, Scripture tells, took place in the presence of the entire Jewish people:

> All the miracles that have occurred or are said to have occurred in any corner of the earth are not to be compared with this great, God-behooving appearance. Also no known testimony of any validity contradicts it.

> Alle Wunder, die irgend in einem Winkel der Erde geschehen sind, oder seyn sollen, sind mit dieser großen, gottanständigen Erscheinung nicht zu vergleichen. Auch wird derselben durch kein uns bekanntes Zeugnis von einiger Gültigkeit widersprochen. (Jub A 7, 88)

This makes it what Mendelssohn calls a "historical matter" (*Geschichtssache,* Jub A 7, 88). But while he observes that this event serves as his orientation point and standard (Jub A 7, 88), he interprets this event as the enunciation of the Law of Moses as historical act. As an act of legislation it does not carry any particular claims for cognitive truth but rather the indisputable act of instituting divine yet particular law. This is why the event at Sinai—singular and incomparable, as Mendelssohn stresses (Jub A 7, 87)—is a historical matter rather than a matter of cognitive truth, however divine it might be.

The revelation at Sinai, this argument suggests, consists thus not in the miracles witnessed at the event but in the dispensation of the law; that is, the revelation is expressed in terms of legislation rather than a form of knowledge. But, and this is only implicitly indicated in this argument, it is this legislation that makes the revelation retrospectively an authentic religious experience. Mendelssohn's stand with respect to miracles, however, is nevertheless no less ambiguous. Their existence remains undisputed, but equally undisputed stands for Mendelssohn the distinction between miracles and religious messages and doctrines. Mount Sinai serves as a paradigm for how miracles function—namely, as sideshows to stage and highlight the importance of revelation, which Mendelssohn clearly distinguishes from the miracles. As a result, revelation is conceived to be independent from the status and nature of miracles:

> A prophet can, therefore, perform the greatest miracles and the most unheard of deeds and find no credence as soon as he contradicts Moses: for we can be assured that his miracles are sorcery or otherwise secret arts.

> [. . .] It has therefore been explicitly commanded to us by God to trust no miracle with the intention to lead us astray from the laws of Moses.
>
> Daher kan ein Prophet die größten Wunder und unerhörtesten Thaten verrichten, und keinen Glauben finden, sobald er dem Moses widerspricht: denn wir können versichert seyn, dass seine Wunder Zaubereyen, oder sonst geheime Künste sind. [. . .] Daher uns von Gott ausdrücklich befohlen worden, keinem Wunder zu trauen, das die Absicht hat, uns von den Gesetzen Moses abzuführen. (Jub A 7, 88)

In addition, this distinction makes it possible to conceive of the message of revelation independently from the discussion on the nature of miracles, and therefore in ways fully compatible with reason. As a consequence, miracles cannot serve any purpose of legitimation.

With the principal refusal of claims simply raised on the fact of reported occurrence of miracles while, at the same time, fully acknowledging the importance of miracles for religion, Mendelssohn takes a critical stand. Resisting the extremes of religious irrationalism and staunch rationalism, he formulates his position of endorsing a purified conception of religion that leaves equal room for both reason and religion. Instead of viewing their relationship as antagonistic, he sees it as mutually supportive. Neither one can be thought to exist for itself without its other, as both are understood to be constitutive for the formation of human civilization.

> Our reason can comfortably depart from the first certain principles of human knowledge and be assured to meet in the end religion on the same road. Here is no struggle between religion and reason, no rebellion of our natural knowledge against the suppressing violence of creed. Their roads are roads of love and all their paths are peace.
>
> Unsere Vernunft kan ganz gemächlich von den ersten sichern Grundbegriffen der menschlichen Erkentnis ausgehen, und versichert seyn, am Ende die Religion auf eben dem Wege anzutreffen. Hier ist kein Kampf zwischen Religion und Vernunft, kein Aufruhr unserer natürlichen Erkentnis wider die unterdrückende Gewalt des Glaubens. Ihre Wege sind liebliche Wege und alle ihre Stege sind Friede. (Jub A 7, 95)

This view anticipates, word for word, the conclusion of *Jerusalem*. But like the argument put forward there, this is not a naive, all-harmonizing plea for tolerance that downplays difference and contradictions. Quite to the contrary, Mendelssohn's unrelenting emphasis on natural religion, his conception of Judaism, and the differentiated understanding of the fundamental role of both religion and reason give sharp profile to his recognition of the dialectics of reason and religion and this dialectic's constitutive role for the foundation of the modern state, culture, and society.

As Mendelssohn himself pursues work on his commentaries on Ecclesiastes and the Psalms, and on the translation of the Psalter and the Pentateuch, he at the same time pursues with undiminished vigor his projects in practical philosophy. The negotiating of this double activity illustrates the concrete, practice-oriented, and practice-based fashion in which Mendelssohn envisions this, his conception of a peaceful and parallel-running, reciprocally cross-fertilizing project of enlightenment. Mendelssohn's particular definitions of reason and religion demonstrate, instead of a false antagonism, their irreducibility and constitutive reciprocity. While this approach is often construed as a somewhat naive oversight of the deeper difficulties and problems at the heart of the Enlightenment conception of reason and religion, Mendelssohn tackles the issue of how to come to terms with both reason and its other in an alternative fashion that in its awareness of the intricately interwoven motives anticipates the best insights of Hegel's analysis of the dialectics of enlightenment and religion and thus still commands attention as it presents a distinctly critical version of the project of enlightenment.

As painful as Lavater's provocation may have been, Mendelssohn's "Gegenbetrachtungen" prove him to be far from any need for apologetic shelter. Instead, Mendelssohn's notes show him addressing the issue of religion in an enlightened age in quite the same way Spinoza had done in his *Theological-Political Treatise* a century earlier. What distinguishes Mendelssohn from Spinoza is a different interpretation of Spinoza's analysis of the social function of religion as one that no longer needs to be thought to undermine all claims of religion but, giving Spinoza's argument a more positive turn, as an analysis that, now, is utilized to provide arguments for a genuine legitimation of a new conception of religiosity that no longer conceives of religion as an instrument for upholding claims or counterclaims but as the space where historical particularity is allowed to express itself.

CHAPTER 9

FRAMING POLITICAL RIGHTS

Mendelssohn's Preface to Manasseh Ben Israel's *Vindication of the Jews*

A DECADE LATER, IN THE CONTEXT OF THE DEBATES on emancipation, the arguments Mendelssohn developed in response to his study of Bonnet come to fruition. Repeatedly asked to either "explain himself," as Lavater had demanded, or to intervene on behalf of Jewish communities facing the threat of expulsion from one or another German state, Mendelssohn increasingly realized that political interventions would not suffice to change the plight of the Jews. Instead, what was needed was, beyond enlightenment in general, a scrutiny of the normative elements informing the discourse on emancipation. Only a critical examination of the silently accepted implications that framed this discourse promised to yield the necessary analytic platform to establish the issue of Jewish emancipation as a concern of direct importance for modern civil society.

The decade of the 1770s had seen the publication of Mendelssohn's translation of the Pentateuch and its commentary, authored by a team of contributors.[1] Mendelssohn had emerged as the celebrated authority of Haskalah, the Jewish Enlightenment, but the years also had made it painfully clear that the political inequality and repression would not cease unless openly challenged. The necessity for a public plea for emancipation became increasingly clear, and to the degree that Mendelssohn had become an internationally acclaimed public figure, answering this call for such an intervention carried, for Mendelssohn, some promise for success. With the publication of *Nathan des Weise* (1779), Lessing's premature death, and Christian Dohm's *Über die bürgerliche Verbesserung der Juden* (1781), the situation had changed. Mendelssohn had been the moving force and source of information behind Dohm, but it was Dohm's own view rather than Mendelssohn's that informs Dohm's call for civil "improvement" and emancipation of the Jews. As this development signaled a shift in the public's attitude with regard to Jewish emancipation, representation of the Jewish position became possible in terms of self-representation. This almost invisible but so crucial sea change in the debate on emancipation, with its transformation from a theological debate to a question of political theory, prepared the ground for Mendelssohn to enter the scene of public discussion as a self-conscious Jew whose voice had become prominent enough to command the attention of the public he had, after all, been instrumental in creating.

Mendelssohn announces this transition with one of his most powerfully formulated contributions, his preface to Manasseh Ben Israel's *Vindiciae Judaeorum* (*Vindication of the Jews*) (London, 1656). This preface to Marcus Herz's translation of Ben Israel's call for granting the Jews admission to England[2] was incorporated by Nicolai as an appendix to the revised edition of Dohm's *Über die bürgerliche Verbesserung der Juden.*

Placed in this way, the preface not only served as introduction to Ben Israel's plea but also came to represent Mendelssohn's supportive response to Dohm. Navigating the difficulties and restrictions that frame the public debate on the plight of the Jews, Mendelssohn's argument underlines that the issue of Jewish emancipation can no longer be contained in isolation but bears directly on how modern civil society is theorized. In arguing for a constitutive linkage between the particular concern of Jewish discrimination and its impact on the constitution of civil society at large, the preface marks an important inaugural step in publicly denouncing the wider implications of marginalization and exclusion as forms of repression with a negative impact on civil society in general. Up to this point, Mendelssohn had appeared in authorial roles that were understood to be mutually exclusive. Either he was writing in the voice of the speculative sage-philosopher and judicious literary critic, and, thus, saluted as the "German Socrates," or he took on the traditional role of the *shtadlan,* or spokesperson for his people, the exemplary representative whose eloquence and sophistication won him wide sympathy as an example for successful assimilation. But as he moved between these two worlds, between rational Enlightenment philosophy and traditional Judaism, both his life and his writing were perceived to bifurcate onto two separate tracks that did not connect. For Mendelssohn, the line between private and public seemed to have split the Jew from the philosopher and literary critic.

With Manasseh Ben Israel, however, Mendelssohn introduces to the Enlightenment debate a modern Jewish authority whose spirited appeal for political recognition defied such compartmentalizing. For in contrast to the rest of Europe, seventeenth-century Holland—where Ben Israel served as rabbi to Amsterdam's Jewish community—stood out as an example of a modern and progressive liberal state where the success of economic and cultural freedom richly rewarded a politics of civil equality and acceptance. In his preface, Mendelssohn thus formulates the explicit argument that the link between the project of enlightenment and the need for civil acceptance of the Jews is of vital importance for society as a whole.

Incidentally, there is also a connection between the history of the publication of Ben Israel's appeal and the fate of Spinoza. In 1656, the year of the publication of Ben Israel's *Vindication of the Jews* during his trip to England on his mission to convince Cromwell of the advantages of opening up Great Britain to the Jews, Spinoza was excommunicated. This highlights a crucial subtext of Mendelssohn's so vigorously expressed rejection of the possibility of any legal theory of a *jus excommunicationis* whatever religious group may argue for such a right to exist.[3]

Mendelssohn exposes the question of how to transform a debate based on ignoring all that is considered foreign to one's own cultural understanding as haunted by a structural predicament. According to him, the dominant culture must extend its hand first toward the minor and take the first step. If this does not happen, tolerance functions in a restricted and selective—and, as a consequence, discriminatory—manner. If Jews are considered a separate colony within the state, as "colonists born in the land" ("eingebohrne Colonisten" [Jub A 8, 5]), they assume a rather precarious status. But if they are treated like a colony that is granted autonomy and self-administration (16), the Jews are only once more exterritorialized by the state in which they live, produce, trade, and pay taxes. Mendelssohn does not openly refute such an approach. He simply shows how the implications of such a model, carried to their conclusions, would play themselves out. For who is a member of a disenfranchised colony to argue with a colonial power? What he can and certainly does give expression to in this text is a series of objections, though mostly implicitly and indirectly articulated—objections raised against the traditional mechanisms of exclusion at work in the debate on the status of the Jews. Aware of the precariously exposed nature of his own position in such a discussion (with a king most unsympathetic toward Jews and toward Mendelssohn in particular), Mendelssohn points to the far-reaching implications this issue has in terms of the practice of enlightenment, shared by both his fellow Jews and by people like Dohm and the Prussian intelligentsia.

Arguing that the utility of people is not a function of their religion but of the political arrangement of a given state, Mendelssohn turns the popular assumption that Jews represent an economically unproductive population into an eloquent and forceful plea for economic liberalism. Arguing that a laissez-faire liberalism will itself establish a working economic order, Mendelssohn concludes: "Whenever human beings become harmful to other human beings in any constitution, the reason is either the laws or the regents" ("So oft Menschen in irgend einer Verfassung, Menschen schädlich werden, liegt es blos an den Gesetzen oder an ihren Verwesern" [Jub A 8, 12]). Not only is the merchant represented as a functional part in the economy, crucial to its functioning, and serving, therefore, as a productive member of society, but he emerges, in Mendelssohn's description, as the central facilitator of a free and smoothly operating market economy. Much like Adam Smith's exaltation of the missionary role of the merchant for civilization, Mendelssohn salutes the merchant as the "true benefactor of the state, and humanity in general" (Jub A 8, 15).[4] This view, combined with a strong stand on natural right as the sole reference point for the constitution of civil society, including its basic model of contract theory, brings Mendelssohn in close proximity to Spinoza's political theory. Mendelssohn's categorical refusal to concede any legitimacy to contractual agreements that cannot be derived from natural law articulates a rigorous critique of the contract theory of political liberalism that echoes Spinoza critical concerns:

> As culture cannot produce a fruit to which nature has not provided the bud; art cannot produce by way of exercise and habituation an arbitrary movement where nature has not provided any muscle; similarly, all contracts and agreements among human beings cannot create a right of which there should be no foundation laid in the state of nature.

> So wenig die Cultur eine Frucht erzielen kan, wozu die Natur nicht den Keim hergegeben; so wenig die Kunst durch Ueben und Gewöhnen eine willkührliche Bewegung hervorbringen kan, wo die Natur kein Muskel hingelegt; eben so wenig können alle Verträge und Verabredungen unter den Menschen ein Recht erschaffen, davon der Grund nicht im Stande der Natur anzutreffen seyn sollte. (Jub A 8, 19)

The formulation of the test of the validity of contracts presents a remarkable application of Spinoza's critique of contract theory: "But where without contract neither duty nor right cannot be thought, all contracts of human beings and their agreements are empty sound and din" ("Wo aber ohne Vertrag, sich weder Pflicht noch Recht denken läßt, da sind alle Verträge der Menschen und ihre Abkommnisse leerer Schall und Ton" [Jub A 8, 20]). Contrary to contract theory, which theorizes that contracts provide their own constitutive power, Mendelssohn, in following Spinoza, revokes this theoretical model as intrinsically flawed. Like Spinoza, he advances an alternative conception of fusion on the grounds of the provisions provided by natural law. Like Spinoza, Mendelssohn does not aim at abolishing or replacing the idea of contract altogether. Both proceed by reframing the theory of contract in a model of natural law that redefines contract as simply the formalization of sociopolitical arrangements conducive to nature in general. By introducing the categories of perfect and imperfect rights, Mendelssohn translates Spinoza's ontology-based theory of natural right into a theory of rights.

Mendelssohn's distinction between perfect and imperfect rights and duties (Jub A 8, 19–20) allows him now to expose the problematic implications of the colonial model, in which the Jewish situation has been theoretically encased, on principal grounds. For this distinction exposes contract theory's conception of political rights merely in terms of contractual agreements. Against such a reductive understanding, Mendelssohn is able to couch his argument in terms of the doctrine of perfect and imperfect rights, arguing that it is only possible to contractually transfer what can be qualified as an imperfect right, which means that only that which preexists as natural right is negotiable for contract.

Based on this distinction, Mendelssohn introduces the fundamental distinction between action and thought. In *Jerusalem* this distinction will serve as the basic foundation for his liberal political philosophy, but here, in the preface to Ben Israel, it functions to critique the colonial model and its false claims to legitimate power and authority. The passage on the perfect and imperfect duties and its implications for distinguishing the different legal status between action and thought leads to the following conclusion:

> Thus, the motherly nation itself has no authority to combine with an agreeable doctrine the enjoyment of a wordly good or advantage, to reward or punish the acceptance or rejection of it, and what it lacks itself, how should it be capable to concede or grant this to the colony?
>
> Also hat die mütterliche Nation selbst keine Befugniß mit einer ihr gefälligen Lehrmeinung den Genuß irgend eines irdischen Guts oder Vorzugs zu verbinden, das Annehmen oder Verwerfen derselben zu belohnen oder zu bestrafen, und was sie selbst nicht hat, wie sollte sie es der Colonie einräumen und gewähren können? (Jub A 8, 20–21)

Such a detachment from the legal power of the mother nation effectively redefines the colonial relationship. The result is a principal dislodging of the paradigm under critique. As a consequence, the colonial model is understood to be devoid of any explanatory, let alone legitimating, power. But the exposure of the problems the colonial paradigm eventually creates gives the situation of the Jews in Germany sharper contours.

This strategy makes it possible for Mendelssohn to approach the debate about the emancipation of the Jews, so fraught with prejudices and dogmatic narrow-mindedness, in a pragmatic manner. Beyond theological and moral concerns, he seems to argue, there is a mechanism of prejudice at work that views and treats Jews—regardless of their religious, moral, and social qualities—as an ontologico-politically different caste. The projective character of prejudices is so deeply seated that when a prejudice is cut off from its roots it finds new grounds elsewhere: "You can cut through all the roots of an obsolete prejudice without completely taking away its nourishment. For in such a case it feeds off the air" ("Man kan einem verjährten Vorurteile alle Wurzeln durchschneiden, ohne ihm die Nahrung gänzlich zu entziehen. Es saugt solche allenfalls aus der Luft" [Jub A 8, 10]). Mendelssohn remains quite aware of the politics of discrimination, exclusion, and disenfranchisement that so seamlessly change from obsolete to more updated versions of justifying ever new forms of rationalizing their fixations. This is why he attempts to avoid the pitfall of apologetic defense. Instead of defending his position, Mendelssohn wants to expose the inconsistencies that haunt the allegations against the Jews. For him it is clear that an apology on behalf of the Jews would backfire, serving only as ultimate demonstration of the resilience of the power of prejudices. Praising Dohm for so circumspectly avoiding this pitfall and for having instead focused on advancing a consistent argument for the significance of Jewish emancipation for society as a whole, Mendelssohn drives home the critical ramifications the debate on the plight of the Jews has for the formulation of the project of enlightenment in general. "Lucky us if this cause becomes at the same time our cause, if one cannot insist on the rights of humanity without demanding at the same time our rights" ("Ein Glück für uns, wenn diese Sache auch zugleich die unserige wird, wenn man auf die Rechte der Menschheit nicht dringen kan, ohne zugleich die Unserigen zu reklamiren" [Jub A 8, 5]). Based on the self-assured reliance on the legitimacy of his Jewish particularity, this universal perspective provides the pragmatic but also theoretically sound grounds for the striking force of Mendelssohn's argumentation. If he praises Enlightenment corrections of historiographic blunders that have transfixed the Jews as evildoers throughout history, his vision points far beyond a thorough revision of history. For the underlying implication consists in the insight that only a practical change, the granting of equal civil rights with no strings or stipulations attached, will lead to a situation in which an enlightened view becomes possible. Mendelssohn thus shares with Spinoza the view that the freedom to philosophize requires not only a fundamental rethinking of political theory but an actual change of the political realities.

Mendelssohn entertains no illusion that law and barbarism may go hand in hand (Jub A 8, 8 and 10). Enlightenment still has to go a long way until all traces of barbarism in history are gone (Jub A 8, 7). Obviously, he seems to imply that enlightenment, left to its own devices, may not prove sufficient to establish effectively civil equality. This is in line with his distinction between thought and action. As long as there are no changes in the political sphere, enlightenment as a practical project is bound to remain an illusion. It is precisely on the grounds of the distinction between thought and action that theoretical enlightenment is thus no longer charged with the task of bringing about change in the world. On the contrary, keeping thought and action separate enables Mendelssohn to argue independently both sides of the divide. In this way he provides a firm grounding both for the claim to full freedom of thought and expression and, at the same time, for the view that change in the political sphere may be aired and envisioned by Enlightenment thought but is eventually brought about only by political change. Insisting on the autonomy of the political thus cuts both ways. It allows him to underline the need for political action by the authorities while it secures everybody's right for freedom of speech.

The question of the right to excommunication illustrates this point in terms of the relationship between religion and political power. For Mendelssohn the assumption of such a right not only betrays a false conception of the role and function of religion but ignores the fundamental difference between thought and action. Against the danger of granting coercive power to religion, Mendelssohn's argument practically captures Spinoza's position:

> The true, divine religion does not arrogate any power with regard to opinions and judgments; does not give us any title on wordly goods, no right to consumption, possession and property; does not acknowledge any other power than the power to win with the help of reasons, to convince, and to make happy by way of conviction. The true, divine religion needs to use neither arms nor fingers; it is pure spirit and heart.

> Die wahre, göttliche Religion maßt sich keine Gewalt der Meinungen und Urtheile an; giebt und nimmt keinen Anspruch auf irdische Güter, kein Recht auf Genuß, Besitz und Eigenthum; kennet keine andere Macht, als die Macht durch Gründe zu gewinnen, zu überzeugen, und durch Überzeugung glückselig zu machen. Die wahre, göttliche Religion bedarf weder Arme noch Finger zu ihrem Gebrauche; sie ist lauter Geist und Herz. (Jub A 8, 18)

In addition to the preface, Mendelssohn supplements the translation of Ben Israel's *Vindication of the Jews* with three footnotes. The way in which they complement the text's course of argument indicates the significance Mendelssohn ascribes to taking an uncompromising stand concerning the debate on emancipation. Whereas Ben Israel, in accord with the tract's diplomatic task of arguing the case for granting Jews permission to enter and live in Great Britain, fashions his account in a manner that offers at times a slightly sanitized version of history, Mendelssohn leaves no doubt that Christian Europe is overcast by a dubious, reprehensible, cruel, and violent past. Certainly, Ben Israel was, with an eye fixed on the urgency for quick action, more inclined to entreat Cromwell's cabinet with an idea of Britain's special calling to finally welcome Jews to their island than to comply with some requirements for historical accuracy. Mendelssohn, on the other hand, is primarily interested in pressing for a discussion that addresses the implications of the whole complex in the broad daylight of the public space. Jewish emancipation, Mendelssohn argues—if it is to be realized in a promising and productive way—is only meaningful if the conditions of its possibility are given careful and thorough examination. For these conditions are, after all, the result of the specific historical circumstances constituting the social, political, legal, and religious environment that functions as the parameters defining the possibility of emancipation. Mendelssohn thus counters Ben Israel's statement that

> It is better, our forefathers said, to live among Edom than among Ismael and thus our captivity among the Muslim has been, as the experience of our nation has taught us, much more burdensome and unbearable than among the Christians who are a more moral, reasonable and better policed people.
>
> Es ist besser, sagten unsere Vorfahren, unter Edom als unter Ismael zu wohnen, und so ist, wie die Erfahrung unsere Nation gelehrt, unsere Gefangenschaft unter den Mahometanern weit lästiger und unerträglicher als unter Christen, welch ein gesitteteres, vernünftigeres und besser policirtes Volk sind.

with a footnote that sets the record straight:

> It may be true in our times that the Jews in Christian states are in better circumstances than im Muslim states; but never have they been so cruelly persecuted, murdered, tortured, burnt, robbed, and chased away naked than by Christian governments and theologians of the Middle Ages. Still nowadays Jews in Turkish lands pay only a moderate head tax and suffer little more than other subjects and as is the consequence of an arbitrary government. The number of Jews in Muslim states is probably higher than in Christian states. Thanks to their excellent skills as physicians and also as state officials they often rise in Muslim states to a position of honor and wealth. Even now the prime minister of the Emperor of Morocco is a Jew called Sumbul.
>
> In den itzigen Zeiten mag es wahr seyn, daß sich die Juden in den christlichen Staaten besser als in den mahometanischen befinden; aber nie sind

> sie doch in diesen so grausam verfolgt, gemordet, gepeinigt, verbrannt, des ihrigen beraubt, nackend verjagt worden, als von den christlichen Regirungen und Religionslehrern der mittleren Zeiten. Noch itzt zahlen die Juden in den türkischen Landen nur ein mäßiges Kopfgeld, und sie leiden wenig mehr als andre Unterthanen und wie es die willkührliche Regirung mit sich bringt. Die Zahl der Juden in den mahometanischen Staaten ist vermuthlich größer, als die in den christlichen. Sie kommen daselbst öfterer durch vorzügliche Geschicklichkeit als Ärzte oder auch Staatsbediente zu Reichthum und Ehren. Noch itzt ist der erste Minister des Kaisers von Marocco ein Jude Sumbul. (Jub A 8, 35 n)

This remark speaks to several points. Besides repeating the argument (already discussed in the preface) that demographic freedom produces economic wealth (Jub A 8, 11–12), Mendelssohn reminds the reader of the murderous danger of theological fundamentalism. But the note on which he concludes his remark, the success story of Sumbul, the Jewish prime minister who serves the Emperor of Morocco, suggests a more philosophical point, for this example challenges the very core of European Christian understanding of the philosophy of history and the precarious "tolerated" status of its Jews. The denial of civil rights and equality to Jews is based on that theological ground that, in the eyes of Christians, Jews represent the millennia-old deniers and denigrators of divine Christian truth. In his comparison of the eighteenth-century Muslim world and its sociopolitical order with Christian Europe, Mendelssohn drives home the perilous consequences of the exclusionary Christian doctrine still dominant in modern Europe: the doctrine of the special onto-theological status of the Jews.

The rank and station of a prime minister transcends the concession of granting personal exception acceptable in extraordinary cases for members of a disenfranchised group marked with onto-theological difference. It reminds the reader of the fact that, in principle, the granting of civil rights to individual members of such a group poses no problems for other cultures. This is the difference Mendelssohn wishes to highlight in comparison to the treatment of Jews in Europe, who may often, as in the case of court Jews, have accumulated formidable wealth but remained despite their economic superiority just as scandalously disenfranchised as their brethren, and—like them—considered onto-theologically different.

As a consequence, Jews in Christian Europe were not only subject to the whims of their rulers and to everyone else who felt called upon to nourish Christian resentment, but they were also strictly excluded from access to the political power, thus lacking the most basic political rights and entitlements provided for by Muslim law to Jews and Christians alike. In this distinction lies the little sting of this footnote: political emancipation is not only possible but already practiced elsewhere, and this not in the advanced West but in countries where "barbarians," or at least "infidels" like Muslims, rule. As a result, one of the key notions underpinning the modern European idea of political order is challenged. Jews' disenfranchisement from the political sphere is exposed as a theological decision that bodes ill for the Christian claim for representing the most humane form of religion of universal love and acceptance.

The second note touches upon another issue central to Mendelssohn's considerations. There is a line spoken in the daily Jewish prayer: "Don't leave any hope to the apostate, destroy all heretics and have all your enemies and all who hate you die. And extinguish the empire of arrogance, weaken and destroy it soon and in our days" ("Lasse den Abtrünnigen keine Hofnung, vertilge alle Ketzer, und alle deine Feinde und alle die dich hassen laß umkommen. Und das Reich des Hochmuths wollest du ausrotten, schwäche und vertilge es bald und in unsern Tagen" [Jub A 8, 47]). Ben Israel argues that it is not the early Christians who are meant with the empire of arrogance, but the Romans. For him, emphasizing the compatibility and affinity of Jewish and Christian culture assumes tactical priority. But in the eyes of Mendelssohn, Ben Israel's interpretation creates another problem. For, Ben Israel understands the meaning of this prayer to refer to a specific historical political reality, namely, the Roman empire (Jub A 8, 48). However, according to Mendelssohn's understanding, such an interpretation of the prayer would commit to a rather unfortunate view linking Jewish religious practice to specific moments in political history. To refute such an ill-fated, constraining understanding, Mendelssohn notes that the "empire of arrogance" does not mean any actual historical empire but is merely meant to denote the abject attitude of those people who, without any cause and with hubris, strive for domination over others.

As Mendelssohn points out, this prayer simply expresses an "innocent wish" that he renders in the following way:

> In this sense this is no curse on a particular kingdom on earth, no wish of the end of any government, and the prayer formula can appropriately be transformed in the following innocent wish: Have presumption (or the

> presumptuous) no longer rule the people but have the violence of arrogance weakened, broken and those who surrender to it soon in our days humiliated.
>
> In diesem Verstande also wird allhier keinem bestimmten Reiche auf Erden geflucht, keiner Regierung der Untergang gewünscht, und die Gebetsformel kann gar füglich in folgenden unschuldigen Wunsch verwandelt werden: Laß den Übermuth (oder die Übermüthigen) nicht länger die Menschen beherrschen; sondern die Gewalt des Hochmuths geschwächt, gebrochen und die sich ihm überlassen, bald und in unseren Tagen gedemüthiget werden? (Jub A 8, 49)

Crowning his hermeneutic efforts, he continues: "wer setzt nicht hier von ganzem Herzen sein Amen hinzu?" ("who does not add here, from the bottom of their heart, their amen?" [Jub A 8, 49]). In this way, Mendelssohn maintains the strict separation between state and religion that Ben Israel's account had threatened to blur.

In a third note, Mendelssohn clarifies another concept central to this understanding of religion that, in Ben Israel's text, may be misconstrued by the reader. When Ben Israel speaks of "conversion," which the German translation renders as *Bekehrung*, this presents for Mendelssohn a potential source of misunderstanding. The term that, according to Mendelssohn, Ben Israel has in mind is *teshuva*, which literally means conversion, or turning around. But it does not mean conversion in the sense of turning to another religion or confession. Instead, *teshuva* signifies the inner moral awakening of one's conscience, a turning away from false involvements and a spontaneous returning to God. Mendelssohn's point is that this means the very opposite of the change of alliance with a particular religion or religious organization. Rather, he underlines the point that from all we can know of providence, the exterior of religious practices shall always remain diverse:

> According to the plan of providence, there will and shall always remain diversity in the external form of religious service. The actual Judaism or content of Jewish customs, laws and testimonies is only supposed to be meant for Jews and Israelites, an inheritance of Jacob's community.
>
> In der äußern Form des Gottesdienstes wird und soll nach dem Plane der Vorsehung, allezeit Mannigfaltigkeit bleiben. Das eigentliche Judenthum,

> oder Inbegriff jüdischer Gebräuche, Gesetze und Zeugnisse soll blos für Juden und Israeliten seyn, ein Erbtheil der Gemeine Jakobs. (Jub A 8, 55)

This point is so crucial to Mendelssohn that he further illustrates its importance for the adequate understanding of religion in general. Thus he argues that, according to Judaism, true religiosity consists in advocating not unity but, instead, diversity of forms for the practice of religion. Mendelssohn's worry about the repeated efforts aiming at religious unification is motivated by the fact that such endeavors necessarily lead to both political and religious catastrophe. This concern presents a constant and guiding idea in Mendelssohn's thought on religion. It attests to Mendelssohn's heightened sensitivity concerning the primary importance of the issue of tolerance and of the virulence of theology's claims for religious hegemony. Continuing his note, Mendelssohn thus discusses the prayer spoken during Rosh Hashanah and Yom Kippur that the nations may turn to acknowledging the Eternal One:

> Here there is no talk of unification of doctrine and law, even less of a so-called religious unification that leads on a direct road to hateful intolerance. All persecutions have always been performed in the name and to the best of such religious unification.

> Hier ist von keiner Vereinigung in Lehr und Gesetz, noch weniger von einer sogenannten Glaubensvereinigung die Rede. Diese führet gerades Weges auf die gehäßige Intoleranz. Alle Verfolgungen sind von je her im Namen und zum Besten dieser Glaubensvereinigung ausgeübt worden.

Mendelssohn's way to cast his arguments may assume the form of an apologetic commentary, as this footnote, which runs over one page, seems to suggest. But an attentive reader, careful enough to follow an overextended footnote to its bitter end, will pick up on the principal rejection of institutional power for religious organizations, as the continuation of the quote illustrates:

> and one has to avoid and prevent this [unification of religions] like the dangerous enemy of humanity and its happiness; for it would, if it ever could be realized, indisputably give way to the old barbarism and the terrible spirit of persecution. Love and hatred are not so different as are the spreading of the knowledge of God and religious unification.

> und man hat diese [unification of religions], wie den gefährlichen Feind des menschlichen Geschlechts und seiner Glückseligkeit zu vermeiden und mit aller Macht zu verhindern; denn sie würde, wenn sie je erhalten werden könte, unstreitig die alte Barbarey, und den schrecklichen Geist der Verfolgung wieder empor bringen. Liebe und Haß sind nicht so sehr verschieden, als Ausbreitung der Erkenntniß Gottes von Glaubensvereinigung. (Jub A 8, 55)

This is quite an unequivocal way to express the threats that haunt the debate on tolerance. Concluding the note with an outspoken reminder concerning the portentous forces at work that "wish to guide, or rather misguide the tolerant attitude of the princes toward unification of the religions" ("Den toleranten Sinn de Großen and Glaubensvereinigung leiten, oder vielmehr verleiten zu wollen" [Jub A 8, 55]), Mendelssohn alerts the reader to the danger that lies hidden behind uninformed good intentions at unification where only self-determination in difference promises true and lasting peace.

Mendelssohn leaves no doubt about the fact that he is far from sharing the traditional concept of tolerance as toleration, Augustinian in its origin and conception. Already "tolerated" in the legal sense of the word,[5] Mendelssohn was understandably reluctant with regard to the blessings tolerance promises. As he wrote in a letter to his friend Herz Homberg on 4 October 1782: "Great thanks for all tolerance if this still implies working on unification of belief!" ("Grossen Dank für alle Toleranz, wenn man dabey noch immer an Glaubensvereinigung arbeitet!")[6]

CHAPTER 10

AN ALTERNATIVE UNIVERSALISM

Jerusalem, or On Religious Power and Judaism

SHORTLY AFTER THE PUBLICATION OF Mendelssohn's preface to Manasseh Ben Israel's *Vindication of the Jews,* an anonymous pamphlet *Das Forschen nach Licht und Recht in einem Schreiben an Herrn Moses Mendelssohn auf Veranlassung seiner merkwürdigen Vorrede zu Manasseh Ben Israel* (The searching for light and right in a letter to Mr. Moses Mendelssohn occasioned by his remarkable preface to Manasseh Ben Israel) appeared.[1] Penned as an open letter, this missive was signed "your most sincere admirer S****" and indicated Vienna as its place of origin (Jub A 8, 87). This pointed to Josef von Sonnenfels, a Jew from Prussia who had advanced to play an influential role in politics at the Vienna court.[2] Given Emperor Joseph II's efforts to introduce a politics of tolerance and to integrate Austrian Jews into civil life, as well as Sonnenfels's prominence, it seemed impossible to ignore this public confrontation. While such masquerading in the guise of respectability may have been the only way for the missive's author, August Friedrich Cranz—a publicist whom Mendelssohn did not hold in too high esteem—to prompt a response, Mendelssohn was now ready to present his answer in terms of a systematically formulated political and legal theory. The time had come to take a clear and firm public stand concerning the question of Jewish emancipation.

The systematic and stringently executed structure of *Jerusalem* suggests that Mendelssohn increasingly felt the need to impart precision and clarity to the emerging debate on the question of Jewish emancipation. While the publication of Cranz's pamphlet urged Mendelssohn to take a position, his strategy marks a deliberate move to counter the missive's attempt at reducing the controversy to a polemic, a polemic in which Mendelssohn would have been fixed in the role of the defendant no matter how unsubstantiated the allegations were. Instead, Mendelssohn responds to the preemptive entreaty of *Das Forschen nach Licht und Recht* with a forthright declaration of Jewish independence, as his *Jerusalem* has rightly been called,[3] as he sets out to take on a rigorous, critical examination of the hidden assumptions informing the missive's claims and expectations. Addressing the question of how to rethink the relationship between state and religion in an unprejudiced manner, fully sensitive to the importance of religion for human happiness while resisting the demands of institutionalized religion for political authority, Mendelssohn formulates a political theory that lays the groundwork for a modern conception of the role and function of religion in state and society.[4]

Already the title *Jerusalem* signals Mendelssohn's pointed response to the hermeneutic restrictions imposed on the discussion of Jewish emancipation during the Enlightenment. The book's concluding line is a quotation from Zechariah: "Love truth! Love peace!"[5] In the continuation of the passage, Zechariah names Jerusalem as the city where many and powerful nations will seek and worship God.[6] He envisions Jerusalem and Judaism as the tangible particularity that represents the universal in its non-representability. Mendelssohn's conclusion alludes thus in a cryptic but easily decipherable way to the prophetic tradition that envisions Judaism's mission to mediate between the particularity of all the nations on earth, their states and cultures, and the project of a universality of worldwide liberation that includes all of humanity without any exception. Jerusalem symbolizes the universal in the shape of the specificity of a locality, history, and particular religion. Reclaiming Jerusalem as a city that is part of the Jewish prophetic tradition, Mendelssohn confronts the Christian hermeneutic of Jerusalem with one whose particularity highlights the limits of a universalism that comes at the expense of the exclusion of Judaism, the very source and origin of the spiritual notion of Jerusalem as universal symbol—a fact to which Mendelssohn's contemporaries turned a blind eye. The title thus pinpoints the contested difference between the attitude the pamphlet *Das Forschen nach Licht und Recht* expresses and Mendelssohn's very different view of his Jewish particularity as the foundation for an alternative form of universalism.

Mendelssohn advances his argument in a bipartite move. The discussion of Judaism is kept for the second part of *Jerusalem.* In a first step, part 1 offers an incisive review of the key doctrines that define the parameters of eighteenth-century political philosophy. This order of procedure allows Mendelssohn to fashion his argument about the modernity of Judaism in a way that engages the challenge of conversion on principally political grounds and to argue that, in the context of modern political theory, such a challenge betrays a misguided desire for homogeneity that runs counter to the basic ideas of modern civil society. Instead, civil society emerges in Mendelssohn's reconstruction as a project that shows strong elective affinity with the central tenets of Jewish tradition. Whereas Spinoza's *Theological-Political Treatise* opened with a discussion of theological aspects and ended with an innovative political theory, Mendelssohn's *Jerusalem* follows the reverse order. But in a remarkable way, the two works follow the same logic of order, foregrounding their discussion in an analysis of what predicates the point under attack: the hermeneutic of scripture in Spinoza's case, political theory in Mendelssohn's case.

Taking his point of departure from the concepts of state and religion—the very opening words of *Jerusalem*[7]—Mendelssohn begins by exhibiting the circular nature of the run of the argument that besets conventional inquiries into the constitutive relationship between the two institutions. Exposing this circle, the discussion returns, after a cursory recapitulation of the main points in Hobbes and Locke where it started out (J 33–38; Jub A 8, 103–8). The approach of Hobbes and Locke[8] thus emerges as incapable of solving the problems created by fundamentalist religious claims for the control of political power. To address this issue Mendelssohn cites the case of Cardinal Bellarmine. Bellarmine had been severely reprimanded by the pope and put on the index of prohibited authors because he had argued for a complete, yet nevertheless only indirect, primacy of papal authority over the temporal—that is, secular—powers (J 39; Jub A 8, 108). In the eyes of the Vatican, however, Bellarmine was seen less as a help for justifying papal sovereignty and viewed more as seriously curtailing absolute ecclesiastic power and authority.

After this circular opening move, Mendelssohn introduces his own version of reconstructing the transition from original to civil state. The crucial difference between him and Hobbes and Locke—but also between him and Rousseau, whose social contract theory requires civil religion as integrative force and social glue—is that Mendelssohn conceives the transition from natural to civil state as one already determined and informed by both social and religious factors. For human beings to unite in order to form a civil state requires, according to Mendelssohn, that their nature is recognized as one that includes as part of their natural needs the spiritual dimension. In acknowledging religiosity as a natural aspect of human nature that classical political theory would otherwise ignore or discount, Mendelssohn provides a version of the model of the transition from natural to civil state that fundamentally recasts the framework of political theory. For, describing the origin of civil society as one that acknowledges the religious and spiritual dimension of human nature as a natural and precontractual given secures Mendelssohn's account against the kinds of instrumentalizations to which the theories of Hobbes, Locke, and Rousseau are subject. Their rigorous radicalism deprives human nature of an understanding that recognizes both its material and spiritual dimensions in equal measure. Instead, their reductionist views lack a deep understanding of individual specificity, which is constituted through the joint aspects of body and mind. However, for Mendelssohn it is precisely this irreducible double aspect of human nature that provides the only source for a meaningful concept of individualism and self-determination.

Mendelssohn's approach not only resolves the religious dilemma exemplified in the case of Cardinal Bellarmine but also rethinks the relationship between state and religion in a more differentiated way, one that is responsive to both the religious and the political concerns of human nature. In defining the aspect of originary religious duties vis-à-vis the creator as fundamental to human nature, Mendelssohn argues that religious duties present a defining moment for theorizing human nature. As a consequence, religious duties may be more effectively fulfilled in society. However, they are understood to already precede the formation of society. Mendelssohn imagines the natural origin of the individual's spiritual and religious dimension as being fully compatible with, and constitutive for, its autonomy, independence, and self-reliance. His view defies all claims from institutionalized religion to reserve the right to determine the content and nature of religion in the state and its institutions. For Mendelssohn the foundations of religion are already laid in the original state (state of nature). Religion, therefore, comes into focus as natural religion independent of, and untrammeled by, any conflicts of interests emerging at the origin of the formation of civil society.

Mendelssohn's account of human nature in the original state leads to an emphasis on the natural religious character and, as a result, to the insight of the originally grounded primacy of the individual in terms of religion and intellectual freedom. It is only then, after the (religious) duties of man are established, that the argument for the constitutive separation between thought and action is introduced.

Introducing duties before rights at the beginning of the version of his account of the state of nature or original state, Mendelssohn reverses the usual order of argumentation. This makes it possible to avoid the problematic consequences of conventional contract theories, for a listing of rights, as progressive and promising as their initial articulation might appear at first sight, institutes a framework whose ramifications entail duties that are no longer negotiable once these rights are ratified. Given the logical structure of this form of argumentation, conventional contract theory runs the risk of creating back doors tacitly admitting unintended obligations of unforeseen consequences. Thus the liberal approach to procure rights before duties produces along with the formulation of rights unanticipated duties whose implications call into doubt the terms on which the model of the social contract theory is based (J 40; Jub A 8, 109).[9]

According to Mendelssohn, it is the fulfillment of our duties that leads to happiness, both on earth and in the afterlife. Therefore, both action and conviction (*Gesinnung*) are necessary to achieve happiness. What duty calls for is enacted through action, while conviction sees to it that action derives from the true source, that is, from unadulterated motives (J 40; Jub A 8, 109–10). This linkage between conviction and action must, therefore, be reflected in the way in which society is constructed. As a result, society can no longer be understood as simply providing a basic legal framework and subsequently leaving its members to their own devices. Besides the office of government and administration, society cannot, therefore, ignore its other obligation, which consists in education. If the first is the task of the state, the second is the responsibility of the church, that is, institutionalized religion. From this view emerges the systematic distinction between state and church, which, joined together, respond to the total of human concerns: "Public institutions for the formation [*Bildung*] of man that concern his relations with God I call *church;* those that concern his relations with man I call *state*" (J 41) ("Oeffentliche Anstalten zur Bildung des Menschen, die sich auf Verhältnisse des Menschen zu Gott beziehen, nenne ich *Kirche;*—zum Menschen, *Staat*" [Jub A 8, 110]). But whereas political liberalism, in a countermove against the concept of civil religion, insists on isolating the temporal from the atemporal, the secular from the spiritual, and whereas the states of eighteenth-century Europe are based on the principle of a state church that guarantees the complete integration of the church in the Christian state, Mendelssohn suggests an altogether different approach. To him, the state's raison d'être cannot be separated from the spiritual character of its members. Thus he continues by proposing a refined conception of the formation of man: "By the formation of man I understand the effort to arrange both actions and convictions in such a way that they will be in accord with his felicity; that they will *educate* and *govern* men" (J 41) ("Unter Bildung des Menschen verstehe ich die Bemühung, beides, Gesinnungen und Handlungen so einzurichten, daß sie zur Glückseligkeit übereinstimmen; die Menschen *erziehen* und *regieren*" [Jub A 8, 110]). In contrast to most definitions of education (*Bildung*), Mendelssohn understands education as formation or development of the individual as a whole and fully rounded being beyond mere instruction of the intellect or the training of the faculties of the mind. Rather than just the outline for a pedagogical project, Mendelssohn's concept of *Bildung* comprehends the political dimension of constructing individuality.[10] As a consequence, *Bildung* takes on a new, distinctly political meaning. Instead of simply representing the result of the interests of the state and society according to which education is supposed to support and enforce the regimen prescribed by those interests, education comes now into focus as a constitutive yet autonomous key element in the foundation of the state and of civil society.

This, of course, poses the question: "Which form of government is the best?" (J 42; Jub A 8, 111). Because each nation's ideal form of government is the one that corresponds best to the cultural level a particular society has reached, there is no absolute standard to determine the best or ideal form of government as such, just as there is not for Spinoza.[11] The preference of a material over a formal type of reasoning leads, according to Mendelssohn, to a form of theorizing that allows assessing the form of government in a way more reflective of the complexity of human nature:

> Under all circumstances and conditions, however, I consider the infallible measure of the excellence of a form of government to lie in the degree to which it achieves its purposes by morals and convictions; in the degree, therefore, to which government is by education itself. (J 42)

> Unter allen Umständen und Bedingungen aber halte ich es für einen untrüglichen Maaßstab von der Güte der Regierungsform, je mehr in derselben durch Sitten und Gesinnungen gewürkt, und also durch die Erziehung selbst regiert wird. (Jub A 8, 111)

The explication of this ground rule for political philosophy makes use of a concept that Mendelssohn had already used extensively in his aesthetics, the concept of intuitive cognition:

> In other words, in the degree to which the citizen is given opportunity to understand vividly (*anschauend*) that he has to renounce some of his rights only for the common good; that he has to sacrifice some of his own advantage only for the sake of benevolence; and that he therefore gains as much, on the one hand, through a display of benevolence as he loses, on the other, by sacrifice. Indeed, that by means of sacrifice itself he greatly adds to his inner felicity, since it enhances the merit and the worth of the benevolent act and therefore also the true perfection of the benevolent individual. (J 42–43)

> Mit andern Worten, je mehr dem Bürger Anlaß gegeben wird, anschauend zu erkennen, daß er auf einige seiner Rechte nur zum allgemeinen Besten Verzicht zu thun, von seinem Eigennutzen nur zum Behuf des Wohlwollens aufzuopfern hat, und also von der einen Seite durch Aeusserung des Wohlwollens eben so viel gewinnet, als er durch Aufopferung verliert. Ja, daß er durch die Aufopferung selbst noch an innerer Glückseligkeit wuchere; indem diese das Verdienst und die Würde der wohlthätigen Handlung und also die wahre Vollkommenheit des Wohlwollens vermehret. (Jub A 8, 111–12)

Intuitive cognition and, along with it, the central role of affects in the formation of intuitive cognition are thus understood to lie at the heart of the conception of a progressive political philosophy. In identifying the chief goal of the state as the government of people through "morals and convictions" (J 43; Jub A 8, 112), Mendelssohn fundamentally changes the approach from the kind of reasoning that defines political thought in Hobbes and Locke. At the same time, he painstakingly avoids association with the sort of well-meaning paternalism advocated by Wolff.[12]

But the formal instruments of power that the state controls, such as the law, penalties, and rewards, do not affect customs, thought, and conviction. Or as Mendelssohn expresses this in a formulation with a Spinozist ring: “Fear and hope are no criteria of truth” (“Furcht und Hoffnung sind keine Kriterien der Wahrheit” [J 43; Jub A 8, 112]). Instead, he insists: “Knowledge, reasoning, and persuasion alone can bring forth principles that, with the help of *authority* and *example,* can pass into *morals*” (J 43) (“Erkenntniß, Vernunftgründe, Ueberzeugung, diese allein bringen Grundsätze hervor, die, durch *Ansehen* und *Beyspiel,* in *Sitten* übergehen können” [Jub A 8, 112]). But such reasoning does not turn into a pedagogical exercise; rather, Mendelssohn’s is a project of self-determination and self-formation with a distinctly individualist note. Mendelssohn’s point is that religion can serve the state to the purpose of “moral support,” in the literal meaning. The church can assume the role of a pillar of civil society. But it is the clearly defined limits of the function of churches that distinguishes the role of the church from a traditional view of its place in society:

> It is the business of the church to convince people, in the most emphatic manner, of the truth of noble principles and convictions; to show them that duties toward men are also duties toward God, the violation of which is in itself the greatest misery. (J 43)

> Ihr [i.e., the church] kömmt es zu, das Volks [*sic*] auf die nachdrücklichste Weise von der Wahrheit edler Grundsätze und Gesinnungen zu überführen; ihnen zu zeigen, daß die Pflichten gegen Menschen auch Pflichten gegen Gott seyen, die zu übertreten, schon an und für sich höchstes Elend sey. (Jub A 8, 112)

The different alignment of the functional divide between state and church responds to the problems in Hobbes and Locke on the one hand and to those the traditional theological arguments would present on the other. Carefully navigating between the dilemmas and paradoxes of political philosophy, Mendelssohn charts an alternative course that foregrounds the necessary theoretical framework to accommodate the new concept of Judaism he is about to develop in the second part of *Jerusalem.*

Certainly, to define religion in such a way may seem a far cry from the reality of which Mendelssohn himself was only, to be sure, too well aware.[13] But his point consists in addressing the disparity so vividly experienced in his own life as more than just a personal problem. This approach allows him to direct critical attention to the responsibility of the politics of institutionalized forms of Christianity as the cause for the repression of Jews and other non-Christians under Christian rule. But more than just articulating a critique of the detrimental consequences of religious discrimination, Mendelssohn formulates a political theory that grasps the role and function of religion to be the legitimation of naturally grown grounds of civil autonomy and independence. For it is in the sphere of religion as an original natural human quality that autonomy and independence are first constituted. This "religious" and still radically modern approach institutes the freedom of thought and conviction on the very basis of taking into consideration the religious aspects of human nature. It thus marks a subtle yet decisive redefinition of political discourse. Now, it is possible to recognize that the "Jewish problem" as a "religious problem" is the by-product of a structural problem generated by the way in which classical political theory is constructed. Contrary to the efforts to abstract from, if not ignore, the role of the religious dimension of human nature distinguishing the constructions of the original state in Hobbes, Locke, and Rousseau, Mendelssohn follows—knowingly or not—the course of argument deployed in Spinoza.[14]

For Mendelssohn, as for Spinoza, the state is no longer understood as the fundament onto which civil life is grafted. Analyzed as "mechanical deeds" ("todte Handlungen") and "works without spirit" ("Werke ohne Geist"),[15] the state provides a neutral framework that needs to be filled with spirit (*Geist*) in order to fulfill its function. And this is the point where religion receives its specific role. Mendelssohn does not imagine the relationship between state and religion to be a clear-cut coordination of two equal institutions. Rather, he argues that their cooperation is to be understood in terms of a framework based on a concept of the political that takes human nature into account in its undiminished complexity. For happiness—the goal and raison d'être of political institutions—cannot be produced or even be forced by "outward felicity and security" (J 44; Jub A 8, 113). And where these are, in fact, enforced while "inner felicity of society" is lacking, religion cannot be employed to simply fill the void and cover up the absence of purpose. "Nor can the state expect any further help from religion, once it can act only by means of rewards and punishments" (J 44) ("Der Staat hat sich auch keine Hülfe mehr von der Religion zu versprechen, sobald er blos durch Belohnung und Bestrafung würken kann" [Jub A 8, 113–14]). The idea of the precarious balance determining the synergy between state and church, necessary for the political sphere to function, thus rejects any instrumentalization of religion and implicitly opposes the idea of a quietist and opportunistic use of religion for political compromises. On the contrary, Mendelssohn's conception of the political underlines the point that the state is not to be reduced to a detached, formalized machine simply running on its own. By emphasizing the equally fundamental spiritual and religious aspects in the genesis of civil society, he formulates a theory of the state which recognizes that religion and individual spiritual happiness are intimately linked to the definition and legitimation of political institutions. With the introduction of spirit (*Geist*) as the power that ultimately brings political structures to life, Mendelssohn adds a crucial aspect to the concept of the political sphere that had otherwise been neglected. In this way, he introduces into political theory a notion of autonomy and self-determination congruent with religiosity understood as an integral part of human experience.

Introducing the concept of spirit to political theory also marks the reclaiming of a principle that had been appropriated by Christian spirituality and subsequently been depoliticized. Returning the notion of spirit to the political arena, Mendelssohn critically responds to the Christian split of human nature into body and soul that even informs the views of Hobbes, Locke, and Rousseau. In clear contradistinction to the Christian notion of spirit, Mendelssohn's use reclaims, from a Jewish point of view, the universal political dimension that Christian dualism had obliterated. Mendelssohn's implicitly counter-theological point resonates with Spinoza's idea that the optimal functioning of the state would appear as an *una mente* consonance of public life and works.[16]

Mendelssohn's juxtaposition of state and religion in a schematic manner might strike us as a somewhat contrived cliché:

> The state gives orders and coerces, religion teaches and persuades. The state prescribes *laws*, religion *commandments*. The state has *physical power* and uses it when necessary; the power of religion is *love* and *beneficence*. (J 45)

> Der Staat gebietet und zwinget; die Religion belehrt und überredet; der Staat ertheilt Gesetze, die Religion Gebote. Der Staat hat physische Gewalt und bedient sich derselben, wo es nöthig ist; die Macht der Religion ist *Liebe* und *Wohlthun*. (Jub A 8, 114)

However, Mendelssohn does not construe love or charity as a stopgap measure to fill in where the arm of the law does not reach. Instead, he sees the state as a precarious, secondary product defined by the original "social contract" that he interprets in his own way. The state's power and authority are balanced by what he terms *Geist,* represented and brought to life by religion. This change in the conception of the state's political legitimation recasts political theory in a way that allows Mendelssohn to present difference in terms of metaphysical preferences as a legitimate political issue. Untrammeled by the force of the historical reality of specific political constellations, this approach is capable of recognizing the private sphere with its individual concerns as genuinely political. Thus, while the state rests on the foundation of positive law that is defined by its temporal character, the state's competence for auto-legitimacy remains checked by the larger, "universal" criteria instantiated through spirit.

This is the motivation for introducing, at this point, the distinction between perfect and imperfect rights and duties. In a digression on the "origin of the rights of coercion and the validity of contracts among men" (J 45ff.; Jub A 8, 114ff.), Mendelssohn presents his own version of a theory of natural rights. Right, as he puts it, denotes the permission or moral faculty to use a thing as a means for one's happiness. "Moral" means in this context that the right is in harmony with the laws of wisdom and of goodness ("Weisheit und Güte"). Duty he defines as the moral necessity, that is, what ought to be done according to those laws. Such an understanding requires that rights and duties be conceived as a harmonious system: "To every right, therefore, there corresponds a duty; to the right to act, there corresponds the duty to suffer [the action], to the right to demand, the duty to perform; etc." (J 46) ("Einem jedem Rechte entspricht also eine Pflicht; dem Rechte zu thun entspricht die Pflicht zu leiden; dem Rechte zu fordern, die Pflicht zu leisten, u.s.w." [Jub A 8, 115]). This makes it necessary to differentiate further the concepts of right and duty. There is, so to speak, a hard and a soft concept of rights and duties. Duties, rights, and contracts are not just conventions but must be based on natural rights. Only where there are "imperfect" rights and duties—that is, where they are grounded in natural right that precedes and constitutes the legal system—can they be transformed into perfect—that is, positive and compulsory—rights and duties. The natural rights basis of this legal theory guarantees that rights and duties remain firmly linked to their foundation within a moral philosophical framework. The unpredictable and uncontrollable dynamics that law may otherwise unleash are thus kept in check.

Siding with Wolff against Thomasius and his school,[17] Mendelssohn privileges a "moral" over a "legal" natural right theory. In doing so, he is able to argue for a resolute understanding of autonomy and conscience (J 52–53; Jub A 8, 120–21). Contracts consist, as a result, in duties and rights transformed from imperfect to perfect ones. What is not an imperfect right or duty cannot become part of a contract and, therefore, cannot be part of the social contract either. As a result, Mendelssohn's theory of natural rights rules out any kind of transfer of competence or authority that would involve moral or religious issues. Mendelssohn thus defines contract as "nothing but the *cession,* by the one party, and the *acceptance,* by the other party, of the right to decide cases of collision involving certain goods which the promising party can spare" (J 54–55) ("nichts anders, als von der einen Seite die *Ueberlassung* und von der andern Seite, die *Annahme* des Rechts, in Absicht auf gewisse, dem Versprecher entbehrliche Güter, die Collisionsfälle zu entscheiden" [Jub A 8, 123]). This—from a juridical point of view rather unusual—definition of the contract makes the transfer of the competence to arbitrate, rather than the transaction of claims, its central moment. As a consequence, what is indisputable for natural right and, therefore, does not represent a possible collision with other claims cannot be transferred. Where there exists no possibility for collision in the state of nature, this definition implies, there cannot exist any contract. This means that the surrender, transfer, or cessation of one's right to moral and religious convictions is made impossible on the grounds of the very nature of the contract, which Mendelssohn conceives here as an extension of natural right rather than its replacement. This allows him to avoid some of the unwarranted implications of contract theory on the very basis of an argumentation grounded in his alternative theory of contract. This view establishes both religious freedom and the right to autonomy and self-determination as indisputable and inalienable rights that precede any contractual agreement and, as a consequence, overwrite any claim to the effect that a transfer of religious or moral rights or duties can be legally possible and therefore admissible.

Drawing the conclusions, the first part of *Jerusalem* culminates in a passionate rejection of any claims for power by the church or any confusion of the strict separation of state and church as running counter to the very concept of natural right. Shown to lack a form of legitimation based in natural rights, such claims can now be refused as incompatible with a consistent form of contract theory.

The rigorous separation of state and church, along with the distinction between the political and religious spheres, thus also sets, in the first part of *Jerusalem,* the stage for a new understanding of religion. With the recasting of the theoretical framework of political philosophy, Mendelssohn breaks grounds for a new approach to theorizing the role of religion as constitutive for civil society. Religion can now be recognized as a crucial and genuine moment of enlightenment itself. This leads to the formulation of a philosophically grounded modern concept of religion. Religion is shown to no longer be opposed to reason but rather to emerge, like reason itself, as a natural and important aspect of human nature.

The emancipatory political philosophy presented in the first part sets thus the stage for introducing a concept of Judaism as a religious practice not only fully compatible with enlightenment but one that represents an important contribution to enlightenment as one of its pillars. Arguing that any suggestion of a *ius circa sacra* (a separate law concerning religious institutions) lacks serious theoretical legitimation, Mendelssohn clears the way for a deliberately nontheological, strictly secularized form of argumentation. Pointing out the difference between the Christian concept of revelation and its Jewish counterpart, he moves the discussion from the dangerous and murky territory of theology to the less contested grounds of philosophical examination. This strategy closely follows the procedure Spinoza deploys in his *Theological-Political Treatise.*

Distinguishing three kinds of truths—eternal necessary truths, eternal contingent truths, and historical truths—Mendelssohn modifies Spinoza's approach in order to later be able to accommodate the notion that scripture contains not only laws, orders, and commands but also universal truths.[18] However, they present no particular part of the law exclusively handed to the Jewish people but are part of the natural religion equally revealed to all through nature in its diverse manifestations. Mendelssohn stresses the point that religious doctrines, truths necessary for salvation, and philosophical propositions are not part of divine legislation revealed through pronouncement and Scripture. The introduction of the notion of historical truths makes it possible to grasp Jewish tradition in its cultural particularity as one devoid of any exclusive, overreaching truth claims and to redeem the religious tradition as particular but, because of this, not only in harmony with enlightenment but one of its most committed champions.

In this way, the revelation at Mount Sinai is interpreted as an event at which divine legislation for a particular mission, that of the Jewish people, is promulgated. Following the argument developed in his "Gegenbetrachtungen," Mendelssohn points out that the recourse to miracles does not provide, in and of itself, legitimation for the truth of the message that might be derived from such an event. Only as a testimony of its historical truth does the revelation at Mount Sinai stand out as a unique event in history whose truth is strictly historical truth.

Thus, Mendelssohn argues in accordance with Spinoza's interpretation, that the Law of Moses requires obedience rather than faith. Commandments, prohibitions, rewards, and punishments only extend to actions and are not articles of faith. But because of its legislative character, the law revealed on Mount Sinai remains, in the eyes of Mendelssohn, irreducible and unchangeable: "But laws cannot be abridged. In them everything is fundamental; and in this regard we might rightly say: to us, all words of scripture, all of God's commandments and prohibitions are fundamental" (J 101–2) ("Aber Gesetze leiden keine Abkürzung. In ihnen ist alles fundamental, und in so weit können wir mit Grunde sagen: uns sind alle Worte der Schrift, alle Gebote und Verbote Gottes fundamental" [Jub A 8, 168]).[19] While for Spinoza the Law of Moses is in force only as long as the theocracy of the Hebrew state existed, thus construing the revealed law as a strictly political one, the destruction of the second temple does not, according to Mendelssohn, imply the end of all ceremonial law as such, as Spinoza had argued. Offering a different interpretation of ceremonial law than the one Spinoza had given, Mendelssohn redeems the role of its religious dimension.[20] He achieves this by means of formulating a theory of culture and tradition based on a theory of semiotics.

In a digression on the origin of language and scripture that contains, in a nutshell, a theory of the genesis and function of tradition, Mendelssohn develops an argument concerning the nature of ceremonial law that, in a countermove to the usual condemnation of ceremonial law as inflexible and petrified, fleshes out the deeper sense potential buried in ceremonies, a sense potential whose infinite meaning words can render only incompletely. While today's culture is predicated on print, and the letter and the book form our minds, Mendelssohn points out, this has not always been the case:

> This was not the case in the bygone days of ancient times. Even though one cannot say that they were better, they were certainly different. One drew

> from different sources, one gathered and preserved in different vessels; and one made one's own that which had been preserved by completely different means. (J 104)

> So war es nicht in den grauen Tagen der Vorwelt. Kann man nun schon nicht sagen, es war besser; so war es doch sicherlich anders. Man schöpfte aus andern Quellen, sammlete und erhielt in andern Gefäßen, und vereinzelte das Aufbewahrte durch ganz andere Mittel. (Jub A 8, 170)

In a reconstruction of the origin of tradition, Mendelssohn traces the central role signs play in the transmission of cultural contents. In his *Essay on the Origin of Human Knowledge* (1746), Condillac had presented a theory of the origin of language that played a seminal role in eighteenth-century discussion of the philosophy of language. Rousseau, Diderot, d'Alembert, but also the secretary of the Berlin Royal Academy of the Sciences, Maupertuis, and Herder take their cues from Condillac's *Essay,*[21] and while Mendelssohn may not have had firsthand knowledge of Condillac, he carefully studied Rousseau's second discourse, which refers to Condillac, and which Mendelssohn translated in 1755 right after its publication. It gave Mendelssohn indirect knowledge of the seminal conception of the origin of language Condillac had introduced.

In his *Essay,* Condillac stresses the fundamental role of signs for the process of cultural development. Defining language as the constitutive faculty of the mind's activity, thinking emerges, Condillac observes, as defined by the limits of language: "[T]he origin and progress of our ideas entirely depends on the manner in which we make use of signs."[22] For Mendelssohn this leads to the view that "without the aid of signs, man can scarcely remove himself the first steps from the sensual" (J 105) ("der Mensch, ohne Hülfe der Zeichen, sich kaum um einen Schritt vom Sinnlichen entfernen kann" [Jub A 8, 172])—an insight which not only proves that language as human artifact is subject to limitations that are constitutive for the preservation and transmission of meaning but also underscores the precarious foundation of language itself.

Already in an early draft "Über die Sprache," presumably written in 1756[23] in the context of his work on Rousseau's second discourse, Mendelssohn offers a detailed account of his view of the origin of language, emphasizing, like Condillac, the natural human faculty for language and speech. Also, similar to Condillac's theory of signs (employed by Rousseau in his discourse translated by Mendelssohn), Mendelssohn addresses the constitutive function signs represent in the formation of language and thought. They enable, facilitate, and expedite the process of knowledge. Like Condillac, Mendelssohn sees language as a necessary precondition for thought.

> What an astonishing speed, with which we follow a series of letters or sounds and how much must thereby the progress of thoughts connected to these signs be advanced! Any other sensory impression would be much too slow for the fast swings of thoughts.

> Mit welcher erstaunlichen Geschwindigkeit verfolgen wir eine Reihe von Buchstaben oder von Tönen, und wie sehr muß dadurch der Fortgang der mit diesen Zeichen verbundenen Gedanken befördert werden! Jeder andere sinnliche Eindruck würde für die *schnellen Schwingungen der Gedanken* viel zu langsam seyn. (Jub A 6.2, 20)

Because of its objective existence, scripture (*Schrift*) is in many ways preferable to speech (*Sprache*), as it is more appropriate for clear cognition (Jub A 6.2, 20). Thus, already at this stage, Mendelssohn recognizes the primary significance of arbitrary signs for the formation of thought and their communication.[24] In *Jerusalem* he now takes this theory a step further, proceeding, as it were, to an archaeological investigation of the history of scripture. Here he interprets the forms of scripture known as alphabetic and hieroglyphic in the light of an altogether different scripture that combines the advantages of arbitrary signs with the capacity for interminable sense production: "a kind of living script rousing the mind and heart" (J 102),[25] free of the pitfalls of alphabetic and hieroglyphic scripture.[26] For they are, as history shows, subject to a dialectics of enlightenment that, in the course of transmission, empties them of their original meaning, often reversing it to its very opposite. In contrast, Mendelssohn argues, ceremonial law produces its own kind of scripture that establishes and secures transmission of meaning through a mediation independent of the unreliable nature of language.

Even such an advanced and profoundly abstract philosophy like the Pythagoreans' had, as Mendelssohn points out, turned into a cult of numbers. Thus, while arbitrary signs are essential for the constitution of language, language that employs conventional scripture would not be able to adequately render the infinite sense potential of divine revelation.

Mendelssohn's point—stressed in the 1756 fragment—that language and scripture are human inventions can now be understood in its deeper theoretical implications. For, while scripture is defined by its fixating character, which ties its contents to the "dead letter" (J 103; Jub A 8, 169), historical change and cultural transformations, removing the interpretation ever further from the original context in which language was laid down, do not reflect, register, or manifest themselves otherwise in scripture. Thus, man-made signs are not capable of transmitting the full semiotic potential of divine revelation, which, through the course of history, unfolds at different stages of culture different aspects of its irreducibly multifaceted meaning with undiminished force.

While the fixation of human language through signs enables the mind to expand its cognitive faculties, scripture, on the other hand, cannot fix meaning in order to preserve the content in unchanged identity over time. Whereas living language continues to develop over time, scripture fixes language at one particular moment in history. As a consequence, the continuous flux of the movement of language makes it necessary that already the next moment requires a recontextualization, and that means a translation of what had been fixed in writing. Thus, in order to transmit revelation without exposing it to the problems of the hermeneutic predicament at the center of all tradition based on semiotic communication, God, according to Mendelssohn, chose the vessel of ceremonial law. Confined to the purpose of commanding actions, ceremonial law creates its own frame of reference, its own semiotics, through the actions that constitute their own ever-adjusting hermeneutics that produce meaning. In this manner, meaning is gained through the practice of ceremonial law. This form of instantiation—a performance of an action rather than the interpretation of fixed signs—remains open to the development of historical and cultural change. It serves as an imaginative and consistent resource for tradition to constantly regenerate.

Mendelssohn thus conceives ceremonial law as a codex of imperatives commanding actions which through their performance produce their own hermeneutics. This hermeneutics' rules are exclusively constituted through practice. Ceremonial law is thus understood as an organon that creatively recasts tradition as a continuous process of dynamic regeneration. This alternative view of the production of meaning through performance proposes a new approach that imagines tradition open to the dynamics of history. Mendelssohn's theory of scripture and transmission provides the theoretical underpinning to conceive tradition as an essentially creative process.

Although Mendelssohn emphasizes the strictly particularist aspect of the unchangeable nature of ceremonial law, he is able, at the same time and on these very grounds, to provide an interpretative model that allows him to avoid the aporia that determine the hermeneutics of interpreting scripture. In rescuing the creative aspect of tradition through a semiotic interpretation of the function of ceremonial law, Mendelssohn implicitly criticizes Bible criticism for missing the true motif of scripture: to serve as law whose text calls less for textual emendation than for hermeneutic activity. It is, then, through the practice of the code of law that meaning is generated. In the course of history, the tradition of the practice of the law produces, in its everyday realizations, a specific and irreducible meaning that, in its continuity and adjustments over the centuries, reflects the infinite sense potential contained in the meaning of the law.

To be sure, this interpretation of ceremonial law poses its own problems, but it sheds some light on the issues of tradition and the preservation, transmission, and function of language and signs. Mendelssohn's emphasis on the vital and creative potential of ceremonial law as an ever-renewing resource that keeps tradition alive and functioning is an attempt at reinterpretation whose critical impulse, however, mostly went unnoticed. Instead, his interest in ceremonial law seemed, in the age of individualism, sentiment, and spirituality, for many an anachronistic obstacle on the road to emancipation. Ironically, the critical considerations underpinning Mendelssohn's interpretation of ceremonial law were overlooked as his position was discarded as a form of obsolete traditionalism. The deliberately critical note of Mendelssohn's reinterpretation, however, highlights the hermeneutic assumptions scripture-based cultures presuppose. The very nature of these assumptions determines the way in which religion and tradition are imagined to function. Mendelssohn thus indirectly but no less powerfully poses the question of the grounds for the hermeneutic legitimacy of traditions in all its urgency. But the originality of his argumentation consists in the innovative theoretical framework it provides for understanding the function of oral tradition, the part of Judaism consistently under attack by traditionalists and modernists alike. Countering the verdict of the backwardness and irrelevance of oral tradition for a proper understanding of Jewish tradition, Mendelssohn's semiotics underscores ceremonial law's constitutive role as that part of tradition which secures the transmission of tradition.[27]

For Mendelssohn, the redeeming factor of ceremonial law consists in its resistance to attempts at unification or any other form of assimilation rationalized by appeal to external norms. Instead it is the particular specificity of such a law that enables him to move toward an alternative approach to a concept of universalism devoid of claims for unity and the desire for unification. This allows Mendelssohn to hold a strong claim to the universal validity of natural religion. Revelations—now understood in his way as always historical in nature—would and could not constitute, define, or ever change the anthropological core of religiosity common to all human beings. Quite on the contrary, such revelations could only reassert the claims of natural religion. As a result, religion in its historical forms can no longer carry universal validity, a claim now strictly reserved to religiosity as a part of human nature that resists any form of institutionalization. By moving in the opposite direction, however, the generation of Mendelssohn's successors was willing to exchange precisely this kind of particularity for a universalism whose hermeneutic assumptions could no longer be addressed in their precarious particularity once Mendelssohn's self-conscious claim for his own particularism was forsaken.

But Mendelssohn's theory of ceremonial law as a kind of living scripture and his conception of Judaism as a religion names the problems a modern theory of tradition and hermeneutics must address. Defining Judaism by three main points—(1) eternal truth inscribed in everyone's soul, at all times legible and understandable, with (2) historical truth as testimony for the historical occurrence of (3) revelation of the laws, rules, and commandments revealed through word and scripture (J 126–28; Jub A 8, 191–93)—Mendelssohn moves the Enlightenment debate on the role of religion to a more differentiated level of theorizing.

For Spinoza, the destruction of the second temple marks not only the demise of the political and national structure of the Hebrew state but also the end of the legitimacy of its theocracy. Mendelssohn's interpretation of ceremonial law, however, argues for a distinction between the political and religious aspects of Judaism that leaves room for the possibility of viewing Judaism as a continuing tradition beyond the destruction of its historical political formation as a state. Underlining the semiotic function of the law as a form of scripture, Mendelssohn makes it possible to attend to religion as what inspires and informs culture and tradition.

His discussion of the origin and history of language and scripture grasps tradition in a way that makes it possible to address the significance of the particularity of ceremonial law as a strength rather than a flaw. Instead of mistaking tradition for a petrified form of obsolete legalism, this approach allows Mendelssohn to interpret ceremonial law as a creative response to the problem caused by the fixation of scripture in hieroglyphs and letters. Mendelssohn's approach exposes the theoretical insufficiency of an unreflected concept of tradition that fails to acknowledge the particularity of the Jewish tradition in its creative aspects. In contrast, he proposes a different view of tradition that replaces the notion of an uninterrupted continuity of reception and transmission with one that addresses the dynamic process of ever new appropriation and realization in the ever changing historical situation of a particular place and time as a constitutive moment of tradition. In Mendelssohn's theory, tradition emerges as the site where tradition's form and content are renegotiated in ever newly constituted continuity, that is, as realization, which means translation of ceremonial law in ever new and different constellations. Continuity and constancy become thus dynamic concepts. Tradition is no longer conceived as a given and fixed content of truth but is now theorized as a process of interpretation always already under way. This allows Mendelssohn to theorize the moment of repetition as creative impulse: as an ever newly constituting transitory act of translation in a present that is grounded in the particularity of history but remains, because of this, open to the future.

While *Jerusalem* marks a key moment in Mendelssohn's Spinoza reception, the question remains as to why his name only occurs once at the beginning of the work. In 1755 the *Philosophische Gespräche* had opened Mendelssohn's—albeit initially anonymous—publicist career with a rescue of Spinoza. There he argues for the groundbreaking step Spinoza had taken to carry Descartes's metaphysics further, thereby making it possible for Leibniz to develop his theory of preestablished harmony (Jub A 1, 3–12). Although anonymously published, this was a bold act of succor for one of the most disreputed figures of philosophy. And thirty years later, in *Morgenstunden* (1785), Mendelssohn was to rescue Lessing for his alleged Spinozism. With the introduction of the concept of "purified Spinozism" as a variety shown to be fully acceptable by sound philosophy and morals, Mendelssohn thought he had succeeded in exonerating Lessing from the accusation of having been a Spinozist.

But both attempts to rescue Spinoza's reputation touch only on a brief discussion of the main aspects of Spinoza's metaphysics, the ontological macrostructure and its implications for the concept of God. Curiously, it is in *Jerusalem,* where Spinoza is mentioned but once, that a profound correspondence of and a productive exchange with his thought can be traced.[28] It seems as if the actual appropriation of Spinoza had to be kept apart from his rescue; that one still was only to use his philosophy as long as no allegiance to his name was made public. In order to grasp the intricate dialectic of silence and acknowledgment at work in Mendelssohn's reception of Spinoza, the discussion of *Jerusalem* must be followed up by an analysis of the rhetorics of the rescue project undertaken in *Morgenstunden.* The constellative character that links the two writings via the downplaying of Spinoza's impact on *Jerusalem,* on the one hand, and the rescue motive in *Morgenstunden,* on the other, will provide a helpful frame of reference to address this question.

In this light, the impassioned defense of Lessing is, not insignificantly, also the cautious defense of a shared concern and, as a result, an indirect self-defense. Mendelssohn's rescue of Spinoza may therefore also be seen as a tacit, coded form of paying tribute to the significance of Spinoza's impact on his own social and political thought culminating in *Jerusalem.* In a remarkably cautiously coded manner, Mendelssohn suggests this himself when he mentions Spinoza for the only time in the opening pages of *Jerusalem.*

The passage is rather baffling. Announcing that despite necessary reservations against Hobbes, Mendelssohn will make use of his philosophy, his defense makes an odd comparison: "In matters of moral philosophy Hobbes has the same merit as Spinoza has in metaphysics. His ingenious errors have occasioned inquiry" (J 36) ("Hobbes hat das Vedienst um die Moralphilosophie, das Spinoza um die Metaphysik hat. Sein scharfsinniger Irrthum hat Untersuchung veranlasset" [Jub A 8, 105–6]). The motive of shrewd error leading to better examination was, to be sure, the argument Mendelssohn had pursued in his 1755 rescue of Spinoza. Nevertheless, the curious asymmetry in the comparison of Hobbes's merits in moral philosophy with Spinoza's in metaphysics demands attention. Lacking a term reserved for political philosophy, the eighteenth-century term "moral philosophy" also included all aspects of political philosophy. And Hobbes certainly was barely hailed in the eighteenth century as a champion of moral reasoning in today's sense of the term. Now, it is certainly Hobbes who prepared the ground for modern political philosophy, and Mendelssohn undoubtedly owes, like all post-Hobbesian thought, much of his own clarity to Hobbes's analytic lucidity. But it is Spinoza who comes closest to Mendelssohn's theorizing and whose *Theological-Political Treatise* serves, if not as model, at least as decisive subtext for the discussion in *Jerusalem.* If Mendelssohn implicitly refers to his 1755 rescue in citing Spinoza's merits regarding the progress of metaphysics, Spinoza's merits for "moral philosophy" are left unmentioned. The irony is that it is in *Jerusalem* that the potential of Spinoza's "moral"—that is, political—philosophy is brought to its impressive realization, albeit without mentioning Spinoza's name. A careful look at the passage suggests that Mendelssohn's passing over the name of Spinoza and the curious quid pro quo with Hobbes suggests a hidden hint expected to stop critical readers in their tracks and make them wonder what the oblique reference to Hobbes and Spinoza is supposed to mean. Venerated for his otherwise so magisterially painstaking precision, Mendelssohn could fairly expect sophisticated readers to pick up on this coded hint to Spinoza. The passage quoted in *Jerusalem* continues:

> The ideas of right and duty, of power and obligation, have been better developed; one has learned to distinguish more correctly between physical and moral ability, between right and might. These distinctions have become so intimately infused with our language that, nowadays, the refutation of Hobbes' system seems to be a matter of common sense, and to be accomplished, as it were by language itself. (J 36)

> Man hat die Ideen von Recht und Pflicht, Macht und Verbindlichkeit besser entwickelt; man hat physisches Vermögen von sittlichem Vermögen, Gewalt von Befugniß richtiger unterscheiden gelernt, und diese Unterscheidungen so innigst mit der Sprache verbunden, daß nunmehr die Widerlegung des hobbesischen Systems schon in dem gesunden Menschenverstande, und so zu sagen, in der Sprache zu liegen scheinet. (Jub A 8, 106)

But it is Spinoza who, more than anyone else, would have to be counted as an instrumental figure in this development. For his philosophy represents, as Mendelssohn's *Jerusalem* so convincingly suggests, a signal moment in the development from Hobbes's concepts of political philosophy to a modern emancipatory theory of politics.

Spinoza's curious absence in name but critical presence in matter sheds a new light on the play between the coded and open use of tradition in *Jerusalem.* Mendelssohn's naming of Spinoza in a marginal aside directs the critical reader's attention to the central position Spinoza takes in a text that is forced to play by rules it critically exposes. This hide and seek of naming what cannot be named without the highest risk highlights the narrowly defined parameters that force political theorists of emancipation and political self-determination such as Mendelssohn to carefully word their thoughts—even at what seems to have been the heights of the Enlightenment.

CHAPTER II

RESCUING LESSING

Mendelssohn's *Morgenstunden*

THE PUBLICATION OF *Morgenstunden oder Vorlesungen über das Dasein Gottes* initiates the final stage of Mendelssohn's Spinoza reception and, along with Jacobi's writings, the onset of the pantheism dispute (or Spinoza dispute). Prior to launching the publication of his conversations with Lessing, Jacobi had, through their common friend Elise Reimarus, investigated whether Mendelssohn knew about Lessing's inclination toward Spinozism. Well aware of the explosive potential of this issue, Jacobi felt the need to inform Mendelssohn about his discovery before breaking the story. Suspecting Jacobi of foul play, Mendelssohn, against the initial plan to coordinate their public debate, was irritated enough to dishonor their agreement and went ahead with publishing his *Morgenstunden*. With this action he hoped to forestall the adverse reactions to be expected from Jacobi's announced disclosure of Lessing's sympathies toward Spinozism. But this drew Mendelssohn further into what was to become one of the most important controversies of eighteenth-century German intellectual history.[1]

From the outset, Jacobi was well aware that, in the eyes of Mendelssohn, such a challenge would imply a direct personal provocation, for it implied that Mendelssohn for most of his life had remained unfamiliar with his best friend's most intimate views and concerns. The two friends, it seemed—celebrated as the foremost literary, aesthetic, and cultural critics of their time—had long parted company. Given the symbolic value this friendship had for Mendelssohn, Jacobi's announcement would—intentionally or not—represent a most cruel blow. What had been for Mendelssohn the most intimate and intense intellectual and affective relationship, his legendary friendship with Lessing, was reduced to a mere illusion that threatened to turn into public embarrassment—the embarrassment that the formative association with Lessing, whose approval had also served as Mendelssohn's legitimation in the eye of the public, was not as close and deep as claimed.

Wary of replaying what he had already experienced ad nauseam in the case of Lavater's and similar earlier attempts at proselytizing, Mendelssohn felt offended in the most personal way.[2] For this time, Christian bigotry of a new kind combined the very personal insinuation that the legendary friendship between Mendelssohn and Lessing had only been a hoax with a relentless attack on Spinoza, the fellow Jew whose philosophy's fatal reputation was to seduce its followers to atheism and immorality.

Thus, Mendelssohn found himself impugned at the heart of his self-understanding. Jacobi's intervention could only mean the merciless attempt at the annihilation of all that Mendelssohn had come to stand for. In a dramatic way that Jacobi diligently tried to exploit, he staged this public showdown as one of the fatal encounters of the new (post-Enlightenment) guard versus the old (Enlightenment) guard. As a consequence, Mendelssohn recognized that the only way to parry this provocation effectively would be by first elucidating the basic concepts that, due to the stir the debate about Spinoza caused, had become confused.

Jacobi's disclosure that Lessing was a closet Spinozist put Mendelssohn in an awkward position, for if he accepted this claim as true he risked giving Jacobi grounds to entrench what in Mendelssohn's view could only be a precarious misrepresentation of Lessing's critical concerns. Furthermore, an unguarded word on Spinoza could lead to an examination of his own work for vestiges of Spinozism. On the other hand, denying the significance of Spinoza altogether would be tantamount to complying with Jacobi's strategy, for such a denial would place Mendelssohn into unwarranted proximity to (for Mendelssohn) Jacobi's deeply suspect agenda. Choosing the middle road, Mendelssohn argued that although Lessing was no Spinozist in the strict sense of naive following, he certainly shared some ideas of a "purified" variety of Spinozism that, essentially, were fully compatible and in accordance with sound reason and morality.

The unusually high emotional toll this controversy took on Mendelssohn—including, as his friends had already pointed out, his untimely death—added to the tensions caused by the self-promoting strategy Jacobi had chosen, making the pantheism dispute one of the key debates in eighteenth-century German culture. In the course of events there was practically no philosopher, poet, or critic who did not take a position in this debate. Even Kant, who persistently tried to stay out of it, was eventually drawn into the arena, called forth to intervene by both sides.[3]

This context accounts for the fact that *Morgenstunden* is a multi-layered text speaking to different issues, all of which it tries to tackle in order to make for a convincing vindication of Lessing and his cause. Thus several issues required attention if Jacobi's challenge was to be met successfully. Mendelssohn tried to respond to this situation by (1) reaffirming a sound and solid fundament for metaphysics, (2) defending Lessing's name, (3) dissolving the allegation of Spinozism by way of introducing a "purified" version of Spinozism, and (4) reasserting the truth of natural religion's universalism against Jacobi's philosophy of faith, which seemed to renounce the achievements of the Enlightenment. As Mendelssohn puts it:

> My intent there [the first part of a two-part plan for *Morgenstunden*] was merely to articulate ideas on the *first grounds of knowledge,* on *truth, illusion,* and *error,* and to attempt to apply them to pantheism. Herr Jacobi, I thought, will perhaps find here the point at which we can convene and from which we can depart so as to bring our contest to an end. This was to take place in my Second Part.[4]

> Meine Absicht war, in diesem Theile [the first part of a two-part plan for *Morgenstunden*] bloß meine Gedanken über die *ersten Gründe der Erkenntniß,* über *Wahrheit, Schein* und *Irrthum* an den Tag zu legen, und die Anwendung davon auf den Pantheismus zu versuchen. Hier findet Herr Jacobi, dachte ich, vielleicht den Punkt, wo wir zusammen kommen, und von welchem wir ausgehen können unsern Wettlauf zu vollenden. Dieses sollte alsdenn von meiner Seite in dem zweyten Theile geschehen.[5]

To divine Mendelssohn's stand on Spinoza in the face of such an entangled situation is thus an altogether forbidding enterprise. While on the one hand the distillation of a purified Spinozism may appear as a methodologically dubious procedure, Mendelssohn's response is to carry out a brave rescue operation of Lessing and Spinoza. This rescue takes place, it must be kept in mind, within the context of the eighteenth-century silence about Spinoza, his controversial reputation, and the period's equation of Spinozism with atheism and immorality. The term "Spinozism" thus serves the purpose of philosophical distinction as well as functioning as a social label that, beyond its strictly philosophical definition, broadcasts suspicion and denunciation. As Jacobi was well aware, the release of the notes of his conversation with Lessing in order to provide evidence for Lessing's Spinozism would therefore have a demolishing effect. Moreover, Jacobi's specifically vested use of the claim of Lessing's allegiance to Spinoza implies that with Lessing the entire movement of progressive, secularized, and critical enlightenment would be put under indictment of leading to the impasse of shallow and sterile rationalism resulting with logical necessity in atheism and immoralism.

While Jacobi's account of his conversations with Lessing could also be read as a not-so-subtle hint that Mendelssohn was, after all, not as familiar with Lessing's most private ideas as assumed, the equally offensive point in Jacobi's challenge consists in the implication that if Mendelssohn would, nevertheless, have been familiar with his friend's Spinozist attitudes, this fact would in turn subject Mendelssohn to the suspicion of sympathy with Spinozism. Consequently, Mendelssohn himself would find himself implicated with the blemish of anti-religious, cold rationalism that the eighteenth century would associate with Spinoza. In his way, Jacobi positions himself to stand for the new guard of the post-Enlightenment generation eager to replace the outlived guard of sclerotic Enlightenment rationalists.

Jacobi explicitly reminded his readers that it was Mendelssohn himself who had demonstrated the importance of Spinoza for Leibniz: "Mendelssohn has clearly demonstrated that the harmonia praestabilita is to be found in Spinoza"[6] ("Mendelssohn hat öffentlich gezeigt, dass die Harmonia praestabilita im Spinoza steht").[7] With this and the proximity to which Jacobi's account brings Leibniz with his predecessor Spinoza, Mendelssohn found himself put on the spot. Now, that Jacobi makes such particular use of Mendelssohn's 1755 rescue of Spinoza, turning what was meant to serve as the rescue of Spinoza into a criticism of Leibniz, the entire metaphysical enterprise as such, and with it Mendelssohn's own thought, was rendered suspicious.

In order to counter this sea change undermining the very foundations of his thought and placing him in the camp of a form of rationalism incapable of theorizing and devoid of religion, Mendelssohn finds himself forced to legitimate the grounds of his philosophy. For it had now become clear that Jacobi moved in altogether different spheres. Returning to the foundation of the first concepts, Mendelssohn tries to identify a common ground of language that would allow a serious exchange and put an end to the pandering of defamatory accusations. Finding the legacy of the project of enlightenment that had defined his life and which he thought to have shared with Lessing for over a quarter of a century under such attack, Mendelssohn responds with a principled reassertion of his philosophical principles.

With Spinoza under attack and Lessing, by implication, exposed to suspicion, the only effective way to react seemed to consist in a preemptive strike rebutting the whole complex of accusations once and for all. Against Jacobi's claim that all metaphysics leads by necessity to nihilism, Mendelssohn responds with a sophisticated and refined version of the demonstration of God's existence. Whereas Jacobi attempts to divide reason and faith as opposites, Mendelssohn reasserts the standpoint that reason and faith are in true harmony.

Refusing Jacobi's allegations of the destructive nature of reason, Mendelssohn frames his response in the cloak of a consistent demonstration of the existence of God. Embedded within this procedure, Mendelssohn addresses the issue of Spinozism in general and the question of Lessing's alleged Spinozism in particular. This framework allows for a discussion of Spinoza that highlights the positive and constructive aspects of his thought rather than the destructive drive Jacobi wishes to identify with Spinoza.[8] Instead, Mendelssohn argues that once some terminological distinctions compatible with, yet absent in, Spinozism proper are made, it is possible to purify Spinozism to the degree that Spinoza's system becomes fully agreeable with sound reason. Furthermore, he argues, once the disagreement with Spinozism is settled, Spinoza can even be embraced as true friend (Jub A 3.2, 130).

Arguing that the technical dimension of terminological usage in metaphysics is always governed by practical knowledge or practical reason, rather than directed, as Jacobi claims, by some ironclad logics of theoretical reason, Mendelssohn puts Jacobi's manner of argumentation in its place. Jacobi's taking Spinozism by its words thus misses the deeper conceptual efforts that drive its formulations. Against Jacobi's binary opposition between reason and religion, which perceives any opposition to its way of reasoning as principally incompetent,[9] Mendelssohn's view suggests that an adequate discussion requires the careful consideration of the entire context of a metaphysical project. Mendelssohn's reconstructive approach introduces a deliberately problem-oriented approach as opposed to Jacobi's tendentiously self-absorbed argumentation. Mendelssohn thus takes a first step to move away from a partisan tactic of using metaphysics in the way Jacobi does for his own religious ends.

Although his reconstructive approach of tackling the problem of Spinozism by way of terminological differentiation may lack the power to cleanse Spinoza from all of Jacobi's criticism, Mendelssohn nevertheless succeeds in steering the dispute into quieter waters. *Morgenstunden* sets the tone for a sovereign framework of a free and critical examination that remains untouched by Jacobi's zealous and manipulative attitude. Whereas Jacobi's language changes from provocative to polemic modes, Mendelssohn's tranquil and reflective procedure makes for a free space of philosophical examination where the issue is not to pass judgment on philosophers but to understand their way of thinking. However, Jacobi and most of his contemporaries showed little sympathy for Mendelssohn's effort to ease the built-up tensions and to exchange the road of polemics for the one of dialogue.

Yet the history of the reception of—or, rather, disregard for—the road taken in *Morgenstunden* has led research to ignore the subtle half tones that define Mendelssohn's deliberate countermove against Jacobi. In the light of this strategy, however, it becomes possible to address the question of Mendelssohn's view of Spinoza more precisely. Unlike Jacobi's polarizing contrast, Mendelssohn's soft, contemplative light produces a Spinoza who is a genuine and resourceful fellow traveler on the arduous road to truth and light. While Jacobi argues that the decision for reason is in itself a terrible mistake, Mendelssohn portrays Spinoza as one of the participants in the project of philosophy that links the chain of thinkers from Plato to the present. In this elevated sphere of intellectual dignity, Spinoza, like everyone else, is protected against the kind of personal allegations that Jacobi raises, for in speculative philosophy arguments only count insofar as they contribute to the promotion of truth. Private moral opinions and theological verdicts do not belong in this sphere; otherwise the truth will suffer contamination from claims alien to reason proper. Independently of the nature of its arguments, the design of *Morgenstunden* thus realizes Lessing's ideal of the discursive open space in which the thought experiment of the rescue of the redeeming aspects of a philosophy under attack is allowed to unfold solely on the strength of its arguments.

This intervention underlines Spinoza's right to dignity as a philosopher even before Mendelssohn engages in a discussion of Spinoza's philosophy itself. For Jacobi, Spinoza represents the most consistent counter-position to his own, but in Mendelssohn's discussion Spinoza emerges simply as one of the key moments in the development of philosophy. This strategic move refutes Jacobi's normative understanding of metaphysics with a historical, evolutionary approach to reason that undermines Jacobi's polarization. In this way, Spinoza's place is firmly grounded. The differences, disagreements, and problems in Spinoza thus appear as consequences that—problematic and even wrongheaded as they might be—are intrinsic to philosophy and do not present an imminent danger. On the contrary, they mark the necessary steps that, though they may retrospectively be recognized as errors or mistakes, are nonetheless understood to serve a necessary function in the advancement of the epistemic process.

While this poses the question of how much of Spinoza might, after all, be left in Mendelssohn's purified version of Spinozism, the attempt to interpret it as a decisive step in the development of modern philosophy implies a recognition of Spinoza that, albeit cautiously phrased, is nevertheless uncompromising in its implications. As one of the links in the chain of thinkers who together prepare the road to philosophical progress, Spinoza no longer appears as Jacobi's demon of reason but rather as an interlocutor no more imperfect than any other. Mendelssohn responds to Jacobi's argument that the absolute consistency of Spinoza's system testifies to reason's ultimate failure by presenting an extensive discussion of the systemic glitches and problems in Spinoza's basic ideas. What for Jacobi appears to be written in stone and can only be either accepted or rejected, Mendelssohn identifies in Spinoza's metaphysics as philosophical options open to negotiation. This leaves enough room for different choices and makes it possible to conceive of a consistent, purified form of Spinozism. Therefore, regardless of the question of whether or not Mendelssohn's version of purified Spinozism stands up to closer examination, this approach proves Jacobi's claim of the monolithic form of Spinoza's philosophy to be false.

In a remarkable turn, Mendelssohn thus counters Jacobi's rejection of Spinoza as the representative of rationalism by pointing out the moments in his system that are not necessarily dictated by reason and which therefore allow for different interpretations of Spinoza's system. In contrast to Jacobi's "perfect" Spinoza, Mendelssohn complicates the discussion in a way that challenges Jacobi's idiosyncratic and tendentious fixation on Spinoza as representative of the ultimate rationalist, fatalist, and atheist position. However, the subtlety of Mendelssohn's defense strategy of indirect argumentation seems to have been lost on most contemporaries and critics. Yet Mendelssohn's own philosophy, whose metaphysics differs from Spinoza but rests otherwise to a large degree on Spinoza's work, prevents him from going any further in his circumspectly balanced rescue of Spinoza.

Immediately after publication of Jacobi's *Über die Lehre des Spinoza* (1785), Mendelssohn replies with what was to be his last word, *An die Freunde Lessings.* Realizing that his *Morgenstunden* had been largely misunderstood, Mendelssohn now spells out what he had left unsaid. Although he now even goes so far as to refer to the "untruth of Spinozism" (Jub A 3.2, 188) from which he clearly distances himself regardless of whoever else might or might not call himself a Spinozist, the underlying religious difference in the dispute with Jacobi is now brought into the open:

> I knew, that in the main, this refined Spinozism can be easily reconciled with Judaism, and that Spinoza, irrespective of his speculative doctrine, could have remained an orthodox Jew were it not that in other writings he had called genuine Judaism into question and in so doing stepped outside the Law. Obviously Spinoza's doctrine would come much closer to Judaism than does the orthodox doctrine of the Christians. If I was able indeed to love Lessing and be loved in return where he was still a strict follower of Athanasius (or was at least considered so by me), then why not all the more where he approximated Judaism, and where I saw in him an adherent of the Jew, Baruch Spinoza? The label of Jew and Spinozist could be for me in no way so startling or so grating as it would seem to be for Herr Jacobi.[10]

> (Ich) wußte, daß sich dieser geläuterte Spinozismus hauptsächlich mit dem Judenthume sehr gut vereinigen läßt, und daß Spinoza, seiner spekulativen Lehre ungeachtet, ein orthodoxer Jude hätte bleiben können, wenn er nicht in andern Schriften das ächte Judenthum bestritten, und sich dadurch dem Gesetze entzogen hätte. Die Lehre des Spinoza kömmt dem Judenthume offenbar weit näher, als die orthodoxe Lehre der Christen. Konnte ich also Lessingen lieben, und von ihm geliebt werden, als er noch strenger Anhänger des Athanasius war, oder ich ihn wenigstens dafür hielt; warum nicht vielmehr, wenn er sich dem Judenthum näherte, und ich ihn als Anhänger

> des Juden Baruch Spinoza erkannte? Der Name Jude und Spinozist konnte mir bey weitem weder so auffallend, noch so ärgerlich seyn, als er etwa dem Herrn Jacobi seyn mag. (Jub A 3.2, 188)

With these words, Mendelssohn points to the subtext that underlies the pantheism dispute but had so far remained unnamed: the scandal of Jewish difference. Mendelssohn now leaves his reserves and names the unavowed complex that, according to his understanding, looms behind Jacobi's argumentation. Spinoza the Jew poses less of a problem for Mendelssohn than it does for Jacobi's form of Christianity. For Mendelssohn, Spinoza's metaphysics does not present any problem for, but is fully compatible with, Judaism. As a matter of fact, it is the opinions Spinoza expresses in other parts of his writings—obviously Mendelssohn thinks here of the *Theological-Political Treatise*—that alienate Mendelssohn from Spinoza's views on Judaism. Ironically, Mendelssohn thus disavows exactly the text that proves so important for the development of his own conception of Judaism, although Mendelssohn is not prepared to acknowledge this fact in this context.

Mendelssohn's pointed irony that Lessing, had he been a Spinozist, would have moved closer to him due to the metaphysical family resemblance of Spinozism with Judaism, returns Jacobi's provocation to his own door. It exposes the more disturbing aspect informing Jacobi's claims that he uses Spinoza to construct the fundamental difference between rationalism and faith as one with profound normative implications leading to a stern indictment of reason and the unrestricted authorization of Christianity as normative religion—a difference that, however, in Spinoza as well as Mendelssohn and Lessing, enables philosophy to address religion as an integral constituent of modernity and its project of enlightenment. In calling attention to the issue of Spinoza's Jewishness, Mendelssohn makes it clear that Jacobi's is less a philosophical strategy than a hidden theological strategy to cleanse culture from un-Christian elements. Mendelssohn's point of contention is not so much that Jacobi publicizes some allegedly concealed opinions of his late friend Lessing but that he makes him a cultural Jew in order to defame not only him but also the reputation and the concerns of the Enlightenment as a whole.

What Mendelssohn sees under attack is therefore genuine religion of reason (Jub A 3.2, 196, 198). As Jacobi appears now as another Lavater, Mendelssohn no longer hesitates to express his alienation. The penultimate paragraph of *An die Freunde Lessings* thus starts:

> I for my part continue in my Jewish unbelief, ascribe *pious and angelic* lips to no mortal. When we are speaking of eternal truths on which man's happiness is founded, I eschew any desire to depend on the authority of even an *archangel;* here either I must fall or I must stand on my own two feet. Or better still, since "we are all of us born within faith," as Herr Jacobi says, I too shall return to the faith of my fathers, which according to the original meaning of the [Hebrew] word, is constituted not by belief in any doctrine or opinion, but by trust in and reliance on the attributes of God.[11]

> Ich von meiner Seite bleibe bey meinem jüdischen Unglauben, traue keinem Sterblichen einen *engelreinen Mund*[12] zu, möchte selbst von der Autorität eines *Erzengels* nicht abhängen, wenn von ewigen Wahrheiten die Rede ist, auf welche sich des Menschen Glückseeligkeit gründet, und muß also schon hierin auf eigenen Füßen stehen oder fallen.—Oder vielmehr: da wir alle, wie H.J. sagt, im Glauben gebohren sind; so kehre auch ich zum Glauben meiner Väter zurück, welcher nach der ersten ursprünglichen Bedeutung des Worts, nicht in Glauben an Lehre und Meinung, sondern in Vertrauen und Zuversicht auf die Eigenschaften Gottes bestehet. (Jub A 3.2, 218)

However, Mendelssohn did not terminate the dispute that in the wake of his death and the posthumous publication of *An die Freunde Lessings* involved practically everyone in German letters from Kant and Herder to Fichte and Hegel. While Spinoza's Jewish identity is referred to only indirectly in this controversy, it figures as the central but suppressed motive in the emergence of German idealism.

If it seemed for an instant that Kant had successfully inaugurated a radically secularized modern philosophy, it soon became clear that secularized Enlightenment and post-Enlightenment philosophy was nevertheless imbued with theological thought. The reliance on Christian faith to confront modernity, however, posed the problem of how to account for radical modern philosophy that would not originate from a Christian-based framework. Lessing's radical form of free thinking presents in this context as much a challenge for people like Jacobi and German idealists as does Mendelssohn's religion of reason.

The problem, however, with Jacobi is not that he chose Spinoza to denounce Judaism or the Jews but that he appropriates him on philosophically dubious grounds to reject a form of reason that, in his eyes, must be incompatible with his faith. For, while keeping the issue of Judaism at bay, Jacobi nevertheless gives it, by implication, enough virulence to have it subliminally define the dispute. The confused obtuseness of this procedure drives Jacobi's argument and demarcates the point at which Mendelssohn must put an end to this discussion by simply stating disagreement, though without the comfort of feeling authorized to expose what for him represents a profound theological confusion.

PART III

SPINOZA THROUGH LESSING

CHAPTER 12

LESSING'S SPINOZIST EXERCISES

WITH THE ANNOUNCEMENT OF LESSING'S alleged confession of Spinozism, Jacobi initiated what was to become the most controversial debate in eighteenth-century German culture. The publication of Jacobi's conversations with Lessing marks a decisive demarcation line that separates the Enlightenment from the new movements, both Sturm und Drang and the emerging German idealism. The disclosure—if it was one—that Lessing died a Spinozist has defined the discussion on Lessing's Spinozism in such a profound way that even most critical accounts find themselves compelled to argue within the Jacobian framework. But Jacobi's particular framing of the debate has only further confused the picture when reaching some degree of clarity seems already difficult enough. Jacobi's self-interested, polemical launching of the discussion in a strictly bipolar scheme, dividing the debate into Spinozist and anti-Spinozist camps, still haunts most of the discussion of Lessing's relationship to Spinoza. From the days Jacobi ignited the controversy by presenting Lessing with Goethe's poem "Prometheus"—the impetus for Lessing's formulation of what seemed to be his Spinozist credo—to the present, critics have regularly addressed the question of Lessing's Spinozism more as a test of Lessing's intellectual competence than as an opportunity to gain an insight into the development and formation of his critical thought.

Although Spinoza, as Lessing would later say in a conversation with Jacobi, was but a "todter Hund" (dead dog),[1] to speak or write about him posed a direct risk to those involved, at least prior to the explosion of the Spinoza controversy, and even sometime after that. The eviction of the paramount philosopher of German early Enlightenment, Christian Wolff, from Halle in 1737 was only the most prominent example of how allegations of Spinozism could threaten the reputation, the career, and even the life of those accused of it.[2] Crypto-Spinozists like Edelmann, mostly residing in Berlin, were living examples of how damaging a careless interest in Spinoza could be. Nevertheless, underground Spinozism was alive and well, especially in eighteenth-century Berlin.

Lessing came into early contact with Spinoza (most likely after 1746), whose reputation must have inspired Lessing's interest in the legendary outcast who was suspected, hated, and vilified for his radical avant-garde stand. But his name is not mentioned by Lessing until 1753. Attempts at periodizing Lessing's Spinoza studies prove somewhat difficult. A first period of the reception starts as early as 1746, but it seems that it is not until the early 1750s that Lessing is ready for a serious study of Spinoza. It well might have been Lessing who introduced Mendelssohn to Spinoza.[3] In the course of their discussions, Spinoza plays a central role. Traces of that early common study, which also plays a crucial part in forging their lifelong friendship, can be found in several publications and the correspondence of that time. The seed that is planted in these early conversations informs their relationship up to their very last publications. In the first half of the 1750s their discussions focus on the metaphysical centerpiece of Spinoza's philosophy: the way Spinoza conceives of God, Nature, and the macrostructure of his ontology. In the second half of the decade, however, in the context of the exchange on tragedy, the discussion shifts, on Mendelssohn's initiative, to the role Spinoza's theory of affects could play in a modern and effective theory of the stage play.

During his time in Breslau (1760–64), Lessing returns to an intensive study of Spinoza. As Lessing engages in a critical study, Spinoza now becomes an important conductor for Lessing's rethinking of his own metaphysical position. In the 1770s Lessing returns to Spinoza once again, but this time it is no longer the metaphysical and ontological conundrums of the *Ethics* that catch his interest but the theory of religion and political theory, with its pioneering formulation of the separation of theology and philosophy put forward in the *Theological-Political Treatise*. With his appointment as chief librarian of the duke of Braunschweig in 1770, Lessing moves in 1777 to a new residence in Wolfenbüttel graced by the magnificent portrait of Spinoza that, hanging in the living room, comes to stand for more than just a household name or conversation piece.

Although Lessing does not mention Spinoza by name until three years later,[4] Lessing's earliest theological writing, "Gedanken über die Herrnhuter" (1750), betrays a remarkable affinity to Spinoza with regard to the question of how to tackle the theological-political complex.[5] Here, Lessing spells out his mission of rescuing the historically weaker yet morally stronger side. Anticipating some of Benjamin's redemptive critique, his attempt at releasing the power of alternative positions that have been repressed in the course of history, Lessing argues that as long as history is only the history of victors, the difference of who is right and who should be right calls for a rescue of the repressed but equally "right" side (L 3, 682). His rescue of the Pietist Herrnhuter is a case in point. Resting on a scheme of history of philosophy and religion reminiscent of the one Spinoza introduces in his *Theological-Political Treatise*, the "Gedanken" display a deep family resemblance with Spinoza's way of rethinking religion in the age of reason. With the underlying distinction between theory and praxis and the idea that laying down clear and simple rules for moral, practical wisdom counts more than correct metaphysical speculation, Lessing depicts an attitude identical with the conceptual framework on which Spinoza based his argumentation in the *Theological-Political Treatise*.[6]

Socrates, in whose mouth Lessing places his convictions, sounds less like the historical Socrates than like Spinoza's version of him:

> Foolish mortals, what is above you is not for you! Turn the gaze inside yourself! Inside you are unexplored depths where you can get lost with use. Here examine the most secret corners. Here learn about the weakness and strength, the hidden corridors and the open explosion of your passions! Build here the kingdom where you are subject and king! Grasp and rule here the only thing that you are supposed to grasp and rule: yourselves.
>
> This is the way Socrates admonished, or rather, God through Socrates.

> Törichte Sterbliche, was über euch ist, ist nicht für euch! Kehret den Blick in euch selbst! In euch sind die unerforschten Tiefen, worinnen ihr euch mit Nutzen verlieren könnt. Hier untersucht die geheimsten Winkel. Hier lernet die Schwäche und Stärke, die verdeckten Gänge und den offenbaren Ausbruch eurer Leidenschaften! Hier richtet das Reich auf, wo ihr Untertan

> und König seid! Hier begreifet und beherrschet das einzige, was ihr begreifen und beherrschen sollt; euch selbst.
>
> So ermahnte Sokrates, oder vielmehr Gott durch den Sokrates. (L 3, 684)

Yet, Socrates' God sounds remarkably like the voice of Spinoza. In fact, the passage could be read as the programmatic summary of Spinoza's theory of affects, his attempt to free man from the domination of the passions and point the way to self-determination.

In contrast to that of the historical Socrates, Lessing's underlying political tone strikes a note that seems to echo a typically Spinozist impulse toward liberation as self-determination. Like philosophy, Lessing points out, religion begins with a few simple principles. And as he is for Spinoza, Christ is for Lessing—and he is careful to repeat this in order to preclude any misunderstanding—"only a God-inspired teacher" (L 3, 686), that is, a teacher of morals and divine obedience rather than an imposer of dogmatic definitions. Lessing's stress on the priority of action over reasoning (*Vernünfteln*) echoes the pragmatist stand of Spinoza: "Man was created to act not to reason" ("Der Mensch ward zum Tun und nicht zum Vernünfteln erschaffen" [L 3, 683]). Thus already in 1750, at the outset of his intellectual career, Lessing articulates a keen interest in distinguishing praxis from theory in order to emancipate the former from the latter very much in the way this separation is formulated by Spinoza.[7]

Conceived in 1749 and published in 1754, Lessing's play *Die Juden* represents a key instance of Spinoza's appearance in the public, albeit in a carefully camouflaged manner. One year after Frederick II promulgated a new law requiring that Jews wear beards for easy identification,[8] Lessing responds with a play that not only proves the absurdity of such a law but also triggers a discussion on Jewish emancipation, a discussion that reaches a new critical stage thirty years later with the release of Lessing's *Nathan the Wise*.[9]

While the play's bearded robbers turn out to be Christians from the village, the mild-mannered and clean-shaven victim of their crime, the traveling gentleman, reveals himself at the end to be the only Jew onstage. Much in the way that the role reversal drives the plot, the plural in the comedy's title *Die Juden* is played out against the singular of one "real" Jew. His noble manners, his Dutch background, and his sophisticated and superior, cultured character all point to Spinoza, the prototype of successful assimilation and cultural refinement.[10] In one of his first comedies, Lessing exposes the psychology of prejudice in a dramatically trenchant manner. From the confusion produced by the thieves masking themselves with beards and the circulation of stolen property (a silver box taken from the traveling gentleman that travels full circle), the traveler—the unnamed but central character of the play—emerges as the point of reference: the calm, enlightened, warm personality standing in for ethical sovereignty in the face of the turbulence that haunts the other characters. His noble attitude echoes the philosophically superior yet nevertheless sympathetic personality of Spinoza, which, the legend reports, is—despite occasional outbursts of passion—best represented by his conception of reason that conceives the world and what inhabits it "sub quadam specie aeternitatis."

It has been argued that given the widespread underground circulation of the Spinoza legend, the play's allusion could not have been more direct without putting the play and its author at risk.[11] Depicting as its protagonist an exemplary Jew, the play manages both to challenge directly the king's legislative wisdom and to expose the mechanism of a popular prejudice. But it is in the discussion following the publication of the play that the connection with Spinoza is made explicit. In a letter to Johann David Michaelis accompanying an essay in which Lessing responds to the former's critical review of the play, an essay that itself includes a touching letter by a Jew (to protect Mendelssohn, Lessing does not mention him by name either in the essay or in the letter) expressing deep disappointment at Michaelis's categorical judgment on the Jewish people, Lessing mentions Spinoza for the first time as a philosopher's ideal that he holds up as a viable possibility despite Spinoza's alleged vicissitudes.

Michaelis's point is that a Jew like the one Lessing places onstage could not possibly exist in the real world. To make it clear that the author of the letter questioning Michaelis's unfair criticism of the Jews is himself a real Jew and contemporary, Lessing writes in a letter to Michaelis:

> He is really a Jew, a man of twenty years who without guidance has achieved great strength in languages, mathematics, in philosophy, and in poetry. I foresee in him the glory of his nation, provided his coreligionists permit him to mature who have always been driven by an unfortunate spirit of persecution against people like him. His honesty and his philosophical mind make me anticipate in him a second Spinoza who in order to equal the first will lack but his errors.

> Er ist wirklich ein Jude, ein Mensch von etliche zwanzig Jahren, welcher, ohne alle Anweisung, in Sprache, in der Mathematik, in der Weltweisheit, in der Poesie, eine große Stärke erlangt hat. Ich sehe in ihm voraus als eine Ehre seiner Nation an, wenn ihn anders seine eigne Glaubensgenossen zur Reife kommen lassen, die allezeit ein unglücklicher Verfolgungsgeist wider Leute seines gleichen getrieben hat. Seine Redlichkeit und sein philosophischer Geist läßt mich ihn im voraus als einen zweiten Spinoza betrachten, dem zur völligen Gleichheit mit dem ersten nichts als seine Irrtümer fehlen werden.[12]

Around the same time, Lessing secures a publisher for Mendelssohn's *Philosophische Gespräche,* whose first two pieces present a Lessing-style rescue of Spinoza. In a review of 1 March 1755, Lessing welcomes Mendelssohn's reassessment of Spinoza's central importance in preparing the ground for Leibniz's concept of preestablished harmony. Although in an earlier review Lessing essentially continues to repeat standard views of Spinoza,[13] the polemical essay *Pope ein Metaphysiker!* (1755), a joint production of Lessing and Mendelssohn, includes a passage on Spinoza that suggests the disinterested distance of the anonymous authors. However, an examination of the passage reminds us that viewing it as a negative comment on Spinoza offers a questionable reading at best.[14] Given the program of this polemics, which argues that Pope's poetry is not to be mistaken for the articulation of a philosophical system but rather as expression of a poet's overflowing sentiments, the authors flatly reject the interpretation of Pope's line "Whose body Nature is, and God the soul" as containing some Spinozist message, as one commentator (Crousaz) would have it. First, they point out that such a statement represents anything but Spinoza's views. As the essay expresses it, the wrongheaded opinion that God is the soul of Nature's body is as removed from Spinozism as it is from the truth (L 3, 662). This has led some critics use this passage as evidence of a negative view of Spinoza and his philosophy.[15] Yet the topological triangle this phrase opens up between truth, Spinozism, and the third opinion expressed by Pope and some wrongheaded philosophers points to a more complex relationship between Spinozism and truth.[16] A careful look at the passage suggests a painstaking equilibrium in evaluating Spinoza that withholds any final judgment on the philosopher. Instead, the text takes the same position that Mendelssohn advanced on Spinoza and is reminiscent of the redemptive strategy pervasive in Lessing. Thus, while the authors concede it to be rather unlikely "that Pope had wished to display a dangerous system in just these letters" ("daß Pope eben in diesen Briefen ein gefährliches System habe auskramen wollen" [L 3, 662]), they nevertheless allow for the view that Pope may not have had a problem with using the language of Spinoza, much as he used the thought of other philosophers to suggest that God is the soul of the world. Painstakingly cautious, the authors simply argue for the poet's legitimate right to use Spinozist language without passing judgment on this "dubbed heretic" ("berufene Irrgläubige" [L 3, 662]). The dangerous and irreligious aspect of Spinoza does not prompt any further comment. But taken as such, these attributes only describe the perception of Spinoza as an anti-religious, even atheistic thinker. They do not imply any other valorization of Spinoza as a philosopher. In the context of the history of Spinozism, however, such an explicit and deliberate silence is a strong indication of Lessing's guarded sympathy.

Whereas in the first phase it may have been Lessing who introduced Mendelssohn to Spinoza, it is Mendelssohn, in the context of a discussion on tragedy, who directs Lessing's attention to the importance of Spinoza as an astute analyst of affects.[17] Mendelssohn did point out that Spinoza's theory of the affects offers more insight into their dynamics, an insight that thus had more to offer the aesthetics of modern theater than the positions of other psychologists, but this was not the only avenue by which Lessing was able to learn from an innovative reception of Spinoza's theory of the affects. Mendelssohn's own emerging aesthetic theory[18] contains enough elements of Spinoza's dynamic conception of the nature of the affects for Lessing, whether consciously or not, to have assimilated a Spinozist impulse while accommodating Mendelssohn's critical suggestions. In any case, it is during the aftermath of the exchange on tragedy that Lessing changes from his early dramaturgic practice to a more sophisticated one that brings a more complex psychology into play.

Following French dramatic models, Lessing's early plays cast a variety of types whose character dispositions present the driving force for plot and action. Situation comedy or tragedy, these plays stage their characters as basically static, "ideal types" of social life. In the tradition of Molière, Lessing's plays run the gamut of the bestiary of different types of characters whose acting combines precisely targeted social observation with carefully indirectly calibrated political critique. With an uncompromising eye for the way the sociology and psychology of prejudice function, the early comedies—*Der junge Gelehrte, Die Juden, Der Misogyn, Der Freigeist,* and *Der Schatz*—expose the mechanisms of prejudice onstage. Academic self-conceit, prejudices against Jews and women, and other stereotyping collapses in the stage light of comic relief that, at the same time, exposes various forms of self-deception as resulting from self-serving rationalizing. Likewise, the early tragedies—*Miss Sara Sampson* and *Philotas*—unfold conflicts that are still removed from a psychodynamic understanding of human nature. However, the situation changes when Lessing goes on to write *Minna von Barnhelm, Emilia Galotti,* and later *Nathan the Wise.*[19] All three plays introduce characters whose particular affective economies, rather than their psychological makeup, determine the dramatic development of the plot.

Written between 1763 to 1767, *Minna von Barnhelm* displays a dramatic emplotment driven by and staged through the dynamics of the protagonists' affects rather than by the motives of the characters alone. The use of accumulation, compression, and release of affective energies help constitute the underlying dramatic motor of the play, distinguishing this comedy from Lessing's earlier plays. *Minna von Barnhelm* marks the transition to the new stage play conceived with a heightened awareness of the fundamental role of the economy of affects as it successfully translates affective dynamics into dramatic performance.

The aesthetic theory Mendelssohn had developed for the tragedy and the stage play in general, based to a decisive degree on an original application of Spinoza's theory of affects, thus acquires an instrumental importance in shaping the new dramatic approach. While Lessing seems at no point to reflect on this connection, it profoundly informs his dramatic achievement in reforming if not revolutionizing the German drama. Spinozist affective theory thereby prepares the ground from which Goethe's conception of classic drama would spring.[20]

Whether this has anything remotely to do with the "Spinozistic exercises" of 1763/64[21] seems questionable. But in any case, even if the preceding discussion of the import of the theory of the affects on Lessing's conception of drama might present a separate instance of Spinoza reception in Lessing, disconnected from the metaphysical thought experiments of the "Spinozistic exercises," Lessing might not have been unaware of the common source of the inspiration for his thought. His partial reception of Spinoza illustrates how different aspects of Spinozist thought might, at the same time, be present in a single author without his necessarily acknowledging this fact. This early stage of Lessing's reception of Spinoza demonstrates the profound effect the particular form of split and discontinuous reception Spinoza enjoys even in thinkers sympathetically disposed toward his thought. A third strand of Spinoza reception in Lessing will not begin to exert its full impact until the 1770s.

During his stay in Breslau, Lessing returns to Spinoza's *Ethics,* to which he now devotes his full critical attention. On the occasion of Mendelssohn's publication of the collection of his *Philosophische Schriften* in 1761, Lessing also rereads Mendelssohn's *Philosophische Gespräche,* which are republished in this early collection of his friend's writings. But now Lessing has second thoughts with regard to Mendelssohn's brave and resolute rescue of Spinoza that he had welcomed a few years earlier.

In April 1763 Lessing questions the presentation Mendelssohn had given Spinoza in the first of his *Philosophische Gespräche.* There, Mendelssohn had argued that Leibniz's concept of preestablished harmony had, in its essential elements, been anticipated by Spinoza.[22] In the short piece "Durch Spinoza ist Leibniz nur auf die Spur der vorherbestimmten Harmonie gekommen,"[23] which seems to have served as a draft for the letter to Mendelssohn Lessing wrote on 17 April 1763, he expresses his reservations about Mendelssohn's claims. In the face of Spinoza's ontological framework, he argues, it seems problematic if not misleading to speak of harmony when, in fact, Spinoza's point is to conceive body and mind as just two different aspects or forms of manifestation of the one and only Substance that, identical in itself, renders superfluous any need to postulate harmony in order to solve the problem of the connection between mind and body in Leibniz. According to Lessing, the different ontological assumptions in Leibniz require him to introduce the notion of preestablished harmony. While Leibniz's system is in need of such an additional assumption, it is one of the strengths defining the architecture of Spinoza's system that it conceives of body and mind as just two attributes of one and the same Substance, thereby obviating any need for a theory of harmony. Instead, Spinoza's ontology tackles the issue more satisfactorily by postulating a deep-structured identity subtending the diversity of all appearances.

In his draft, Lessing attempts to capture the difference between Leibniz and Spinoza in a striking image that he, however, leaves unfinished. In the letter, however, he does not mention this simile but, interestingly enough, uses an ambiguous reason for ending his letter somewhat abruptly:

> But Leibniz?—I am prevented from continuing. And now I wish I had not written at all! Still, this does not amount to much more than nothing.—Farewell, beloved friend, farewell!

> Aber Leibnitz?—Ich werde abgehalten, weiter zu schreiben. Und nun wollte ich, daß ich gar nicht geschrieben hätte! Noch ist es auch nicht viel mehr als gar nichts.—Leben Sie wohl, liebster Freund, leben Sie wohl! (Jub A, 12.1, 8)

What at a first reading might look like an external interruption is, according to the inner logic of the course of argument, very likely Lessing's not so accidental reason for breaking off at this point: "Ich werde abgehalten, weiter zu schreiben." Having arrived at the end of his argument, the continuation would lead to a transition to another level of reasoning. For while Mendelssohn was primarily concerned with the attempt to vindicate Spinoza within the given framework of unquestioned Leibnizianism, the continuation of Lessing's draft ceases to address Mendelssohn's redemptive strategy and instead proceeds to a head-on confrontation with the content of the philosophies of Spinoza and Leibniz:

> Would you like to allow me a simile? Two savages who for the first time see their image in the mirror. The wonder has passed and they now begin to philosophize about this phenomenon. The mirror image, they both say, performs the identical movements a body performs and just in the same order. Consequently, both conclude, it must be possible to explain the effect of the movements of the image and the effect of the body's movements with one and the same reason.

> Wollen Sie mir ein Gleichnis erlauben? Zwei Wilde, welche das erstemal ihr Bildnis in einem Spiegel erblicken. Die Verwunderung ist vorbei, und nunmehr fangen sie an, über diese Erscheinung zu philosophieren. Das Bild in dem Spiegel, sagen beide, macht eben dieselben Bewegungen, welche ein Körper macht, und macht sie in der nämlichen Ordnung. Folglich, schließen beide, muß die Folge der Bewegungen des Bildes, und die Folge der Bewegungen des Körpers sich aus einem und eben demselben Grunde erklären lassen. (L 8, 518)

Now it seems clear that the continuation of the simile argues for Spinoza's theoretically more satisfying and hence philosophically superior view of the matter. This becomes obvious when we follow Danzel's suggestion to complete the simile for ourselves:

> It is clear how Lessing wanted to continue: "But they will disagree about the reason itself; one will say: my body moves for itself and so does the mirror image, but they are designed by a hidden power in such a way that they have to agree, and the other will propose: that only *one* movement takes place which one simply sees in two different places: the first view corresponds to Leibniz's school, the other to Spinozism."

> Es ist klar, wie Lessing fortfahren wollte: "Aber über den Grund selbst werden sie uneinig sein; der eine wird sagen: mein Körper bewegt sich für sich selbst und das Bild im Spiegel ebenfalls, sie sind aber durch eine verborgene Macht so eingerichtet, daß sie übereinstimmen müssen, und der andere wird behaupten: Es finde nur *eine* Bewegung statt, die man nur zweimal an verschiednen Orten erblicke: die erstere Ansicht wird dem Leibnizianismus, die andere dem Spinozismus entsprechen."[24]

In his response, Mendelssohn carefully reiterates his point. What remains unsaid in Lessing's simile and what Danzel has filled in, Mendelssohn—unaware of the simile Lessing had noted for himself—formulates in his letter with impeccable clarity. Spinoza, he reminds Lessing, has, regardless of his friend's reluctance to acknowledge this, formulated in his *Ethics* a metaphysical system that not only points the way to the notion of preestablished harmony, as Lessing concedes, but more importantly, expresses this conception in its very architecture. The point Mendelssohn's argument suggests by implication is that Spinoza provides the purer version of that harmony.[25]

It is often ignored in discussions of Lessing and Mendelssohn's exchange that what separates them is less their assessment of Spinoza's metaphysical edifice than their rather different concerns. Whereas Mendelssohn's primary interest seems to be in rescuing Spinoza on the basis of Leibniz's philosophy, which he applies as the standard of contemporary thought, Lessing at this stage is no longer interested in keeping within the limits of this philosophical standard. Rather, he takes the discussion a step further. With Spinoza as his critical lever, Lessing seeks to flesh out the weaknesses of Leibniz's metaphysical conception. Mendelssohn and Lessing have different theoretical interests at this point, and this brings Lessing to halt his discussion precisely when he is about to leave the grounds of Mendelssohn's argument. If Mendelssohn is concerned with assimilating Spinoza to the generally accepted thought of

Leibniz,[26] thereby permitting him to deploy Spinoza's philosophy in an innocuous yet productive way, Lessing is now more interested in a view of Spinoza that would make Mendelssohn's defensive maneuvers obsolete, allowing Spinoza to be discussed as a philosopher in his own right.

This is why Mendelssohn and Lessing take different yet equally tenable positions, both of which reject any easy solution. Mendelssohn is interested in introducing Spinoza as a philosopher whose thought fully meets the demands of the traditional metaphysical school of thought, personified in Leibniz. Thus he formulates his own philosophy through implicit agreement, rejection, and reformulation of Leibnizian philosophy. Lessing, on the other hand, calls for a more challenging display of unorthodox thinking. In contrast to Lessing, Mendelssohn's precariously marginal position as a cultural outsider prevents him from displaying himself with the kind of bold move that the provocative position of Lessing undertakes. Lessing thus neither adds to nor corrects, in this Spinozist exercise, anything Mendelssohn has said. More significantly, he changes the trajectory in which he would like to lead the discussion of Spinoza.[27]

This becomes clear in the second "exercise," which takes up the discussion in Mendelssohn's second philosophical conversation.[28] In "Über die Wirklichkeit der Dinge ausser Gott," Lessing's response to Mendelssohn's explanation of the difference between Spinoza and Leibniz[29] is couched in terms of Leibniz's two-world theory. According to Leibniz, God chooses from all the possible worlds the best one, and as his choice is a divine decree, it becomes reality. Leibniz is thus able to introduce a theory of the different modalities of the possible, the actual, and the necessary.[30] Now, Mendelssohn argues that Spinoza can be made compatible with Leibniz if his system is understood to represent the world, not how it is "outside" of God, but the way it exists prior to its reality within divine understanding. From a Leibnizian point of view, Mendelssohn suggests, Spinoza is not entirely wrong but correct as long as his ontological framework is understood to describe that part of the world that is within God's understanding.

Lessing, on the other hand, now picks up where Mendelssohn had left off. Pushing Mendelssohn's argument to its logical conclusion, Lessing unfolds Spinoza's position as, again, the theoretically more satisfactory and more convincing one. Already his first statement articulates Lessing's critical attitude toward Leibniz: "I may explain the reality of things outside of God however I wish, I still have to confess that I cannot have a concept of this" ("Ich mag mir die Wirklichkeit der Dinge außer Gott erklären, wie ich will, so muß ich bekennen, daß ich mir keinen Begriff davon machen kann" [L 8, 515]). Henry Allison points out that Lessing's argument for immanence receives its importance from the fact that he links it with an interesting critique of Leibniz's notion of actuality, or, as Allison puts it, his *Wirklichkeitsbegriff:*

> To be sure, [Lessing] begins by accepting this concept [of actuality], but this is only for the purpose of developing a *reductio*. In fact, Lessing's argument can be seen as an anticipation of Russell's contention that the assumption that existence is a predicate (which is the heart of the Leibnizian conception of actuality) leads necessarily to the conception of God "as the only substance, as an immanent pantheistic God incapable of creation."[31]

The "Spinozistic thrust"[32] of this argument points to the internal contradictions caused by the metaphysical distinction between things existing in the mind of God and the actual reality of things outside God's mind. For Lessing, the Spinozist framework has the advantage of not having to double the world in the way Leibniz's system seems to suggest.[33]

In turning around Mendelssohn's strategy, Lessing opens the way to a new appreciation of Spinoza's metaphysics,[34] an assessment leading to the recognition of Spinoza's undiminished potential for critical thought. Although Mendelssohn is well aware of Spinoza's importance as a philosophical critic, he is, unlike Lessing, not prepared to deviate from the Leibnizian path as far as the framework of metaphysics and ontology is concerned.

CHAPTER 13

TOWARD A NEW CONCEPT OF TRUTH

THROUGH THE 1760S, IT IS THE *Ethics* that seems to determine Lessing's reception of Spinoza. On the one hand, its innovative ontological framework draws the attention of Mendelssohn and Lessing; on the other hand, its theory of the affects, along with Mendelssohn's version of it, comes to play a crucial role in the redefinition of the stage and of dramatic theory. Spinoza's other key work, the *Theological-Political Treatise,* comes to take center stage in Lessing's thought only in the context of his renewed interest in theology and the philosophy of religion and history.

At the same time that Mendelssohn intensified his preoccupation with the central issues of Spinoza's *Treatise* in the work that would lead up to his *Jerusalem,* the trajectory taken by Lessing's studies of the 1770s follows the path staked out by the complex of concerns the *Treatise* raises. The critical agenda of Spinoza's *Theological-Political Treatise* can be found in the activity and ensuing debates set off by Lessing's publication of selected sections from the "fragmentist" Hermann Samuel Reimarus's *Apologie oder Schutzschrift für die vernünftigen Verehrer Gottes* and its discussion of theological, philosophical, and religious issues.[1] Lessing, who creatively used his recently assumed position as chief librarian of the ducal library at Wolfenbüttel, claimed to have "found" Reimarus's papers among the treasures of the library, treasures that he hurried to bring to the attention of the public along with his commentaries, his "counter-observations." The way in which Reimarus's work poses the problem of interpreting history, justice, revelation, secrecy, and the role of political institutions shares its critical angle with Spinoza's *Theological-Political Treatise,* philosophically the most consistent and compelling theoretical groundwork for the critical study of the Bible and the socio-political study of religion of the time.

In Lessing, the specifics and, more crucially, the overall method of theorizing theological-political issues all take their cue from Spinoza, for Spinoza's reformulation of the theological-political nexus provides a platform allowing Lessing to present the intricacies of current theological debates in a new and theoretically productive light. In a way, the development of Lessing's writing in the 1770s, leading up to *Ernst and Falk, Nathan the Wise,* and the *Education of the Human Race,* can be described as the unfolding and productive reception of Spinoza that carries out the consequences of the argument presented in the *Theological-Political Treatise.*

In this last phase, Lessing reaches a stage of critical reflection that produces a theoretical framework clarifying what he had practiced all along in his publicistic, dramaturgic, poetic, and philological career, making it apparent that his diverse literary, scholarly, and polemical projects together form a comprehensive attempt to achieve a critical understanding of praxis, an understanding that leads to a profound re-conceptualization of history, tradition, reason, and religion. Lessing's uncompromising search for the nature of truth, his enduring concern for the public and the practice of free and transparent dialogue, and his radical rethinking of the question of history and tradition thus emerge as elements of the single concern around which his thought revolves: his attempt to realize the full potential of the radical and hidden core of the nexus of the theological and the political. The virulence of the question of what constitutes history, tradition, truth, and the public that runs through Lessing's work suggests less the turbulence of a restless, ever-struggling mind, as is often claimed, than an unflagging commitment to look critically at the factors that constitute culture in its constantly shifting shapes.

At the heart of Lessing's concerns stands the question of the nature and status of truth. Although it was already a crucial, focal theme in Lessing's first writings, the notion of truth and the question of the conditions for its constitution reaches a new stage in his late thought. In his analysis of the elements that define history, tradition, culture, and the public, Lessing breaks new ground for a critical and challenging reexamination of the philosophical underpinnings of the constitutive elements of the idea of truth. He bases his approach on the recognition that truth consists in a specific effect of certain constellations rather than in an ensemble of fixed contents. The traditional concept of truth is thus replaced by a view that responds to the question of truth by examining the conditions that establish the parameters for determining an answer. By introducing the deep dimension of historicity and the dialogical in place of the dialectical view of what determines the historical coordinates defining "truth," Lessing formulates a new approach. This understanding is dialogical in that answers responding to the question of the historicity of characteristics of truth-defining conditions are seen as hinging on the way the question frames the answer. A great deal of Lessing's polemics against theologians and philologists alike aims at simply exposing and removing the hidden presuppositions that predetermine the outcome and thus render any critical investigation impossible. This dialogical approach allows Lessing to address the dynamic, context-dependent nature of a conception of history in which it is only the specific conditions of a given point in time and space that allow an accounting of those conditions necessary for truth.

Lessing proceeds in a step-by-step fashion. In the face of the dispute on the "fragmentist" and other polemics challenging the assumptions of both traditional and modern theological claims, he does not base his own stand on an abstract philosophical system but rather advances it as an engaged dialogical response. He thus seeks less to establish a final and eternal truth than to investigate the limit-conditions of truth, in order to forestall the closure of disputation over claims and counterclaims. The stress on the dynamic and complex meaning of truth finds expression in the classic formulation of the *Duplik* that already anticipates crucial aspects of the pragmatist concept of truth.

In the *Duplik* (rejoinder), Lessing answers accusations raised against his publication of selections from the "fragmentist," the late Reimarus. In order to prevent critics from simple *ad hominem* refutations that would reduce a serious matter to a witch-hunt, and in order to secure a level of objective discussion whose sole object is to discuss the question at hand without the impingement of larger (ecclesiastic) interests, Lessing refers to the author as the "unnamed." Although this bold move—placing the focus solely on the logic of the argument itself, regardless of personal implications that might be implied—would also put Lessing's own name at risk, it illustrates how little interest Lessing has in a particular outcome of the discussion over the "fragments." Rather than represent an interested party, Lessing sees himself as the facilitator of the truth-finding process, or as he calls himself, the *Wärtel:* "The *warder* (Kampfwärtel) was a court attendant; and I don't judge no one in order not to be judged by anyone" ("Der *Kampfwärtel* war eine Gerichtsperson; und ich richte niemanden, um von niemanden gerichtet zu sein" [L 8, 30]). This same emphasis on the epistemological level is expressed in the epigraph taken from the *Diktys* of Crete and ascribed to a legendary participant in the Trojan War, though it seems to have been derived from a description of this war by Septimus Lucius:[2] "Contestandi magis gratia, quam aliquid ex oratione promoturus" ("More to determine the matter of contest than to prove anything by his speech"). Lessing's interest in first examining the respective "standpoint" (L 8, 30) of the parties involved is, however, often mistaken for a defensive tactic, when in fact it implies an epistemological shift. Parallel to a similar development Kant's thought was making at the same time, Lessing moves toward an epistemological-critical mode. Like Kant in his *Critique of Pure Reason,* Lessing aims at clarifying the legitimacy of claims and counterclaims. The underlying assumption is that clarification of the parameters and validity of arguments brought to bear in a dispute can render the status of a dispute's legitimacy transparent as such an examination helps to flesh out the axiomatic presuppositions that define the conflict. Lessing's move to the meta-level of critical reflection in the theological debate thus aims not to "solve" problems by offering definitive answers to metaphysically ponderous questions but to provide a theoretically sound framework for examining claims that would otherwise simply be continually asserted and repeated in the battles over principles and worldviews.

Lessing's continuing stress on the fact that truth as such—truth as unmediated, abstract essence—is unattainable must therefore be understood as a clear rejection of the traditional concept of truth as fixable content. The difficulty that arises in interpreting Lessing's argument is that he is forced to deploy two different notions of truth at once, a traditional, "old" concept and a new concept of truth as defined by its functional, operative assignments. Lessing's otherwise paradoxical-sounding proviso points to a deeper meaning when it outlines a new understanding of truth beyond tactical considerations:

> A man who seeks to push through untruth in good intention, and while he is convinced of the opposite, in a clever as well as modest manner, is infinitely more valuable than a man who defends the best and most noble truth out of prejudice in an everyday manner and while decrying his adversaries.
>
> Ein Mann, der Unwahrheit, unter entgegengesetzter Überzeugung, in guter Absicht, eben so scharfsinnig als bescheiden durchzusetzen sucht, ist unendlich mehr wert, als ein Mann, der die beste edelste Wahrheit aus Vorurteil, mit Verschreiung seiner Gegner, auf alltägliche Weise verteidiget. (L 8, 32)

Whereas for tactical and *ad hominem* reasons the two sentences that precede this passage argue that the justice due a person is something altogether different from the justice owed the question at hand, the quoted passage pushes the argument still further. For now such a man, wrongheaded though he may be, is not only excused for his "false" opinions but is presented as "infinitely more valuable" than someone who merely follows the truth without examination.

If we now revisit the classic passage on truth and the aporia of its possession, the synergy of the two layers—deliberate religious modesty, on the one hand, and the recognition of truth not as an "answer" to a question, or as a definitive formula, but rather as a synergetic effect of discursive activity, on the other hand—calls forth a powerful image:

> Not the truth that is possessed or fancied to be possessed by any human being but the sincere effort he has made to get behind the truth makes the worth of a human being. For it is not because of the possession but because of the examination of truth that his potential expands wherein alone his ever growing perfection lies. Possession makes calm, inert, proud—
>
> If God held in his right hand all truth and in his left the unique, ever active spur for truth albeit with the stipulation to err in eternity, and spoke to me: choose! I would fall with humility for his left hand and say: Father, give! For the pure truth is anyway just for you alone!
>
> Nicht die Wahrheit, in deren Besitz irgend ein Mensch ist, oder zu sein vermeinet, sondern die aufrichtige Mühe, die er angewandt hat, hinter die Wahrheit zu kommen, macht den Wert des Menschen. Denn nicht durch den Besitz, sondern durch die Nachforschung der Wahrheit erweitern sich

> seine Kräfte, worin allein seine immer wachsende Vollkommenheit bestehet. Der Besitz macht ruhig, träge, stolz—
>
> Wenn Gott in seiner Rechten alle Wahrheit, und in seiner Linken den einzigen immer regen Trieb nach Wahrheit, obschon mit dem Zusatze, mich immer und ewig zu irren, verschlossen hielte, und spräche zu mir: wähle! Ich fiele ihm mit Demut in seine Linke, und sagte: Vater gib! die reine Wahrheit ist ja doch nur für dich allein! (L 8, 32–33)

At first glance this passage appears to advance an argument not about truth itself but rather about the subjective role truth plays in the individual's affective economy. It seems more a statement about the dynamics of growth in intrasubjective psychology. Yet such an exclusive reading cannot account for Lessing's final line. Instead, it only emphasizes the fact that absolute consciousness alone has access to pure truth. But more than religious truth is at stake here, for Lessing's introduction of this fictitious dialogue with God represents more than a theological grace note: it points instead to the distinction between finite and infinite knowledge, a distinction that carries epistemological consequences as well. Since "pure truth" is available only to God, any claim to possess it is, by implication, inexcusably arrogant. Confined to the realm of finite consciousness, the individual must therefore determine what kind of truth remains for us; by syllogism, this is obviously only "impure truth."

The imagery used in this context points to the constructivist aspect of Lessing's conception of truth. Lessing fleshes out this constructivism in a passage that addresses what is quite literally the "fundamentalist" understanding of truth, which ignores the intricately circular nature of any epistemological grounding, mistaking it for a simple and static given. Lessing thus asks:

> —Which fool digs curiously in the ground of his house just to convince himself of the quality of the house's foundation?—The house had first to settle here and there.—But that the foundation is good, I now know, since the house has been standing for such a long time, more convincingly than those could know who saw it being laid.

> —Welcher Tor wühlet neugierig in dem Grunde seines Hauses, bloß um sich von der Güte des Grundes seines Hauses zu überzeugen?—Setzen mußte sich das Haus freilich erst, an diesem und jenem Orte.—Aber daß

> der Grund gut ist, weiß ich nunmehr, da das Haus so lange Zeit steht, überzeugender, als es die wissen konnten, die ihn legen sahen. (L 8, 39)

Lessing's crucial insight here is that grounding truths have no a priori basis and that they would not enjoy metaphysical dignity unless they had been *made* through the passage of time, that is, in the course of history. Only by fulfilling the functions that they assumed over time, that is, in history, do these "grounds" become grounds. In other words, a ground becomes a ground only once a "house" is built upon it. Dialectically, only the building that covers the ground and makes it disappear creates its grounding character and sets it to use. That is, its grounding function is produced only retrospectively, through history. It is the use that gives grounds their constitutive function. Grounds are, therefore, to use a term introduced by Freud, a result of *Nachträglichkeit,* an a posteriori construction.

To illustrate this point, Lessing introduces the parable of Diane's temple in Ephesus. Let us assume, he suggests, that the temple still stands in all its beauty, but some old tradition (*alte Nachrichten*) would have it that the temple rests on a foundation of coals (L 8, 39). And let us further assume that it was never fully clear what type of coals establish the "grounds" for this temple. Coals from olive trees, oaks, or alders? Obviously, Lessing points out, coals—rotten, crumbling, and absorbing humidity—do not make for an ideal base. And yet, he asks, who would be mad enough to begin excavating samples to probe the coal's texture, simply to determine the kind of trees they came from? "O such archfools who rather fight about a polyvalent texture of coals than would wish to admire the great and pleasing proportions of the temple!" ("O der Erztoren, die lieber über eine vieldeutige Textur von Kohlen streiten, als die großen Ebenmaße des Tempels bewundern wollten!" [L 8, 40]). This image captures the fundamentalist's paradox perfectly. While one may engage in a study of the coal's complex (*vieldeutige*) texture—literally, the many possible meanings of that texture—such a study offers no explanation whatsoever that would grasp the temple's structure and proportion (*Ebenmaße*), that is, the architecture of the house of the goddess. Lessing leaves no doubt: "I praise what stands on the earth and not what is hidden beneath the earth!—Pardon me, dear constructor, that I do not want to know more than that is has to be well built and solid. For it holds and has been holding so long" ("Ich lobe mir, was über der Erde steht, und nicht, was unter der Erde verborgen liegt!—

Vergib es mir, lieber Baumeister, daß ich von diesem weiter nichts wissen mag, als daß es gut und fest sein muß. Denn es trägt, und trägt so lange" [L 8, 40]). Now emerging as a function rather than an ontologically verifiable—or falsifiable—essence, only the pragmatic effect is important as far as the examination of the ground is concerned. The rest, hidden and inaccessible to discursive investigation, Lessing demonstrates, has no impact on determining the ground's consistency, its carrying capacity, or reliability in supporting something, and thereby becoming its ground.

In the context of the *Duplik,* this argument is played out first with regard to the meaning of miracles. Miracles, though inexplicable and discursively evasive, may well have some historical veracity. But the ability to affirm or negate them conclusively is beyond our ken. All we can be certain of is that because of our inability to verify or falsify miracles, they cannot serve as grounds for religious truth, despite the fact that they are used in this way. If historical space and time are the ground on which the edifice of religion rests, miracles represent the scaffold of that edifice. Yet—and this is Lessing's point—the scaffold, too, is irrelevant where the structure and veracity of a religious edifice is concerned: "The scaffold is destroyed as soon as the construction is completed" ("Das Gerüste wird abgerissen, sobald der Bau vollendet ist" [L 8, 41]). In other words, historical proofs do not provide any grounds for religious truth, for its structure is considered in the same fashion as a building, as an "edifice is judged according to the agreed rules of good architecture" ("den Bau selbst nach den eingestandenen Regeln eines guten Architekts zu prüfen" [L 8, 41]).

Lessing's use of architectural imagery illustrates his move away from an ontology-based, substance metaphysics toward a proto-pragmatist mode of thought. His new approach views religion more in terms of its functions than in terms of a metaphysical essence. In considering the functional aspect as the decisive feature, Lessing prefigures the pragmatist turn to empirically accessible praxis as the sole criterion for constructing truth. In this he is antedated by Spinoza alone, who established the crucial separation of praxis from theory in the *Theological-Political Treatise.* It is interesting to note that Kant's critical move performs a very similar intervention that, in revolutionary fashion, recasts the theory/praxis divide anew. But Mendelssohn's stress on the priority of common sense over speculative reason also signals the same refusal to submit to pure speculative thought where truth is concerned.[3]

From a very different point of departure, Lessing simultaneously performs another move, one that, interestingly enough, winds up at practically the same conclusion. In the wake of the publication of the fragments of the "unnamed," the theologian Johann Daniel Schumann, whose *Ueber die Evidenz der Beweise für die Wahrheit der Christlichen Religion* appeared in the fall of 1777, ventured a first response. Lessing's reply consists of two parts. The first part, "On the Proof of the Spirit and the Power" ("Über den Beweis des Geistes und der Kraft"), examines Schumann's claim that the historic age of the Bible, along with its miracles and prophecies, testifies to the truth of the Christian religion. Against this view, Lessing maintains that any kind of proof for any historical truth remains altogether impossible, for anything that is brought forward as possible evidence is already implicated in the infinite regress of contingency to which all historical knowledge is subject. The evidence of historical truth is thus itself historical in nature. And while it may well be true on its own terms, for such evidence to serve as proof for the truth of a particular belief would mean to subject it to the mistake of confusing categories, for what has happened historically always remains contingent. This dependency on contingency makes it impossible to ground any necessary truth on it; that is, truth that is supposed to be removed from and independent of the process of history cannot be grafted on the contingent nature of history. To do this would mean to mistake categories of historical truth for logical truth. Lessing succinctly summarizes this categorical difference in the following formulation: "[A]ccidental truths of history can never become the proof of necessary truths of reason" (C 311) ("[Z]ufällige Geschichtswahrheiten können der Beweis von notwendigen Vernunftswahrheiten nie werden" [L 8, 12]). So, even while the reported facts—the occurrence of prophecies and miracles—may have taken place (and who could deny or reconfirm these occurrences except by recourse to historical documents, that is infinite hermeneutic regress), brute facticity in history—if such a thing existed—or the veracity of the stories does not per se carry implications as far as the truth of what they might signify is concerned.

But this is only half of Lessing's argument. The other half is contained in the appendix, "The Testament of John" ("Das Testament Johannis"). This is a dialogue between the author (*Ich*) and some interlocutor, simply referred to as he (*Er*). The dialogue picks up where the short essay left off. Brief, laconic, and almost a bit abrupt, this is an exercise in restrained talk and in holding back one's words—in short, in practicing what it preaches. The three-word sermon at the center of this dialogue—which presents, according to the narrator-author, the testament of St. John—is stylized into an irritating, even annoying reminder. The mere repetition of it seems to render it, if not absurd, into a stingingly reverberating memento. The author's refusal to engage in anything more than simple repetition of John's little sermon creates a vacuum of sense that, by its sheer, monotonous abstention from uttering anything more, raises all the more urgent suspicion on the part of the reader that this gestural silence and repetition should be recognized as a carefully coded hermeneutic message.

This is a text that marks the vanishing point of itself as text, signaling the pointed and ultimately rather eloquent, although monosyllabic, resignation that preaches by reducing its message to a single point. At the end of his days, the reader learns, John the Baptist had really just one thing to say, which he indulged himself by continually repeating his three-word message: "Kinderchen, liebt euch!" ("Little children, love one another!" [C 316–17]). With such preaching, he has left a naive understanding of language far behind. The relentless repetition stages a play on and with self-referentiality that also plays with both St. John's audience and the reader's patience; has St. John lost his mind?

The repetitive monotony of this "Kinderchen, liebt euch!" that mercilessly and continually resurfaces in the dialogue, however, curiously dwells at the threshold that divides and connects speech and action. The tireless reiteration that conjures the purity of the word at the same time reveals itself as the speech act that puts an end to words and calls for action. The mocking undertone and the comic effect of the absurd (is this John just a man who has lost his marbles and his audience but has not realized this yet?), however, is not a gesture that undermines the person or his message. Rather, and more importantly, this comic insistence exerts a powerful resistance to exegetical takeover. The self-referential character both saps such attempts and, at the same time, sends the reader on a search for the obviously necessary underlying subtext to "make sense" of the author's use of John's testament in the context of his dispute.

The text this incantation invokes is none other than Spinoza's *Theological-Political Treatise*.[4] The result of Spinoza's Bible interpretation in the *Treatise* is that (1) religion is indifferent to cognitive content, and its sociopolitical function as institution can be reduced to the guarantee of obedience; and (2) the moral content of both the Old and the

New Testaments can be identified in the command to love one's neighbor as oneself. In a way, then, Lessing's St. John converges exactly with Spinoza's *Theological-Political Treatise*. Both stress piety and love as the exclusive and central teaching. This might come as a surprise, but the version of St. John and his testament as it is expounded in Lessing does nothing less than suggest precisely such a connection.

This is no coincidence. Spinoza's *Treatise* bears its "pantheist" creed right on its title page: "Through this, we know that we remain in God and God remains in us: that he has given us of his Spirit" (1 John 4:13). And now the interplay of the two halves of Lessing's response to pastor Schumann reveals its deeper motivation through this two-faced appearance. The hermeneutic circle that is opened by the circular way historical evidence is produced reads like an abbreviated, brief, and condensed, yet illuminating variation of Spinoza's discussion. For one of Spinoza's main points in the *Treatise* is precisely to demonstrate that miracles and prophecies cannot prove anything and that, therefore, their actual occurrence provides, at best, historical veracity. Yet that veracity is tied to the infinite regress that can only provide proof through witnessing, that is, from other texts. In no case, however, would such historical occurrence—if it were shown to have taken place—provide anything like a proof for the truth of this or that claim made by this or that religion or religious institution.

Taken together, the two parts of Lessing's response represent the double move operating in Spinoza's *Theological-Political Treatise:* on the one hand, the argument of the limits of historical truth, and on the other, the radical and emancipatory fashion in which Spinoza conceives religion not as a reservoir of doctrine but as praxis. St. John's testament presents the praxis-based and praxis-oriented form of religiosity. In his response, Lessing thus gives Spinoza's separation of philosophy and religion, reason and belief, theory and praxis, a formally stringent actualization. Together, both halves of Lessing's answer, then, represent a remarkable reformulation of the central argument of the *Theological-Political Treatise*.

CHAPTER 14

THE SECRET OF THE PUBLIC

The Dialogues on Freemasonry, *Ernst and Falk*

FROM THE START OF HIS CAREER as a playwright, reviewer, publicist, and poet, Lessing displays an intimate grasp of the way publicity works. The consideration of its constitutive role for the functioning of civil society and the development of the individual presents a recurrent theme in Lessing and informs his style. But it is in *Ernst and Falk,* his *Dialogues for Freemasons,* that he addresses the problem of the public and publicity in programmatic manner. Yet, Lessing's *Dialogues* do not simply propose a theory of the public but proceed by way of investigating the opposite or reverse aspect of the public, its hidden presupposition and underpinning: the secret and the structure of secrecy. Already the subtitle of the dialogues, dedicating them to Freemasons, hints at everyone's entitlement to imagine himself a Freemason. For Freemasonry, the beginning of the first dialogue argues, has always existed as a necessary correction to civil society, one without which civil society cannot exist. It is so intimately connected with civil society that both are thought to be possible only when conceived as necessary factors of one phenomenon.

Although Reinhart Koselleck and Jürgen Habermas have offered pioneering studies of the formation of the public sphere,[1] linking it to the emergence of the bourgeoisie (suggestive and crucial as it may have been) has led to a limited understanding of the complexity involved in this process.[2] Central to the debate initiated by these two studies is how to translate the term *Öffentlichkeit.* Taking its cue from the translation of Habermas's study, the debate in political theory and intellectual history generally has opted for "public sphere." Although this seems to do full justice to the notion Habermas employs, it loses the connotations of publicity and publicness that, while not central to Habermas's argument, nevertheless retain in the German term *Öffentlichkeit* options for a more complex understanding.[3] Focusing on the "public sphere," the American debate has defined this issue in its own way. The reification of a concept that in the eighteenth century only served as a model for the self-constitutive discourse the philosophers envisioned has imposed its own epistemic interests. Instead of following these interests, however, the reexamination of the eighteenth century discussion about the public allows us to grasp the critical impulse that informs the Enlightenment concepts of the public and publicity.

The claim that Enlightenment philosophers argue for an elitist notion of the "public sphere" ignores the resolute efforts to formulate a theory of the public capable of accounting for civil society as the very medium through which the public alone is thought to constitute itself. Some of the eighteenth-century theorists are interested precisely in articulating a theory that grounds the concept of the public in the new sovereign it strives to install: the people. Whatever these thinkers might have conceived under this rubric, to interpret their move as elitist is to miss their trajectory at its very core.

Georg Simmel recognized the sociologically complex implications which determine the social relations that crystallize in the concepts of publicity and secrecy as mutually constituting elements of social interaction. In addressing the implications of the sociological dynamics at work in the act of letter writing, which hinges on the social consensus to honor the secrecy of what is communicated, Simmel points out that it is in sociological terms, ultimately, that the intrinsically public character of the private act of writing leads to the social, "public" cultivation of secrecy: "In the first place, writing is opposed to all secrecy. [. . .] The written form [. . .] involves an unlimited, even if only potential, 'publicity.'"[4] Simmel's reminder argues for an implicit dynamic between the two poles of the oppositional pair secret/public, a dynamic that obviates any further theorizing of the public sphere as a simple, clear-cut, and stable concept at the end of the eighteenth century. Instead, secrecy is the limit concept defined by publicity, just as the reverse is true for publicity. Neither exists as an independent concept; both are constituted by their mutually delimiting power. Thus to begin with assumptions that take either secrecy or publicity as a given sphere for formulating political theory[5] is to operate within a static framework that predetermines the subject. By contrast, eighteenth-century theorists such as Lessing and Kant[6] offer an approach that reveals a surprisingly self-reflective awareness.[7]

It is, however, the specific literary strategy in which Lessing has the theme take its course that makes for an intriguing intervention. Exposing the problematic nature of the naive understanding of the secret and the public, he replaces it with a model of mutually constitutive reciprocity that determines the public and the secret as dynamic and relational constituents that, in dialectical exchange, shape the tenuous construct of the oppositional pair secret/public. In developing this, the interlocutors espouse views that sound surprisingly similar to the central assumptions in Spinoza's political theory.[8] This is no coincidence, for it is only in the context of a critical political theory that it is possible to subject the function of the secret/public divide to a critical examination.

The opening dialogue of *Ernst and Falk* starts with the theme of the universal character of the spirit of Freemasonry. Falk—the one who betrays advanced knowledge of the secrets but remains reluctant to share his experience too quickly—is about to discuss the problem of the gap between the aspirations of Freemasons and the dire restrictions dictated by the world as it presents itself in reality when he interrupts the conversation to pursue a butterfly. Tellingly, his attempt to catch this symbol of beauty, spirituality, and airy evasiveness fails once the butterfly sets across a nearby creek and thus reaches the safety of inaccessibility. While such metaphysical chase is shown to lead nowhere, or rather, to come to an abrupt end at the unbridgeable abyss symbolized by the creek, Ernst—the soon-to-be novice—turns his attention to the observation of ants. Falk's hunting for a butterfly that metamorphoses from the curious caterpillar Wolfsmilchraupe (a name that might contain a wordplay on classic political theories that operated with the wolf/sheep paradigm) alludes to Falk's play with the promise of power that, correctly understood, carries the potential to turn into something as beautiful, poetic, and light-winged as a butterfly. It may be that the sphinx euphorbiae, whose colors change before it transforms into a colorful butterfly (another name in German, indicative of what Lessing has in mind here, is Wolfsmilchschwärmer), alludes to its feeding habits.[9] Since it feeds off plants of the family of the toxic *Wolfsmilch* or *Euphorbia*, its appearance may just visualize Falk's point that although the foundation of life may sometimes be poisonous, proper digestion produces the most beautiful results—freedom, for instance. At the same, this image invokes the danger involved in such metaphorical-metaphysical daydreaming. In contrast, Ernst's admiration of the social life of ants stands for his political down-to-earth approach of the commonsense standpoint that what you see is what you get.[10]

Naturally, or so it seems, the interest in these self-governing insects leads to some rather conspirational thoughts whose anarchist undercurrent forms the key passage on political theory, which in turn provides the theoretical framework for understanding the function of the construction of the oppositional pair secret/public:

> ERNST. The goings-on in and around this anthill here. What activity, and yet what orderliness! Everyone is carrying or dragging or pushing something, and not one gets in the other's way. Just look there. They're even helping one another. (Z 284)

> ERNST. Das Leben und Weben auf und in und um diesen Ameisenhaufen. Welche Geschäftigkeit, und doch welche Ordnung! Alles trägt und schleppt und schiebt; und keines ist dem andern hinderlich. Sieh nur! Sie helfen einander sogar. (L 8, 458)

Taking its cue from Proverbs 6:6–8, the passage alludes to the differentiated notion of change brought about not by great state actions but by the total accumulation of minuscule yet steady and incessant work "here and now." The ants' restless, steady, and harmonious work symbolizes the "Leben und Weben" of nature in general, a striking metaphor for the course "nature" takes when granted free reign. In a move that highlights Ernst's critical distance to classic political philosophy, the dialogues further unfold the metaphor of the ant-hill. As Falk comments upon Ernst's observation on the ant-hill with the remark: "Ants live in society like the bees" (Z, 284) ("Die Ameisen leben in Gesellschaft, wie die Bienen" [L 8, 458]), Ernst's reply lays the stress on the difference between the bee state and the society of ants. Critical of Hobbes's critique of Aristotle that had rejected any similarity between the social life of animals and human society,[11] Ernst's reply leads the way to some bold political conclusions: "And yet in an even more amazing society than bees. Because they don't have anybody among them who keeps them together and governs them" (Z, 284) ("Und in einer noch wunderbareren Gesellschaft als die Bienen. Denn sie haben niemand unter sich, der sie zusammenhält und regieret" [L 8, 458]). The critique of Hobbes could not be more poignant. But this remark aims at the same time at those political models—progressive or reactionary—that consider the individual as a mere functionary of the collective. Falk's conclusion that Ernst seems to suggest that order might very well exist without government prompts Ernst to note: "If every individual knows how to govern himself, why not? (Z, 284) ("Wenn jedes einzelne sich selbst zu regieren weiss: warum nicht?" [L 8, 458]). This exchange rehearses the key oppositions that stand at the center of modern political thought—individual versus society, contract versus natural association, top-down government versus self-determination, and, if you will, freedom versus necessity—with a critical purpose where the ant-hill serves as Lessing's counter-image for the state, his non-state, or "non-governmental organization" that literally self-organizes political life from the ground up.

The ideal of the self-organized cooperation that acts as if guided by a single mind echoes the key formula of Spinoza's *Political Treatise,* namely, that a well-organized state functions as if guided "una veluti mente."[12] Spinoza's *Ethics*, his *Theological-Political Treatise,* and the *Political Treatise* all articulate the same critical approach to classic political philosophy that Lessing advances in his dialogues. Both philosophers pose the problem of civil society and its foundations with strikingly similar urgency. Like Spinoza, Lessing argues that the natural state serves as the inalienable ground for the legitimation of the civil state and its institutions that will not be superseded or obliterated by civil society. And both take an uncompromising stand on the question whether civil society is to be considered as a means or an end in itself—that is whether human beings are meant to serve the state or the state is meant to serve human beings, and this means, all human beings as the distinction between the bee state and the ant-hill so pointedly suggests. But the argument takes a more challenging turn as the interlocutors come to address the ultimate challenge of civil society and a fundamental paradox in political thought: the fact that what unites people also separates them. Or even more paradoxically, as Ernst formulates Falk's insight: "mankind can be united only by division" (Z 289) ("die Menschen sind nur durch Trennung zu vereinigen" [L 8, 464]). This is Lessing's dialectic way to articulate a powerfully liberating if not revolutionary insight into the constructedness of political structures, an insight that directly translates into the idea that what is man made can, as a matter of consequence, also be changed by man. The point that uniting people means always at the same time dividing them implies that each and every political form of statehood has its own to structural flaws. In other words, the dialectics between state and society is necessary but it also points the way toward freedom and progress. Falk describes this dialectic in terms of the fire that can only be domesticated, channeled, and made powerful when a chimney absorbs its smoke and thus enables the fire. If fire requires a chimney for smooth operation, so—Falk argues—civil society requires some political institutions. His use of the fireplace expresses in no uncertain terms how he theorizes the relationship between state and society, a trope that implies that nature remains the ultimate authority over man made constructions, which, as a consequence, must always remain open to renegotiation and reinvention. It is no wonder that such a view required the kind of careful packaging Lessing's dialogues provide as they dress this point in one of the period's favored costumes, that of Freemasonry.

Falk articulates a view of the task of the state that formulates the criteria of its quality in exactly the same way Spinoza's *Political Treatise* does:

> The sum of the individual happiness of all members is the happiness of the state. Beyond this, there is none whatsoever. Every other happiness of the state, by which however few individual members suffer or *are compelled* to suffer, is a cover-up for tyranny. Nothing else! (Z 285)

> Das Totale der einzeln Glückseligkeiten aller Glieder, ist die Glückseligkeit des Staats. Außer dieser gibt es gar keine. Jede andere Glückseligkeit des Staats, bei welcher auch noch so wenig einzelne Glieder leiden, und leiden *müssen,* ist Bemäntelung der Tyrannei. Anders nichts! (L 8, 459)[13]

Tellingly, Ernst agrees but worries about Falk's boldness to speak his mind. And this reservation makes him in Falk's eyes already half a Freemason: "Because you already recognize truths which are better left unsaid" (Z 285) ("Denn Du erkennst ja schon Wahrheiten, die man besser verschweigt" [L 8, 459]). But before the question of keeping quiet about such issues in public is addressed, the dialogue continues on another topic. In continuing the discussion that forms of governments are just means to pursue human happiness, the friends arrive at the agreement that, as a consequence, forms of governments are just "means of man's invention" (Z 285; L 8, 459). Thus identified as a human invention, they by definition lack perfection. Although they certainly can be optimized, the fact that they are man-made makes it impossible that even the best form of government—if there were such a thing—would be faultless (Z 287; L 8, 461).[14]

Here, Falk introduces a striking argument. For if we hold that there were such a thing as the best form of government, and if we further assume that all human beings of the world would live under this best form of government, we still could not imagine that there would only be a single state constituted by all of humanity (Z 287; L 8, 461). In other words, civil society in its various political forms of state organization is only possible in the plural of different particular realizations of a universal idea. Because human beings do not exist in civil society as natural individuals but always already in socially and historically particular forms of existence, any effort to join them also calls forth structures of division (L 8, 462). This idea is so central to Falk that he repeats it and expands on its implications. The paradox of civil society, then, is: "It cannot unite men without dividing them; not divide them, without establishing rifts between them, without putting walls among them" (Z 289) ("Sie kann die Menschen nicht vereinigen, ohne sie zu trennen; nicht trennen, ohne Klüfte zwischen ihnen zu befestigen, ohne Scheidemauern durch sie hin zu ziehen" [L 8, 463]). It is this paradox that calls forth its corrective countermovement—a movement that much later is given the name of the Freemasons. Whether or not Lessing's theory about the origin of Freemasonry is correct[15] is of little importance as far as the argumentative trajectory of the dialogues is concerned, for Freemasonry serves here as the colorful and playful backdrop for a discussion of the dialectics of the universal and the particular in the socio-theologico-political sphere. In bringing into play the question of secrecy and publicity, Lessing enacts the dynamic dialectics of the constitutive reciprocity of the oppositional pair secret/public. But Falk makes it clear that to arrest these dialectics at an arbitrary moment in order to exploit them for the purpose of particularist interests would be to misunderstand his point altogether. Well coded as the political sympathies are, Lessing leaves no doubt as to where his sympathies lie: "It's very much to be wished for that there might be in every state men who were above the prejudices of the populace and who would know exactly where patriotism ceases to be a virtue" (Z 290) ("Recht sehr zu wünschen, daß es in jedem Staate Männer geben möchte, die über die Vorurteile der Völkerschaft hinweg wären, und genau wüßten, wo Patriotismus, Tugend zu sein aufhöret"

[L 8, 465]). Contrary to the still popular opinion that patriotism serves as an uncontested value that, in whatever refined and "universalized" form, rules supreme, Lessing has Falk speak a clear and unequivocal language. It is thus, as Falk puts it, the mission of the wise men free of prejudices with regard to historical religions ("angeborne Religion") and free of prejudices with regard to class and rank ("welche bürgerliche Hoheit nicht blendet, und bürgerliche Geringfügigkeit nicht ekelt" [Z 290; L 8, 465]) to transcend the historically sedimented particularist divisions. Leaving such divisions behind, these wise men direct people toward a society and states whose specific particularity nevertheless allows for some refined form of universalism, despite, and possibly because of, a critically understood form of particularism.

> FALK. What if it were the Freemasons, who were to make it *just* one of their endeavors to draw those divisions, whereby men become so alien to one another, as close together as possible? (Z 291)

> FALK. Wie, wenn es die Freimäurer wären, die sich *mit* zu ihrem Geschäfte gemacht hätten, jene Trennungen, wodurch die Menschen einander so fremd werden, so eng als möglich wieder zusammen zu ziehen? (L 8, 465–66)

At this point, however, Falk interrupts himself and has Ernst follow him to join the others for breakfast. Not until that night can Ernst get a hold of Falk, when he finally, excited by the morning discussion, follows Falk into his bedroom. For, the whole day while they were in company participating in social diversions that had "joined" but also separated the two friends in society and thus prevented them from pursuing their subject, they had no opportunity to continue their dialogue. Now, however, in private, they are able to resume their conversation. Yet, Falk's observations remain just general and abstract enough to spurn Ernst's enthusiasm without obstructing it with the gray shades of reality. As a consequence, between the third and fourth dialogues Ernst joins the Freemasons, only to suffer from sobering disillusion for which he now blames his friend Falk.[16] For, in his view, Falk had let him indulge in childlike dreaming without clear warning about the illusionary hazards awaiting those admitted to a Freemasons lodge.

However, it is not until after having had this experience—which occurs, so to speak, outside the text and between the lines—that Falk, who has long left the circles of the carefree social life of the Freemasons, is prepared to touch on the issue of secrecy. To make his point, he distinguishes between the making of secrets by simple hiding (*Heimlichkeiten;* "private matters") and the secret (*Geheimnis;* "mystery") (L 8, 476; Z 298). This makes it possible to now express the decisive difference between those *Heimlichkeiten* that can very well be expressed but are kept secret due to envy, fear, or caution (*Klugheit*) and the true secret of Freemasonry, which the Freemason could not express even if he wished to.

At the beginning of the third dialogue, Ernst summarizes in passing Falk's point on the secret, a point Falk himself has, so far in the dialogue, not really cared to express with such clarity:

> FALK. Well then? In the intoxication of that Pyrmont mineral water we were drinking, I didn't reveal the mystery to you, did I?
> ERNST. Which, as you say, can't be revealed anyhow. (Z 292)

> FALK. Nun?—Ich habe dir im Rausche des Pyrmonter doch nicht das Geheimnis verraten?
> ERNST. Das man, wie du sagst, gar nicht verraten kann. (L 8, 466)[17]

The full meaning of this point is now further developed in the fourth and fifth dialogues. While the holding back of *Heimlichkeiten* presupposes and maintains a static framework of a fixed division into distinct spheres of the public and the secret whose borderlines can be crossed at will, the secret that cannot be expressed challenges such a nondialectical conception of secrecy. Only now, after Falk has clarified the difference between *Heimlichkeit* and *Geheimnis,* he sees that the time has come to launch a discussion on the historical origins of Freemasonry. And not surprisingly, the study of that history displays more of *Heimlichkeiten* than of *Geheimnis.* Active in the world of politics and power, Freemasonry, like any other organization, follows the laws of institutional self-assertion. This leads to the need to distinguish the institution from its idea.[18]

In this context, Lessing introduces his well-proved opposition between spirit and letter. In our case, Falk couches his application of this distinction in the following way: the lodge of the Freemasons relates to Freemasonry the way the church relates to belief (Z 301; L 8, 478). Lessing's previous writings have left no doubts as to what the second half of this clause means. His writings consistently differentiate between, on the one hand, the institutionally manifest realizations of Christianity as the result of church organization and, on the other hand, the spirituality, purity, and profundity of the religion of Christ.[19] The conceptual explosive of this distinction also effectively relativizes the claims of the business of Freemasonry, at that time a growing, widespread pastime of the emerging bourgeoisie. Again, just after having shared with Ernst some of his critical insights, Falk demands that during lunch with his guests there will not be any talk about this subject. The fifth dialogue will reveal the irony implied in this request to keep quiet with regard to such matters when at the table.

As soon as they meet again in private, Ernst urges Falk to return to their subject. Tired of the company they enjoyed during lunch, Ernst complains about one of the fellows, but when Falk comments that this man belongs to those "who fight in Europe for the Americans," Ernst replies: "This would not be the worst side in him."[20] From the start, this concluding dialogue makes it clear that the political fight for freedom is, while intimately connected to the cause of Freemasonry, nevertheless not simply identical with it. What this means becomes clear only when Lessing outlines his critical genealogy of the Freemasons. He not only destroys the myth of the Freemasons as builders and architects, as has often been observed, but more importantly offers a commentary on social contract theories. Rather than originating from a secret, Falk explains, Freemasonry originates from small social gatherings that, in turn, serve as the social cells out of which civil society constitutes itself. Instead of being thought to be adversarial in nature and solely bound by the introduction of (the fiction of) a social contract, individuals form society through a bond based on sociability. Like publicity, sociability is anything but a utopian ideal. It is the very foundation on which human life rests. Contrary to the contract models of Hobbes, Locke, and Rousseau, this model, based on social fusion, highlights the noncontractual nature of civil society's foundations.

In its critical distinction from Hobbes, Lessing's dialogue points to Spinoza, who identifies in fusion or union the initial moment of the constitution of civil society. Operating outside the framework of compact or contract, Spinoza's theory of social association allows for a political theory of rights that, contrary to those defined by theories of contract, refuses to acknowledge the transfer of power and rights to a third party as a necessary precondition for the foundation of a civil state. In contrast to the classic view of contract theory, Spinoza holds: "If two men come together and join forces, they have more power over Nature, and consequently more right, than either one alone; and the greater the number who form a union in this way, the more right they will together possess."[21] In the light of this subtext, Lessing's dialogues suggest more than a harmless conversation. They articulate a pointed political vision that conveys an eminently Spinozist concern for a politics of universal emancipation. When Falk discloses the "secret" history of the Freemasons, Ernst reacts with a question: What prevents this disclosure from being written down? (Ironically, Lessing has just done so!) Falk retorts: There will be no more secrets. But what if Falk's disclosure is only conjectural? Where is the evidence for putting an end to all secrets? Falk refers to his library.[22] But what is crucial is the way he thinks about the books that serve as evidence for his claims. It is precisely the scriptural materiality—publicity in its material form, not as ideal, but as potentiality in the sense of Simmel—that provides the concrete and self-evident proof: proof for publicity as the foundation of social and political life. Referring to the books, Falk's penultimate sentence is: "You shall see and grasp it in my books."[23] The conclusion the reader is invited to draw is that publicity is initiated behind closed doors, in private, in the study. That is, it is through the study—through the written word, that which can be spread, circulated, and disseminated—through the private space, that publicity comes into being.

Secrets are secrets because they are publicity contained, postponed, supplemented, displaced, exchanged, and contorted. Publicity is the secret of being wary of this, of acknowledging that to be in the know implies a relational, sociological act that lives off the virtuality of the very concept of publicity it posits for its grounding, whether or not and in whatever way it may be delimited.

In this, rather than in the whole debate about the various forms of *Heimlichkeiten* that the history of Freemasonry provides in such abundance, consists the theoretical critique these dialogues articulate. They address the constructed and therefore infinitely perfectible nature of civil society with a radically emancipatory interest that displays a profound resemblance with Spinoza's theory of the political constitution of civil society and the state.

Lessing's reflections on the intimate reciprocity that constitutes the private and the public unfolds its critical potential along the lines of a discussion of the key concepts of Spinoza's political theory. Lessing's pronounced advocacy for understanding publicity in its intrinsically dialectic tensions that drive the oppositional pair secret/public thus sheds light on Spinoza's emphasis on the fundamental role of public discourse. While the *Theological-Political Treatise* deploys a powerful argument for the necessity of a culture of public debate that Lessing artfully recirculates through the idioms of his time, Lessing's insight about the constitutive role of publicity in the search for truth finds its prefiguration in the argument with which Spinoza had grounded his advocacy for freedom of thought and its expression: "The fact is that men's wits are too obtuse to get straight to the heart of every question, but by discussing, listening to others, and debating, their wits are sharpened, and by exploring every avenue they eventually discover what they are seeking, something that meets with general approval and that no one had previously thought of."[24]

CHAPTER 15

THEORIZING THE ENLIGHTENMENT

Spinoza in *The Education of Mankind*

IN THE CONTEXT OF HIS OBJECTIONS to the fragments of the "unnamed," Lessing develops his own views with regard to religion, revelation, history, and individualization. Having formulated them as a critical response to the ideas put forward in the fragments, Lessing starts out publishing the first fifty-three paragraphs of *The Education of Mankind* in 1777 as an anonymous text he inserts in his "Objections by the Editor" that appear as an appendix to the fragments of the "unnamed."[1] In 1780, again just posing as its editor, Lessing publishes the complete draft of one hundred paragraphs along with a motto from Augustine and an introductory note.

Conceived as a thought experiment, the *Education* bears some resemblance to the Spinozistic exercises of the 1760s. In one instance the text even takes up the discussion where two decades earlier the exercises had left off. While already early on interpreted as Lessing's testament,[2] such an interpretation ignores the fact that the *Education* is foremost a contribution to a debate in which the author's point is not to reach final conclusions but to ignite debate. The author's gesture of leaving a legacy, his announcement of the third age and its new testament, serves as literary device to rethink the implications of the specific forms of religious discourse at stake. To equate Lessing's authorial role play with the assumption of authorship of a testament would be tantamount to ignoring the elaborate staging of the editorial framing of a text that, rather, broaches the question how testaments operate. However, despite all the precautions taken, the quasi-canonical status attributed to this text has led most commentators to neglect the significance of its distinct epistemological critical impulse. But it is precisely the critique of theological speculation—although innocuously clothed in the mantle of theological speculation—that lies at the heart of the *Education.*

The text's form, style, and diction make it clear that its mode is experimental, probing, suggestive, and inquisitive rather than assertive or affirmative.[3] Toying with the loftiest ideas of human speculation about God, man, history, and immortality, the text creates a free discursive space that allows for the possibility of thought experiments unfettered by the constrictions of theological expectations and commitments. The experimental mode of the *Education* resists all attempts to press for precocious conclusions, which, as far as the text itself is concerned, would be only of interest as problems, questions, and suggestions provoking a further examination to demarcate the limits of the grounds of reason. Paragraph 31 expresses this most clearly when it observes that "to think over an idea about which before no one troubled himself in the least, is halfway to knowledge" (Z 325) ("in Überlegung ziehen, warum man sich vorher ganz und gar nicht bekümmerte, ist der halbe Weg zur Erkenntnis" [L 8, 497]). Lessing's one hundred theses invoke literary reminiscences of such models as Luther's historic Wittenberg theses and the church fathers' style of writing. Yet the *Education*'s intertextual play with theological form and style artfully signals the critical difference at the heart of Lessing's piece. The sheer "contemporariness of the non-contemporary" that this text stages clothes its ideas in a historic patina that seems to command the reader's uncompromising attention. Rather than a theological speculation, it suggests a critical reflection on the theological-political implications of the relationship between reason and belief, philosophy and religion. This is also why, instead of presenting a full treatment of the crucial theological issues, the *Education* addresses a particular set of points. This set follows—with the exception of the complex of immortality and metempsychosis—point for point the trajectory of the argument so effectively deployed in Spinoza's *Theological-Political Treatise.*[4] Yet, while most studies acknowledge one or another striking similarity (or occasionally an entire catalog of such similarities) between Lessing and Spinoza, the specific critical achievement of Lessing's productive Spinoza reception and its larger implications for the history of philosophy and the interpretation of the development of enlightenment remain curiously unappreciated. However, it is precisely the philosophically stringent attempt at a reformulation of Spinoza under the sign of the emerging but already critically conceived historicism that makes Lessing's *Education* a decisive moment in the reception of Spinoza.

Often mistaken for a contribution to theology,[5] the work's opening paragraphs signal a very different take. In a nutshell, they introduce Spinoza's argument of the separation of reason and belief, religion and philosophy. The functional equation of education with revelation at the very start sets the tone for the contemplative and, at the same time, poignantly dialectical mode of these theses. For education, it soon becomes clear, is in this context exclusively understood to stand for moral education, not for intellectual training or transfer of information and knowledge. What may look like a theological point thus betrays, from the start, a distinctly theology-critical note. The theory of Moses' mission is only the first stage of teaching, exclusively conceived for the Jewish people of that time. It is a mission that provides the Jews with an *Elementarbuch* (basic textbook) that leaves room enough for future speculations, much the way any sound basic textbook is supposed to introduce, rather than close off, vistas unto new fields. And if such a textbook does not itself already spell out more advanced insights, it also does not preclude any future interpretation leading to the discovery of such insights as are already contained in the original revelation itself (esp. §§26 and 68–69). The praise for the "heroic obedience" of the Jewish people for their continuous adherence to the God-decreed laws and commandments (§§32 and 33) is not only an homage to the loyalty of an ancient people but also a reference to Spinoza's sociological insight that the function of religion consists in obedience and obedience alone.[6]

The functional notion of divine revelation as a sociopolitical institution to stabilize humanity on its course through history is different both from a salvation history and from its secularized version as transformation into a history of progress. Rather, it is—and the pervasiveness of the author's stress on the functional role of revelation throughout the *Education* bears a clear Spinozist ring—a meditation on the implications inherent in any construction of individualization and history. If we read the text in this way, it becomes clear that the weak structure of the argument presented is strong enough to sustain this point, whereas a reading that would mistake it for a claim to theological validity would bring it to collapse under the heavy weight of such an expectation.[7]

Also, Lessing's emphasis that the New Testament replaces the Old entails the tacit corollary that in function and principle the two testaments differ in no way from each other. This idea is based on Spinoza's hermeneutic reduction of both religions to one common core, which he identifies in their shared task to guarantee obedience and the principle of the command to love one's neighbor as oneself. Whereas the historicizing scheme that informs the *Education* presents the order of different stages of revelation according to the Augustinian tripartition of history into the scheme of child-youth-adult, this view is based on the assumption that functionally the more refined version replaces its precursor precisely because, in terms of performance, their difference consists only in degree but not in substance and function.[8] In a way, then, the *Education* is to be read not only in terms of what it says but equally in terms of what it leaves unsaid yet what it nevertheless tacitly, albeit no less distinctly, seems to suggest. This is, however, no esotericism[9] but rather the kind of dialogical exchange that presupposes a reader who rethinks the proposed arguments in order to contradict, complement, and add what the text in its innocuous and unassuming but no less challenging manner projects as possibilities for contemplation.

Paragraph 73 commands particular attention for its sheer length, which sets it apart from the otherwise briefly and laconically worded paragraphs. Contrary to the pointed diction of the rest of the text, this paragraph contains an essay in itself. On the surface it appears to offer an interpretation of trinity, but Lessing employs the seemingly innocuous appearance of a discussion about trinity to revisit ideas earlier developed in "Das Christentum der Vernunft" (1753) and in his Spinozistic exercises of 1764. Paragraph 73 presents, however, a new stage in Lessing's speculation on trinity. If in 1753 the examination of the idea of trinity was the subject of Lessing's attempt at formulating a rational theology of Christianity,[10] he addressed the philosophical implications of Spinoza's ontological formulation of the problem a decade later in "Über die Wirklichkeit der Dinge außer Gott" and the exchange with Mendelssohn.[11] In order to highlight the problem of the Leibnizian two-world theory when compared with Spinoza's ultimately more convincing solution he had discussed with Mendelssohn, Lessing now submits trinity to an allegorical application. In this context, trinity becomes the heuristic vehicle to examine the metaphysical implications of the difference between Spinoza and Leibniz, between the framework of a philosophy of immanence and one of transcendence.[12] And it is, therefore, not without pointed irony that Lessing cites trinity in support for the idea of immanence. As a consequence, trinity is redefined in a crucial way. It is now no longer just a theological figure that commands intellectual submission lending itself to ridicule such as Heine's observation, "that the multiplication table [. . .] suspiciously collides with the sacred doctrine of trinity" ("daß das Einmaleins [. . .] doch mit der heiligen Dreiheitslehre bedenklich kollidiert").[13] Rather, and very much in the way "revelation" is understood to be education, it now serves as vehicle to inquire into the question of how God and creation relate to each other, or in other words, how transcendence can be conceived within a theoretically consistent framework of immanence. To have trinity support a Spinozist argument is one of those sublime theological pranks Lessing enjoys playing. But its rather serious consequence consists in a liberatory reassignment of trinity, which no longer serves just as symbol for an article of faith or doctrine but is now deployed as an elucidating model to probe the metaphysical implications of the difference between an immanent and a transcendent model of world explanation.

Lessing's introduction of the image of the mirror illustrates with its doubling of images the aporetic implications to which the concept of God as extra-mundane transcendence finally leads. Lessing had used the same image already in his draft "Über die Wirklichkeit der Dinge außer Gott." And as the discussion of 1764 illustrates, the mirror image is an unambiguous pointer for the demonstration of the superiority of Spinoza's philosophy of immanence over Leibniz's solution to introduce a complicated two-world explanation to resolve the problems produced by his metaphysics.

Jacobi, who can easily be accused of having misunderstood Spinoza, and sometimes Lessing too, observes, however, with regard to §73, and in this case remarkably to the point:

> I would like to know how anyone can make sense of this passage without recourse to Spinozist ideas. With these, however, the commentary becomes straightforward. Spinoza's God is the pure principle of reality in all that is real, the principle of being in all that exists, entirely without individuality, simply and plainly infinite.[14]

> Ich möchte wissen, ob sich jemand diese Stelle anders, als nach Spinozistischen Ideen deutlich machen kann. Nach diesen aber wird der Commentar

> sehr leicht. Der Gott des Spinoza, ist das *lautere* Prinzipium der Würklichkeit in allem Würklichen, des *Seyns* in allem Daseyn, durchaus ohne Individualität, und schlechterdings unendlich.[15]

While it is certainly true that Jacobi had his own hermeneutic agenda, his pointing out of the Spinozist implications of this passage exposes what most critics have glossed over: the Spinozist undercurrent of §73. In principle, Jacobi is correct if one adds that, rather than replacing a Christian with a Spinozist point of view, Lessing engages Spinoza's metaphysics in order to expose the systemic problems traditional metaphysics is bound to incur.

Jacobi was further on the mark to recognize that by following the cue that his interpretation of §73 represents, he was able to shed elucidating light on "the whole essay, thought through with such profundity."[16] For this paragraph formulates the basic conceptual structure on which the speculation on the concept of its philosophy of history hinges. The meditation on the monist principle as model for the understanding of creation and, as a consequence, of the structure of nature in general thus also serves as the link between metaphysics and the concept of history. In this context, the paragraph grounds the reflection on how the genetic principle of the concept of a philosophical-historical model can be formulated in a fully secularized framework.[17] In this way the paragraph serves as the crucial axis that connects Lessing's concept of history with Spinozist metaphysics. For if history is what emerges from the difference between nature as the creative force of divinity and the mirror-like representation of it as self-consciousness, the genetic concept of history can now be theorized on the solid grounds of history as embedded in, and thus based on, a conception of God that is both consistently monist and immanent.

A conventional attack against a purely immanent understanding of the *Education* is often launched by juxtaposing §§4 and 77.[18] While, at the outset, Lessing equates revelation and education in a way that takes all transcendent otherworldliness from the notion of revelation, §77 seems to oppose such a radical interpretation. There, Lessing notes that revelation leads us to better notions which reason alone might not have discovered. However, Lessing phrases this whole paragraph as a question. And for Lessing—and this point cannot be overstated—not all questions are rhetorical and come with clear-cut answers. Rather, as he observes at one point, writing serves for him the purpose of experimentation for the sake of self-clarification. How intimately Lessing experiences the connection of thought experiment and his writing is expressed in a telling paradox, if it is one:

> What a pity I cannot think without the pen in my hand! What pity! I only think for my own instruction. If my thoughts satisfy me, I tear the paper apart. If they don't, I have it printed.

> Nur Schade, daß ich nicht nachdenken kann, ohne mit der Feder in der Hand! Zwar was Schade! Ich denke nur zu meiner eigenen Belehrung. Befriedigen mich meine Gedanken am Ende: so zerreiße ich das Papier. Befriedigen sie mich nicht: so lasse ich es drucken.[19]

As the following paragraphs of the *Education* demonstrate, as well as the critical continuo running through the whole piece, §77 does pose a question—a question, however, that it by no means attempts to answer:

> And why should not we too, by means of a religion whose historical truth, if you will, looks dubious, be led in a similar way to closer and better conceptions of the divine Being, of our own nature, of our relation to God, which human reason would never have reached on its own? (C 331)

> Und warum sollten wir nicht auch durch eine Religion, mit deren historischen Wahrheit, wenn man will, es so mißlich aussieht, gleichwohl auf nähere und bessere Begriffe vom göttlichen Wesen, von unsrer Natur, von unsern Verhältnissen zu Gott, geleitet werden können, auf welche die menschliche Vernunft von selbst nimmermehr gekommen wäre? (§77)

Henry Allison has convincingly argued that a simple juxtaposition of this paragraph and §4 ignores the dialectical development that the concept of revelation is subject to undergo in the course of the *Education*—a development wherein the old concept of revelation eventually overcomes itself.[20] The implicit point of the *Education* would, after all, as Allison observes, be a difficult one to reconcile with the idea of conventional transcendence of revelation: "Thus, the defense of revelation offered in *The Education of the Human Race* does, indeed, issue in the complete rejection of the traditional conception."[21] Allison cites §§72 and 75 to illustrate his point. In addition, a key for this question can be found in §§36 and 37, which highlight the dynamic dialectic that casts revelation and education as reciprocally constitutive concepts. Paragraph 36 reads: "Revelation had guided their [i.e., the Jewish people's] reason, and now, all at once, reason gave clearness to their revelation" (C 325) ("Die Offenbarung hatte seine Vernunft geleitet, und nun erhellte die Vernunft auf einmal seine Offenbarung"). Lessing's compelling argument here is that the encounter with advanced civilizations during the Babylonian exile led the Jewish people to refine their notions of revelation on the newly acquired ground of autonomous reason. Already at this early stage, therefore, the concept of revelation undergoes a decisive transformation. Paragraph 37 summarizes this historic development and highlights the dialectical character of the relationship between revelation and education:

> This was the first reciprocal influence which these two (reason and revelation) exercised on one another; and so far is such a mutual influence from being unbecoming to the author of them both, that without it either of them would have been useless. (C 325)

> Das war der erste wechselseitige Dienst, den beide einander leisteten; und dem Urheber beider ist ein solcher gegenseitiger Einfluß so wenig unanständig, daß ohne ihm eines von beiden überflüssig sein würde. (§37)

Paragraph 73 and its Spinozist point can now be understood as a coded yet challenging plea for a consistent conception of immanence.

But the critical impulse not only informs the trajectory of Lessing's argument but also articulates itself explicitly in the pointed and resolute stand on liberty of thought eloquently taking on the politically radical thrust articulated in Spinoza's *Theological-Political Treatise.* In §78, Lessing expresses the critical concern that lies at the heart of the *Education.* Just after §77, quoted above, he continues with what is his very own declaration of intention:

> It is not true that speculations upon these things have ever done harm or been injurious to civil society. Reproach is due, not to these speculations, but to the folly and tyranny which tried to keep them in bondage; a folly and tyranny which would not allow men to develop their own thoughts. (C 331–32)

> Es ist nicht wahr, daß Spekulationen über diese Dinge jemals Unheil gestiftet, und der bürgerlichen Gesellschaft nachteilig geworden.—Nicht den

> Spekulationen: dem Unsinne, der Tyrannei, diesen Spekulationen zu steuern; Menschen, die ihre eigenen hatten, nicht ihre eigenen zu gönnen, ist dieser Vorwurf zu machen. (§78)

Read together with the succeeding paragraph, this passage almost literally echoes the program announced in the declaration of the content of Spinoza's *Theological-Political Treatise* as proclaimed on its title page. There, Spinoza spells out the practical core concern of his treatise, namely, to convince the reader not only of the feasibility but, more importantly, of the fundamental necessity of *libertas philosophandi,* the freedom to think and express one's thoughts freely, as the condition for peace, stability, and productivity: "Theologico-Political Treatise containing some Dissertations by which it is shown not only that the Freedom of Philosophizing can be Granted in keeping with Piety and the Peace of the Republic, but that it cannot be Removed unless along with that very Piety and the Peace of the Republic." This is an argument that, indeed, informs the whole of the *Treatise* and gives it its poignant acuity—a programmatic declaration that both opens and concludes the work.[22] As Lessing continues in §79, now explicating the second part of the *Treatise*'s program:

> On the contrary, though they may in individual instances be found wanting, speculations of this sort are unquestionably the most fitting exercises of the human reason that exist, just as long as the human heart, as such, is capable to the highest degree of loving virtue for its eternal blessed consequences. (C 332)

> Vielmehr sind dergleichen Spekulationen—mögen sie im Einzeln doch ausfallen, wie sie wollen—unstreitig die *schicklichsten* Übungen des menschlichen Verstandes überhaupt, so lange das menschliche Herz überhaupt, höchstens nur vermögend ist, die Tugend wegen ihrer ewigen glückseligen Folgen zu lieben. (§79)

That the radical nature of freedom of thought invoked here is indeed grounded in Spinoza is made explicit in §80. In contrast to the French and British materialist, empiricist, and sensualist conceptions of Enlightenment and in distinction to the German versions of reform Enlightenment which aim at reform and modernization of theology,[23] Lessing calls for unrestricted enlightenment which does not limit itself at simply investigating "which concerns our bodily needs" ("was unsere körperlichen Bedürfnisse betrifft"). For to limit reason in such a way would entail its subjection to dullness instead of honing the mind's capacities. Understanding (*Verstand*), Lessing emphasizes,

> is absolutely necessary . . . to be exercised on intellectual [Z has: spiritual] objects, if it is to attain its complete enlightenment [Z has: perfect illumination], and bring out that purity of heart which makes us capable of loving virtue for its own sake alone. (C 332)

> will schlechterdings an geistigen Gegenständen geübt sein, wenn er zu seiner völligen Aufklärung gelangen, und diejenige Reinigkeit des Herzens hervorbringen soll, die uns, die Tugend um ihrer selbst willen zu lieben, fähig macht. (§80)

This is a clear reference to the *Ethics*' notorious concluding and key proposition that true virtue is its own reward (E5P42). The deliberate citation of this proposition highlights Lessing's approach of bringing together religious and philosophical concerns without causing a standstill of the dialectics at work in his conception of history. Thus the political, ethical, metaphysical, and religious strands of Spinoza's philosophy of immanence combine here in a program of philosophy of history that refuses to sacrifice the individualism of the individual but regards the moment of enlightenment as the moment of the realization of individual virtue under the sign of social and historical fulfillment.

The next paragraph, which consists of one question, transforms the question of enlightenment into one of philosophy of history: "Or is the human species never to arrive at this highest step of enlightenment [Z has: illumination] and purity?—Never?" (C 332) ("Oder soll das menschliche Geschlecht auf diese höchste Stufen der Aufklärung und Reinigkeit nie kommen? Nie?" [§81]). Yet such a "never," Lessing insists, would be unacceptable. "Education has its goal" (§82), and this goal lies in the future. However—and this is the crucial turning point in Lessing's considerations on philosophy of history and the radical impulse of the conception of enlightenment now possible on the grounds of such historical awareness—the future itself, though a firm guiding point, can no longer rule the present and serve legitimatory purposes. As Lessing puts his rejection of teleological arguments:

> No! It will come! it will assuredly come! the time of the completion [Z has: perfecting], when man, the more convinced his understanding feels about an ever better future, will nevertheless not need to borrow motives for his actions from this future; for he will do right because it *is* right, not because arbitrary rewards are set upon it, which formerly were intended simply to fix and strengthen his unsteady gaze in recognizing the inner, better, rewards of well-doing. (Z 332)

> Nein, sie wird kommen, sie wird gewiß kommen, die Zeit der Vollendung, da der Mensch, je überzeugter sein Verstand einer immer bessern Zukunft sich fühlet, von dieser Zukunft gleichwohl Bewegungsgründe zu seinen Handlungen zu erborgen, nicht nötig haben wird; da er das Gute tun wird, weil es das Gute ist, nicht weil willkührliche Belohnungen darauf gesetzt sind, die seinen flatterhaften Blick ehedem bloß heften und stärken sollten, die innern bessern Belohnungen desselben zu erkennen. (§85)[24]

The philosophical-historical potential of Spinoza's conclusion of the *Ethics* is thus unfolded in its radical, uncompromising, and emancipatory implications. The notion of enlightenment that originates in this anti-teleological move is anything but naively progress-oriented. Instead, it presents a profound critique of any legitimation inclined to turn to the future in order to legitimate the present, whether such reasoning be theological or secularized. In a remarkable twist, then, Lessing points out that the time of fulfillment will be the time which realizes that fulfillment always takes place in the present. A truly Spinozist thought, indeed.

The argument of the *Education* thus projects itself less as a theological exercise than as a principal challenge to theological thinking. The thrust of the philosophical thought of immanence unfolds by way of a reflection of philosophy of history that energetically replaces the figure of teleological thought with a grasp on history that proposes, at the same time, an interpretation of Spinoza that does full critical justice to the exigencies of emerging historicism. Thus, at the threshold of historical consciousness, Lessing broaches the problem of the status of narrative constructions of history in the form of heuristic fiction. That this is expressed by way of an appropriation of Spinoza attests both to the challenging potential of Spinoza's thought and to Lessing's critical perceptiveness.

CHAPTER 16

NEGOTIATING TRUTH

On Nathan's Business

THE POLITICS OF READING AND STAGING *Nathan the Wise* have come to brand the play as extraordinary, exceptional, extreme, and unique. Yet such a reception has led to the appraisal of the drama as the product of an anemic humanism, curiously removed from the historical conflicts of the time. To detach and isolate Lessing's last great production and analyze it separately, as is often done, would be tantamount to heaving out the cornerstone of an arcade in the desire to celebrate it all by itself, leaving the arcade in rubble.

However, viewed in the context of the trajectory of Lessing's thought, the play emerges as the site where enlightenment, emancipation, and the problems of a liberal constitution of modern civil society are injected onto the scene of the public. Paying attention to the role of the specifically Spinozist aspects in the drama leads to a better grasp of this drama as a crucial juncture in Lessing's development.

Nathan the Wise stands at the end of a rich series of productions, and if we follow their development a trajectory becomes visible that allows us to understand why *Nathan* is not an exception or a piece of self-transcendence but rather the last and most gripping and conclusive realization of Lessing's project. This is a project, as we have seen, in search of new modes of representations of—one could say—representation, a project of critically rethinking what truth and truth value are and what the functions, operations, and pragmatics of truth are. In this context,

Lessing's project emerges as an enterprise to stage, rehearse, deliberate, play with, and reflect upon the implications and ramifications of the functions of writing, acting, and thinking. It is this concern that determines Lessing's writing and produces its surprising consistency in the face of all the diverse issues tempting Lessing in different directions and into a variety of disciplines and genres.

Yet it is this "philosophy in action," as Jaspers calls it, that unites a body of work normally compartmentalized into theology, aesthetics, drama, poetry, literary criticism, satires, and polemics.[1] For it is not the heroic enthusiasm for truth and the just cause—a simplistic view of the Enlightenment that betrays its anti-Enlightenment resentment—that distinguishes Lessing, but rather this project of scrutinizing the concept of truth itself on every level, in every regard, and in every dimension that lies at the heart of his efforts. This is why Lessing's project implicates aesthetics and semiotics while it transcends them at the same time.

If Lessing moves with apparent ease from discussing technical questions in Greek, Latin, or Hebrew philology to questions of aesthetic representation or to literary criticism, or if he slides back into personal polemics, this happens because, for him, everything is connected to everything else, and questions of truth, verification, and veracity cannot be as easily separated from one another as one might wish. He is not so much the brave knight-errant who wagers his superior virtuosity on behalf of whatever cause he comes across, be it the critique of prejudices, opinions, assumptions, metaphysical fallacies, philological blunder, or Hauptpastor Goeze. Rather, his hyperactive agility aims at what they all have in common: reason gone out of control and reduced to mere instrumentality in the service of the dogmatic.

To thus reduce *Nathan* to a plea for tolerance or freedom of religion would be to trivialize crucial moments of the play and screen out the farther-reaching implications of the metaphorical-philosophical connection it stages. Yet to address the play as "Toleranzstück" has become the lens through which it is still read.[2] To read *Nathan* in such a way, however, forces us to ignore some of the dramatic moments at the center of the play. Both supporters and critics of such readings who identify the issue of tolerance as the central concern of the drama seem to imply that the play unequivocally argues for tolerance. For some, such tolerance seems to call for assimilation and surrender of tradition. Such readings opt for an interpretation that reads *Nathan* as a play written in the normative mode and/or take its protagonist for an assimilated Jew who is forced to deny and abandon his Judaism. However, such readings lack sufficient textual evidence. They seem to be the result of a hermeneutic transference pattern that has, in the last two hundred years or so, formed a canonical reading whose own concerns overwrite critical textual analysis. However, contrary to such attempts, Lessing's *Nathan* is one of the first texts to address the transformation of tradition into a modern concept.[3]

It seems obvious that rather than arguing for an Augustinian model of tolerance—and religious tolerance is, after all, an Augustinian concept[4]—*Nathan,* in the spirit of Spinoza, plays out an argument for freedom of religion, speech, and opinion with no restrictions whatsoever. The play sends a clear signal when it has the Templar burst out in rage, calling Nathan "the tolerant babbler" ("der tolerante Schwätzer"). This is the only time the word occurs onstage. And I would argue that rather than merely inverting the negative into a simply positive meaning, the play expresses a deliberate critique of tolerance as just another exclusionary mechanism.[5] Instead of presenting an argument that tolerance is great—great for business and for Jews, on the condition, of course, that they are rich, useful, and hence tolerable—Lessing's project aims to challenge the traditional epistemological framework altogether.[6]

Lessing's experimenting with truth conditions—the staging and playing out of the question "What constitutes truth?"—resembles the attitude of pragmatism as it is formulated later. For Lessing, what comes into focus is no longer truth per se, as if it could any longer be thought of as a substantial thing in itself, but rather the status of truth functions. How is truth to be construed? How is it constructed—socially, politically, legally? What are the consequences of truth? These are the kinds of questions that emerge more and more clearly as the leading concern of Lessing's project.

The extreme emphasis on contingency as a decisive element in almost all of Lessing's plays and its theoretical conception in his writings on philosophy of religion illustrate how rigorously he tries to strip truth of all preestablished, presupposed assumptions and how emphatically he presses the issue of the fragility of what he calls in *Nathan* the "old" concept of truth. Thus it becomes increasingly obvious that truth is not an intrinsic quality but rather the moment of insight and observation which arises out of realization and praxis.

The transactions at the center of action in Lessing's plays (e.g., in *Die Juden, Minna von Barnhelm*) or in his critical writing (e.g., in *Laokoon*) enact exchanges that constitute and reconstitute descriptions of reality in more than casual ways. The questions reiterated throughout his oeuvre raise issues of evidence and truth and of how they are produced. The dramatic and critical drive of these writings aims at more than merely rendering suspect the way truth may become subject to manipulation. Rather, and more radically, motivation and artistic tension are derived from the fact that ultimately the concept of truth itself is exposed to critique.

The sign of truth—and here the dramatic, critical, philological, aesthetic, and philosophical writings have their common ground—is for Lessing contingent, arbitrary, and subject to coincidence. The sign of truth is not truth itself but merely its signifier. It is only (as Claudia Brodsky Lacour's study of *Laokoon* shows)[7] the realization of the sign in its circulation of use, as the sign is brought into the circuit of action, into the process of validation—it is only the sign's verification within a frame of reference that can be empirically or narratively shared. In brief: the functional meaning of the sign is only constituted through its history, only its contingent application rules.[8] To argue that *Nathan* "recognizes but deftly sidesteps the problem of what truth is, just as the fable [i.e., the *Märchen* of the rings] sidesteps the problem of which religion is true,"[9] assumes that to move an issue to another level and to recast it in a different way is to circumvent it.[10] This, however, seems a rather curious position to take when the examination and reformulation of the problem of the nature and conditions of truth constitutes the philosophical project in the late eighteenth century. The accusation that Lessing or, for that matter, Nathan skews Saladin's blunt question for the truth—if, in truth, this is Saladin's question—is as old as the play's reception. But such an argument precedes rather than results from a careful reading of the story of the rings. The play itself does not provide any evidence that would allow us to view Nathan as a philosophical escapist. Rather, the *Märchen* of the rings suggests the opposite. To rate *Nathan* in such a light as a "work of pseudophilosophy"[11] merely perpetuates the canonized reading uncritically.

In *Nathan,* however, the validation process for the new concept of truth—its pragmatic functionalization—comes to play a key part in the plot. The process-like character of truth constitution is not a matter of representation alone. It produces the subsequent question of how truth must be conceptualized at a moment when conventional metaphysical assumptions of the ontological-teleological discourse have been rendered, if not obsolete, then at least questionable.

If Lessing's project is theorized in such a way, the poetological functioning of *Nathan the Wise* emerges more clearly in its complex weave of tropes, metaphors, and logical reasoning. As a result, the roles religion, miracle, economy, politics, and the question of genealogy assume in this drama become perceptible as an orchestrated staging of Lessing's argument for a new and critical concept of truth as praxis-oriented wisdom—in short, as a pragmatism of sorts.

Thus, to interpret *Nathan* as a plea for tolerance, for equality of religions or cultures, or for freedom of thought would not only precociously instrumentalize the concept of reason that the play introduces but would also leave the interpretation of the poetic economy of the drama in a hermeneutic deficit. The dramatic makeup of the play seems to refuse any quick resolution. The poetic energy it displays may well receive its power from biographical experience,[12] but it cannot be reduced to this. The resistance the play seems to exert against any attempt at reduction, no matter how forceful the hermeneutic virtuosity of the interpreter, should not be ignored, but deserves to be recognized as one of the play's strong points.

There are four important moments in *Nathan* that, although often downplayed, prove to be crucial for an understanding of the play:

1. The miracle discourse of the first act.[13]
2. The economic metaphor comprising the coin/truth metaphor, Nathan's occupation as a businessman, trader, and financier.[14]
3. Nathan's Job-like suffering.[15]
4. The open-ended, transitory ending and what we could call the genealogical paradox of Nathan.

And, Nathan himself seems to present one of the—if not the foremost—interpretational embarrassments in German literary criticism: a wealthy, economically successful, powerful, proud, self-consciously religious Jew. In a variation of Adorno's epithet about Heine, one could speak of Nathan the wound.[16] Nathan represents the German Jewish complex in its unavoidable fixation. To declare Nathan—as some have suggested—as really a Protestant and the play as one inviting the application of Max Weber's *Protestant Ethics and the Spirit of Capitalism*[17] may have produced a knowing laugh from Hermann Cohen, who argued, one hundred years after Lessing, that German Jews were actually Protestants;[18] or it may solicit the commentary that rather than Weber it should be Werner

Sombart's answer to Weber, *Die Juden und das Wirtschaftsleben,* that one needs to refer to; but it is a telling example of how deep this complex really runs.[19]

It is no accident that Nathan is a Jew—and a Jewish merchant for that matter. In the Bible, his namesake, the prophet, is sent by God to explain to King David why he has not been called upon to build the sanctuary in Jerusalem. Nathan does this in a speech Martin Buber calls "one of the strongest and most important speeches of God in Scripture," at the center of which stand "the two key words of the thornbush speech: 'my people' and 'I will be with thee.'"[20] In *Nathan the Wise* this signals Nathan's distinct sense of nationhood and religious autonomy. His existence is rooted in the same historical continuity as his predecessor and namesake. Nathan the Wise picks up where Nathan the Prophet left off as he points out the limits of political power to Saladin, and the moment of repetition gives Nathan the Wise a historical dimension that makes him anything but a lifeless figure. Likewise, the location plays an important role. To speak of Jerusalem in eighteenth-century German culture was to speak of Jews. Mendelssohn gave his groundbreaking book on the question of Jewish emancipation the title *Jerusalem or On Religious Power and Judaism.*[21] And Kant, for example, like many others, thought of Jews as Palestinians who lived among the Germans in temporary exile. Kant was also convinced the Jews were a nation of usurers and fraudulent merchants:

> The Palestinians living among us have, for the most part, earned a not unfounded reputation for being cheaters, because of their spirit of usury since their exile. Certainly, it seems strange to conceive of a *nation* of cheaters; but it is just as odd to think of a nation of merchants, the great majority of whom, bound by an ancient superstition that is recognized by the State they live in, seek no civil dignity and try to make up for this loss by the advantage of duping the people among whom they find refuge, and even one another.[22]

> Die unter uns lebenden Palästiner sind durch ihren Wuchergeist seit ihrem Exil, auch was die größte Menge betrifft, in den nicht ungegründeten Ruf des Betruges gekommen. Es scheint nun zwar befremdlich, sich eine *Nation* von Betrügern zu denken; aber eben so befremdlich ist es doch auch, eine Nation von lauter Kaufleuten zu denken, deren bei weitem größter Teil durch einen alten, von dem Staat, darin sie leben, anerkannten Aberglauben

> verbunden, keine bürgerliche Ehre sucht, sondern dieser ihren Verlust durch die Vorteile der Überlistung des Volks, unter dem sie Schutz finden, und selbst ihrer untereinander, ersetzen wollen.[23]

It is significant that Nathan has been represented in German literary criticism by the contrary image: that of the anemic, idealistic character with his head in the clouds—"da liegt man nicht eng" (Celan)—when the intertextual indicators point instead to a concrete, socially committed, politically engaged individual steeped in history, speaking a clear and uncompromising language.

In the same way that the question of Nathan's identity resists trivialization, the miracle debate of the first act frames and motivates the play. It sets the tone and establishes another important intertextual frame of reference, which, although it has eluded scholarly recognition of its relevance to the dramatic organization of the first act, presents itself in a precise, indicative manner.[24] As Lessing sat writing his *Nathan* he faced the famous radiant portrait of Spinoza, hanging in the house that had served as the private quarters of the Wolfenbüttel librarian since 1777.[25] Both Spinoza's *Ethics* and his *Theological-Political Treatise* function as subtexts. Reverberating throughout the play, their resonance creates the inspired and sublime timbre that gives this drama its unique philosophical foundation. Spinoza's revolutionary biblical hermeneutics resurfaces word for word in *Nathan* as the miracle debate unfolds onstage.[26] The pedagogical program proceeds precisely along the lines of both the conception of religion in the *Theological-Political Treatise* and of Spinoza's theory of the affects. This psychology breaks with naive rationalism. It realizes that gaining knowledge is not a process that can be conceived as detached from the affective, emotional household of the soul but rather is one that conceptualizes knowledge as the highest form of affective life. Such knowledge can be achieved by way of an economy of transferring emotions into new, purified affects that eventually will transform themselves into intellectual knowledge. And as in Spinoza, it is a hermeneutics of signs with a purpose, namely, to recast the issue of religion and truth as issues calling for epistemological reflection. Both Lessing and Spinoza arrive at the same conclusion: the differentiation of theology and religion from philosophy and reason. Nathan advocates precisely Spinoza's distinction between religion and superstition, defining the latter as grounded in ignorance while the former is grounded in wisdom.[27] His religiosity consists in a rather Spinozist-sounding, praxis-oriented, emancipatory kind of wisdom. Consequently, truth becomes an aspect of praxis and performance. Its criterion is no longer derived from a metaphysics-based logic but consists in the concrete, immanent, practical, and pragmatic proof any truth claim must be able to furnish.

The miracle debate, with its almost Masonic cleansing of the passions and its initiation-like introduction to reason, thus charts the dramatic course of this philosophical drama as a drama of philosophy. In correspondence with Spinoza's distinction between three levels of knowledge, the first act represents the transition from the first to the second level. Recha's rescue by the Templar and Daja's attempts to make use of it for the purpose of proselytizing a confused Recha with her own version of a superstitious kind of Christianity rehearses Spinoza's "ex auditu aut ex aliquo signo" hermeneutics ("from report or from some conventional sign") as Recha goes through the emotional ordeal of the commotions caused by an episode of "random experience" ("experientia vaga").[28] The origin of such "experientia vaga" springs "from singular things which have been represented to us through the senses in a way that is mutilated, confused, and without order for the intellect" ("ex singularibus, nobis per sensus mutilate, confuse, & sine ordine ad intellectum repraesentatis" [E2P40 schol 2; CW 477]) just the way Recha describes her experience. The *Ethics* lists this as the first and lowest form of knowledge. To this, Spinoza adds in the *Ethics* the imagination-driven interpretation of signs, which is already one step removed from the uncoordinated perceptions of sense data and, therefore, already more "sophisticated." This more complicated form of knowledge—which, therefore, is also more likely subject to errors of misinterpretation—describes the state of Daja's mind.[29]

The second form of knowledge is represented in the drama by the metaphor of economy. Delimited by utility in the strict philosophical sense, this is the realm of instrumental reason. Not only is Nathan an extraordinarily successful businessman, a merchant trading and, to the dismay of some critics, even collecting debts,[30] but he also *enjoys* his business activities. Unlike the members of his household, *his* joy of return is mitigated by the joy of a fulfilled life in the business world. Obviously, alienation, exploitation, and capitalist market economy are not exactly the categories that can be applied as is to twelfth-century Middle Eastern economy. Economic theory in Lessing's time ascribes to trade rather than to production and labor the primary importance of economy. Three years before Lessing composes *Nathan the Wise,* Adam Smith's *Wealth of Nations* identifies exchange and circulation as the primary sources for wealth and prosperity, and the merchant as their facilitator.[31] Smith and a whole school of economic thought unite in saluting the merchant as the benefactor of society and commercial activity as a social, even to some degree civilizing, mission. Smith recognizes a universal trait in the merchant. The need to engage to some degree in the activities of trade in order to provide for life's necessities accounts for the fact that everyone is forced to exchange and barter goods or skills. Trading, therefore, constitutes a basic aspect of human existence.[32]

An experienced, successful, and renowned businessman, Lessing's friend Moses Mendelssohn responds three years after the publication of *Nathan* in the preface to his edition of Manasseh Ben Israel's *Vindication of the Jews* to the stereotyping of the commercial activities of Jews as unproductive and parasitic. He answers the accusation of Jewish exploitation of labor with a resolute plea for the recognition of trade and commerce as productive labor equivalent to any other form of production: "The smallest trading Jew is in this regard not just a consumer but a useful denizen (I must not say citizen) of the state, a real producer."[33]

Nathan is just such a businessman, though of a rather wealthy sort, who is well aware that it is the market that creates value and that somebody's gain ultimately means everybody's—that is, society's—gain.[34] The conception of money as an instrument of commerce that lacks character but amplifies one's own character is an insight developed in the *Ethics*. There, Spinoza acknowledges the fact that money has become the universal standard, but he sees this to be a problem when money is mistaken to represent a value in and for itself. The son of a merchant and living in a community actively engaged in overseas trade and well familiar with seventeenth-century world economy,[35] Spinoza shares this view of the instrumental character of money with Nathan, who seems to lead his life according to Spinoza's maxim: "Those, however, who know the true use of money, and set bounds to their wealth according to need, live contentedly with little."[36] Before we discuss the role of the economic paradigm in *Nathan* it is necessary to assess its functioning in the play. *Nathan* lives off the various meanings the word *handeln* carries: to deal, bargain, negotiate, trade, and traffic, but also to act.[37] At the heart of the allegory of trading lies the mediating ability of Nathan. He is the one who gets things done because he brings opposite interests together and mediates them in such a way that he produces the sort of surplus only *handeln* in its semiotic polyvalence makes possible.

Nathan's short soliloquy, the prologue to the ring *Märchen,* introduces the image of the old and the new coin as allegories of the old and the new truth. With the juxtaposition of the two truth concepts in terms of substance versus function, Lessing foreshadows the theme of pragmatism. To represent truth as money is not unconventional, but whereas substance metaphysics would validate only the old coin, whose identity of being and representation represents the ideal of truth-by-correspondence-to-reality, Nathan now validates, in a countermove, that new form of truth defined by the function of circulation and exchange. Hobbes had already cautioned about the limits of the "new" money when he wrote: "But that Coyne, which is not considerable for the Matter, but for the Stamp of the place, being unable to endure change of ayr, hath its effect at home only; where also it is subject to the change of Laws, and thereby to have the value diminished, to the prejudice many times of those that have it."[38] In Kant's *Metaphysics of Morals* money and thought are categorized under the same legal status right on the border between private and public right. For Kant, both money and books are defined by the interfacing of the public and the private sphere.

> The intellectual concept under which the empirical concept of money falls is therefore the concept of a thing which, in the circulation of possessions (permutatio publica), determines the *price* of all other things (goods), among which even the sciences belong, insofar as they would not otherwise be taught to others.[39]

> Der intellektuelle Begriff, dem der empirische vom Gelde untergelegt ist, ist also der von einer Sache, die, im Umlauf des Besitzes begriffen (permutatio publica), den Preis aller anderen Dinge (Waren) bestimmt, unter welche letztere so gar Wissenschaften, so fern sie anderen nicht umsonst gelehrt werden, gehören.[40]

Nathan's prologue to the ring story thus announces the transformation or, as it were, transaction in which intrinsic value is exchanged for functional currency. But it does so in a complicated double move, for the oppositional pair "old" versus "new" coin is introduced as an opposition that remains unstable. Rather than simply offering an alternative of either the old or the new coin as the symbol for truth, Nathan questions such an approach as wrongheaded, as his soliloquy illustrates:

H'm! h'm!—how strange!—I'm all confused.—What would
The Sultan have of me?—I thought of money;
And he wants—truth. Yes, truth! And wants it so—
So bare and blank—as if the truth were coin!—
And were it coin, which anciently was weighed!—
That might be done! But coin from modern mints,
Which but the stamp creates, which you but count
Upon the counter—truth is not like that!
As one puts money in his purse, just so
One puts truth in his head? Which here is Jew?
Which, I or he?—But stay!—Suppose in truth
He did not ask for truth!—I must admit,
Suspicion that used the truth as trap
Would be too small by far.—Too small? What is
Too small for one so great?—That's right, that's right:
He rushed into the house incontinent!
One knocks, one listens, surely, when one comes
As friend.—I must tread warily!—But how?—
To be a Jew outright won't do at all.—
But not to be a Jew will do still less.
For if no Jew, he might well ask, then why
Not Mussulman?—That's it! And that can save me!
Not only children can be quieted
With fables.—See, he comes. Well, let him come! (M 230–31)

Hm! hm!—wunderlich!—Wie ist
Mir denn?—Was will der Sultan? was?—Ich bin
Auf Geld gefaßt; und er will—Wahrheit. Wahrheit!
Und will sie so—so bar, so blank—als ob
Die Wahrheit Münze wäre!—Ja, wenn noch
Uralte Münze, die gewogen ward!—
Das ginge noch! Allein so neue Münze,
Die nur der Stempel macht, die man aufs Brett
Nur zählen darf, das ist sie doch nun nicht!
Wie Geld in Sack, so striche man in Kopf
Auch Wahrheit ein? Wer ist denn hier der Jude?
Ich oder er?—Doch wie? Sollt' er auch wohl
Die Wahrheit nicht in Wahrheit fordern?—Zwar,
Zwar der Verdacht, daß er die Wahrheit nur

Als Falle brauche, wär' auch gar zu klein!—
Zu klein?—Was ist für einen Großen denn
Zu klein?—Gewiß, gewiß: er stürzte mit
Der Türe so ins Haus! Man pocht doch, hört
Doch erst, wenn man als Freund sich naht.—Ich muß
Behutsam gehn!—und wie? wie das?—So ganz
Stockjude sein zu wollen, geht schon nicht.—
Und ganz und gar nicht Jude, geht noch minder.
Denn, wenn kein Jude, dürft er mich nur fragen,
Warum kein Muselmann?—Das war's! Das kann
Mich retten!—Nicht die Kinder bloß, speist man
Mit Märchen ab.—Er kömmt. Er komme nur![41]

It is the "ancient" ("uralte") coin, long obsolete, that would have been acceptable if it were still possible to use it—not so much, the passage indicates, because of its substance but because of its historical dimension. The operative clause here is "which was weighed" ("die gewogen ward"), but is no longer weighed and pondered. Compared to the old coin, whose value is determined on the grounds of the custom and habit that present the framework of historical continuity, the new coin appears in a questionable light. Its value determined by stamp and denomination, that is, convention and currency exchange rate, Nathan cautions against confusing the new and purely empirical truth with metaphysical truths. And it is in this context of refusing such a criterion as a standard for truth that Lessing has Nathan reverse the charge concerning his Jewish identity in a remarkable turn: "Which here is Jew?"

Nathan's soliloquy can now be understood in its multilayered function. In a dramatic manner, it joins the issues of truth, negotiation, religion, and personal identity into a single image. From this overdetermination the play derives its dramatic energy, making the choice between the coins, the old one and the new one, its driving allegory as it prepares for Nathan's gambit.[42] But, the passage does not force the conflict between the "old" and the "new" to a solution. To charge this passage, however, with being a diversion ignores the fact that it is precisely the suspension of a resolution that produces the dramatic potential of the scene. What the interpreter is left with is not the resolution about which coin to prefer but the recognition that, if there is such a thing as truth, it consists in a differential value between the old and the new coin. The new coin thus represents not truth as such but instrumental reason in its pragmatic use, which carries its uncontested value as long as it remains restricted to its own limits.

Nathan's monologue presents him thinking aloud, so we get glimpses of his thoughts—moments that indicate the turning points in his deliberations rather than a discursive order. In this way, the monologue frames, prefigures, comments, and reflects upon the dramatic development of the play itself. Nathan ends this moment of collecting himself and reviewing his arguments by naming the strategy he is about to espouse in order to answer Saladin's challenge: "Not only children can be quieted with fables." This line has almost exclusively been read as paralipsis, which would have it expose the underlying paternalist current in Nathan's, or for that matter Lessing's, thought. But this line seems to invoke another point. Besides the rigorous legal course of arguments pitched against one another, the Talmud contains the aggadah, a repository of stories and similes, dense and rich in meanings. These *Märchen* are not for children but offer accounts of complex thoughts that point beyond simple solutions to enigmas and paradoxes that only the form of narrative improvisation can address.

In Lessing's age, the term *Märchen* had not yet received its narrow modern meaning of fairy tale but still denoted any type of little tale, fable, or story. It is such a little piece of narrative, abundant with biblical and rabbinical allusions, rather than a New Testament–style didactic parable, that Nathan is about to present to Saladin.

With the coin metaphor signaling the end of substance metaphysics, the issue in *Nathan* is no longer the truth of a or any religion. The truth of religion is now altogether removed from the sphere of instrumental reason regulated by the laws of economy, and the question rather has become how to accommodate religion conceived of as a religion of reason within the limits of experience.[43] For the gambit with which Nathan has opened his response prepares the grounds for the effective counterattack, making the end game an interactive exchange of both parties involved.[44] This line of argument is drawn to its logical-political conclusion in the *Märchen* Nathan is about to tell Saladin. Against the conventional use of the term "parable" when speaking of the ring story, the transformative character of its narrative aims at more than just a parable. Whereas the parable proposes a didactic approach to truth, the ring story introduces a new understanding of truth that points beyond parabolic truth to the constitution of truth as a process through which the understanding of truth itself is renegotiated. Staging this conceptual change as a transaction, Lessing abandons the genre of the parable for the possibility of a more dynamic presentation. Beyond parabolic closure that calls for a clear-cut conclusion, the *Märchen* stages through its narrative enactment truth as a process. The double feature of the *Märchen* represents both the performance of an account of change and the change it enacts by way of redefining the concept of truth.[45]

In Lessing's own terminology, the appropriate term for the ring story would be the fable. In his 1759 *Abhandlungen über die Fabel,* Lessing illustrates the distinction between the parable and the fable in the following way: in order to turn a parable into a fable the author has to remove all generality and, instead, give the text individuality.[46] Lessing underscores here the constitutive link between the fable and the presentation of knowledge. The general or universal, Lessing observes, can only be recognized as intuitive cognition in the form of the particular (L 5, 382). The particular must be imagined as real, not just possible, in which case it would still be an unspecified universal. Lessing concludes his remarks on the fable with the following statement:

> If we reduce a general moral proposition to a particular case and give this particular case reality, inventing a story whereby one recognizes the general proposition by way of intuitive cognition: this invention is called a fable.
>
> Wenn wir einen allgemeinen moralischen Satz auf einen besonderen Fall zurückführen, diesem besonderen Falle die Wirklichkeit erteilen, und eine Geschichte daraus dichten, in welcher man den allgemeinen Satz anschauend erkennt: so heisst diese Erdichtung eine Fabel. (L 5, 385)

This move from the general to the particular, addressed in his theory of the fable, is now put onstage in and through the dramatic presentation of a fable. Designed as fable rather than parable, the particularity of the ring story produces just such an effect of intuitive cognition. The epistemological implications of Lessing's theory of the fable come now into play as the transformative power of intuitive cognition. Presented to the sultan, the fable of the rings thus argues a point whose theoretical significance is most effectively communicated through the telling of a fable.

Just as the biblical Nathan pronounces David's limits, so the speech of Lessing's Nathan puts Saladin—that is, state power—in its place.[47] Nathan's new economics announces circulation and exchange as the new paradigm for the epistemological process of truth production. The

Märchen stages the narrative of this transmutation from metaphysical truth based in substance to the new, functional, circulatory concept of truth. Rather than a device for diversion and escape, the *Märchen* marks an argumentative intervention. Saladin is no fool, and Nathan would risk his life if he attempted to lead him on. Nathan is no fool either. He realizes that the only way to convince Saladin is by way of exposing the problematic nature of the assumption underlying Saladin's challenge. Surprised and, at the same time, deeply touched to meet his equal, Saladin acknowledges the superior power of both the logic of Nathan's argument and his moral integrity. For Nathan, the consistency of intellectual integrity remains the only way left to respond, in a convincing, consistent, and dignified manner, to the dilemma he confronts. There is surely irony in the fact that some critics have turned precisely this integrity against Nathan and made it into his ultimate *pseudos*. Yet it is not true that the *Märchen* leaves the question as to the truth, the truth of the rings, or the concept of truth itself unchanged.[48] For this narrative performs a challenging transformation of the concept of truth. As a result, the validity of metaphysical concepts is exchanged for a critical verification process that introduces a new notion of truth.

The renunciation of all metaphysical-theological claims in *Nathan* has become irrefutable since Rüdiger Zymner's insistence that the fiction of a perfect imitation of the ring can no longer be upheld. Before the twentieth century it simply was technically impossible to artificially synthesize opals, and since there exist no two identical opals in the world, Lessing must have wished to block an easy way out of the *Märchen*'s dilemma.[49]

Too often, it seems, the little clause about the probable loss of the original ring has been ignored,[50] leading to the ironic twist that some readers consider themselves to have been singled out as heirs to the original ring. If this were the *Märchen*'s message, then, indeed, the play would be only about tolerance. Yet the story leaves no doubt that there is no longer anyone who could lay valid claim to the original.[51] Even if the existence of the original could have been assumed at one point in time, however far removed this might be, the line of the story is that there no longer exists any such thing as an original. Instead, its place is now taken by the manufactured, fabricated replacement. Substance and "weight" are exchanged for a concept of truth that is determined by currency gained through circulation. The *Märchen* thus marks the transition to a functional understanding of truth. Truth emerges from Nathan's account at the moment when all parties involved are connected in praxis. Truth's criterion is, for all practical purposes, instrumental utility. That which has no effect on our lives here on earth transcends human knowledge and therefore cannot be granted any hold over this praxis, for such speculative, transcendent truths do not necessarily constitute intersubjective consensus. Because of this they must remain suspect.[52] The fundamental shift the *Märchen* enacts announces the transition toward the new conception of truth that Kant's critical project will formulate two years later in his *Critique of Pure Reason*.[53]

The theory of tradition that the ring *Märchen* proposes attends to the fact that repetition is only possible as repetition in difference and that the concept of tradition—itself a product of the transition to modernity—implies the replacement of the authentic by the continually reappropriated that subsequently undergoes constant transformation. The *Märchen* can thus be seen as one of the first literary instantiations of a modern conceptualization of tradition. In telling his story of the ring *Märchen,* Nathan performs the transmutation of truth into a plurality of traditions. They now come to present the historical contingencies of human existence. As such, they are now understood to be manufactured like the rings. As fabrications, however, they are equally part of and subject to the history they reflect. The moment tradition is pluralized, they undergo a conceptual change. When conceptualized, traditions come into view as products of history and can therefore no longer carry any normative significance. The *Märchen* functions in this context as the effective narrative passage that connects the transformation from authenticity to the contingent character of the status quo. This state no longer falls under the atemporal category of an a priori given but can now be addressed as a particular tradition, that is, a product of historical contingency.

To arrive at a critical understanding of the drama, however, it is crucial not to confuse the *Märchen* with the play as a whole. Although the *Märchen* performs the transformation of the truth concept, the dramatic unfolding of the plot takes the protagonists by way of a cleansing of their affects through a development that has them progress from false forms of rationalizing determined by impulse, emotions, and imagination to a liberated, autonomous use of reason. In this way the play's trajectory stages the process of enlightenment in a manner closely reverberating with Spinoza's theory of enlightenment. An often-invoked comparison with the *Education of Mankind* is thus only meaningful when it relates to the drama as a whole instead of the *Märchen* of the ring story, which presents only a specific, albeit decisive, moment in the dramatic development of the plot. For the *Märchen* concerns itself not with history or the history of religions but exclusively with the way we conceive of or manufacture truth. The ring story thus does not so much address tolerance as it replaces it with a more refined, critical understanding of the nature and function of truth. On the other hand, the drama as a whole stages the implications of the concept of enlightenment, a concept now informed by a sophisticated theory of the affects. If we compare the play's plot development (rather than the functionally differently working *Märchen*) with the *Education of Mankind,* the often-stated incompatibility fades and gives way to a deeper consistency.[54] Both introduce the same kind of transformed conception of revelation, the same refined conception of religion, and a similarly differentiated theory of enlightenment.

But while, in the *Education of Mankind,* the impulse of enlightenment appears in theological guise, Nathan stresses the affective and epistemological drama that defines the Enlightenment. For the play's dramatic unfolding enacts the process of recognizing truth as multilayered. Structure, architecture, and development of the plot stage the distinction between different types of truth. Besides the emotive-affective, doctrinary approach to truth represented by figures such as Daja, the Templar, and the patriarch, there is the cognitive-instrumental understanding. Yet the drama makes clear that Nathan is only capable of holding up the pragmatic notion of truth because his reason is grounded in a third kind of certainty, or rather, trust. This third kind also hints at the role of the third level of knowledge introduced in Spinoza's epistemology as *scientia intuitiva.*

Thus, Nathan is not only a successful businessman. There is a deeper aspect to his truth negotiations. It is telling that in the dramatic course of events the audience is introduced only late in the play to the decisive moment in the formation of Nathan's wisdom. Significantly, this episode is presented only as flashback, commenting, as it were, on the representational problem of historical truth. The insertion of Nathan's Job-like sufferings after the miracle debate and the ring story thus gives the role of Spinoza's third kind of knowledge dramatic importance. This kind of knowledge is not the crowning of the drama but rather its grounding. As such, it does not, as in Spinoza, introduce a new truth. More decisively, it delineates the limits of instrumental reason. The allusion to Job's challenge of God and its response, Job's speechless vision of God as the unspeakable ground of being, appears in *Nathan* as the dramatization of the third kind of knowledge, which Spinoza calls—in distinction to the instrumental form of rationality—intuition.

Thus the truth and scope of Nathan's pragmatism is clearly defined. And as if to obviate a self-satisfied, naive humanist reading, the play ends with a final scene whose asymmetry once more underlines Lessing's point: that if there is anything we should know about truth, it is the fact that as far as existential truths are concerned, there will always remain an unresolved remnant, a difference that resists complete explanation. The genealogical paradox of Nathan as the one who remains outside any attempts at total genealogical unification illustrates this point dramatically.

To then call Lessing a philosophical pragmatist is not as far-fetched as it may seem. In his lectures on *Pragmatism,* the only example William James takes from literature to make his point is a nonsensical epigram by Lessing. James quotes from Mach an epigram that, however, in the course of transmission must have undergone some change.[55] Lessing's own version of "Hänschen Schlau" goes as follows:

> As Hans Smart told his Cousin Fritz,
> It's actually quite funny,
> That the richest people have their mitts
> On most of the world's money.[56]

> "Es ist doch sonderbar bestellt,"
> Sprach Hänschen Schlau zu Vetter Fritzen,
> "Daß nur die Reichen in der Welt
> Das meiste Geld besitzen."[57]

James uses the epigram to illustrate the absurdity of what he calls "the stock rationalist trick of treating the *name* of a concrete phenomenal reality as an independent prior entity, and placing it behind the reality as its explanation."[58]

Such anecdotal connection aside, it is striking that the descriptions of pragmatism by Peirce, James, and to some degree by Rorty sound as if they were talking about Lessing. Peirce cites Spinoza, along with Kant, as one of the philosophers whose experiment-oriented method he finds congenial to his own.[59] His famous and often-repeated definition of pragmatism sounds as if it were to sum up the result of Nathan's *Märchen* with regard to the limits of metaphysics and religion for understanding: "Consider what effects, which might conceivably have practical bearings, we conceive the object of our conception to have. Then, our conception of these effects is the whole of our conception of the object."[60] And likewise, James's lectures read at times as if they were a commentary on Lessing's thought and method.[61] James cites Socrates, Aristotle, and Locke—the mentors he shares with Lessing. The pragmatist revolution in thought by which "theories [. . .] become instruments, not answers to enigmas, in which we can rest"[62] emphasizes the "'instrumental' view of truth" itself.[63] "Truth for us is simply a collective name for verification-processes. [. . .] Truth is *made* [. . .] in the course of experience."[64]

If until now neither philosophers nor literary critics have taken Lessing's pragmatism seriously, it is simply because labels like "pragmatism" and "utilitarianism" only seem to be good for one purpose in Continental thought: to wipe out somebody's reputation.[65] Already one year after the publication of James's *On Pragmatism,* Ludwig Stein countered with the following comment: "[W]e predict for this fashion in philosophy not certainly a long life, but a life which is all the more intensive for its not being long."[66] Like James's "fashion," Rorty's insistence on pushing the anti-essentialist agenda of pragmatism[67] and his emphasis on the contingent character of language and discursive makeups[68] are likewise very much in the spirit of Lessing. Both Lessing and to some degree his protagonist Nathan are "ironists" in the Rortyan sense. Both qualify to be called "sufficiently historicist and nominalist."[69] In that sense, Nathan is very much a pragmatist and not surprisingly so. If Rorty presents the paradox that we never can tell when we have arrived at truth, even if this were possible, his statement is reminiscent of the celebrated passage in Lessing's answer to Goeze, that it is preferable to forsake truth in favor of the search for it: "The problem with approaching truth is that if one, indeed, were to reach it one would not know when this would happen" ("Das Mißliche am Anvisieren der Wahrheit ist, daß man, wenn man sie tatsächlich erreichte, nicht wüßte, wann man es geschafft hat").[70] This epistemological predicament of the lack of any a priori criterion that could indicate the point at which the process of knowledge comes to its completion is expressed in a letter to Mendelssohn, where Lessing expresses this dilemma in a strikingly similar way: "It is infinitely difficult to know when and where one should stop, and for thousands the end of their thinking is the point where they have become tired of it" ("Es ist unendlich schwer zu wissen, wenn und wo man bleiben soll, und Tausenden für einen ist das Ziel ihres Nachdenkens die Stelle, wo sie des Nachdenkens müde geworden").[71]

Peirce, James, and their critics, like Stein, repeatedly point out that pragmatism is not to be considered a new philosophy: "There is absolutely nothing new in the pragmatic method."[72] Rather, it is an old concern formalized within a generalized philosophical framework. It is therefore not a question of retrospectively reclaiming Lessing's poetics and poetic praxis for a certain school, in this case the pragmatists, but rather of reconsidering Lessing's role as a philosopher. His place marks the moment of transition when the concept of truth undergoes a paradigm shift. The place at a crucial juncture in the history of philosophy which *Nathan the Wise* occupies accounts for the enormous hermeneutic difficulties its poetics has presented for an audience still caught in the framework of the old concept of truth. But that poetics also places *Nathan* right at the crossroads of this historical moment. The play itself acts as the scene where this paradigm shift is epistemically reflected as it is acted out.

Beneath the layers of religious, humanist, and historical patina that generations of critics have laid upon the play, constructing a canonized reading of *Nathan the Wise*, a transaction or exchange of truth—of the very concept of truth—is at work in the text. There is no reason to neglect any longer the pragmatic impulse at work in the heart of the dramatic poetics of the play.

If Peirce's listing of Spinoza as one of his predecessors might seem perplexing at first, Spinoza's *Ethics* does, indeed, provide a remarkably thorough philosophical grounding for its pragmatic conception of utility. Utility, Spinoza argues, consists, if understood correctly, in self-preservation. Self-preservation, however, in Spinoza does not denote a narrow, egotist striving but the positive concept of dynamic self-realization guided by the full potential of reason: "what is really useful (is) [. . .] that everyone should strive to preserve his own being as far as he can" (CW 555) ("utile est [. . .] ut unusquisque suum esse, quantum in se est, conservare conetur").[73] Moreover, this conception of utility is closely linked to virtue in the sense defined in the *Ethics:* "The more each one strives, and is able to seek his own advantage (utile), i.e., to preserve his being, the more he is endowed with virtue; conversely, insofar as each one neglects his own advantage (utile), i.e., neglects to preserve his being, he lacks power."[74] As a consequence, utility is not alien to sociability but, on the contrary, defines the very criterion for true community: "Things which are of assistance to the common Society of men, or which bring it about that men live harmoniously, are useful; those, on the other hand, are evil which bring discord to the State."[75] In the *Theological-Political Treatise,* utility becomes the criterion for the validity of the social contract. As a consequence, the contract or compact is nothing but the legal-political expression of the optimal form of utility: "no compact can have force unless for the reason of utility"[76] ("pactum nullam vim habere posse nisi ratione utilitatis").[77] What is so remarkable about *Nathan the Wise* is then not just the many traces of Spinoza echoing the *Ethics* and *Theological-Political Treatise* alike but the creative use the play makes of them. Nothing could attest more impressively to the decisive place Spinoza occupies in Lessing's thought than this play's dramatic plotline. Beyond a mere rehearsal of practically all important critical elements of Spinoza's philosophy, the drama breathes the invigorating air of Spinoza's thought as this thought is brought to stage for a unique dramatization of Spinozist ideas. Taking Spinoza's philosophy onstage, the play advances a vigorously liberal, progressive conception of an uncompromisingly radical program of enlightenment. Grounded in Spinoza, Lessing thus articulates a theory and praxis of enlightenment that—beyond the limiting scope of the pantheism dispute that will later define the post-Enlightenment criticism of enlightenment—brings Spinoza's thought into play as a catalyst for modern critical thinking.

PART IV

SPINOZA'S NEW PLACE

CHAPTER 17

HEINE'S DIS/ENCHANTMENT OF HEGEL'S HISTORY OF PHILOSOPHY

WITH HEINE, SPINOZA RECEPTION REACHES a new stage. Ironically, Heine's outspoken advocacy on behalf of his *Unglaubensgenosse* (fellow nonbeliever) has gone virtually unnoticed except for his Jewish readers from Moses Hess to Sigmund Freud.[1] This is mostly due to readings that have been oblivious to the philosophical sophistication of a writer whose artful staging of his narrative as chance and free association has concealed the theoretical implications of his so palatably wit-wrapped critique. Yet with his intervention in the reception of Spinoza, Heine reclaims the revolutionary potential of a philosopher who, as a result of his appropriation by German idealism from Fichte to Hegel and Schelling, had, in the wake of Jacobi, been "spiritualized" and dehistoricized. With Heine's reclamation, Spinoza assumes a central position in the emergence of modern thought. Yet, Heine broaches his reappropriation in an ingenuously framed challenge of the historiography of philosophy in general. This makes it possible to expose the underlying assumptions that inform and cripple the historiography of philosophy, which, in the case of Spinoza, has led not only to the oversight of his role in the shaping of modern thought but even to the denial of his specificity.

Heine's *On the History of Religion and Philosophy in Germany* marks a rather curious point of transition in German letters. At the crossroads of philosophy and literature, it is alternately trivialized or charged with cryptic meanings. If Heine obviously engages Hegel's philosophy, the question of whether he simply appropriates or rejects the philosophical paradigm of his time overlooks the carefully targeted argument Heine brings into play in this work. Some critics have called attention to the fact that the poetological ramifications of this text are crucial. Yet discussions regularly overlook what seems to lie at the heart of Heine's project.

The claim that *On the History of Religion and Philosophy in Germany* was written solely to provide the French audience with a popularized introduction to German thought misses the critical thrust that transcends the humor and gives the whimsical presentation its deeper meaning. This text stages an open challenge that takes the historiography of philosophy to task, exposing in an unforgiving way the strings and ropes that move religion, philosophy, and politics. Yet Heine's text is not simply a parody that ridicules the sublime and deflates the hot air of both idealism and empiricism for the sake of entertainment. Heine's project is philosophical in a distinctly critical way. It challenges the positions and opinions that have assumed canonical status.[2]

As Heine rewrites the history of philosophy as one of a not so mythological reality, he launches into reinventing in a playful way a mythology and genealogy, constructing a monumental history while at the same time constantly undoing such mythologization. If on the historical stage tragedy is followed by farce, as Heine notes[3]—a remark picked up by Marx, certainly one of the more attentive readers of Heine's radical critique of ideology—this is certainly the hermeneutic-critical principle Heine brings to bear on the history of philosophy. His farcical style Disneyfies culture with a critical intent. This approach sets in motion a dynamic that demythologizes philosophy.

Exposing the mythological fundament of philosophy's self-fashioning in Hegel, Heine pushes the tendency of the self-mythologization of philosophy to its extreme. Rewriting the history of philosophy as mythology forces the framework of the history of philosophy and, as a consequence, of history to its cataclysm. The application of the Hegelian model of philosophy of history to itself reveals the problematic nature of the assumptions on which it is based. Heine cannot attack Hegel's philosophy of history from outside but has to critique him from within if he is to challenge it on its own grounds. Heine's intervention thus recasts Hegel's vision as a farce. Yet it is a farce that subverts the entire Hegelian setup, leaving no room for even a partial redemption of Hegel's claims.

Despite all his ambivalent admiration, Heine leaves no doubt about his view of Hegel. If in his 1852 preface to the second edition of *On the*

History of Religion and Philosophy in Germany his famous verdict on Hegel is unequivocal, it only makes even more explicit what Heine's overall approach to Hegel had already intimated from early on. Admittedly, the constant ridiculing of the old professor in Berlin betrays some personal knowledge of Hegel the man, but this should not be mistaken, as it often is, for unreflected identification. Rather, it signals the small yet crucial difference between the poet and the philosopher:

> There are, indeed, many other fine and curious stories in the Bible which deserve their [the Young Hegelians'] attention; right at the start, for example, you have the story of the forbidden tree in Paradise and the snake, the little lecturer, who expounded the entire Hegelian philosophy six thousand years before Hegel's birth. This blue-stocking without legs demonstrates very acutely how the absolute consists in the identity of being and knowing, how man becomes God through knowledge, or, what is the same thing, how God becomes conscious of himself in man. This formula is less clear than the original words: "If ye eat of the tree of knowledge ye shall be as God!" [. . .] O Paradise! It is strange, as soon as woman attains intellectual self-awareness, her first thought is a new dress! This Bible story, too, especially the speech of the snake, haunts my mind, and I should like to prefix it to this book as a motto, just as you often see outside prince's estates a board with the warning: "Man-traps and spring-guns in operation." (R 202; B 3, 510–11)

This warning points to the poetic snare within the text that so artfully deconstructs its own images, much in the way Abraham in *The Rabbi of Bacherach* destroys in Sara's dream the idols that, in turn, constantly recompose themselves.

Heine's constant oscillation between truth, fiction, and trivilization and his subversive wit and irony bracket the claims to univocal truth as he exposes their ulterior motives. Posing as the narrator who is about to let us in on what Heine calls the "secret of German philosophy" (*Schulgeheimnis*), which, as he divulges, consists in German philosophy's or Hegel's hidden atheism, Heine calls attention to the latent political character of German speculative thought. On the other hand, it is Heine himself who makes equally clear that there is no such thing as a "trade secret" of German philosophy. It is a phantasm, and its polemical use serves to expose the esotericism of idealist ideologues such as Madame de Staël, whose book *De l'Allemagne* presents the foil against which

Heine aims his comments. If some contemporary critics expressed their disapproval of Heine's presentation, to quote one, of "how profound subjects are presented in such a pleasant and joking way, that even young boarding girls and seamstresses [Pensionärinnen und Nähmamsells] can read [it] with pleasure and then say: Now we understand the whole philosophy,"[4] they only underscore the point Heine drives home—namely, that there are no secrets in all of this inflated philosophical posturing. The secret, as this farce makes abundantly clear, is that there are no secrets behind the veil of esoteric speculation of philosophy. For philosophy and the critical exchanges it requires are precisely based on publicity, whereas reason limited to secret circles could only mean, as Heine knew from Kant and Hegel, forms of particularisms that countered all that reason would stand for.

Some critics have complimented Heine for his fine achievements as a dilettantish philosopher,[5] while others have argued that he must be taken seriously as a critic of Hegel. Yet little or no attention has been given to the central concerns of Heine's critique. If some critics have identified the passage on Kant as the crux of Heine's presentation,[6] others focused on the Hegel discussion,[7] while still others have viewed its political aspects—Heine's prophecy of a German revolution of literally spectacular dimensions—as the center around which the text is organized. And, of course, there is the motif of pantheism, in all its varieties, that pervades the entire text and interconnects it as a whole. But if, like Heine, one is suspicious of scholarly profundity, then one can recognize in his use of pantheism more than merely a compositional device, for it operates as a kind of code name for a complex that cannot otherwise be explicitly expressed. Heine's so often celebrated and deplored courage may obfuscate the fact that a self-imposed form of censorship is still at work in his writings, and has to be, even if it is not directed at the explicit politics of the day. Yet if one looks at the literature on Heine, one could get the impression that his one and only interest was to produce an entertaining conversation piece on German philosophy.[8] The literature on Heine instructs us that, after Luther, the best and greatest man for Heine is Lessing,[9] in short, that Luther and Lessing are the high points of Heine's narrative.[10] And we are told that "Heine's interests focus on the most important events in the German history of ideas: the Reformation and the philosophical revolution introduced by Kant."[11]

Thus the uniquely critical role Heine ascribes to pantheism falls by the wayside, making pantheism more a peculiar hobbyhorse of poetic imagination than a serious concern of the philosopher.[12] For, according to such a scheme, pantheism could not possibly express any serious philosophical or political content but would function merely as a literary device for the narration of the liberation of the senses.[13]

Indeed, the sedimentation of canonical interpretation under which Heine has been buried has taken hermeneutic virtuosity to remarkable heights of oversight. The degree of disinterest, if not repression, is formidable with regard to a text that has been acknowledged as central to Heine's writing. But what has been repressed here has a name: Baruch de Spinoza.[14]

It is telling that even the name itself, where it is not repressed, presents a problem. Hegel, for instance, suggests that Spinoza had "altered"[15] or "changed"[16] (*verwandelt*)[17] his first name from Baruch to Benediktus, and a German standard pocket encyclopedia of philosophy, the *Kröner Lexikon der Philosophie,* still suggests his name was Bento, "with the sacral first name [mit sakralem Vornamen]" Baruch.[18] Thus, even the fact of simply translating his name from Hebrew to Latin is construed as a name change that seems to suggest more then simply this, namely, the philosopher's amorphous and ever-changing, chameleon-like nature that warrants alertness.

Heine introduces Spinoza in the second of three books, precisely at the center of the text. The passage comprises 10 pages of a 120-page text, but Heine presents virtually everything that follows this passage as informed in one way or another by Spinoza's thought. Kant, by comparison, gets only one page more than Spinoza but, like Hegel, who actually receives no fuller discussion, is for obvious reasons introduced only late in the game, in the third book. If one were to single out a figure looming large at the horizon of Heine's account it would be Goethe, around whom Heine constructs the development of German intellectual history. With the identification of Goethe as the culmination of modern pantheism, Heine—who sees himself as the heir to Goethe—suggests with this narrative that he is the one to lead German poetry into the future. But most strikingly, the introduction of Spinoza results in a radical transformation of conventional historiography. Placed in the middle of the three books on German religion and philosophy, the introduction of Spinoza effectively decenters and rearranges the focus on German matters of the entire work.

One of the endemic problems in discussing Spinoza has always been how and where to situate him within the narrative of the history of philosophy. Spinoza is usually positioned at one of its important intersections, somewhere among Descartes and Locke, Hobbes and Leibniz, a sort of stand-in in the series of European masters. The very problem of placing him thus poses a principal question, and how one answers this question determines the understanding and interpretation of his philosophy. Heine performs a rather elegant move to address this exigency. He first treats Descartes, goes on to discuss Locke, and then turns to Leibniz, thereby outlining a development that leaves a void at its center. It is not until this frame is established with an open space at its center that Heine introduces Spinoza as that "providential man" ("providentieller Mann") who fills this central position and "nowadays is attaining the sole supremacy over people's minds" ("in unseren heutigen Tagen zur alleinigen Geisterherrschaft emporsteigt").[19] Notice the innocuous-sounding present-tense use of the indicative. It illustrates Heine's virtuoso play with language to inform views through fiction as he describes the status quo by what pretends to function as simple narrative but in fact presents an underhanded siding with the movement of progress and liberation—in the guise of mere description. This fiction of the factual projects the imagined as that which is already presented as reality and thus silently argues the case for alternative possibilities. Besides explicit criticism, such well-concealed moves deploy the political force that drives Heine's narrative.

Heine speaks about Spinoza with unequaled engagement and sympathy.[20] Already in *The Romantic School,* Heine had asserted a year earlier, in 1833:

> Once one rescues Spinoza from the rigid format of obsolete mathematical Cartesianism and makes him accessible to the large public, it will perhaps turn out that he more than anyone else would have the right to complain of plagiarism. All our contemporary philosophers, perhaps often without knowing, see the world through lenses that were ground by Spinoza.

> Wenn man den Spinoza einst aus seiner starren altcartesianischen, mathematischen Form erlöst und ihn dem grossen Publikum zugänglicher macht, dann wird sich vielleicht zeigen, daß er mehr als jeder andere über Ideendiebstahl klagen dürfte. Alle unsere heutigen Philosophen, vielleicht oft ohne es zu wissen, sehen sie durch die Brillen die Baruch Spinoza geschliffen hat. (B 3, 433–34)

In *On the History of Religion and Philosophy in Germany,* Heine picks up where he had left off a year before. Located at the axis of this work, the "Pantheist excursion"—as he calls the extended digression on Spinoza at the heart of the book—pays tribute to the origins of the modern ideas that German philosophy and literature will, in turn, bring to fruition. Heine's excursus provides the cornerstone for the philosophical distinction between sensualism and spiritualism—between materialism and idealism—that constitutes the crucial critical category of his project of demythologizing the history of philosophy and thus the philosophy of history, for Spinoza's philosophy comes to denote the site where the aporias of Cartesian and empiricist models are resolved on the grounds of a new ontology.

In a passage whose rich intertextual allusions recall both the biblical language of the Prophets and Goethe's classic acknowledgment of his indebtedness to Spinoza in his autobiographical *Truth and Fiction,*[21] Heine celebrates Spinoza as the source of modern inspiration par excellence:

> His mathematical form gives to Spinoza a dry, uninviting appearance. But this is like the sour exterior of the almond: the core is all the more pleasing. Reading Spinoza, we feel as though we are contemplating great nature in her most vital repose. A forest of sky-high thoughts, whose blooming crowns are in surging motion, while their immovable trunks are firmly rooted in eternal earth. There is in Spinoza's writings a certain inexplicable atmosphere, as though one could feel the breeze of the future. Perhaps the spirit of the Hebrew prophets still rested on their late descendant. At the same time, he has a gravity, a confident pride, an intellectual *grandezza,* that likewise seems hereditary; for Spinoza belonged to one of those families of martyrs that were expelled from Spain by the Most Catholic Kings. He also had the patience of the Dutchman, and this quality was never absent from either his writings or his life.
>
> It has been established that Spinoza's life was wholly blameless, as pure and spotless as the life of his divine cousin Jesus Christ. Like him, Spinoza suffered for his teaching; like him, he wore a crown of thorns. Wherever a great mind utters its thoughts, there is Golgotha. (R 242–43; B 3, 561–62)

Quite adroitly, Heine points to the critical stage Spinoza initiates. Spinoza, Heine argues, is opposed equally to the materialism of Locke and the idealism of Leibniz. Heine makes clear that he is less interested in

Spinoza's system per se than in the kind of *Anschauungsweise* (approach) Spinoza inaugurates, which Heine subsequently calls "pantheism." This much ignored differentiation is the critical lever for Heine's use of pantheism: "In what follows, I shall apply the term pantheism not so much to Spinoza's system as to his manner of apprehending things" (R 245) ("Ich werde in der Folge weniger das System als vielmehr die Anschauungsweise des Spinoza mit dem Namen Pantheismus bezeichnen" [B 3, 565]). Pantheism—and this is one of the points of the digression at the center of *On the History of Religion and Philosophy in Germany*—is Heine's other name for Spinoza, or rather for Heine's progressive interpretation of Spinoza.

More than a simple pagan or hedonistic creed, pantheism entails for Heine the full potential of Spinozist philosophy—a philosophy, Heine is eager to stress, that carries powerful political and emancipatory implications underneath its metaphysical coat. Heine's interpretation of Spinoza therefore represents an innovative and bold intervention, repeated and taken to new heights by Moses Hess[22] and carried on in the wake of Althusser by Balibar, Negri, Moreau, and Deleuze, among others. The political interpretation of pantheism produced by this line of thinkers descends in one way or another from Heine's original contribution.

In order to introduce the *modern* meaning of the concept of pantheism Spinoza formulates, Heine employs a particularly dramatic device. Playfully casting pantheism as primitive, chthonic force—a pagan tradition that mobilizes the return of the repressed—Heine conjures a nightmarish version of an original, archaic pantheism in order to enact the staging of its name. Cheerfully recounting ghost stories about sprites, imps, goblins, poltergeists, and witches, Heine underlines the importance of these homegrown forms of pantheism as the German variety of Pantheism. In this Walpurgis Night–like setting, Pan's frenzied cult of vitality intrudes upon the classic schemes of Greek philosophy and Christianity, thereby creating a discursive space for a kind of thinking previously covered up by the Hegelian construction of world history. For, in Heine's presentation, pantheism functions precisely not as a unified mode of thought but rather as that disturbance in our thought whose nightmarish resurfacing signals the return of the repressed in all its unspecificity. No wonder that the Saint-Simonists did anything but appreciate the "wild" side of Heine's work.[23] Yet it is this passage through a fantasized history of pantheism that clears the way for Spinoza. Heine's free-handed mixing of the various brands of pantheism functions as poetic play aimed at disengaging fixed notions of pantheism before he has Spinoza take center stage.

Heine's emphasis on the primitive and ghoulish forms of pantheism in Germany prepares the ground for an argument concerning the profound affinity between this primitive variety and Spinoza's sophisticated, modern concept of pantheism, which points with its dynamic view of nature beyond the classic dualism of idealism versus materialism to a critical rehabilitation of the flesh without, however, succumbing to doctrinary materialism. This comparison thus further underlines that the very modernity of German history of religion and philosophy is intimately connected with and indebted to Spinoza.

As a result of this poetic enactment or staging, Heine's reinterpretation of Spinoza dislodges the Hegelian scheme in which Spinoza, like all other philosophers, is reduced to playing a bit part in the great script of the unfolding of the absolute spirit, a grandiose drama whose denouement finds that spirit knocking at the door of one Professor Hegel in Berlin. Yet underneath the inherently philosophical dimension of Heine's attempt to undo Hegel's philosophical claims from within, there is another dimension to his rewriting of the history of philosophy.

When, in his lectures on the history of philosophy, Hegel reiterates the Jewish aspect of Spinoza's lineage to suggest that it was precisely this Jewish identity that makes for Spinoza's peculiar positioning in that history, he is merely repeating a topos as old as Spinoza reception itself. From the day Spinoza entered the scene of the republic of letters, his biography was fashioned into the defining narrative for his philosophy. Of course, his biography could assume different, even contradictory forms, but it was the label of the Jew who was expelled by his community—the "Jew of the Jews," so to speak—that occupied already the imagination of his contemporaries. Spinoza came to represent, on the one hand, the possibility that a Jew could fully qualify as a philosopher in Western philosophy. On the other hand, this also meant that any Jew who aspired to be a philosopher was henceforth perceived as another Spinoza—although, one hoped, a Spinoza without the mistakes of Spinoza himself. So when, for instance, Moses Mendelssohn began his career as a philosopher, this was precisely the contention he faced. As Spinoza assumed generic significance historically, his name became the signature for the predicament faced by every Jew who wished to participate in the project of modern philosophy. And certainly the penchant for orientalizing helped to reinforce this phenomenon. Hegel's introductory passage to the chapter on Spinoza in his lectures on the history of philosophy expresses this tendency to orientalize in classic fashion:

> The philosophy of Descartes underwent a great variety of unspeculative developments, but in Benedict Spinoza a direct successor to this philosopher may be found, and one who carried on the Cartesian principle to its furthest logical conclusions. [. . .] The dualism of the Cartesian system Spinoza, as a Jew, altogether set aside. For the profound unity of his philosophy as it found expression in Europe, his manifestation of Spirit as the identity of the finite and the infinite in God, instead of God's appearing related to these as a Third—all this is an echo from Eastern lands. The Oriental theory of absolute identity was brought by Spinoza much more directly into line, firstly with the current of European thought, and then with the European and Cartesian philosophy, in which it soon found a place.[24]

> Die Spinozistische Philosophie verhält sich zur Philosophie des Descartes nur als eine konsequente Ausführung, Durchführung [. . .] Den Dualismus, der im Cartesischen System vorhanden ist, hob Benedikt Spinoza vollends auf,—als ein Jude. Diese tiefe Einsicht seiner Philosophie, wie sie in Europa sich ausgesprochen, der Geist, Unendliches und Endliches identisch in Gott, nicht als einem Dritten, ist ein Nachklang des Morgenlandes. Die morgenländische Anschauung der absoluten Identität ist der europäischen Denkweise und näher dem europäischen, Cartesischen Philosophieren unmittelbar nähergebracht, darein eingeführt worden.[25]

But if already in 1827 Heine had called Spinoza his *Unglaubensgenosse* (fellow nonbeliever), Heine's Spinoza of 1827 was a philosopher of a distinct political profile, thus clearly pointing beyond Hegel's idiosyncratic interpretative efforts at reducing Spinoza to metaphysics.[26] In contrast to Hegel, whose interpretation of Spinoza turned on an exclusively metaphysical argument, Heine highlights the revolutionary political theory that provides a coherent theory of freedom of religion, free speech, and self-determination and a potentially subversive concept of power. Heine leaves no doubt about the significance of Spinoza's political theory. In the French edition, he is even more explicit, recommending that his readers read Spinoza's *Political Treatise* ("Lisez son *Tractatus politicus*").[27]

Hermann Cohen is the only one who has stressed the point that Heine's Judaism or Jewish identity is essentially determined by his Spinozist concept of pantheism, and that it is in Heine's Spinozism that his

Jewish identity finds its expression.[28] Capitalizing on the affinity between the monotheistic and the Spinozist pantheistic strands, Cohen argues that it is the monotheistic core of that pantheism that accounts for Heine's progressive and socialist tendencies. Whereas the often-cited Hellenism and other non-Spinozist forms of pantheism celebrate political and social stasis, it is only in Spinoza that messianic hope finds its modern transformation into a conceptually convincing philosophy based on a consistently dynamic concept of nature. Ignoring this connection has led historically to a misunderstanding of Heine's use of pantheism. While most often taken for a reverential bow to the Saint-Simonists—a coquettish gesture it certainly may have also performed—the motive for pantheism was a more serious one. If we grant Heine the philosophical sophistication of a genuine thinker—and there is no reason we should not, especially given the fact that in Heine we face the person who has effectively done away with any kind of esoteric philosophical presumptions—then the importance of the innovative interpretation of Spinoza he introduces in *On the History of Religion and Philosophy in Germany* can no longer be doubted.[29]

To take on the cause of Spinoza therefore means to invoke the issue of Jewish emancipation. More than a pastime, proving Spinoza's philosophical and theoretical independence, equality, and revolutionary relevance was tantamount to a declaration of Jewish independence. In order to fully realize the degree of the challenge that Heine first formulates, one must remember that Hegel's scheme of the history of philosophy presented a particular predicament to the Jews among his students and followers, especially those who gathered in the Verein für Cultur und Wissenschaft der Juden where Heine met people like Leopold Zunz, Eduard Gans, and his friend Moses Moser. For each nation had, according to Hegel, one shot at playing a historical role, after which it would sink into oblivion, or to express this in more dignified terms, be sublated in history's progress. Obviously, that left the Jews in the cold as far as the modern world was concerned. And for Hegel this simply meant that they had better learn this lesson fast and merge with the demands of history without dallying, that is, strip themselves of the obsolete national features that for Hegel constituted Judaism itself.

For Heine's generation, this call to leave "their nation" behind was especially difficult to ignore because Hegel's argument carried all the weight and authority of conviction, progress, and promise. Only a refutation of the Hegelian model from within would suffice in response.

This is why Heine assumes in *On the History of Religion and Philosophy in Germany* the persona of a Hegelian, whereas he was otherwise anything but a Hegelian, and too much of an anarchist to be counted among the Young Hegelians, except with a grain of salt. His was what we might call a strategic Hegelianism, which, while quite contrary to the philosophical positions we find elsewhere in Heine's work, allows him to undo Hegel's model of history on its own terms. Only such a refutation could stand up to the criteria of critical philosophy formulated by Hegel himself. Yet such a refutation, if convincing, would at the same time demonstrate that Jewish identity offers an equally viable realization of modernity.

In this light we can view the full significance of Heine's "Spinozist pantheism." That which might otherwise appear to be an erratic changing of sides from radical materialism to a conversion of homey traditionalism, including the restitution of the old God who just had been declared dead[30]—all this can now be understood as a coherent and consistent project. Once Spinoza is recognized as the radical philosopher whose uncompromising thought breaks ground for modernity, the Jew by implication no longer signifies a relic that begs for tolerance and respite. Rather, Jewish culture then emerges as viable and even progressive, carrying the promise of the future.[31]

Heine's so-called conversion at the end of his life is then not a return to the Jewish self-consciousness he never really had abandoned[32] but rather another staging of a strategy for unfolding the power of Spinozism, a mode of thinking that is neither anti-religious nor anti-spiritual. On the contrary, Spinoza's is the only modern philosophy that makes religion possible for modern consciousness. For how else are we to understand the subtle and playful irony that infuses even the most religious and touching moments in Heine's haggling with God?[33]

Placing Spinoza at the heart of the Hegelian argument results in a carefully crafted implosion of the claims of Hegel's scheme of history. Such a placement suggests a revolutionary reflection on the place of Jews in Hegel's society, and this means in the modern nation-state in general. Heine formulates Jewish emancipation very much in the way Mendelssohn had done half a century earlier, namely, not by seeking to secure rights extended by the state to special interests but by postulating them as the necessity of the state and society as such. Whereas in Mendelssohn's day state and society were still thought to be identical, Heine, in the wake of Hegel, faces a world in which state and society have become antagonistic forces. While emancipation thus represented for Mendelssohn a primarily legal issue, it becomes for Heine a matter of sociopolitical urgency Mendelssohn could not have predicted.

The eccentric anomaly of Heine's *On the History of Religion and Philosophy in Germany*—its placement of a Dutch Jew at the center of a decentered history of German philosophy—is more than just the whimsical prank of a student of Hegel. It is Heine's radical critique of mythologizing German philosophy and performance of its demythologization. Its liberating and emancipatory result effectively undermines the calamities to which conventional emancipation projects are subject, for Heine does not aim simply at reverting the historical order but at reinventing the script for the story of progress and liberation itself.

CHAPTER 18

TRADITION AS INNOVATION IN HEINE'S "JEHUDA BEN HALEVY"

Counterhistory in a Spinozist Key

FAR FROM ARGUING THAT ASSIMILATION, or its opposite, would provide the Jewish answer to the challenge of modernity, Heine instead plays out the charged tension of the nineteenth-century cultural contradictions that helped shape the dialectics of the German Jewish experience. He responds to this challenge with a keen critical awareness of the need to rethink tradition in a new way that captures the double aspect of cultural transmission as the site of preserving the old through its ever new reinvention.

Heine's project of reconceptualizing history and historiography articulates a new understanding of tradition as formative and constitutive yet simultaneously fluid and open to constant new reinscriptions. Tradition emerges in Heine as both foundational and the site of permanent innovation, and both in equal measure. Differential in character, tradition for Heine is what links the old with the new, the connecting element that enables change as much as it may seem to block it. As the poetic theory and practice of writing counterhistory, Heine's *Romanzero* introduces an array of ideas that pose a challenge to any inquiry into how to represent past and present, and not only in poetry. It is in the concluding section, "Hebrew Melodies," that poetological self-reflection combines with free poetic imagination to pose the question of tradition as the question of modernity. At the center of the "Hebrew Melodies" stands "Jehuda ben Halevy," a poem that projects Jewish tradition as no longer just a question of the past but as the vital force that carries the poet's voice into the future. Resolutely unapologetic, "Jehuda ben Halevy" rests on a concept of tradition that critically reflects the dialectics of cultural transmission.

Heine's self-conscious presentation of Jewish tradition owes—through the mediation of the Verein für Cultur und Wissenschaft der Juden—much to Mendelssohn's initiative to propose a modern concept of Judaism that would not only meet the standards of modernity but was understood to be a crucial force in bringing about this modernity in the first place. There was, in Heine's eyes, no reason to be shy about Judaism's universal cultural importance, which Heine, in typical fashion, expresses in dialectical manner:

> Striking, indeed, is the deep affinity which prevails between these two ethical nations, Jews and old Germans. [. . .] Fundamentally, the two peoples are alike—so much alike, that one might regard the Palestine of the past as an Oriental German—just as one might regard the Germany of today as the home of the Holy Word, the mother-soil of prophecy, the citadel of pure spirituality. But it is not Germany alone which possesses the features of Palestine. The rest of Europe too raises itself to the level of the Jews. I say raises itself—for even in the beginning the Jews bore within them the modern principles which only now are visibly unfolding among the nations of Europe.[1]

> Es ist in der Tat auffallend, welch innige Wahlverwandtschaft zwischen den beiden Völkern der Sittlichkeit, den Juden und Germanen besteht. Diese Wahlverwandtschaft [...] hat einen tiefern Grund, und beide Völker sind sich ursprünglich so ähnlich, daß man das ehemalige Palästina für ein orientalisches Deutschland ansehen könnte, wie man das heutige Deutschland für die Heimat des heiligen Wortes, für den Mutterboden des Prophetentums, für die Burg der reinen Geistheit halten sollte.
>
> Aber nicht bloß Deutschland trägt die Physionomie Palästinas, sondern auch das übrige Europa erhebt sich, denn die Juden trugen, schon im Beginne das moderne Prinzip in sich, welches sich heute erst bei den europäischen Völkern sichtbar entfaltet. (B 4, 257–58)

While the association with the project of the Verein für Cultur und Wissenschaft der Juden and Mendelssohn's mostly unacknowledged role in foregrounding the expectations of the Verein's generation have defining importance for the development of Heine's argument, Spinoza's free and untrammeled thought presents the theoretical framework. A "pantheist of the joyful sort" ("ein Pantheist der heitern Observanz"),[2] Heine has notions of tradition and history that take their cue from the free-spirited philosophical sovereignty and self-reliance paradigmatically advanced in Spinoza. Spinoza thus not only makes his appearance in Heine's theoretical views but infuses his poetic practice in exactly the way in which Heine argues in *On the History of Religion and Philosophy in Germany* that Spinoza assumes a central role in the emergence of modern German poetry. In this way, Spinoza's critical spirit provides the theoretical viewpoint from which it becomes possible to conceive culture, tradition, and history no longer as merely determining human existence but rather as social constructions that call for renegotiation.

In recovering the pointedly Spinozist impulse, the deeper critical motivation behind Heine's seemingly lighthanded poetic playfulness comes to the fore. What appears as frivolous lightness that carries the winged horse of poetry—in "Jehuda ben Halevy" the poet makes free use of his Pegasus as a means of transport—emerges as the critique of a culture that refuses to take notice not only of Jewish history and tradition but of what it signifies in the modern European context: freedom of religion and of cultural expression, creativity, and self-determination. The spatiotemporal interweaving in "Jehuda ben Halevy" of different places (Toledo, Jerusalem, Berlin, Paris), cultures (Greek, Babylonian, medieval Spanish, modern French and German), and periods (biblical times, antiquity, Middle Ages, modernity) creates a turbulent mix whose bewildering simultaneity calls attention to the fact that history is always written backwards, from the future into the past. It is the retrospective look into history that allows the cauldron of the past to release its shapes in recognizable forms. But, Heine's poem makes clear, it is only such recourse to the past that provides the grounds for conceiving the future at all. In order to understand the significance of what takes place in "Jehuda ben Halevy," it may be helpful to use the conceptual pair of categories of "space of experience" (*Erfahrungsraum*) and "horizon of expectation" (*Erwartungshorizont*) that Reinhart Koselleck employs to capture historical thinking.[3] Koselleck's hermeneutic categories allow us to recognize that in historical constructions the past is always foreshadowed as the future. With the help of this distinction, "Jehuda ben Halevy" can be described as the site where the relationship of these two categories, constitutive for thinking history, is reconstituted from the bottom up. Heine's poem redefines the way the two categories relate to each other, representing counterhistory as the ever-necessary corrective to any historiography whatsoever, even the most progressive form. For it is the impossibility of fixing any unchangeable point in history that would, in the end, preclude the possibility of arriving at any definitive version of the past. Instead, it is the open-ended future that calls for ever-new interpretations of history.

Given this paradox of historiography, it comes as little surprise that Heine gives direct expression to this aporia. He does this in the way he describes cultural transmission as a creative, fragile, and artistic enterprise rather than simply a mechanical task. It is no coincidence that on the two occasions when the poem speaks of forms of transmission, this happens in a dichotomous manner, pointing to a split in culture that characterizes both forms of transmission. Both times, each side of the cultural divide represents complementary aspects of the other: the first time as halakha/aggadah, the second time as the form/content of Darius's jewel box.

The poem's powerful opening with a full stanza citing in direct quotation Psalm 137, the incantation of the psalm "By the waters of Babylon," transports the reader into the world of memory and imagination intimately tied to the power of poetry. Switching the order of the verses from the original, the poem's version stresses the constitutive role of memory for poetic imagination:

Dry with thirst, oh let my tongue cleave
To my palate—let my right hand
Wither off, if I forget thee
Ever, O Jerusalem—[4]

Lechzend klebe mir die Zunge
An dem Gaumen, und es welke
Meine rechte Hand, vergäß' ich
Jemals dein, Jerusalem— (B 6.1, 129)[5]

Heine thus both expresses a poetological reflection and performs its imperative in one and the same speech act. With these lines, the poem not only recalls the biblical tradition, the Babylonian exile, and Yehuda Halevi's ode to Zion but also refers to the role this quotation had played in the Berlin days when this psalm had served as watchword for Heine and his friends from the Verein für Cultur und Wissenschaft der Juden.[6] In a rather intriguing manner, then, the incantation of biblical poetry plays out the constructive aspect in the concept of time that allows us to imagine the past through the present, and thus it can in turn only be expressed through the work of remembering the past. It is through the melodious humming of the psalm in prayerlike meditation that the poem's narrator connects with tradition and leads the way to the world of dream figures (*Traumgestalten,* B 6.1, 130).[7] There the narrator encounters Yehuda Halevi, the greatest Jewish medieval poet, yearning for Zion. In what is presented as the history of Halevi's education, the poem gives its own account of the formation of the great poet. This account recasts the relationship to Jewish tradition in an innovative manner. In Heine's poem, the talmudic tradition, categorically rejected by early-nineteenth-century reform Judaism as an obsolete form of thinking that would lock Jews in an anachronistic worldview, undergoes an interesting revalorization. While Heine joins his contemporaries in criticizing the halakha for its anachronistic outlook, he highlights the creative potential represented in the Hagada.

Leopold Zunz's view of the Hagada as the expression of the free and innovative principle of Judaism and the vital counterforce against the restrictive, law-oriented mode of rabbinical thinking may have inspired Heine. In his *Die gottesdienstlichen Vorträge der Juden,* Zunz makes the Hagada a crucial part of Jewish tradition that guarantees its future development.[8] For Zunz, Halacha and Hagada relate to each other much like head and heart.[9] While Halacha represents the "organ of the law," Hagada functions as the "organ of freedom," representing the free word of the individual.[10]

Taking the cue of Babylon, the Talmud—which at that time was still predominantly associated with the Babylonian version—reconnects the reader to a tradition whose known version constitutes itself in the Babylonian exile. This is expressed in the daringly bold comparison of the Hagada to the hanging gardens of Queen Semiramis, where beauty is created in the garden of fantasy suspended in the air.[11] This presentation of the Hagada as "a garden of such childlike airy fancy" ("ein Garten / Solcher Luftkindgrillenart" [HD 658; B 6.1, 133]) allows Heine to position Jewish parabolic narrative as an alternative origin of poetry. The poetry of Halevi, a Jew, is described as originating from a Jewish tradition that flourished, throughout history, in exile, a site where cultural creativity is associated with cross-cultural fertilization.[12] In this way, the poem points out, Halevi is to be hailed not only as a great scholar of Scripture but also as a master of poetry and a great poet.

Describing Halevi as a master not only of reason and the word but also of the song, Heine highlights the ideal of well-rounded *Bildung* as one already prefigured in Jewish tradition. For Halevi plays an important role not only as the poet of the odes to Zion, the poem rightly reminds us, but also as the author of the *Kitab Al Khazari,* or *Sefer Ha-Kuzari,* a key text for medieval Jewish self-assertion. There, the master greets the disciple's conclusion that we should not rely on Aristotle's findings with a resolute "yes, this follows from it."[13]

As a synthesis of the scholar, the religious man, and the poet, Heine's Halevi represents the personification of his ideal of art's inventive approach to tradition, an approach that recognizes tradition as a productive rather than simply reproductive activity. Halevi's key import for rethinking Jewish tradition, the poem suggests with such eloquent enchantment—an enchantment based on poetic chant—consists in Halevi's sovereign attitude to literally bring that tradition to play. It is this concept of poetic sovereignty that returns at the conclusion of the first part of the poem in the form of full-fledged poetic autonomy as the poet is equated with a king of the realm of ideas answering to God alone. Here, as throughout the poem, aesthetic, cultural, religious, and political themes are brought together and interwoven in a fashion that makes for the contrastive effect of the poetological and cultural-political reflections that highlight each other in a highly artistic blend of themes.

Although the implications of Halevi's artistic mastery are fully unfolded in this conclusion of part 1 of the poem, the significance of Halevi's art is recounted—or, more precisely, finds its melodious image—early on when the poem tells of the beautiful manner in which Halevi was trained to recite scripture. For Halevi possessed the gift of singing the cantillation called shalshelet, a birdlike flourish in the recitation. Shalshelet, though rarely used, may nonetheless have once been sung by Heine himself if, indeed, he did sing the parsha on his bar mitzvah.[14] But, more interesting than such a potentially self-referential allusion,[15] shalshelet signals a profoundly gripping semantic field of meaning: the Hebrew word means first "chain," used in the context of recitation of the aforementioned type of cantillation, but "chain" in Hebrew can also refer to either "tradition" or to the kind of necklace introduced in part 3 of the poem.

In the image or sound—or rather sound image—of shalshelet, Heine illustrates the profound connection of tradition and innovation as different aspects of one and the same historical process. The poem's use of Schalscheleth thus condenses both the meaning of space of experience (*Erfahrungsraum*) and horizon of expectation (*Erwartungshorizont*) into a single word. This poetic move not only brings tradition's and art's autonomy into a new and productive relation but also opens the door to a principal reconsideration of the fundamental significance of tradition for modern art (and vice versa). Moving beyond a stale concept of secularism, Heine's poetry attends to the full intricacy of the foundational complex that surrounds the issue of tradition, repetition, and transmission in modernity. The poem's use of shalshelet opens the interpretative framework to an understanding that allows his poetry to acknowledge the foundational yet nevertheless necessary act that lies in what becomes tradition only through recovery, repetition, and continuity. As a performative act, such intervention is artistic in character—which means, for Heine, aesthetic and, therefore, poetic.

With this emphatically poetic yet equally profoundly critical reconceptualization of tradition, transmission, and enactment in mind, the signal import of the poem's central metaphor—or rather, to be precise, metonymy—of shalshelet becomes clear: the artistic flourish and embellishment of the free singer's voice makes a point as distant from a frivolous *l'art pour l'art* symbolism as it is from an "art with a purpose" point of view. Heine's shalshelet denotes the unbound freedom of art that brings life to tradition in the first place as it links the past with the future, a tradition that makes the new possible as it reconnects it—that is anchors or roots it—in the past it critically reimagines.

Part 3 of the poem introduces a variation of the shalshelet motif that unfolds its meaning by outlining two different modes of cultural transmission and historiography. This part also serves as a point of departure from which Heine launches a discussion of poetry's role. In his victory over Darius and the Persians, Alexander the Great, the poem recounts, won Darius's valuable jewel box. As Alexander distributes the content of the box to his heroes, he hands a marvelous chain of pearls to a beautiful dancer, Thais. From Thais the pearls are, by way of detour, passed on to Cleopatra, to later resurface at the turban of the Calif of Cordova. From there the pearls are passed on to the crown jewels of Castille and, later, to the kings of Spain. There, Mendizabel, the Spanish finance minister of Jewish origin, sells them to cover the debts of the court. Finally, the pearls appear in Paris as decoration around the neck of Baroness

Salomon (i.e., Betty Rothschild). While the history chronicled seems to represent an uninterrupted chain of transmission, it may be as complete as it is trivial in its truth. The case is different with the jewel box itself. Alexander held onto the jewel box to store the songs of Homer, and at night the songs' heroes would visit him in his dreams. At this point, the poem switches to the subjunctive, as the narrator fantasizes how—were he only able to gain possession of the box, and rich enough not to have to hawk it—he would use it to store the poems of Yehuda Halevi. Unlike the pearls the box would originally contain, Halevi's poems represent something infinitely more precious: they are the pearls of tears shed at the fall of Jerusalem. These "pearly teardrops, strung together / By a golden thread of verses" make the song produced "in the poet's golden forge" (HD 668; B 3, 173–75).

While the content/form problem finds expression in the metaphor of the box's classical shape and poetic content,[16] the imagery also describes two alternative forms of historiography, the chronicle as distinguished from poetic imagination of the past. Each implies a different set of epistemic and ethical categories. Heine plays this out in the fourth, concluding part. The poem returns to the poet's domestic scene in Paris, where his wife shows little sympathy with her husband's wish to hold on to his treasure when a truly "religious" spouse would hasten to turn such a treasure into money. Mathilde's profound ignorance of Halevi in particular and Jewish tradition in general serves as a springboard for a sharp critique of the repression of Europe's own history: the West, the poem points out, cannot be contained within the narrow boundaries of Christian culture. Launching into a eulogy of the Sephardic school of poets celebrating the tripartite stellar constellation Halevi, Salomo ben Gabirol, and Moses ben Esra leads to a genealogy that stamps the poet as schlemiel. While the second part had shown the superior literary tradition of Halevi when compared with the emerging medieval forms of troubadours, the last part turns to the genealogy of the poet as schlemiel. For is not Apollo, the God of poetry, the poem insinuates, reduced to just such a (divine) schlemiel when he is tricked into chasing the lovely nymph Daphne? But the origin of all schlemiels is to be found elsewhere, as is the origin of poetry, this alternative account suggests.

With the introduction of the genealogy of the schlemiel as the line of parentage for poetry, Heine performs a double move, both proposing a counterhistory of the origin of poetry and at the same time reclaiming citizenship for the Jewish contribution to European culture—and in the same act, actual citizenship for the Jews themselves.[17] In the schlemiel's counternarrative's reminder that the pressure to assimilate to a Christian-dominated culture represents a repression of Christian culture's own origins, Heine brings to bear his poetic conception of shalshelet as the free-spirited approach to tradition. As he rewrites his poetic version of the history of schlemiels, Heine not only frees Jewish marginality from its shadow existence (embodied in Chamisso's strikingly universal man without shadow, Peter Schlemihl) but also reasserts himself as both a modern and a consciously Jewish poet, and both irreducibly so.

Not surprisingly, then, the schlemiel anti-mythology Heine playfully introduces here presents us with two aspects that are crucial in their contradictory consequences. As before, the ambivalent potential of tradition is played out in a critical manner. On the one hand, one might emphasize the fact that such a fanciful genealogy points to the tenuous nature of any kind of foundational narrative, thus performing a masterful play of supplemental difference—a play whose counterhistorical narrative brings home the point that the writing of history is itself always based on the narrative of one or the other sort of schlemiel. On the other hand, the mock lineage of the schlemiel reasserts the idea expressed in the poetic use of shalshelet as the tradition/flourish. In this sense, the mock family tree of the schlemiel suggests that the deeper meaning of history can best be grasped in the counter-image that does not replace history with its opposite but instead engages tradition in a critical dialogue. Here, countertradition is figured as a poetic transcription, inaugurating a dialectical understanding of tradition characterized by a continually reconstituted subject that engages itself in history as a process both open-ended and continuous. Heine's whimsical celebration of the schlemiel poetically reflects how the best-bet scenario of the precarious subject position occupied by Jews in modern European culture might look and suggests that even the most diluted and assimilated version still owes its life force to the—albeit repressed—tradition it seems to deny. Heine captures this in his play on Isaak Itzig turned Julius Hitzig, whose assimilation causes him to repress the memory of the schlemiel narrative until the narrator's blasphemous cursing forces Hitzig/Itzig to come to terms with the poem's version of the lineage of schlemiels. In the supplemental H that turns Itzig into Hitzig, Heine figures the sign of assimilation that blocks the Jew from openly acknowledging his origins.

By exposing the schlemiel as the figure for countertradition, and thus connecting it with Jewish identity through the ages in a deeper sense than any conventional sense of tradition would dare, Heine presses home his point: that while the particular form of his subjectivity is neither going away nor likely going to be dissolved into a Christian-defined, secular, European culture, the pressure to do so will only reinforce his cultural identity all the more. The universal, critical, and emancipatory impulse of poetry is hence firmly linked to its constitutive foundation in the freedom that reclaims the schlemiel from his universal emplotment as everyman and instead frees him to be seen as the prefiguration of the poet whose Jewish identity no longer needs to be suppressed, ignored, or masked.[18] In this final acceptance, the poem seems to signal, poetry would fulfill one if not its most universal mission: to speak the word of the individual in an untrammeled, uncensored, and liberating way.

Heine's "Jehuda ben Halevy" thus performs a striking intervention in the nineteenth-century debate at the junction of historicism, fiction, and the function of poetry. Heine's answer to this problematic, so central to an emerging modernity, is not just another question but one that stresses the questionable implications of the problematic fictional character of what pretends to be seemingly straightforward, objective, "scientific," and, therefore, unquestionable prose. Against such a position, the dynamic fluidity of Heine's poetry—for which generations of linguistic purifiers have taken him to task—maintains that reality and its constructions are ultimately the result of the work of poetic imagination.

With the figure of shalshelet, Heine gives Spinoza's insight into the hermeneutic foundation of tradition poetic expression. And he does so in playing to the themes of Spinoza's progressive philosophy. If Goethe was the Spinoza of poetry and all his poems are infused with the spirit of Spinoza, as Heine declares (B 3, 618), this insight carries for Heine, who saw himself as Goethe's legitimate successor, the implications of a genealogical link that captures the poetics of his own poetry: "Yet Goethean pantheism finds its expression in the purest and most endearing form in his little songs. Spinoza's doctrine has emerged from its mathematical chrysalis and floats among us as Goethean song" ("Aber am reinsten und lieblichsten beurkundet sich dieser Goethesche Pantheismus in seinen kleinen Liedern. Die Lehre des Spinoza hat sich aus der mathematischen Hülle entpuppt und umflattert uns als Goethesches Lied" [B 3, 620]).[19] In the light of Heine's Spinoza interpretation, Heine's own writings assume sharper profile. The critical impulse of Heine's pointed wit receives its deeper philosophical meaning from his original appropriation of Spinoza. Both Heine's philosophy and his poetry represent a powerful realization of the modern potential of Spinoza's thought. A new and rejuvenated Spinoza finds entrance to modernity in both. Through Heine a new view of the revolutionary power of Spinoza's thought radiates forward to Moses Hess and a line of progressive thinkers who—knowingly or not—discover through Heine the critical potential of Spinozist thought.

NOTES
BIBLIOGRAPHY
INDEX

NOTES

INTRODUCTION. THE SCANDAL OF SPINOZA'S JEWISHNESS

1. For a comprehensive overview see Manfred Walther, "Spinoza und das Problem einer jüdischen Philosophie," in *Die philosophische Aktualität der jüdischen Tradition,* ed. Werner Stegmaier (Frankfurt: Suhrkamp, 2000), 281–330, and his essay "Spinozas Philosophie der Freiheit—eine 'jüdische Philosophie'?" *Edith Stein Jahrbuch* 3 (1997): 99–133. See also Steven B. Smith, "How Jewish Was Spinoza?" in *Piety, Peace, and the Freedom to Philosophize,* ed. Paul J. Bagley (Dordrecht: Kluwer, 1999), 191–208. On Spinoza's contested place in Jewish philosophy see Willi Goetschel, "'Jüdische Philosophie'—ein Querverweis," *Babylon* 14–15 (Winter 1994–95): 119–32.

2. The most prominent cases of outright rejection of Spinoza for his apparent apostasy are those of Hermann Cohen and Emmanuel Levinas. Levinas follows Cohen's (and possibly Harry Austryn Wolfson's) cue in condemning Spinoza. See Cohen's "Spinoza über Staat und Religion, Judentum und Christentum," in his *Jüdische Schriften,* ed. Bruno Strauss (Berlin: Schwetschke, 1924), 3:290–372, and Franz Rosenzweig's remarks in his preface, ibid., 1:xiii–lxix. See also Ernst Simon, "Zu Hermann Cohens Spinoza-Auffassung," in his *Brücken: Gesammelte Aufsätze* (Heidelberg: Lambert Schneider, 1965), 205–14. For Wolfson see his magisterial study *The Philosophy of Spinoza: Unfolding the Latent Processes of His Reasoning* (1934; Cambridge: Harvard University Press, 1983) and also his *From Philo to Spinoza: Two Studies in Religious Philosophy* (New York: Behrman, 1977). For Levinas see the polemical piece "The Spinoza Case" in his *Difficult Freedom: Essays on Judaism,* trans. Séan Hand (London: Athlone Press, 1990). Directly opposed to such a view stands the majority of modern German

Jewish tradition beginning with the Verein für Wissenschaft und Cultur der Juden, whose members Wolf and Heine celebrate Spinoza as a champion of Jewish thought and modernity (see chapters 17 and 18). From Moses Hess to Martin Buber and Leo Baeck, Spinoza has great symbolic significance for the articulation of German Jewish identity. Leo Strauss's Spinoza project is representative of the prominent place of Spinoza for Jewish self-understanding in Wilhelmine and Weimar Germany.

In his *Das Vermächtnis des deutschen Judentums,* Hermann Levin Goldschmidt stresses Spinoza's central role for the development of modern Judaism. Goldschmidt, *Das Vermächtnis des deutschen Judentums, Werke,* vol. 2 (Vienna: Passagen, 1993). For a discussion of Goldschmidt's view of Spinoza see Willi Goetschel, "Spinozas Modernität: Kritische Aspekte seiner politischen Theorie," in *Ethik, Recht, und Politik bei Spinoza,* ed. Marcel Senn and Manfred Walther (Zurich: Schulthess, 2001), 209–24.

3. For an incisive study see Geneviève Brykman, *La judéité de Spinoza* (Paris: Vrin, 1972); other, more recent exemplary essays are Shlomo Pines, "Spinoza's *Tractatus Theologico-Politicus* and the Jewish Philosophical Tradition," in *Jewish Thought in the Seventeenth Century,* ed. Isadore Twersky and Bernard Septimus (Cambridge: Harvard University Center for Jewish Studies, Harvard University Press, 1987), 499–521; Eduard Field, "Spinoza the Jew," *Modern Judaism* 9 (1989): 101–19; Isaac Franck, "Was Spinoza a 'Jewish' Philosopher?" *Judaism* 28 (1979): 345–52, and his equally polemical essay "Spinoza's Onslaught on Judaism," *Judaism* 28 (1979): 177–93. The publication of Yirmyahiu Yovel's two-volume study *Spinoza and Other Heretics* (Princeton: Princeton University Press, 1989) brought the issue of Spinoza's Jewish background back as a central issue. An intriguing contribution to the argument that Spinoza's Jewishness is a key to properly understanding his role as innovative pioneer of modern critical thought is provided in José Faur's chapter "Spinoza and the Secularization of Western Society" in his *In the Shadow of History. Jews and Conversos at the Dawn of Modernity* (Albany: State University of New York Press, 1992), 142–75. Steven Nadler, *Spinoza's Heresy: Immortality and the Jewish Mind* (Oxford: Clarendon Press, 2001) and Heidi M. Ravven and Lenn E. Goodman, *Jewish Themes in Spinoza's Philosophy* (Albany: State University Press of New York, 2002) appeared after completion of this book.

4. Faur, "Spinoza and the Secularization of Western Society."

5. Friedrich Heinrich Jacobi, *Schriften zum Spinozastreit,* ed. Klaus Hammacher and Irmgard-Maria Piske, in Jacobi, *Werke, Gesamtausgabe* (Hamburg and Stuttgart: Meiner and Frommann-Holzboog, 1998), 1:347.

6. Pagan theories of theogony are easily lumped together with Kabbalist traditions ("die philosophische Emanationslehren der Juden," ibid., 346), renewing the old claim that Spinozism is a variation of Kabbalist philosophy. For a discussion of this question see Alexander Altmann, "Lessing und Jacobi: Das Gespräch über den Spinozismus," in his *Die trostvolle Aufklärung: Studien zur Metaphysik und politischen Theorie Moses Mendelssohns* (Stuttgart–Bad Cannstatt:

Frommann-Holzboog, 1982), 50–83; and Gershom Scholem's introduction to Abraham Cohen Herrera, *Das Buch Pforte des Himmels* (Frankfurt: Suhrkamp, 1974), 7–67, on Spinoza: 41–64; and Scholem, "Die Wachtersche Kontroverse über den Spinozismus unf ihre Folgen," in *Spinoza in der Frühzeit seiner religiösen Wirkung,* ed. Karlfried Gründer and Wilhelm Schmidt-Biggemann (Heidelberg: Lambert Schneider, 1984), 15–25.

7. In a footnote to this passage, Jacobi explains that the late Mendelssohn seems to have taken offense with Jacobi's communication that Lessing had excused him and that, were Mendelssohn still alive, he would not insult him with this explanation. But now, after Mendelssohn's death, no longer bound by ethical décor, he seems eagerly willing to share his information. In the first edition of his letters *Über die Lehre des Spinoza,* the original wording of this statement was differently distributed among the interlocutors, Jacobi expressing his surprise that "a man of such bright and accurate understanding like Mendelssohn" ("ein Mann von so hellem und richtigem Verstande wie Mendelssohn") would have taken interest in the Cartesian demonstration of the existence of God, and Lessing simply excusing Mendelssohn (9).

8. Altmann points out that the judgment that Mendelssohn was no metaphysical mind is obviously Jacobi's own rather than Lessing's ("Lessing und Jacobi," 51).

9. For recent critical studies on the early German reception of Spinoza see Winfried Schröder, *Spinoza in der deutschen Frühaufklärung* (Würzburg: Epistemata, 1987), and Rüdiger Otto, *Studien zur Spinozarezeption in Deutschland im 18. Jahrhundert* (Frankfurt: Lang, 1994). See also Hanna Delf, Julius H. Schoeps, and Manfred Walther, eds., *Spinoza in der europäischen Geistesgeschichte* (Berlin: Hentrich, 1994).

10. Althusser's intuitive reading prepared the way for the critical renewal of Spinoza studies. Cf. his statement: "The first man ever to have posed the problem of *reading,* and in consequence, of *writing,* was Spinoza, and he was also the first man in the world to have proposed both a theory of history and a philosophy of the opacity of the immediate." Louis Althusser and Étienne Balibar, *Reading Capital,* trans. Ben Brewster, 2nd ed. (London: Verso, 1983), 16. For a representative sample of new readings see Warren Montag and Ted Stolze, eds., *The New Spinoza* (Minneapolis: University of Minnesota Press, 1997); cf. also Warren Montag, *Bodies, Masses, Power: Spinoza and His Contemporaries* (London: Verso, 1999). For a fresh look at Spinoza see Moira Gatens and Genevieve Lloyd, *Collective Imaginings: Spinoza, Past and Present* (London: Routledge, 1999); Genevieve Lloyd, *Part of Nature: Self-Knowledge in Spinoza's "Ethics"* (Ithaca: Cornell University Press, 1994); and Moira Gatens, *Imaginary Bodies: Ethics, Power, and Coropreality* (London: Routledge, 1996). With the release of the new biography by Steven Nadler, *Spinoza: A Life* (Cambridge: Cambridge University Press, 1999), which synthesizes new historical research of the last half century or so, Spinoza emerges for the first time in historically sharp contour. The magisterial study by Jonathan I. Israel, *Radical Enlightenment: Philosophy*

and the Making of Modernity, 1650–1750 (Oxford: Oxford University Press, 2001) appeared after the completion of this book.

11. Manfred Walther, "Spinozismus ille Spinoza oder wie Spinoza zum 'Klassiker' wurde—zur Etikettierungs-, Rezeptions-, und Wirkungsgeschichte Spinozas im europäischen Vergleich," in *Beobachter und Lebenswelt: Studien zur Natur-, Geistes-, und Sozialwissenschaft,* ed. Helmut Reinalter (Thaur: Thaur, 1996), 183–238. For Walther's numerous publications on Spinoza see the bibliography.

12. See my review essay on recent Mendelssohn research, "Neue Literatur zu Moses Mendelssohn," *Lessing Yearbook* 29 (1998): 199–208, and my "Moses Mendelssohn und das Projekt der Aufklärung," *The Germanic Review* 71 (1996): 163–75. Most recently, Carola Hilfrich, in *"Lebendige Schrift": Repräsentation und Idolatrie in Moses Mendelssohns Philosophie und Exegese des Judentums* (Munich: Wilhelm Fink, 2000), has added the first in-depth study that fully embraces the critical theoretical implications of Mendelssohn's *Jerusalem, or On Religious Power and Judaism.*

13. Heine, *Ludwig Börne: Eine Denkschrift,* in B 4, 18.

CHAPTER 1. THE NEW METAPHYSICAL FRAMEWORK OF ONTOLOGY

1. For the idea that Spinoza's *Ethics* contains two different kinds of texts see Gilles Deleuze, *Spinoza et le problème de l'expression* (Paris: Les Éditions de Minuit, 1968), 318ff., and Deleuze, "Spinoza and the Three 'Ethics,'" in Montag and Stolze, *The New Spinoza,* 21–34; Edwin Curley, *Behind the Geometrical Method: A Reading of Spinoza's "Ethics"* (Princeton: Princeton University Press, 1988).

2. For a good discussion of this aspect of Spinoza's philosophy see Pierre-François Moreau, *Spinoza* (Paris: Seuil, 1975).

3. Spinoza is early on associated with materialism. Cf. J. G. Walch's 1726 *Philosophisches Lexikon* s.v. Materialism. The historian of materialism's original plan to devote a special chapter to Spinoza "had, however, to be abandoned in order not to swell the book unduly, and prevent its varying from its original character"; Frederick Albert Lange, *The History of Materialism and criticism of its present importance,* trans. Ernest Chester Thomas (New York: Humanities Press, 1950), 2:35 n. According to Lange, the connection of Spinozism with materialism proper has been overestimated, as is illustrated by the history of Spinozism in Germany, where Spinozism became associated with idealistic strands of thought; ibid., see also 2:147. For the role of Spinoza for the materialist tradition in France see Paul Vernière, *Spinoza et la pensée française avant la Révolution,* 2nd ed. (Paris: Presses universitaires de France, 1982). See also Olivier Bloch, *Le matérialisme* (Paris: Presses universitaires de France, 1985), 63–66. For the materialist implications of Spinoza see Louis Althusser, "The Only Materialist Tradition," in Montag and Stolze, *The New Spinoza,* 3–19;

Athusser, "Sur Spinoza," in his *Éléments d'autocritique* (Paris: Hachette, 1974), 65–83; Emilia Giancotti, "The Birth of Modern Materialism in Hobbes and Spinoza," in Montag and Stolze, *The New Spinoza,* 49–63; and André Tosel, *Du Matérialisme de Spinoza* (Kimé: Paris, 1994).

4. The term "pantheism" was not introduced until 1709 by the Dutch theologian J. De la Faye in a critique of Toland, who seems to have first mentioned the doctrine of the pantheists in his *Socinianism truly stated* (London, 1705), 7. See the entry on pantheism by Winfried Schröder in *Historisches Wörterbuch der Philosophie* (Basel: Schwabe, 1989), 7:59.

5. For an incisive discussion of Spinoza's reinscription of metaphysics see Manfred Walther, *Metaphysik als Anti-Theologie: Die Philosophie Spinozas im Zusammenhang der religionsphilosophischen Problematik* (Hamburg: Meiner, 1971).

6. For a good discussion of why Spinoza cannot be considered as pantheist, see Jean Axelrad Cahan, "Spinoza's Theory of Immanence Reconsidered," *Journal of Jewish Thought and Philosophy* 5 (1995–96): 81–98. See also Hermann Levin Goldschmidt, "Stoa Heute," in *Aus den Quellen des Judentums: Aufsätze zur Philosophie, Werke,* vol. 5 (Vienna: Passagen, 2000), 21–83.

7. Max Scheler speaks of the "marble like propositions" of the *Ethics.* Scheler, *Gesammelte Werke,* ed. Manfred S. Frings (Bern: Francke, 1976), 9:182.

8. Edmund Husserl, *Die Krisis der europäischen Wissenschaften und die transzendentale Phänomenologie* (Hamburg: Meiner, 1977), 71 (Husserl's emphasis).

9. Cf. the discussion of the link between subjectivity and self-preservation as a specifically modern one in Spinoza in *Subjektivität und Selbsterhaltung: Beiträge zur Diagnose der Moderne,* ed. Hans Ebeling (Frankfurt: Suhrkamp, 1976), esp. the essay by Robert Spaemann, "Bürgerliche Ethik und nichtteleologische Ontologie," 76–96.

10. For a good discussion see Giancotti, "The Birth of Modern Materialism in Hobbes and Spinoza."

11. Dieter Henrich, "The Basic Structure of Modern Philosophy," *Cultural Hermeneutics* 2 (1974): 1–18.

12. Hans Blumenberg, "Selbsterhaltung und Beharrung: Zur Konstitution der neuzeitlichen Rationalität," in Ebeling, *Subjektivität und Selbsterhaltung,* 144–207. This volume centers around a discussion of the relationship between subjectivity, self-consciousness, and self-preservation. For another critique of Dilthey see Goldschmidt, "Stoa Heute."

13. Spaemann, "Bürgerliche Ethik und nichtteleologische Ontologie," 80.

14. Blumenberg, "Selbsterhaltung und Beharrung," 146; Henrich, "The Basic Structure of Modern Philosophy," 106.

15. The discussion about the meaning and function of the geometric order is as old as Spinoza's philosophy. See on this point Lodewijk Meyer's preface to Spinoza's first publication, *Renati Des Cartes Principiorum Philosophiae Pars I et II, More Geometrico demonstratae.* Cf. Wolfson, *The Philosophy of Spinoza,* 1:32–60; Osamu Ueno, "Mentis oculi ipsae demonstrationes: Jouissance et

démonstration dans l'Éthique de Spinoza," in *Spinoza: Puissance et Ontologie,* ed. Myriam Revault D'Allonnes (Paris: Kimé, 1994), 73–84; Efraim Shmueli, "The Geometrical Method, Personal Caution, and the Ideal of Tolerance," in *Spinoza: New Perspectives,* ed. Robert W. Shahan and J. I. Biro (Norman: University of Oklahoma Press, 1978), 197–215.

16. Cf. Pierre Macherey's remarks in "The Problem of the Attributes," in Montag and Stolze, *The New Spinoza,* 65–95, 86.

CHAPTER 2. UNDERSTANDING UNDERSTANDING

1. For a suggestive reading of the affinity between Vermeer and Spinoza see Hubertus Schlenke, *Vermeer, mit Spinoza gesehen* (Berlin: Mann, 1998).

2. Hermann Ulrich Asemissen, *Die Malkunst: Aspekte eines Berufsbildes* (Frankfurt: Fischer, 1988), 50.

3. The model carries all the trappings traditionally associated with Clio, the Muse of historiography. But in Vermeer's painting the Muse no longer appears as an Olympian deity. Rather, Vermeer highlights the human features of the model. For an interpretation of the possible political and aesthetic implications of the painting see Asemissen, *Die Malkunst.*

4. Asemissen speaks of the painting's concern for the question of representation of representation. Ibid., 51.

5. See Edwin Curley in his edition of *The Collected Works of Spinoza,* CW xiii. Nadler, *Spinoza,* 175, follows.

6. Cf. TTP, chapter 6, note VI, 197; Y annotation 6 to 6.1.22.

7. For an in-depth study of the comprehensive project of the epistemological treatise see Pierre-François Moreau, *Spinoza: L'expérience et l'éternité* (Paris: Presses universitaires de France, 1994).

8. For a discussion of the complicated role of the autobiographical narrative in Descartes see Claudia Brodsky Lacour, *Lines of Thought: Discourse, Architectonics, and the Origin of Modern Philosophy* (Durham, N.C.: Duke University Press, 1996).

9. For a incisive discussion of the classical background of the TIE, see Moreaux, *Spinoza: L'expérience et l'éternité.*

10. TIE §108.5, CW 44; see also E2P44 Corol 2.

11. For this much-liked expression of Spinoza's critique of the illegitimate claim of human nature to a special ontological status see E3 Praefatio; TTP 548/550, Y 17.12.51 and 54; TP II§6.

12. Cf. Etienne Balibar, "L'institution de la vérité: Hobbes et Spinoza," in *Hobbes and Spinoza: Science and Politics,* ed. Daniela Bostrenghi (Naples: Bibliopolis, 1992), 3–22, 18.

13. Ernst Cassirer, *Das Erkenntnisproblem in der Philosophie und Wissenschaft der neueren Zeit,* 3rd ed. (1922; reprint, Darmstadt: Wissenschaftliche Buchgesellschaft, 1974), 2:84–96.

14. Cf. Marcelo Dascal, "Spinoza and Leibniz: Language and Cognition," *Studia Spinozana* 6 (1990): 103–45.

15. For a similar use of a circular argument in Spinoza see Etienne Balibar, "A Note on 'Consciousness/Conscience' in the *Ethics*," *Studia Spinozana* 8 (1992): 37–53, 42–43.

16. The view that Spinoza's epistemology is based on his ontology is shared by most interpreters; see, e.g., Errol E. Harris, "Method and Metaphysics in Spinoza," *Studia Spinozana* 2 (1986): 129–50; Francis S. Haserot, "Spinoza and the Status of Universals," in *Studies in Spinoza: Critical and Interpretive Essays*, ed. S. Paul Kashap (Berkeley: University of California Press, 1972), 43–67; Don Garrett, "Truth, Method, and Correspondence in Spinoza and Leibniz," *Studia Spinozana* 6 (1990): 13–43.

17. Haserot argues this point in "Spinoza and the Status of Universals."

18. Harris, "Method and Metaphysics in Spinoza," points out its dialectical character.

19. Haserot, "Spinoza and the Status of Universals."

20. Cf. Louis Althusser, "The Only Materialist Tradition," 11, and Althusser, "Sur Spinoza," 75. Cf. also Montag, *Bodies, Masses, Power*, 68–69. See also Lloyd's discussion of Spinoza's way of thinking sameness and difference in her *Part of Nature*, 149–68, which points in the same direction.

21. Spinoza refers here to E2P38 Corol, E2P39 and Corol, and E2P40. This amounts to a sophisticated qualification as to the status of the general notions of the third kind, effectively linking them through the cited "renvois" to a nominalist position.

22. For a brief discussion of Spinoza's nominalism see Jean-Pierre Osier, "L'herméneutique de Spinoza et de Hobbes," *Studia Spinozana* 3 (1987): 319–47, 325, 328ff.; Moreau, *Spinoza*, 54, 60. In his review essay, Manfred Walther points out that "a thorough monographic treatment of the nominalist heritage in Spinoza's philosophy and his possible reservations against it presents one of the most urgent tasks of research." Walther, "Spinoza als Kritiker der Neuzeit?" *Philosophische Rundschau* 28 (1981): 274–300, 285.

23. Balibar speaks of "un nominalisme de la singularité"; see "L'institution de la vérité," 21.

24. See also the corresponding passage in E2P49 Schol.

25. Cf. David Savan, "Spinoza and Language," in Kashap, *Studies in Spinoza*, 236–48: "Spinoza explicitly rejects the semantic theory of truth" (239). Cf. also Balibar, "L'institution de la vérité," 18.

26. Charles S. Peirce, *Selected Writings*, ed. Philip P. Wiener (New York: Dover, 1966), 183.

27. Peirce's rule for defining truth goes as follows: "Consider what effects, which might conceivably have practical bearings, we conceive the object of our conception to have. Then, our conception of these effects is the whole of our conception of the object" (ibid., 124, repeated on 192, 204.)

28. For a good description of Spinoza's attempt at holding a middle ground, see Dascal, "Spinoza and Leibniz."

CHAPTER 3. A PSYCHODYNAMIC THEORY OF AFFECTS

1. Sigmund Freud, *Vorlesungen zur Einführung in die Psychoanalyse,* 18th lecture, *Studien Ausgabe* (Frankfurt: Fischer, 1969), 1:283–84. For a brief discussion of the debate on the significance of Spinoza for Freud and psychoanalysis cf. Michèle Bertrand, "Spinoza et la psychanalyse," *Studia Spinozana* 8 (1992): 171–90. For an early appraisal see Bernhard Alexander, "Spinoza und die Psychoanalyse," *Chronicon Spinozanum* 5 (1927): 96–103, rpt. in *Almanach für das Jahr 1928* (Vienna: Internationaler Psychoanalytischer Verlag, 1928). Cf. also Lothar Bickel, "Über Beziehungen zwischen der Psychoanalyse und einer dynamischen Psychologie" (1931), in *Spinoza in neuer Sicht,* ed. Leo Sonntag und Heinz Stolte (Meisenheim am Glan: Anton Hain, 1977), 145–68; Walter Bernard, "Psychotherapeutic Principles in Spinoza's *Ethics,*" in *Speculum Spinozanum 1677–1977,* ed. Siegfried Hessing (London and Boston: Henley and Routledge & Kegan Paul, 1977), 63–80; the chapter on Spinoza and Freud in Yovel, *Spinoza and Other Heretics,* 136–66; Frank Burbage and Nathalie Chouchan, "Freud et Spinoza: La question de la transformation et le devenir actif du sujet," and Bertrand Ogilvie, "Spinoza dans la psychanalyse," both in *Spinoza au XXe siècle,* ed. Olivier Bloch (Paris: Presses universitaires de France, 1993), 527–48 and 549–75. For a brief but interesting discussion of Spinoza's importance for Lacan see Elisabeth Roudinesco, "Lacan et Spinoza: Essai d'interpretation (1916–1964)," ibid., 577–88. The affinity between Freud and Spinoza consists also in the fact that both fashioned their contributions as therapies. Already the specific Spinozist ring of the title of a book by Spinoza's friend and student Ehrenfried Walter von Tschirnhaus brings this out most clearly: his *Medicina Mentis* (1687) accentuates the specifically therapeutic aspect that informs Spinoza's *Ethics.* For a brief discussion of Tschirnhaus see Cassirer, *Das Erkenntnisproblem in der Philosophie und Wissenschaft der neueren Zeit,* 2:191–211.

2. Hegel's eloquent silence on this point certainly deserves attention as instrumental for the particularly tendentious reception of Spinoza. Hegel's exclusive focus on the macrostructure of Spinoza's ontology—here following in Jacobi's steps—while ignoring the innovative aspects of the theological-political and the political theory as well as the theory of affects has been formative for modern historiography of philosophy. For Heine's challenge of Hegel's biased view of Spinoza see below chapters 17 and 18. But in the nineteenth century, Spinoza did not have to wait for the recognition of the pioneering role of his psychology by Nietzsche. Johannes Müller acknowledged it already in 1826 when he incorporated Spinoza's theory of affects word for word in his *Handbuch der Physiologie des Menschen* (Coblenz: Hölscher, 1834–40), 2:543–48. Cf. Reiner Wiehl, "Die Vernunft in der menschlichen Unvernunft: Das Problem

der Rationalität in Spinozas Affektenlehre," in *Metaphysik und Erfahrung: Philosophische Essays* (Frankfurt: Suhrkamp, 1996), 277–332, 285.

An interesting case is Wilhelm Dilthey, whose ambivalent attitude articulates itself in placing Spinoza squarely at the center of the development of modern philosophy but admitting his originality only under erasure, as he interprets his thought as strictly following the Stoics. Dilthey, "Die Autonomie des Denkens, der konstruktive Rationalismus, und der pantheistische Monismus nach ihrem Zusammenhang im 17. Jahrhundert," in *Gesammelte Schriften* (Leipzig and Berlin: Teubner, 1914), 2:285ff. Cf. also his comments in other essays in the same volume, 342–43; 464–65.

3. Zeno, the founder of the Stoics, defines affect as "perturbatio aversa a recta animi contra naturam animi," cf. Cicero, *Tusc.* IV, 9, and Diogenes Laertius, *Life and Opinions of Famous Philosophers,* VII, 110ff.; Dilthey, "Die Autonomie des Denkens," 293.

4. Plato, *Phaedo,* but see also the parable of the cave in the *Republic.*

5. See Wiehl, "Die Vernunft in der menschlichen Unvernunft," for an elucidating study of how Spinoza's theory of affects allows us to grasp the rationality of affects.

6. Marx Wartofsky, "Action and Passion: Spinoza's Construction of a Scientific Psychology," in *Spinoza: A Collection of Critical Essays,* ed. Marjorie Grene (Notre Dame: University of Notre Dame, 1979), 329–53.

7. For a good discussion of the parallelism between body and mind see Curley, *Behind the Geometrical Method,* 60ff. Montag argues to drop the notion of parallelism altogether as body and mind are attributes of the substance and thus only linked through the substance. The notion of parallelism implies some sort of causal nexus, whereas Spinoza's solution does not allow for a causal link between mind and body and allows therefore for a more complex relationship between body and mind. See Montag, *Bodies, Masses, Power,* 42. For a complex view on the mind-body relationship with an elucidating application on the question of sexual difference see also Lloyd, *Part of Nature,* 154–68.

8. Lloyd, *Part of Nature,* 154.

9. For a detailed study see Dilthey, "Die Autonomie des Denkens."

10. See ibid.

11. Curley's emphasis.

12. For Spinoza's innovative concept of individuality see Moreau, *Spinoza,* and Lloyd, *Part of Nature.*

13. Joy represents an individual's transition from less to more perfection, sadness represents the transition from more to less perfection, and desire consists in the nature of the individual itself insofar as the individual is determined by it to act (Def 1–3 of appendix Affectuum Definitiones of E3). Desire (*cupiditas*) is appetite/instinct with the consciousness of it (E3P9 Schol).

14. Wiehl, "Die Vernunft in der menschlichen Unvernunft," 322.

15. Ibid., 288.

CHAPTER 4. SPINOZA'S THEORY OF RELIGION, HERMENEUTIC, AND TRADITION

1. For outstanding studies see Manfred Walther, "Biblische Hermeneutik und/oder theologische Politik bei Hobbes und Spinoza: Historische Studie zur Theorie der Ausdifferenzierung von Religion und Politik in der Neuzeit," in *Hobbes e Spinoza,* ed. Daniela Bostrenghi (Naples: Bibliopolis, 1992), 623–69; and Brayton Polka, "Spinoza's Concept of Biblical Interpretation," *Journal of Jewish Thought and Philosophy* 2 (1992): 19–44. See also Osier, "L'herméneutique de Spinoza et de Hobbes"; and Norman O. Brown, "Philosophy and Prophecy: Spinoza's Hermeneutics," *Political Theory* 14 (1986): 195–213. For an engaging critique of Strauss and readings informed by Strauss and a fresh look at Spinoza see Nancy Levene, "Ethics and Interpretation, or How to Study Spinoza's *Tractatus Theologico-Politicus* without Strauss," *Journal of Jewish Thought and Philosophy* 10 (2000): 57–110.

2. I would like to thank Martin Yaffe for letting me use his forthcoming translation of Spinoza's *Theologico-Political Treatise.* Y refers to his translation, followed by the number of the chapter.paragraph.sentence. Y, Preface 4.8.

3. References to the Latin text of the *Tractatus theologico-politicus,* ed. Günter Gawlick and Friedrich Niewöhner (Darmstadt: Wissenschaftliche Buchgesellschaft, 1979), are indicated as TTP and page number. TTP 14.

4. Hermann Cohen, *Religion of Reason Out of the Sources of Judaism,* trans. Simon Kaplan (Atlanta: Scholars, 1995), preface.

5. For the historical background of the identification of prophets with "recipients of revelation" see Herbert Donner, "Prophetie und Propheten in Spinozas *Theologisch-politischem Traktat,*" in *Theologie und Wirklichkeit: Festschrift für Wolfgang Trillhaas,* ed. Hans Walter Schütte and Friedrich Wintzer (Göttingen: Vandenhoeck & Ruprecht, 1974), 31–50.

6. For a brief discussion of navi see Spinoza's own annotation to this passage (Y annotation to 1.1.3; TTP adnotatio I, 30).

7. For Spinoza's critique of miracles see Manfred Walther, "Spinozas Kritik der Wunder—ein Wunder der Kritik? Die historisch-kritische Methode als Konsequenz des reformatorischen Schriftprinzips," *Zeitschrift für Theologie und Kirche* 88 (1991): 68–80. See also Leo Strauss, *Spinoza's Critique of Religion,* trans. E. M. Sinclair (New York: Schocken, 1965).

8. Berel Lang, "The Politics of Interpretation: Spinoza's Modernist Turn," in *The Anatomy of Philosophical Style* (Oxford: Basil Blackwell, 1990), 221.

9. James C. Morrison, "Spinoza and History," in *The Philosophy of Baruch Spinoza,* ed. Richard Kennington (Washington, D.C.: Catholic University of America Press, 1980), 173–95; Wilhelm G. Jacobs, "Spinozas *Theologisch-Politischer Traktat* und das Problem der Geschichte," in *Tradition und Innovation,* ed. Wolfgang Kluxen, XIII Deutscher Kongreß für Philosophie (Hamburg: Meiner, 1985), 82–89; and André Tosel, "Théorie de l'histoire ou philosophie

du progrès historique chez Spinoza?" in Tosel, *Du Matérialisme de Spinoza,* 79–103.

10. Pierre-François Moreau, "Fortune and the Theory of History," in Montag and Stolze, *The New Spinoza,* 97–106.

CHAPTER 5. A NONCONTRACTUAL THEORY OF THE POLITICAL ORDER

1. While the *Theological-Political Treatise* advances already in 1670 a radical political philosophy introducing a comprehensive theory of democracy, it is in the *Political Treatise* that Spinoza formulates a theory of the political.

2. For a discussion of the role of Hobbes in Spinoza's thought see the essays in the volume *Spinoza and Hobbes* of *Studia Spinozana* 3 (1987). On Spinoza's political theory see the essays by Manfred Walther, "Die Transformation des Naturrechts in der Rechtsphilosophie Spinozas," *Studia Spinozana* 1 (1985): 73–104; Walther, "Politik, Moralität, und Freiheit in der Philosophie Spinozas," in *Selbstbehauptung und Anerkennung: Spinoza, Kant, Fichte, Hegel,* ed. Helmut Girndt (St. Augustin: Academia, 1990), 7–23; Walther, "Institution, Imagination, und Freiheit bei Spinoza: Eine kritische Theorie politischer Institutionen," in *Politische Institutionen im gesellschaftlichen Umbruch: Ideengeschichtliche Beiträge zur Theorie politischer Institutionen,* ed. Gerhard Göhler, Kurt Lenk, Herfried Münkler, and Manfred Walther (Opladen: Westdeutscher Verlag, 1990), 246–75; Etienne Balibar, *Spinoza et la politique* (Paris: Presses universitaires de France, 1985); Lucien Mugnier-Pollet, *La philosophie politique de Spinoza* (Paris: Vrin, 1976); Fatma Haddad-Chamakh, *Philosophie systématique et système de philosophie politique chez Spinoza* (Tunis: Université de Tunis, 1980). For a challenging attempt at appropriative interpretation see Antonio Negri, *The Savage Anomaly: The Power of Spinoza's Metaphysics and Politics,* trans. Michael Hardt (Minneapolis: University of Minnesota Press, 1991). See also the discussion in Henry E. Allison, *Benedict de Spinoza: An Introduction* (New Haven: Yale University Press, 1987), chapter 6, "The Individual and the State."

3. Cf. C. B. Macpherson, *The Political Theory of Possessive Individualism: Hobbes to Locke* (Oxford: Oxford University Press, 1962).

4. For the most recent critical edition see Baruch de Spinoza, *Politischer Traktat/Tractatus politicus,* trans. and ed. Wolfgang Bartuschat (Hamburg: Meiner, 1994). Cf. also Bartuschat's concise introduction, vii–xliv. Cf. now also Spinoza, *Political Treatise,* trans. by Samuel Shirley, introduction and notes by Steven Barbone and Lee Rice (Indianapolis and Cambridge: Hackett, 2000).

5. For this equation see also *Theological-Political Treatise,* chapters 16 and 20 (Y 16.2.3 and 20.2.2; TTP 466 and 602).

6. Cf. Balibar, *Spinoza et la politique,* 72–78; Walther, "Transformation des Naturrechts."

7. It is noteworthy that Spinoza, if he speaks of a contract at all, hastens to equate it with laws. Cf. TP IV§6; Shirley 60.

8. While Spinoza speaks in the *Theological-Political Treatise* of a contract (*pactum*), he describes it as defined by reason and the golden rule (Y 16.5.4; TTP 472). For Spinoza the contract is predicated on utility: "pactum nullam vim habere posse nisi ratione utilitatis." The validity of the contract remains only as long as the prospect of danger and the utility continue (Y 16.5.5–14, Y 16.7.7; TTP, chapter 16, 472, 474, 486).

9. Balibar, *Spinoza et la politique,* 69, 76ff.; Douglas J. Den Uyl, "Sociality and Social Contract: A Spinozistic Perspective," *Studia Spinozana* 1 (1985): 19–51; Mugnier-Pollet, *La philosophie politique de Spinoza,* 116ff.; Allison, *Spinoza,* 185; Walther, "Transformation des Naturrechts"; Walther, "Politik, Moralität, und Freiheit in der Philosophie Spinozas"; Walther, "Institution, Imagination, und Freiheit bei Spinoza"; see also Alexandre Matheron, *Individu et communauté chez Spinoza* (Paris: Minuit, 1969), 307–30; Sylvain Zac, "État et nature chez Spinoza," in *Philosophie, théologie, politique dans l'oeuvre de Spinoza* (Paris: Vrin, 1979), 117–43, 133–34; Jean Préposiet, *Spinoza et la liberté des hommes* (Paris: Gallimard, 1967), 198–202; Negri, *The Savage Anomaly,* trans. Michael Hardt (Minneapolis: University of Minnesota Press, 1991), 194–95.

10. Thomas Hobbes, *Leviathan,* ed. C. B. Macpherson (Harmondsworth: Penguin, 1968), chapter 17, 227–28.

11. Balibar, *Spinoza et la politique,* 84; Balibar, "Spinoza, the Anti-Orwell: The Fear of the Masses," in *Masses, Classes, Ideas: Studies on Politics and Philosophy before and after Marx* (New York: Routledge, 1994), 3–37; see also Alexandre Matheron, "The Theoretical Function of Democracy in Spinoza and Hobbes," in Montag and Stolze, *The New Spinoza,* 207–17; and Antonio Negri, "*Reliqua Desiderantur:* A Conjecture for a Definition of the Concept of Democracy in the Final Spinoza," in Montag and Stolze, *The New Spinoza,* 219–47, esp. 229–37. For a discussion of Spinoza's theory of sovereignty see Thomas Heerich, *Transformation des Politikkonzepts von Hobbes zu Spinoza: Das Problem der Souveränität* (Würzburg: Königshausen & Neumann, 2001).

12. For an elucidating reading of this trope see Etienne Balibar, "Potentia multitudinis, quae una veluti mente ducitur," in *Ethik, Recht, und Politik bei Spinoza,* ed. Marcel Senn and Manfred Walther (Zurich: Schulthess, 2001), 105–37.

13. Cf. Thomas Hobbes, *On the Citizen,* trans. Richard Tuck and Richard Silverthorne (Cambridge and New York: Cambridge University Press, 1998), chapter 1, section 12, and Hobbes, *Leviathon,* ed. C. B. Macpherson (Harmondsworth: Penguin, 1968), 186.

14. Spinoza may have had in mind Tacitus's quip that the Romans announced peace and delivered subjection. See Tacitus's commentary about the discrepancy between the Romans' foreign politics and their rhetoric: "Solitudinem faciunt, pacem appellant" (They make a desert, and call it peace). Tacitus, *Agricola,* 30.

15. Balibar, *Spinoza et la politique,* 84ff.; Balibar, "Spinoza, the Anti-Orwell," 24–25; see also Negri, "*Reliqua Desiderantur:* A Conjecture."

16. Cf. André Tosel, "La théorie de la pratique et la fonction de l'opinion publique dans la philosophie politique de Spinoza," *Studia Spinozana* 1 (1985): 183–208.

17. Walter Eckstein, "Rousseau and Spinoza: Their Political Theories and Their Conception of Ethical Freedom," *Journal of the History of Ideas* 5 (1944): 259–91; see also Vernière, *Spinoza et la pensée française avant la Révolution,* 485–86.

18. For the consequences of Spinoza's thought with regard to political institutions see Walther, "Institution, Imagination, und Freiheit bei Spinoza."

CHAPTER 6. FROM THE MARGINS OF PHILOSOPHY

1. See the pioneering studies by Alexander Altmann: *Moses Mendelssohn: A Biographical Study* (Tuscaloosa: University of Alabama Press, 1973), *Moses Mendelssohns Frühschriften zur Metaphysik* (Tübingen: Mohr, 1969), and *Die trostvolle Aufklärung: Studien zur Metaphysik und politischen Theorie Moses Mendelssohns* (Stuttgart–Bad Cannstatt: Frommann-Holzboog, 1982).

2. See the studies of Edward Breuer, *The Limits of Enlightenment: Jews, Germans, and the Eighteenth-Century Study of Scripture* (Cambridge: Harvard University Press, 1996); Amos Funkenstein, *Perceptions of Jewish History* (Los Angeles: University of California Press, 1993); Arnold Eisen, "Divine Legislation as 'Ceremonial Script': Mendelssohn on the Commandments," *Association for Jewish Studies Review* 15 (1990): 239–67; Arnold Eisen, *Rethinking Modern Judaism: Ritual, Commandment, Community* (Chicago and London: University of Chicago Press, 1998); Michael L. Morgan, "History and Modern Jewish Thought: Spinoza and Mendelssohn on the Ritual Law," in *Dilemmas in Modern Jewish Thought: The Dialectics of Revelation and History* (Bloomington: Indiana University Press, 1992), 14–26; David Sorkin, *Moses Mendelssohn and the Religious Enlightenment* (Berkeley: University of California Press, 1996).

3. For a view that highlights Mendelssohn as commentator see Sorkin, *Mendelssohn and the Religious Enlightenment.* For commentary as a preoccupation of "Jewish" intellectual praxis see Gershom Scholem, "Revelation and Tradition as Religious Categories in Judaism," in *The Messianic Idea in Judaism* (New York: Schocken, 1995), 282–303: "Commentary thus became the characteristic expression of Jewish thinking about truth" (290).

4. Cf. Bamberger in his introduction to the early writings, Jub A 1, xlv.

5. These notes seem to have been jotted down immediately following the reading of the second discourse and may have preceded Mendelssohn's detailed critique of Rousseau published in 1756 and written after Lessing had left Berlin for Leipzig in October 1755. We may therefore assume that the cited entry dates from 1755.

6. Altmann makes the most convincing case in tracking, point for point,

Mendelssohn's involvment with the views and methods of Leibniz and Wolff. See esp. his *Mendelssohns Frühschriften zur Metaphysik.*

7. Altmann, *Mendelssohn: A Biographical Study,* 5, 7; cf. Sorkin, *Mendelssohn and the Religious Enlightenment,* xvii, xx.

8. Ludwig Stein, *Leibniz und Spinoza: Ein Beitrag zur Entwicklungsgeschichte der Leibnizischen Philosophie* (Berlin, 1890); Georges Friedman, *Leibniz et Spinoza* (Paris: Gallimard, 1962); cf. also *Studia Spinozana* 6 (1990), which is dedicated to the theme "Spinoza and Leibniz."

9. Hegel simply represents the view that had gained popularity in the course of history when he introduces Spinoza in his history of philosophy as the representative of the oriental principle. See *Hegel's Lectures on the History of Philosophy,* trans. E. S. Haldane and F. H. Simson (1896; reprint, London and New York: Routledge and Kegan Paul and Humanities Press, 1963). The passage is discussed in chapters 17 and 18 below.

10. Husserl, *Die Krisis der europäischen Wissenschaften,* 71.

11. See Lessing's letter to Michaelis, 16 October 1754, in *Briefe,* ed. Helmuth Kiesel (Frankfurt: Deutscher Klassiker Verlag, 1987), 58.

12. Jub A 1, 1–19; D 96–111.

13. For Henry Allison's important discussion of Lessing's "Spinozist Exercises," see chapter 12 below.

14. Mendelssohn changed the name of Palemon in the 1761 revised edition into Theokles to indicate the difference of Theokles' position from the one of Palemon, like Theokles a Shaftesbury character. Euphranor is also the pseudonym chosen by Georg Friedrich Meier for his essay "Versuch einer philosophischen Abhandlung von dem Mittelmässigen in der Dichtkunst," as Altmann points out (*Mendelssohns Frühschriften zur Metaphysik,* 112).

15. "einige Betrachtungen über die *Natur der vermischten Empfindungen,* die aus Lust und Unlust zusammen gesetzt sind, und über die erstaunliche Gewalt, mit welcher sie in die Seele würken" (Jub A 1, 229–30).

16. "Wenn wir den Sturm einer unangenehmen Leidenschaft besänftigen wollen; so befiehlt uns die Vernunft, über die Ursachen unsres Mißvergnügens nachzudenken, und die Begriffe aufzuklären. Nur diese finstere Wolken sind es, aus denen das Ungewitter entsteht; und so bald es in unsrer Seele heiter wird, so verschwindet das Toben der Leidenschaft" (Jub A 1, 240–41).

17. It is important to note that Mendelssohn uses here *Affekt* (affect) rather than *Leidenschaft* (emotion): "Der Affekt verschwindet, sobald die Begriffe aufgekläret werden" (Jub A 1, 241).

18. Jub A 1, 49. In the caption heading, Mendelssohn gives this version: "Der Affekt verschwindet, wenn alle Begriffe deutlich werden" (Jub A 1, 240).

19. Altmann, *Mendelssohns Frühschriften zur Metaphysik,* 114.

20. For Spinoza's point that the more we recognize individual things the more we recognize God see E5P24. With regard to Mendelssohn's attitude to the question of miracles see his 1753 fragment "Von den ohngefähren Zufällen" (Jub A 2, 3–5).

21. It is important to note that Rousseau's *perfectibilité,* though similar to

Mendelssohn's, lacks the specific ontological grounding of a dynamic conception of nature that points back to Spinoza.

22. "Die reine Seelenlust, als eine Bestimmung des Geistes betrachtet, und abgesondert von ihrer fleischlichen Begleiterinn, von der sinnlichen Wollust, muß in den positiven Kräften unserer Seele, und nicht in ihrem Unvermögen, nicht in der Einschränkung dieser ursprünglichen Kräfte gegründet seyn" (Jub A 1, 248).

23. "Allein die wahre Vollkommenheit ist eine lebendige Flamme, die immer um sich greift, und immer stärker wird, je mehr sie um sich greifen kann. Die Neigung sich mitzutheilen, um das Gute, dessen man geniesst, zu vervielfältigen, ist der Seele so eingepflanzt, als der Trieb sich zu erhalten. Wir werden vollkommener, wenn alles, was uns umgiebt, vollkommen ist; wir werden glückselig, wenn wir alles, was um uns ist, glückselig machen können" (Jub A 1, 406). The urge to communicate what one has recognized as truth is a central idea in Spinoza's understanding of human nature. See E4P37.

24. "Dieses allgemeine Gesetz, diese Nerve der Glückseligkeit läuft durch alle Theile der Schöpfung, blühet in der Rose, regt sich im Wurme, und denket, will und fühlt sich seelig im Menschen" (Jub A 1, 408). For Werther see especially the letter from 10 May, Johann Wolfgang Goethe, *Die Leiden des jungen Werther,* in *Sämtliche Werke,* ed. Ernst Beutler (Zurich and Munich: Artemis and Deutscher Taschenbuch Verlag, 1977), 4:384–85.

25. Bamberger, introduction to Jub A 1, xxxvi.

26. "Man lerne die wahre Würde des Menschen kennen, und die Erhabenheit seiner sittlichen Natur in dem gehörigen Lichte betrachten" (Jub A 1, 420).

27. "Ein jeder habe vor sich selbst geziemende Achtung, sagt ein alter Weltweiser, so wird er desto geneigter seyn, der Stimme der Tugend zu gehorchen. Der nächste Weg zum sittlichen Verderben ist die Geringschätzung der menschlichen Natur" (Jub A 1, 420).

28. "Sie [die menschliche Natur] zeigt sich Anfangs unter der Gestalt der Selbsterkentniß, der Demuth; allein sie ist betrüglich, so bald sie mehr auf das menschliche Geschlecht, als auf unser Individuum, mehr auf das gehet, was wir Menschliches, als auf das, was wir Eigenthümliches haben. Sie erzeugt alsdenn Menschenhaß, statt der Selbsterkenntniß, Kleinmüthigkeit, statt der Demuth, schlägt die Kräfte des Gemüths zu sehr nieder, und macht uns fast gleichgültig gegen das Gute und Böse" (Jub A 1, 420).

29. "Man darf, mit wahrer Demuth im Herzen, auf die Würde des Menschen und auf den Rang, den er in der Schöpfung einnimmt, stolz seyn. Wir müssen in unseren Augen etwas wichtiges, und unser Thun und Lassen von einiger Bedeutung seyn, wenn wir uns des Guten mit Eifer und Nachdruck annehmen sollen" (Jub A 1, 420–21).

CHAPTER 7. THE EXCHANGE ON TRAGEDY

1. For a comprehensive discussion of the exchange see Schulte-Sasse's detailed commentaries in his edition of Gotthold Ephraim Lessing, Moses Mendelssohn, and Friedrich Nicolai, *Briefwechsel über das Trauerspiel* (Munich: Winkler,

1972). See also Robert Petsch's introduction to his edition of *Lessings Briefwechsel mit Mendelssohn und Nicolai über das Trauerspiel,* Phil. Bibl. Bd. 121 (Leipzig: Dürr, 1910), ix–lv; Fred O. Nolte, "Lessing's Correspondence with Mendelssohn and Nicolai, August 31, 1756 to May 14, 1757," *Harvard Studies and Notes in Philology and Literature* 13 (1931): 309–32; Max Kommerell, *Lessing und Aristoteles: Untersuchungen über die Theorie der Tragödie,* 3rd ed. (Frankfurt: Vittorio Klostermann, 1960); Peter Michelsen, "Die Erregung des *Mitleids* durch die Tragödie: Zu Lessings Ansichten über das Trauerspiel im Briefwechsel mit Mendelssohn und Nicolai," *Deutsche Vierteljahrsschrift* 40 (1966): 548–66; Jost Schillemeit, "Lessings und Mendelssohns Differenz: Zum Briefwechsel über das Trauerspiel (1756/57)," in *Digressionen: Wege zur Aufklärung: Festschrift für Peter Michelsen,* ed. Gotthardt Frühsorge, Klaus Manger, and Friedrich Strack (Heidelberg: C. Winter, 1984), 79–92; Hans-Jürgen Schings, *Der mitleidigste Mensch ist der beste Mensch: Poetik des Mitleids von Lessing bis Büchner* (Munich: Beck, 1980); and Henrik de Wild, *Tradition und Neubeginn: Lessings Orientierung an der europäischen Tradition* (Rodopi: Amsterdam, 1986). With the exception of Schulte-Sasse and de Wild, most discussions treat the exchange from Lessing's perspective, framing it in a somewhat slanted manner, for rather than simply utilizing his friends as critics for feedback when formulating his budding views on tragedy, Lessing engages in a genuine dialogue that will affect the formulation of his mature theory of tragedy in his *Hamburgische Dramaturgie* a decade later. While most critics maintain that Lessing does not change his views from his early to his later stage, or only with regard to aspects that will not bear on the main conception of tragedy (Nolte calls the correspondence "an early and spirited rehearsal" ["Lessing's Correspondence," 332]), I argue that changes in Lessing's understanding can be traced in both the later presentation of his theory of tragedy in the *Hamburgische Dramaturgie* and, more interestingly, in the development of his playwriting from *Minna von Barnhelm* to *Nathan der Weise.*

2. Dahlstrom's translation continues here following the addition in the revised edition of Mendelssohn's dialogues in his *Philosophische Schriften* of 1771, Jub A 1, 290.

3. Schulte-Sasse, ed., *Briefwechsel über das Trauerspiel,* 11–44, esp. 12, 17, 31.

4. Petsch speaks of Lessing's project as one of "Erziehung zum Mitleid" (*Lessings Briefwechsel,* xlix).

5. Cf. Mendelssohn's "Sendschreiben an den Herrn Magister Lessing" ("Open Letter to Magister Lessing"), where Mendelssohn voices his critique of Rousseau's second discourse, which he had translated following Lessing's suggestion. There Mendelssohn notes only a few months prior to the exchange on tragedy: "Pity itself, this human sentiment [. . .] is not an original inclination as [Rousseau] had seen it. Our natures are not specifically designed to produce displeasure at the feebleness of other creatures. No! pity is grounded in love, and love is grounded in the pleasure at harmony and order. Where we recognize

perfections we wish them to grow; and as soon as they show a deficiency we develop a feeling of displeasure which we call pity." ("Das Mitleiden selbst, dieses menschliche Gefühl [...] ist keine ursprüngliche Neigung, dafür er [Rousseau] es angesehen hat. In uns lieget keine ausdrückliche Bestimmung, an den Schwachheiten anderer Geschöpfe Mißvergnügen zu haben. Nein! Mitleiden gründet sich auf Liebe, Liebe gründet sich auf die Lust an Harmonie und Ordnung. Wo wir Vollkommenheiten erblicken, da wünschen wir sie wachsen zu sehen; und sobald sich ein Mangel bey ihnen äus[s]ert: so entspinnet sich bey uns darüber eine Unlust, die wir Mitleiden nennen" [Jub A 2, 86]).

6. Lessing seems to agree with Rousseau's identification of pity as the source of all social virtues. See Jean-Jacques Rousseau, *Discourse on the Origin of Inequality*, in *The Basic Writings*, trans. Donald A. Cress (Indianapolis and Cambridge: Hackett, 1987), 25–109, 53ff.

7. Nolte maintains that the correspondence on tragedy presents some sort of tug-of-war where "Mendelssohn frequently succeeded in drawing the debate to his side of the line, but in so doing he invited sheer dialectics" ("Lessing's Correspondence," 313). Petsch points out that Mendelssohn, however, not only has often the more convincing arguments but that Lessing owes the flexibility to a more open view during the exchange to Mendelssohn (Petsch, *Lessings Briefwechsel,* xlv). While Nolte concedes that Mendelssohn is at times "closer to the truth" (330), he notes "the inability of the two disputants to meet confidently on common ground that gave to the correspondence its most unsatisfactory aspect" (313). For the fact that the suggestions of both Mendelssohn and Lessing are in the end faulty see 330. For a generally more balanced view of the shortcomings of both correspondents see de Wild, *Tradition und Neubeginn,* 228–87.

8. For a commentary on the full irony of the subtext for this reference to Mendelssohn see Schings, *Der mitleidigste Mensch,* 39.

9. "Moral taste" ("moralischer Geschmack") is defined as "the faculty of the soul that works by means of intuitive cognition so that it will abhor vices, love virtue, and experience displeasure at those physical imperfections that, in a subject, are associated with virtue" ("das Vermögen der Seele, vermittelst der anschauenden Erkenntniß Laster zu verabscheuen, die Tugend zu lieben, und über die physikalischen Unvollkommenheiten, die mit der Tugend in einem Subjekt verknüpft sind, Unlust zu empfinden" [Jub A 11, 128–29]).

10. For a discussion of Mendelssohn's semiotics see David Wellbery, *Lessing's "Laocoon": Semiotics and Aesthetics in the Age of Reason* (Cambridge: Cambridge University Press, 1984).

11. Wellbery acknowledges the transcendental character of this move (ibid., 65).

12. Altmann, *Mendelssohns Frühschriften zur Metaphysik,* 137–38.

13. See the discussion of the letter to Lessing cited earlier (Jub A 11, 149) in which it is argued that to be oneself, to bring about one's perfection, and *suam realitatem conservare* (to preserve one's reality) all express the same idea of self-determination and self-realization.

14. For a discussion of this prize essay see Altmann, *Mendelssohns Frühschriften zur Metaphysik*, 252–391, and my discussion of Kant's submission, which, despite its equal if not superior quality, only came in second; Willi Goetschel, *Constituting Critique: Kant's Writing as Critical Praxis* (Durham, N.C.: Duke University Press, 1994), 49–52.

15. D 305–6; Jub A 2, 327–28.

16. For the contrary view of the philosophical uselessness of examples and the importance of maxims stands Kant.

17. Dahlstrom ends his translation of *On Evidence in Metaphysical Sciences* with this sentence.

18. Lessing, *Hamburgische Dramaturgie, Werke,* ed. Herbert G. Göpfert (Munich: Hanser, 1979), 4:577.

19. Ibid., 588.

20. Ibid., 579–91; number 75 to 77.

21. Claudia Brodsky, "Lessing and the Drama of the Theory of Tragedy," *Modern Language Notes* 98 (1983): 426–53, esp. 444.

22. Schings points out the two friends' remarkable affinity in difference: "Man gewinnt den Eindruck, dass Mendelssohn durch Trennung und Distinktion der Sphären erreichen möchte, was Lessing nur durch ihre Vereinigung in einem gemeinsamen Ursprungsphänomen garantiert sieht—die Aufwertung der Kunst und der Tragödie" (*Der mitleidigste Mensch,* 35).

CHAPTER 8. STAKING OUT GROUNDS FOR PUBLIC REASON

1. Published in 1767, the first edition was sold out within four months. New editions followed from 1768, 1769, etc. The book was translated into Danish, Dutch, English, French, Hebrew, Hungarian, Italian, Polish, Russian, and Serbian. For a complete listing of the editions see Hermann M. Z. Meyer, *Moses Mendelssohn Bibliographie: Mit einigen Ergänzungen zur Geistesgeschichte des ausgehenden 18. Jahrhunderts* (Berlin: de Gruyter, 1965), 39–44.

2. Moses Mendelssohn, *Phaedon; or, the Death of Socrates,* trans. Charles Cullen (London: J. Cooper, 1789), viii–ix.

3. Lavater's letter in Jub A 7, 3. For an exact reconstruction of the history and prehistory of this exchange see Altmann, *Moses Mendelssohn: A Biographical Study,* 201–63. For the background see also Simon Rawidowicz's introduction to Jub A 7, xi–lxxx.

4. Cf. the use of this passage, almost word for word, in *Jerusalem,* Jub A 8, 161, 194.

5. At the junction of post-Humean and post-Voltairean thought, Bonnet, Lavater, and many of their contemporaries reacted to the rationalist forays with renewed interest in spiritual aspects of faith. Rather than being shunned, the discussion of miracles assumes increased prominence with the progress of the Enlightenment. The interest in the nature and meaning of miracles is reflected in various ways, from credulity to reflectiveness to unambiguous irony and plain

mockery. But however the views of that generation would be defined in the individual cases, miracles commanded central importance. For a discussion of the background to the miracle debates of the Enlightenment cf. Ernst Cassirer, *Die Philosophie der Aufklärung*, 3rd ed. (Tübingen: Mohr, 1973), 178–262; Peter Gay, *The Enlightenment: An Interpretation: The Rise of Modern Paganism* (New York: Knopf, 1966), 145–59; and Panajotis Kondylis, *Die Aufklärung im Rahmen des neuzeitlichen Rationalismus* (Munich: Deutscher Taschenbuchverlag, 1986), 361–81.

6. For Spinoza's treatment of miracles, which anticipates Mendelssohn's conclusions point for point, see Spinoza, *Theological-Political Treatise*, chapter 6, and my discussion in chapter 4 above.

7. Cf. for the view of the prophet as interpretor/translator of miracles Spinoza, *Theological-Political Treatise*, beginning of chapter 1.

CHAPTER 9. FRAMING POLITICAL RIGHTS

1. For a discussion of the Bible translation see the important study of Breuer, *The Limits of Enlightenment*. For its reception see Nils Römer, *Tradition und Akkulturation: Zum Sprachwandel der Juden in Deutschland zur Zeit der Haskalah* (Münster: Waxmann, 1995).

2. The translator may have been Henriette Herz. In a conversation, Eva Engel pointed out that several faulty renderings due to a weak command of English may point to Henriette rather than Marcus Herz as the translator.

3. While there is no historic evidence for the view that the absence of Manasseh from Amsterdam can be brought in direct connection with the excommunication of Spinoza, the absence of Manasseh, who was more liberal than the chief rabbi of the Amsterdam Portuguese Jewish community, Saul Levi Mortera, might have contributed to the ease with which the excommunication was handled. For a detailed discussion of the background of Spinoza's excommunication see Nadler, *Spinoza*, chapters 5 and 6.

4. Cf. Adam Smith, *An Inquiry into the Nature and Causes of the Wealth of Nations*, ed. Edwin Cannan (Chicago: University of Chicago Press, 1976). For Smith, "the propensity to truck, barter, and exchange" (I, 17) plays the key role in making possible the division of labor, which, Smith argues, drives the economy: "every man thus lives by exchanging, or becomes in some measure a merchant, and the society itself grows to be what is properly a commercial society" (I, 26).

5. The predicate "tolerated" was used for one of the lower-ranking categories for granting privileges of residence to Jews in Prussia.

6. Jub A 13, 83.

CHAPTER 10. AN ALTERNATIVE UNIVERSALISM

1. Rpt. in Jub A 8, 73–87.

2. See Altmann's introduction, Jub A 8, xxiv–xxvi and his introduction to the English translation of *Jerusalem*, J, 7–8.

3. See Goldschmidt, *Das Vermächtnis der deutschen Judentums,* 25, and Goldschmidt, "Moses Mendelssohns geschichtliche Bedeutung," in *"Der Rest bleibt," Aufsätze zum Judentum, Werke,* vol. 4 (Vienna: Passagen, 1997), 165–79, 173–74.

4. For the study of *Jerusalem* see Alexander Altmann's pioneering work in *Mendelssohn: A Biographical Study* and *Die trostvolle Aufklärung;* see also his "Moses Mendelssohn's Concept of Judaism Reëxamined" in his *Von der mittelalterlichen zur modernen Aufklärung: Studien zur jüdischen Geistesgeschichte* (Tübingen: Mohr, 1987), 234–48.

5. J 139; "Liebet die Wahrheit! Liebet den Frieden!" (Jub A 8, 204). The passage is from Zechariah 8:19.

6. Zechariah 8:20–23.

7. "Kirche und Staat" are the first words of Mendelssohn's draft for *Jerusalem* (Jub A 8, 95). For the English translation see J 247.

8. Rousseau is not mentioned here, but Mendelssohn seems to imply the generic identity in the way the basic framework for their respective political theories is formulated.

9. It is interesting to note that Simone Weil's analysis of political theory leads to a similar privileging of duties over rights in order to guarantee the humanity and progressive impulse of the jurisprudential aspect of the argument. For a detailed discussion of Weil's theory of rights and obligations see Maja Wicki-Vogt, *Simone Weil: Eine Logik des Absurden* (Bern: Haupt, 1983).

10. This is important in order to grasp the political connotations of the central role the concept of *Bildung* plays in Mendelssohn's essay "On the Question: What Is Enlightenment?" There, as in *Jerusalem, Bildung* is anything but just an aesthetic or cultural concern but has direct political implications. See Jub A 6.1, 113–19. For an English translation see James Schmidt, ed., *What Is Enlightenment? Eighteenth-Century Answers and Twentieth-Century Questions* (Berkeley: University of California Press, 1996), 53–57.

11. For Spinoza see Idit Dobbs-Weinstein, "Rereading the *Tractatus theologico-politicus* in Light of Benjamin's 'Theologico-Political Fragment,'" in Bagley, *Piety, Peace, and the Freedom to Philosophize,* 67–89.

12. See Mendelssohn's discussion of the duty of parental care that he defines to be—in contrast to most accounts of the origin of family and family right—grounded in the intention of both parents to have and raise children together. The emphasis on the consent of two human beings to found a family effectively does away with the privileging of the paterfamilias in both paternalist and possessive individualism. See J 49–50; Jub A 8, 118–19.

13. See, e.g., his acknowledgment of the existence of views more in line with Cranz's own: J 85–86; Jub A 8, 153.

14. Cf. Julius Guttmann, "Mendelssohns *Jerusalem* und Spinozas *Theologisch-Politischer Traktat,*" *48. Bericht der Hochschule für die Wissenschaft des Judentums* (Berlin, 1931), 31–67.

15. J 44; Jub A 8, 113.

16. See the discussion of the idea of a society guided *una veluti mente,* that is, as if by one spirit, in chapter 5 on Spinoza's political theory.

17. See Altmann's commentary to this passage in Jub A 8, 308–9, J 174–76.

18. J 90–93; Jub A 8, 157–60.

19. For a discussion of Mendelssohn's reservations against modern Bible criticism see Breuer, *The Limits of Enlightenment.*

20. See Eisen, "Divine Legislation as 'Ceremonial Script'" and *Rethinking Modern Judaism*; Morgan, *Dilemmas in Modern Jewish Thought,* chapters 1–3; and Edward Breuer, "Politics, Tradition, History: Rabbinic Judaism and the Eighteenth-Century Struggle for Civil Equality," *Harvard Theological Review* 85 (1992): 357–83.

21. The primary importance of Condillac for the eighteenth-century debate on the origin of language is discussed in Hans Aarsleff, "The Tradition of Condillac: The Problem of the Origin of Language in the Eighteenth Century and the Debate in the Berlin Academy before Herder," in his *From Locke to Saussure: Essays on the Study of Language and Intellectual History* (London: Athlohe and University of Minnesota Press, 1982), 146–209. See also Ulrich Ricken, "Sprachauffassung und geschichtliches Menschenbild der Aufklärung," in *Logos Semantikos: Studia Linguistica in honorem Eugenio Coseriu,* ed. Horst Geckeler et al. (Madrid and Berlin: Gredos and de Gruyter, 1981), 1:41–55.

22. Etienne Bonnot de Condillac, *An Essay on the Origin of Human Knowledge,* trans. Thomas Nugent (1756; reprint, New York: AMS Press, 1974), part 2, section 2, chapter 14, §53, 338.

23. See Eva Engel in her introduction, Jub A 6.2, xviii.

24. Mendelssohn develops his theory of signs early on; see his essays "Über die Quellen und die Verbindungen der schönen Künste und Wissenschaften" (Jub A 1, 174 and 180ff.) and "Gedanken vom Ausdrucke der Leidenschaften" (Jub A 2, 259–65, 264). For a brief discussion see Otto F. Best's introduction to Moses Mendelssohn, *Ästhetische Schriften in Auswahl* (Darmstadt: Wissenschaftliche Buchgesellschaft, 1974), 20–21; and Funkenstein, *Perceptions of Jewish History,* 222–29. Cf. also Hilfrich, "*Lebendige Schrift,*" 58–66.

25. "eine lebendige, Geist und Herz erweckende Art von Schrift" (Jub A 8, 169).

26. For the background of the eighteenth-century debate on hieroglyphs to which Mendelssohn's remarks implicitly but pointedly refer, see Jan Assmann, *Moses the Egyptian: The Memory of Egypt in Western Monotheism* (Cambridge: Harvard University Press, 1997).

27. Cf. Breuer, "Politics, Tradition, History," esp. 379–83.

28. Cf. Guttmann, "Mendelssohns *Jerusalem* und Spinozas *Theologisch-Politischer Traktat.*"

CHAPTER 11. RESCUING LESSING

1. Cf. Strauss's introduction to Jub A 3.2, xii–cx; Altmann, "Lessing und Jacobi"; Frederick C. Beiser, *The Fate of Reason: German Philosophy from Kant*

to Fichte (Cambridge: Harvard University Press, 1987), chapters 2 and 3; George di Giovanni, "The First Twenty Years of Critique: The Spinoza Connection," in *The Cambridge Companion to Kant,* ed. Paul Guyer (Cambridge: Cambridge University Press, 1992), 417–48. Kurt Christ's study *Jacobi und Mendelssohn: Eine Analyse des Spinozastreits* (Würzburg: Königshausen & Neumann, 1988) argues the need for an unbiased treatment of the dispute. His own discussion, however, suffers from a portrayal of Mendelssohn fraught with inaccuracies that produce a stereotypical impression. His claim that Mendelssohn emerged as the clear victor in this debacle is as misguided as his curious assumption that Mendelssohn lacked a deeper familiarity with Spinoza's philosophy. For a more balanced, careful reconstructive approach see Sylvain Zac, *Spinoza en Allemagne: Mendelssohn, Lessing, et Jacobi* (Paris: Méridiens Klincksieck, 1989).

2. Jacobi's repeated citing of Lavater and the religious undertones had, in Mendelssohn's ears, certainly a rather incendiary ring.

3. See Mendelssohn's indirect request, Johann Erich Biester's request, Christian Gottfried Schütz's entreaty, and the correspondence between Marcus Herz and Kant of 27 February and 7 April 1786, Immanuel Kant, *Briefwechsel,* ed. Otto Schlöndörffer and Rudolf Malter, 3rd ed. (Hamburg: Felix Meiner, 1986), 272, 273, 283, 285, 292–93, 299–305, 309. See also the journal style reports from Hamman in his letters, and also Hippel, collected in Rudolf Malter, ed., *Immanuel Kant in Rede und Gespräch* (Hamburg: Meiner, 1990), 270–75, and the discussion of Kant's position in Goetschel, *Constituting Critique,* 155–57.

4. Gérard Vallée, ed., *The Spinoza Conversations between Lessing and Jacobi* (Lanham, Md.: University Press of America, 1988), 145.

5. Mendelssohn, *An die Freunde Lessings,* Jub A 3.2, 213.

6. Vallée, *The Spinoza Conversations,* 92.

7. Jacobi, *Werke,* 1:24.

8. Jacobi's peculiar weave of philosophical, metaphysical, moral, and theological strands of arguments allows him to address Spinoza's philosophy with the missionary zeal that brings the Enlightenment debate down to the level of Jacobi's particular conception of moral-theological truth defined by the somewhat obtrusive militancy of his concept of Christianity. See Jacobi, *Werke,* 1:115ff., 136–46. This tendency becomes more outspoken in Jacobi's writings published after Mendelssohn's death. See *Werke,* 1:179, 304ff., and esp. 342ff.

9. See esp. Jacobi, *Werke,* 1:116, 342–53.

10. Vallée, *The Spinoza Conversations,* 130.

11. Ibid., 149.

12. This is an allusion to Lavater, whose pious, angelically pure mouth Mendelssohn mentions in the sentence preceding the quote. Jacobi had concluded his *Über die Lehre des Spinoza* with a long quote from Lavater which he introduced invoking Lavater himself: "let me, sincere Lavater, bless and seal my work with a word from your pious, angelically pure mouth" ("laß mich, redlicher Lavater, mein Werk mit einem Wort aus Deinem frommen Engelreinem Munde segnen und versiegeln" [Jacobi, *Werke,* 1:145]).

CHAPTER 12. LESSING'S SPINOZIST EXERCISES

1. Jacobi, *Über die Lehre des Spinoza,* in *Werke,* 1:27.

2. For a discussion of the background of the intrigues that led to Wolff's expulsion see the introduction by Michael Albrecht in his edition of Christian Wolff, *Rede über die praktische Philosophie der Chinesen* (Hamburg: Meiner, 1985).

3. While it is often assumed that it was Lessing who introduced Mendelssohn to Spinoza, some critics claim that it was Mendelssohn who introduced Lessing to Spinoza. See Hans Schmoldt's *Der Spinozastreit* (Würzburg: Triltsch, 1938), which highlights Mendelssohn's key role in the reception of Spinoza; Detlev Pätzold, "Lessing und Spinoza: Zum Beginn des Pantheismus-Streits in der deutschen Literatur des 18. Jahrhunderts," in *Aufklärung-Gesellschaft-Kritik: Studien zur Philosophie der Aufklärung,* ed. Manfred Buhr and Wolfgang Förster (Berlin: Akademie-Verlag, 1985), 298–355, thinks that, in the beginning, Mendelssohn may have had superior knowledge of Spinoza (312, 320); see now also Pätzold, *Spinoza—Aufklärung—Idealismus: Die Substanz der Moderne* (Frankfurt: Peter Lang, 1995). Clear evidence as to which of the two friends introduced the other to Spinoza is lacking. The attempt to answer the question of priority implies therefore options that reflect more the critics' preferences than anything else. Although Lessing was, by the time he met Mendelssohn, familiar with the Spinoza legend from his study of Bayle and his discussions with free spirits such as his mentor Mylius and others, Mendelssohn may likewise have encountered Spinoza on his own. The fact that Lessing describes Mendelssohn as a second Spinoza may have been occasioned either by Mendelssohn's identification with Spinoza or by Lessing's perception alone. Most likely they both had, by the time they met, some interest in Spinoza that sparked their early discussions.

4. For a discussion of the 1753 review of the *Oeuvres mêlées* by Abbé de Bernis (L 3, 172) and the 1754 review of John Leland's *Abriß der vornehmsten Deistischen Schriften* (Lessing, *Sämtliche Schriften,* ed. Karl Lachmann and Franz Muncker, 3rd ed. [Stuttgart: Göschen, 1890], 5:443–45), see Martin Bollacher, *Der junge Goethe: Studien zur Geschichte des Spinozismus in der Epoche des Sturms und Drangs* (Tübingen: Niemeyer, 1969), 196 and 200; Pätzold, "Lessing und Spinoza," 318–19, and Pätzold, *Spinoza—Aufklärung—Idealismus,* 110–11.

5. See also Pätzold, "Lessing und Spinoza," 313–14, and Pätzold, *Spinoza—Aufklärung—Idealismus,* 107–10, 114.

6. See also T. C. van Stockum, *Spinoza—Jacobi—Lessing: Ein Beitrag zur Geschichte der deutschen Literatur und Philosophie im 18. Jahrhundert* (Groningen: P. Noordhoff, 1916), 56–57; Pätzold, *Spinoza—Aufklärung—Idealismus,* 105–6.

7. While some critics seem to identify precipitations of Spinozism in this early piece, I solely wish to highlight the interesting similarity of Lessing's original point of departure prior to a critical engagement with Spinoza. Although Pätzold,

Spinoza—Aufklärung—Idealismus, 106–7, rightly cautions against the mistake of taking as evidence for a Spinozist influence what can be described as Pietist thinking, the text's framing of the relationship between theory and praxis, reason and faith, reveals a striking affinity to the thought of Spinoza. This affinity explains the natural attraction to Spinoza's philosophy that Lessing was to experience later.

8. Selma Stern, *Der preussische Staat und die Juden,* part 3, first half volume of documents (Tübingen: J. C. B. Mohr [Paul Siebeck], 1971), 208.

9. For a discussion of the play see Willi Goetschel, "Lessing and the Jews," in *A Companion to Lessing,* ed. Barbara Fischer and Thomas Fox (Columbia, S.C.: Camden House, forthcoming).

10. See Karl S. Guthke, "Lessing und das Judentum. Rezeption. Dramatik und Kritik. Krypto-Spinozismus," *Judentum im Zeitalter der Aufklärung: Wolfenbütteler Studien zur Aufklärung,* Bd. 4, ed. Günter Schulz (Wolfenbüttel: Jacobi, 1977), 229–71, 253; and Samuel Modlinger, *Lessing's Verdienste um das Judenthum* (Frankfurt: Selbstverlag, 1869), 12–13.

11. See Guthke, "Lessing und das Judentum."

12. Letter to Michaelis, 16 October 1754, Lessing, *Briefe,* 58.

13. See the review of Abbé de Bernis's *Oeuvres mêlées* in nr. 81 of *Berlinische Privilegirte Zeitung,* 7 July 1753 (L 3, 172).

14. Johannes Hoops, "Lessings Verhältnis zu Spinoza," *Archiv für das Studium der neueren Sprachen und Litteraturen* 86 (1891): 1–28, is a sort of unfortunate polemic trying to argue that Lessing was clean of Spinozism; for the text in question, see 2–3. For a more differentiated view see van Stockum, *Spinoza—Jacobi—Lessing,* 59–60; Bollacher, *Der junge Goethe,* 197–98; Pätzold, "Lessing und Spinoza," 320–21; Pätzold, *Spinoza—Aufklärung—Idealismus,* 111–13.

15. Cf. Hoops, "Lessings Verhältnis zu Spinoza," and van Stockum, *Spinoza—Jacobi—Lessing,* 59–60.

16. Cf. Bollacher, *Der junge Goethe,* 197–98; Pätzold, "Lessing und Spinoza," 320–21; Pätzold, *Spinoza—Aufklärung—Idealismus,* 111–13.

17. The exchange on tragedy is discussed in detail above in chapter 7.

18. For a discussion of the Spinozist elements contained in Mendelssohn's aesthetic theory see chapters 6 and 7.

19. Written in 1771, *Emilia Galotti* presents an exception. The plot's conception, presupposing a still more static understanding of human psychology, goes back to 1754. Yet, the affective dynamics that leads to the tragic ending displays an eruption of violence that suggests a psychodynamic conception of the economy of the affects.

20. For the role of the theory of affects in the formulation of Lessing's dramatic theory see his *Hamburgische Dramaturgie.*

21. This is Henry Allison's expression. See his excellent essay "Lessing's Spinozistic Exercises" in *Humanität und Dialog: Lessing und Mendelssohn in neuer Sicht,* ed. Ehrhard Bahr, Edward P. Harris, and Laurence G. Lyon (Detroit and Munich: Wayne State University Press and edition text + kritik, 1982), 223–33.

22. Jub A 1, 3–12.
23. L 8, 517–18.
24. Th. W. Danzel, *Gotthold Ephraim Lessing, sein Leben und sein Werk*, vol. 2.2 completed by G. E. Guhrauer based on Danzel's manuscripts (Leipzig: Dyk, 1854), 112. Danzel continues: "It is also [. . .] obvious to which side the scale tips; the savage, whose view is analogous to Spinoza's, explains the phenomenon according to the true situation; the other proposes a forced theory."
25. Cf. Altmann's peculiar comment on Mendelssohn's overkill based on a mistaken rendering of the passage (*Mendelssohns Frühschriften zur Metaphysik*, 24). From Mendelssohn's point of view, Lessing's point can easily be accepted. The difference is not so much one of philosophical opinion as of different argumentative strategies.
26. While the Berlin academy under the leadership of Maupertuis and the French contingent certainly rejected Leibniz, the dominance of Christian Wolff in German universities made Leibniz the central figure and Wolffianism the intellectual frontier in German philosophy from 1720 until the rise of Kantianism. That Mendelssohn holds on—and does so, as is often stated with some amazement, with a certain stubbornness—to Leibniz at a time when the trend in most of his contemporaries is to move away from him can be interpreted as an example of the phenomenon that the public demeanor of someone forced into the position of what to the outside appears as cultural assimilation often seems to lag behind the new trends of a culture.
27. Bollacher, *Der junge Goethe*, 207–8, sees Mendelssohn and Lessing at opposite ends, not realizing that not only Lessing, whom he likes to see as the superior of the two thinkers, but also Mendelssohn pursues a strategy. Because of this, the dialectics of Mendelssohn's reading is lost on him. For a disparaging assessment of Mendelssohn see van Stockum, *Spinoza—Jacobi—Lessing*, 66. Also Pätzold, *Spinoza—Aufklärung—Idealismus*, 123, cheerfully casts the difference of viewpoints as one of philosophical competence: "At the same time, Lessing emerges as far more knowledgeable on Spinoza's philosophy than Mendelssohn.
28. Cf. Allison, "Lessing's Spinozistic Exercises," 223–33. See also Gideon Stiening, "'Werden Sie lieber ganz sein Freund': Zur Bedeutung von Lessings Spinoza-Rezeption," in *Spinoza im Deutschland des 18. Jahrhunderts: Zur Erinnerung an Hans-Christian Lucas (1942–1997)*, ed. Eva Schürmann, Norbert Waszek, and Frank Weinrich (Stuttgart–Bad Cannstadt: Frommann-Holzboog, 2002), 193–220, esp. 205–15.
29. Jub A 1, 17–18.
30. For an elucidating discussion of the different motives coming together in this issue, see Allison, "Lessing's Spinozistic Exercises," 226–30.
31. Ibid., 232 n. 21 (for the quote from Russell see Bertrand Russell, *A Critical Exposition of the Philosophy of Leibniz*, 2nd ed. [London, 1937], 185).
32. Ibid., 227.
33. Bollacher, *Der junge Goethe*, 209, also comes to the conclusion that Lessing now resolutely, and in no way only experimentally, joins Spinoza: "The

positive effect of Lessing's Spinozism reflects the importance of Spinozist doctrine for the Enlightenment as a whole: negatively, it signals a series of ruptures in the system of orthodox theology."

34. Cf. Danzel, who states that Lessing, "though he has not written a rescue for Spinoza has laid the ground for it in world history, and, thus, one of philosophy itself" (*Lessing*, 112). Guhrauer sums up his own view: "thanks to Spinoza, Lessing has gained the deeper and more comprehensive understanding of Leibniz that enabled him to achieve a final breakthrough to his own particular results in philosophy and their applications to religion and theology" (Danzel, *Lessing*, 114). Cf. also Allison, "Lessing's Spinozistic Exercises," 230: "Spinoza emerges as something more than a stepping stone to Leibniz." Pätzold also concludes that the two "Spinozistic exercises" document a decisive change in Lessing's view of Spinoza (*Spinoza—Aufklärung—Idealismus*, 114–23). Cf. also Stiening, "'Werden Sie lieber ganz sein Freund.'"

CHAPTER 13. TOWARD A NEW CONCEPT OF TRUTH

1. The first complete edition of this work, published on behalf of the Joachim-Jungius-Gesellschaft der Wissenschaften Hamburg, did not appear until 1972. Hermann Samuel Reimarus, *Apologie oder Schutzschrift für die vernünftigen Verehrer Gottes*, ed. Gerhard Alexander (Frankfurt: Suhrkamp, 1972).

2. See the editor's commentary in L 8, 625.

3. Mendelssohn, *Morgenstunden*, chapter 10, reports the "allegorical dream" that formulates Mendelssohn's preference of common sense over speculative contemplation. While Kant's essay "What Is Orientation in Thinking" ("Was heisst sich im Denken orientieren?") takes issue with Mendelssohn's seemingly blunt privileging of common sense over contemplation, Kant's version of practical reason does not seem to be that much different from Mendelssohn's common sense.

4. See also Edward S. Flajole, "Lessing's Retrieval of Lost Truths," *PMLA* 74 (1959): 52–66, 59. Bollacher speaks of the "spinozistische Filiation der Lessingschen Johannesexegese" (*Der junge Goethe*, 222). See also Pätzold, *Spinoza—Aufklärung—Idealismus*, 133.

CHAPTER 14. THE SECRET OF THE PUBLIC

1. Reinhart Koselleck, *Critique and Crisis: Enlightenment and the Pathogenesis of Modern Society* (1959; Cambridge: MIT Press, 1988); Jürgen Habermas, *The Structural Transformation of the Public Sphere: An Inquiry into a Category of Bourgeois Society*, trans. Thomas Burger with the assistance of Frederick Lawrence (1962; Cambridge: MIT Press, 1989). Already Ernst Manheim's study, *Aufklärung und öffentliche Meinung: Studien zur Soziologie der Öffentlichkeit im 18. Jahrhundert*, ed. Norbert Schindler (1930; Stuttgart–Bad Cannstatt: Frommann-Holzboog, 1979), 99, notes that the public sphere of the emerging

bourgeois society is steeped in and the result of the structure of its esoteric societies.

2. For good discussions see Anthony J. La Vopa, "Conceiving a Public: Ideas and Society in Eighteenth-Century Europe," *Journal of Modern History* 64 (1992): 79–116; Dena Goodman, "Public Sphere and Private Life: Toward a Synthesis of Current Historiographical Approaches to the Old Regime," *History and Theory* 31 (1992): 1–20. See also the contributions by Jochen Schulte-Sasse in *Aufklärung und literarische Öffentlichkeit,* ed. Christa Bürger and Peter Bürger (Frankfurt: Suhrkamp, 1980), 12–38, 83–115. For a discussion of Habermas see *Habermas and the Public Sphere,* ed. Craig Calhoun (Cambridge: MIT Press, 1992), which also contains Habermas's own suggestions for revision of his model, "Further Reflections on the Public Sphere" (421–61), and the transcript of a discussion with Habermas.

3. Onora O'Neill speaks of "publicity" in Kant in *Constructions of Reason: Explorations of Kant's Practical Philosophy* (Cambridge: Cambridge University Press, 1989); Ernest J. Weinrib uses the term "publicness" in "Publicness and Private Law," *Proceedings of the Eighth International Kant Congress,* ed. Hoke Robinson (Milwaukee: Marquette University Press, 1995), 1:191–201.

4. Georg Simmel, *The Sociology of Georg Simmel,* ed. Kurt Wolff (Glencoe, Ill.: Free Press, 1950), 352.

5. It is interesting to note the agreement on this by theorists holding such opposed views as Carl Schmitt and Habermas. For Schmitt see G. L. Ulmen's discussion of the *arcanum* in his introduction to Carl Schmitt, *Roman Catholicism and Political Form,* trans. G. L. Ulmen (1923; Westport, Conn.: Greenwood, 1996).

6. For Kant's use of the secret clause in *On Perpetual Peace* see Willi Goetschel, "Kritik und Frieden: Zur literarischen Strategie der Schrift *Zum Ewigen Frieden,*" in *Proceedings of the Eighth International Kant Congress,* ed. Hoke Robinson (Milwaukee: Marquette University Press, 1995), 2:821–27.

7. Hans-Georg Werner, "Zum Verhältnis zwischen 'öffentlicher' und 'privater' Sphäre im dichterischen Weltbild Lessings," in *Humanität und Dialog,* ed. Ehrhard Bahr, Edward P. Harris, and Lawrence G. Lyon, 83–102, argues that the tragic moment in Lessing's plays manifests itself in the reiteration of the antinomy between the absolutist public sphere and the virtuous private existence (96) and thus stages the dualism of the private/public dichotomy dramatically. For the mutually constitutive character of the two categories in Lessing see also John McCarthy, "'Das sicherste Kennzeichen einer gesunden, nervösen Staatsverfassung': Lessing und die Pressefreiheit," in *Lessing und die Toleranz,* ed. Peter Freimark, Franklin Kopitzsch, and Helga Slessarev (Detroit and Munich: Wayne State University Press and edition text und kritik, 1986), 225–44.

8. Hermann Timm, *Gott und die Freiheit: Studien zur Religionsphilosophie der Goethezeit,* vol. 1, *Die Spinozarenaissance* (Frankfurt: Klostermann, 1974), recognizes the affinity between Spinoza's political philosophy and Lessing's "ideal of a democratic pantheism" (129). But while he highlights the "structural

analogy" between *Ernst and Falk* and Spinoza's *Ethics* and *Theological-Political Treatise,* his discussion focuses on the ethical aspects of Lessing's political philosophy. But it is, remarkably, Spinoza's *Tractatus politicus* that foregrounds the theoretical conceptualization of the key idea of the Freemasons' "unspeakable secret," that is, the fact that it is neither social divisions nor simply their abolition that will solve the paradoxical nature of the constitution of social and political structures but a working within and against historically contingent, particular forms of social and political structures in order to envision a true form of cosmopolitanism grounded in the knowledge of both the necessity and the limitation of any particular form of social and political arrangement.

9. For Wolfsmilchschwärmer see for instance the 1935 edition of the Brockhaus dictionary.

10. L 8, 457–58; Z 277–306, 283–84. For a discussion of this passage see also John McCarthy, *Crossing Boundaries: A Theory and History of Essay Writing in German, 1680–1815* (Philadelphia: University of Philadelphia Press, 1989), 226ff.; and Peter Michelsen, "Die 'wahren Taten' der Freimaurer: Lessings 'Ernst und Falk,'" in his *Der unruhige Bürger: Studien zu Lessing und zur Literatur des 18. Jahrhunderts* (Würzburg: Königshausen & Neumann, 1990), 137–59, esp. 143–44.

11. For Hobbes's critique of Aristotle's categorization of bees as political beings see Hobbes, *On the Citizen,* chapter 5, section 5, 71, and Hobbes, *Leviathan,* 225.

12. TP II§16 and III§5 and §7; and see the discussion in chapter 5. Cf. E4P18 Schol.

13. See Spinoza's vindication of the nontransferability of an indivdual's natural right: "for every man's natural right (if we consider the matter correctly) does not cease in civil order" (Shirley, 49) ("nam jus naturae uniuscujusque [si recte rem perpendamus] in statu civili non cessat" [TP III§3]). For the general purpose of the state to protect a thick concept of peace as the life under the guidance of reason, which means that everyone's potential is given room to realize itself, see section 5 of the *Political Treatise,* esp. §§1–5. Cf. also *Theological-Political Treatise,* chapters 16 and 20. Asked about the difference between his and Hobbes's political theories, Spinoza observes: "With regard to political theory, the difference between Hobbes and myself, which is the subject of your inquiry, consists in this, that I always preserve the natural right in its entirety, and I hold that the sovereign power in a State has right over a subject only in proportion to excess of its power over that subject. This is always the case in a state of nature." Ep. 50, 2 June 1674, Spinoza, *The Letters,* trans. Samuel Shirley (Indianapolis: Hackett, 1995), 258. In *Lessing and the Enlightenment: His Philosophy of Religion and Its Relation to Eighteenth-Century Thought* (Ann Arbor: University of Michigan Press, 1966), Henry Allison seems to qualify his assertion that "Falk's (Lessing's) conception of a civil state is thoroughly within the Lockean, liberal tradition" (136) when, following the quote from Falk, he notes as crucial point in this passage: "However, and this is the important

point, the state as a purely human institution is by nature imperfect" (137). This stipulation relativizes Locke's strictly contract-based construction of civil society and the political state and motivates the reader to look for another model of political theory, more congenial to Falk's "anarchist"—or at least strongly autonomist—streak.

14. All of Spinoza's political theory informs the view that governments are products of human invention that require change if they no longer serve their original purpose and the idea that there is no "best government" but only approximations serving a specific people living within a specific cultural framework whose changes demand also respective changes in their political regimes. See *Theological-Political Treatise,* chapters 16 and 20; for the argument of the state of the Hebrews as example for a successful government dependent and based on the people's needs and interest, see chapters 17 and 18. Contrary to Hobbes's, Locke's, and even Rousseau's, Spinoza's is the model of a "user-friendly" political theory. For the limits of the power of governments see, e.g., TP IV§4 and §6.

15. See Heinrich Schneider's discussion of possible sources for Lessing's view on the origins of the Freemasons and semantic meaning of the word "Masonry." Heinrich Schneider, "Lessing und die Freimaurer," in his *Lessing: Zwölf biographische Studien* (Francke: Bern, 1951), 166–97; see also Michelsen, "Die 'wahren Taten' der Freimaurer," 156–57, on Lessing as the probable source for Justus Möser's Masonry hypothesis.

16. While Allison identifies in Falk Lessing's own position, Ernst's episode of joining a lodge and his subsequent disappointment with the organization of Freemasonry hints at Lessing's own experience and disillusion with the contradiction between idea and reality of Freemasonry at the time. For a good discussion see Schneider, "Lessing und die Freimaurer."

17. The joke that Falk might have given away the secret while having drunk too much of the Pyrmonter, the carbonated soda water from the springs of Pyrmont, highlights the superior soberness of Falk's thoroughly enlightened character.

18. For a discussion of the historical background see Schneider, "Lessing und die Freimaurer."

19. See esp. his "Die Religion Christi" (L 7, 711–12) and other writings related to church history, e.g. "Theses aus der Kirchengeschichte" (L 7, 606–13), "Über die Entstehung der geoffenbarten Religion" (L 7, 282–83), and "Von der Art und Weise der Fortpflanzung und Ausbreitung der christlichen Religion" (L 7, 283–301). The spirit/letter theme also receives thorough dramatic staging in *Nathan the Wise.* It is practically omnipresent in Lessing's writings. Cf. Klaus Bohnen, *Geist und Buchstabe: Zum Prinzip des kritischen Verfahrens in Lessings literarästhetischen und theologischen Schriften* (Cologne: Böhlau, 1974), specifically on *Ernst and Falk,* 176–84.

20. L 8, 480; Zwiebel (303) translates this passage as "he is one of those who do their fighting for America over here in Europe," and Ernst's retort as: "That's probably not the worst thing about him." He adds in a footnote that Falk points

to the revolutionary fight "far from the scene of battle" (ibid.), whereas the German seems to suggest a less ironic and more poignant idea: Lessing's coded support for revolutionary tendencies in Europe. It is interesting to note that, for Lessing, it seems only possible to express revolutionary ideas by way of projecting them into the scene of the "New World."

21. TP II§13, Shirley, 43; see also Spinoza's circumspect wording of the conditions that need to be met to keep a contract valid and his theory of theocracy of the state of the Hebrews, which presents a direct critique of Hobbes's view of total transfer of rights to a third party, the sovereign. See *Theological-Political Treatise,* chapters 16 and 20, and for his discussion of the state of the Hebrews see chapters 17 and 18. According to Spinoza, contracts are only as good as the reality that stands behind such compacts: "no compact can have force unless by reason of utility" (Y 16.5.14) ("pactum nullam vim habere posse nisi ratione utilitatis" [TTP 474, 474]).

22. H. B. Nisbet, "Zur Funktion des Geheimnisses in Lessings *Ernst und Falk,*" in *Lessing und die Toleranz,* 291–309, notes the provocative character of Lessing's mystification tactics. Lessing's teasing hide-and-seek game of pretending to present esoteric knowledge makes readers realize the problematic nature of instituted thought and spurs their interest to think for themselves (306).

23. L 8, 488 (Zwiebel cuts off five pages earlier). The sentence's unusual diction ("Unter meinen Büchern sollst du sehen und greifen") communicates something of the dialectics Lessing has in mind here. When read together with Simmel's statement quoted above, it sheds light on the intricate connection that informs the public/secret sphere in a most intimate way.

24. Shirley, 126; TP 9§14. See also page 80 above in chapter 5.

CHAPTER 15. THEORIZING THE ENLIGHTENMENT

1. See L 7, 476–88.
2. See commentary in L 8, 709.
3. Already the motto taken from Augustine's *Soliloquies* signals this mode of discourse, for Lessing's use of the passage gives Augustine's words a different turn, implying practically the opposite of what Augustine had in mind. While Augustine, preparing for his baptism, looks for the support of reason to bolster his newly espoused faith, Lessing plays with another implication of Augustine's words as he points to the purely heuristic character of the model for the interpretation of history he is about to introduce. Cf. Eckhard Heftrich, *Lessings Aufklärung* (Frankfurt: Klostermann, 1978), 42–45.
4. See also van Stockum, *Spinoza—Jacobi—Lessing,* 80–88; Allison, *Lessing and the Enlightenment,* 147–61; Bollacher, *Der junge Goethe,* 211–14; Pätzold, "Lessing und Spinoza," 346–55; Pätzold, *Spinoza—Aufklärung—Idealismus,* 135–42; and Monika Fick, *Lessing-Handbuch: Leben—Werk—Wirkung* (Stuttgart: Metzler, 2000), 425–33. Flajole, in "Lessing's Retrieval of Lost Truths," proposes a reading that views Lessing as one who, thanks to Spinoza, rediscovers

the virtues of Christianity. Although Flajole is one of the first critics to have attended to the correspondences between the writings of Spinoza and Lessing, his approach simplifies matters in that it presents a Lessing who returns to Christianity. Stressing some differences between Spinoza and Lessing, Flajole's biased approach produces a questionable reading of Lessing that loses sight of the crucial similarities of Lessing and Spinoza.

5. For one of the most recent examples of such a reading see the commentary by Erwin Quapp, *Lessings Theologie statt Jacobis "Spinozismus": Eine Interpretation der "Erziehung des Menschengeschlechts" auf Grundlage der Formel "hen ego kai pan"* (Bern: Peter Lang, 1992).

6. See also van Stockum, *Spinoza—Jacobi—Lessing,* 84 (TTP chapter 14).

7. Cassirer's point that the *Education* presents a reconciliation between the religious and the historical dimension rests on the premise that its theses can be taken at face value. The tentative, deliberative, and expository mode of writing, however, makes such a reading problematic. Instead, the text appears to address the precarious fragility of the attempts at such reconciliatory gestures and poses the question of the problematic nature of the desire to arrive at such solutions. Cassirer, *Die Philosophie der Aufklärung,* 257 and 308.

8. For Augustine's view on history see St. Augustine, *Concerning the City of God against the Pagans,* trans. Henry Bettenson (Penguin: London, 1984), book 10, chapter 14, 392.

9. Not surprisingly, the debate about Lessing's esotericism has over the last two centuries not been able to produce a consistent way to distinguish the oppositional pair esoteric/exoteric that would hold up to critical scrutiny. The suspicion that such a distinction is doomed to collapse seems not without justification as such an approach does not provide any assistance to a critical interpretation.

10. Lessing, "Das Christentum der Vernunft," L 7, 278–81.

11. See the discussion in chapter 12.

12. For a discussion of this paragraph see also Pätzold, "Lessing und Spinoza," 350–55; Pätzold, *Spinoza—Aufklärung—Idealismus,* 139–41; Bohnen, *Geist und Buchstabe,* 207; Stiening, "'Werden Sie lieber ganz mein Freund,'" 215–20.

13. B 2, 113.

14. Vallée, *The Spinoza Conversations,* 101–2.

15. Jacobi, *Werke,* 1:39. Thielicke rejects Jacobi's claim that §73 is Spinozist on grounds that hinge on a restrictive reading of Lessing. While Lessing's point is without any doubt clearly not limited to a Spinozism in the narrow, technical sense of the term, using, as Thielicke points out, a metaphysical framework that contains non-Spinozist elements, Thielicke ignores the decidedly Spinozist angle Lessing takes in arguing in a non-Spinozist framework. For Thielicke's reductive argumentation see his *Vernunft und Offenbarung* (Gütersloh: Bertelsmann, 1936), 102ff. For a curious comment of this passage in Jacobi, see Thomas P. Saine: "One would have to torture and procrusteanize the text of §73 of *The*

Education of Mankind considerably to fit it into the interpretation of Spinoza's concept of God that Jacobi proceeds to spin out in his letter to Mendelssohn. Probably Jacobi fully understood neither Spinoza nor Lessing's §73, which is frankly a speculation about a speculation." Saine, *The Problem of Being Modern, or The German Pursuit of Enlightenment from Leibniz to the French Revolution* (Detroit: Wayne State University Press, 1997), 224. While the last part of the last sentence is correct, Saine does not grasp the extent to which this "speculation about a speculation" serves a thoroughly critical purpose. Saine's conclusion is even more apodictic: "This is a perfect example of how competing misreadings (or misunderstandings) can muddy the waters and influence generations of scholarship. By asserting, with the support of one quite obscure and highly speculative paragraph in *The Education of Mankind* (§73), that Lessing was a Spinozist, Jacobi led Mendelssohn to claim that the early fragment 'The Christianity of Reason' demonstrated that Lessing from early on had played with pantheistic ideas which he had then never completely put aside" (ibid., 226).

16. Vallée, *The Spinoza Conversations,* 154; "das Ganze dieses tief durchdachten Aufsatzes"; Jacobi, *Werke,* 1:311.

17. Timm, *Die Spinozarenaissance,* 106–28, gives a thoughtful reconstruction of this nexus and the systematic function of §73 in the argument of the *Education.* However, Timm's stress on reading the *Education* as a renewal of Leibniz's *Theodicy* firmly frames this piece as a theological rather then a theological-political exercise and thus privileges a theological reading at the expense of the distinctly critical engagement in a reflection on the conditions and parameters of enlightenment that the text suggests.

18. Thielicke, *Vernunft und Offenbarung,* 68. For a sharp rebuttal of Thielicke's claim see Bohnen, *Geist und Buchstabe,* 198 n. 80. But Bohnen does not pay attention to the transformation to which Lessing subjects revelation in the course of his argument. For a good discussion of this issue see Henry E. Allison, "Lessing's Conception of Revelation as Education," *Studies in Eighteenth Century Culture* 4 (1975): 183–93.

19. Lessing, "Über eine zeitige Aufgabe," L 8, 549. On Lessing's essayistic style of writing see my entry on Lessing in *Encyclopedia of the Essay,* ed. Tracy Chevalier (London: Fitzroy Dearborn, 1997), 476–78.

20. Henry E. Allison, "Lessing's Conception of Revelation as Education," 183–93, cf. 189. For an earlier discussion by Allison see his *Lessing and the Enlightenment,* 158–59.

21. Ibid.; Martin Bollacher, *Lessing, Vernunft und Geschichte: Untersuchungen zum Problem religiöser Aufklärung in den Spätschriften* (Tübingen: Niemeyer, 1978), 298ff., offers another explanation to refute the argument that §§4 and 77 contradict each other. Although he points to Lessing's recognition of the historical dimension to which reason is subject, he does not acknowledge the full extent of the role Lessing's dialectical procedure plays for a satisfactory interpretation of the *Education.* Pätzold, *Spinoza—Aufklärung—Idealismus,* 141–42, seems to follow Bollacher.

22. Cf. Spinoza, *Theological-Political Treatise,* title page, preface, and conclusion (Y 20.7.1–8.1; TTP 618–620).

23. For a discussion of the reform character of most of German Enlightenment see Werner Schneiders, *Hoffnung auf Vernunft: Aufklärungsphilosophie in Deutschland* (Hamburg: Meiner, 1990); for a brief but helpful survey of the different varieties of European Enlightenment in France, Great Britain, and Germany see his *Das Zeitalter der Aufklärung* (Munich: C. H. Beck, 1997).

24. For a discussion of the Spinozist elements in §85 see Allison, *Lessing and the Enlightenment,* 160; for §§80–85 see Bollacher, *Der junge Goethe,* 212–14.

CHAPTER 16. NEGOTIATING TRUTH

1. Karl Jaspers, *Die grossen Philosophen: Nachlass,* ed. Hans Saner (Munich: R. Piper, 1981). Jaspers counts Lessing among the "great philosophers" and devotes a whole chapter to this "awakener [Erwecker]," as he calls him. See 1:346–415, 2:726–63, quote on 749. While Jaspers's perceptive reconstruction of Lessing's thinking offers one of the best treatments of Lessing as philosopher, Lessing research has, unfortunately, paid little attention to his discussion.

2. For a notable exception see Franz Rosenzweig's notes for a speech "Lessing's Nathan" in *Zweistromland: Kleinere Schriften zu Glauben und Denken. Gesammelte Schriften,* vol.3, ed. Reinhold and Annemarie Mayer (Dordrecht, Boston, Lancaster: Martinus Nijhoff, 1984), 449–53, and my discussion in Goetschel, "Lessing and the Jews."

3. See Willi Goetschel, "The Differential Character of Traditions," *Telos* 95 (1993): 161–70. Ludwig Kahn, "The Changing Image of the Jew: Nathan the Wise and Shylock," in *Identity and Ethos: A Festschrift for Sol Liptzin on the Occasion of His Eighty-fifth Birthday,* ed. Mark H. Gelber (New York: Peter Lang, 1986), cites the conservative Austrian Jewish writer Friedrich Torberg, who thinks he can detect anti-Semitic traces in *Nathan.* Kahn, like many other readers, does not seem to realize that because of the dramatic nature of the play the characters do not simply stand for certain views and positions but represent lively figures interacting with each other. What they say cannot be reduced to statements on issues but is predicated by the stage situation—that is, to whom they speak and at which point or turn in the play.

4. It is often overlooked that the point of tolerance in the traditional sense is only to grant individuals the right to err but not to acknowledge their views, which are simply considered to be errors. Such errors represent heretical ideas that call for rigorous persecution. Tolerance thus is only granted under the condition that the incriminated views be abandoned.

5. Cf. the way in which Lessing exposes the Templar's misled understanding of enlightenment in his attempt to disguise Nathan when he triumphantly announces: "The tolerant babbler is unmasked!" ("Der tolerante Schwätzer ist entdeckt!") (IV, 4). Scenes 3–5 of act 4 have been cut in Bayard Quincy Morgan's English translation, which is used otherwise.

6. The politics of the discourse of tolerance was clear to people like Moses Mendelssohn, who knew from his own experience the semantic stretch the term "tolerance" could be subjected to. Cf. his letter to Herz Homberg (4 October 1782) quoted at the end of chapter 9. How little Mendelssohn was off the mark in his cautionary warning is substantiated in Kant's congenial congratulations a year later upon the publication of Mendelssohn's *Jerusalem, or On Religious Power and Judaism*. Even there Kant maintains that in terms of all the crucial points, all religions will eventually reunite. See Kant to Mendelssohn on 16 August 1783, Kant, *Briefwechsel*, 236. Cassirer distinguishes two forms of tolerance. Against the tolerance of the age of Enlightenment, which he calls a tolerance of pity, Lessing's is a tolerance of respect based on modesty, reflecting Lessing's deep religiosity. See Cassirer, "Die Idee der Religion bei Lessing und Mendelssohn," in *Festgabe zum zehnjährigen Bestehen der Akademie für die Wissenschaften des Judentums, 1919–1929* (Berlin: Akademie Verlag, 1929), 22–41, 34–35.

7. Claudia Brodsky Lacour, "'Is That Helen?' Contemporary Pictorialism, Lessing, and Kant," *Comparative Literature* 45 (1993): 230–57.

8. For a discussion of the current debate of the concept of truth in Lessing see my review essay on the volume *Streitkultur: Strategien des Überzeugens im Werk Lessings*, ed. Wolfram Mauser and Günter Saße (Tübingen: Max Niemeyer, 1993), in *Lessing Yearbook* 26 (1994): 145–50.

9. Marc Shell, "'What Is Truth?': Lessing's Numismatics and Heidegger's Alchemy," in *Money, Language, and Thought: Literary and Philosophical Economies from the Medieval to the Modern Era* (Berkeley: University of California Press, 1982), 162.

10. Stuart Atkins, "Die Ringparabel in Lessing's *Nathan der Weise*," in *Lessings "Nathan der Weise,"* ed. Klaus Bohnen (Darmstadt: Wissenschaftliche Buchgesellschaft, 1984), 161, calls this the "diversionary function of his [Nathan's] parable." Peter Heller, "Paduan Coins," *Lessing Yearbook* 5 (1973): 163–71; Jay Newman, "The Parable of the Three Rings in *Nathan der Weise*," *Mosaic* 12, no. 4 (1978–79): 1–8; and others seem to share the interpretation of Nathan as a sly character.

11. Shell, "What Is Truth?" 162.

12. See, e.g., Jill Anne Kowalik, "*Nathan der Weise* as Lessing's Work of Mourning," *Lessing Yearbook* 21 (1989): 1–17, for *Nathan* as Lessing's working through his own experience of loss and suffering. See also the discussion in Thomas Koebner, "*Nathan der Weise:* Ein polemische Stück?" in *Interpretationen: Lessings Dramen* (Stuttgart: Reclam, 1987), 138–207, esp. 164 and 173.

13. Lessing follows here almost word for word Spinoza's chapter on miracles in his *Theological-Political Treatise*. Spinoza is not entirely ignored in Lessing research, but I have so far not been able to locate any references beyond Spinoza's *Ethics*. This is surprising given the fact that some of the material most relevant for Lessing is only found in the *Treatise* among other writings of Spinoza. For an exception see van Stockum, *Spinoza—Jacobi—Lessing*, 89–90;

Roger Bauer, "Spinoza-Reminiszenzen in Lessings 'Nathan der Weise'?" *Festschrift für Herbert Kolb,* ed. Klaus Matzel and Hans-Gert Roloff (Bern: Peter Lang, 1989), 1–20; and Bauer, "Du 'Tractatus Theologico-Politicus' à 'Nathan der Weise,'" *Comparatistica* 5 (1993): 55–74.

14. In the final analysis even detailed discussions of the economic complex have not been satisfying. Peter Demetz, "Lessings 'Nathan der Weise': Wirklichkeiten und Wirklichkeit," in *Lessings "Nathan der Weise,"* ed. Bohnen, 168–218, esp. 199ff. (first in his edition of *Nathan der Weise* [Frankfurt: Ullstein, 1966]), sees in the coin metaphor the key to the interpretation of the "ring parable" (204). Cf. Hans-Jürgen Schlütter, "'. . . als ob die Wahrheit Münze wäre': Zu *Nathan der Weise* III, 6," *Lessing Yearbook* 10 (1978): 65–74; Mark Lehrer, "Lessing's Economic Comedy," *Seminar* 20 (1984): 79–94; Helmut Göbel, "Die Bildlichkeit im 'Nathan,'" in *Lessings "Nathan der Weise,"* ed. Bohnen, 228–66, esp. 250–64; Shell, "What Is Truth?"; Wolf Wucherpfennig, "Nathan, der weise Händler," in *Jahrbuch für Internationale Germanistik* 8.4. Akten des VI. Internationalen Germanistenkongresses, Basel 1980, ed. H. Rupp and H.-G. Roloff (Bern: Peter Lang, 1980), 57–64, argues that it is through the economic metaphor that the play stages the question of truth and validity.

15. For exceptions see Hermann Levin Goldschmidt, "Von der Toleranz zur Dialogik—Lessings und Mendelssohns Herausforderung zum christlich-jüdischen Gespräch," *Frieden ohne Menschenrechte? Aspekte einer Politik für den Menschen* (Aachen: Einhard, 1981), 186–99, reprinted in Goldschmidt, *Aufsätze zur Philosophie, Werke,* vol. 5 (Vienna: Passagen, 1999); Ingrid Strohschneiders-Kohrs, *Vernunft als Weisheit: Studien zum späten Lessing* (Tübingen: Niemeyer, 1991).

16. Theodor W. Adorno, "Heine the Wound," in *Notes to Literature,* trans. Shierry Weber Nicholsen (New York: Columbia University Press, 1991), vol. 1, 80–85.

17. Paul Hernadi, "Nathan der Bürger: Lessings Mythos vom aufgeklärten Kaufmann," in *Lessings "Nathan der Weise,"* ed. Bohnen, 341–49. Hinrich C. Seeba, *Die Liebe zur Sache: Öffentliches und privates Interesse in Lessings Dramen,* Untersuchungen zur deutschen Literaturgeschichte, vol. 9 (Tübingen: Niemeyer, 1973), 80, seems to endorse such a view. I do not know exactly what to make of an interpretation that speaks of Nathan as "the Protestant in Jewish disguise" and declares *ex cathedra* "the appropriateness of Hernadi's appeal to Max Weber" (Lehrer, "Lessing's Economic Comedy," 90, 91). This is not the place to enter a debate over whether or not Nathan "expounds a basically Protestant philosophy" (ibid., 90), whatever such a proposition may imply. Let me just state the obvious, that Nathan is introduced as a Jew and that the entire dramatic energy of the play hinges on this fact. To claim that Nathan is actually a Jew who is no longer a Jew, as even a diligent and exemplary reader like Peter Demetz has suggested ("Lessings 'Nathan der Weise,'" 169), takes the reader to hermeneutic netherlands I would prefer to avoid. Hans-Friedrich Wessels, *Lessings "Nathan der Weise": Seine Wirkungsgeschichte bis zum Ende*

der Goethezeit (Königstein: Athenäum, 1979), 305–53, gives a balanced account on *Nathan* in the context of the emancipation of Jews in Germany. For a survey of some nineteenth-century voices on this issue see Arnold Bodek, "Warum ist Nathan ein Jude? Stimmen aus der Lessing-Literatur," *Lessing-Mendelssohn-Gedenkbuch,* ed. Deutsch-Israelitischer Gemeindebund (Leipzig, 1879), 350–76.

18. See Cohen's 1880 essay "Ein Bekenntnis in der Judenfrage," *Der Berliner Antisemitismusstreit,* ed. Walter Boehlich (Frankfurt: Insel, 1965), 124–49. Cf. Willi Goetschel, "Models of Difference and Alterity: Moses Mendelssohn, Hermann Cohen, Franz Rosenzweig, Martin Buber, and Hermann Levin Goldschmidt," in *The German-Jewish Dilemma: From Enlightenment to Shoa,* ed. Edward Timms and Andrea Hammel (Lewiston, N.Y.: Edwin Mellen Press, 1999), 25–38.

19. On Sombart as response to Max Weber's *Protestant Ethics* see Alex Bein, *Die Judenfrage: Biographie eines Weltproblems* (Stuttgart: Deutsche Verlagsanstalt, 1980), 1:75ff., 2:83–85.

20. Martin Buber, *On the Bible: Eighteen Studies,* ed. Nahum N. Glatzer (New York: Schocken, 1968), 90.

21. Published in 1783, Mendelssohn's book can, to some degree, also be seen as a response—part critique, part reconfirmation and continuation of the ongoing discussion between the two friends. In this context, *Nathan* presents Lessing's last offshoot of the project the two friends had shared in an exchange of twenty-five years.

22. Immanuel Kant, *Anthropology from a Pragmatic Point of View,* trans. Mary J. Gregor (The Hague: Martinus Nijhoff, 1974), footnote to §46, 77.

23. Immanuel Kant, *Anthropologie* §43 fn., *Werke,* ed. Wilhelm Weischedel (Frankfurt: Insel/Suhrkamp, 1964), 12:517–18. See also Chaninah Maschler, "On the Wisdom of Nathan," *Interpretation* 15 (1987): 347–65. This passage of Kant's presents the harshest statement on Jews in his body of writing, and it is noteworthy that it contradicts his own otherwise strict, critical standards of theorizing.

24. For an exception see van Stockum, *Spinoza—Jacobi—Lessing,* and the two papers by Bauer (see note 12 above).

25. The portrait is by an unknown master of the seventeenth century. See, e.g., *Baruch de Spinoza, 1677–1977: Werk und Wirkung,* Ausstellungskataloge der Herzog August Bibliothek, vol. 142, ed. Wilhelm Schmidt-Biggemann (Wolfenbüttel, 1977). For a possible identification of the painter with Spinoza's friend Lodewijk Meyer see Baruch de Spinoza, *Lebensbeschreibungen und Dokumente,* ed. Manfred Walther (Hamburg: Felix Meiner, 1998), 52.

26. See esp. *Theological-Political Treatise,* chapter 6, "Miracles," and chapter 7, "The Interpretation of Scripture"; for Spinoza see also Walther, "Spinozas Kritik der Wunder—ein Wunder der Kritik?" and "Biblische Hermeneutik und/oder theologische Politik bei Hobbes und Spinoza"; Osier, "L'herméneutique de Spinoza et de Hobbes."

27. For Spinoza's distinction between religion based on wisdom and superstition based on ignorance, see his correspondence, Ep. 73, in Spinoza, *The Letters*, 333.

28. For Spinoza's distinction of forms of knowledge see *Tractatus de intellectus emendatione* and *Ethics*. Baruch de Spinoza, *Traité de la réforme de l'entendement*, ed. A. Koyré (Paris: Vrin, 1979), §§19ff., 16ff., where Spinoza distinguishes four steps of knowledge: (1) hearsay (*ex auditu, aut ex aliquo signo*), (2) random experience (*experientia vaga*), (3) inadequate perception, and (4) adequate perception. In the *Ethics* Spinoza combines the first two steps he distinguishes in his epistemological treatise and replaces it with a three-step model. Whereas notions we construct from vague experience or signs present the first step of knowledge, which Spinoza calls opinion or imagination, the second step is defined by common notions and adequate ideas of the properties of things. This level is what for Spinoza represents reason. The third level Spinoza then calls intuitive knowledge (*scientia intuitiva*). It transcends rationality as it reaches adequate understanding of the nature of things. This stage represents the ultimate achievement of the sage (*sapiens*). Cf. E2P40 Schol 2. For an in-depth study of the comprehensive philosophical compass of Spinoza's epistemological treatise see Moreau, *Spinoza: L'expérience et l'éternité.*

29. See E2P40 Schol 2, CW 477–78.

30. Hernadi, "Nathan der Bürger," 342; Seeba, *Die Liebe zur Sache*, 80.

31. Smith, *Wealth of Nations.*

32. Ibid., I 26.

33. "Der geringste Handelsjude ist in dieser Betrachtung kein bloßer Verzehrer, sondern ein nützlicher Einwohner (ich darf nicht sagen, Bürger) des Staats, ein wirklicher Hervorbringer." Mendelssohn, Jub A 8, 16.

34. See also Helga Slessarev, "Nathan der Weise und Adam Smith," in *Nation und Gelehrtenrepublik. Lessing im europäischen Zusammenhang*, ed. Wilfried Barner and Albert Reh (Detroit and München: Wayne State University Press and edition + kritik, 1984), 248–56.

35. See Nadler's description of Spinoza's background as a merchant of Amsterdam in his *Spinoza*, 80–115.

36. E4 Caput 29, cf. also Caput 28, CW 593.

37. Thus *handeln* is also the first word of Kant's categorical imperative: "Handle, dass die Maxime deines Willens jederzeit zugleich als Prinzip einer allgemeinen Gesetzgebung kann gelten können." Kant introduces this and similar formulas in the second section of his *Grundlegung zur Metaphysik der Sitten*, *Werke*, 7:51, 61, 70ff.; Kant, *Foundations of the Metaphysics of Morals*, trans. Lewis White Beck (New York: Macmillan, 1990), 38, 46, 54ff. What remains through all the reformulations through which Kant takes the formula is, of course, the beginning "Handle."

38. Hobbes, *Leviathan*, 301.

39. Immanuel Kant, *The Metaphysics of Morals*, trans. Mary Gregor (Cambridge: Cambridge University Press, 1996), 70.

40. Kant, *Die Metaphysik der Sitten, Werke,* 8, 403. For a discussion of money and books as the two constituants of the public sphere see Goetschel, *Constituting Critique.*

41. L 2, 274–75; act III, scene 6.

42. James L. Hodge, "The Parable in *Nathan* as a Gambit," *The Germanic Review* 55 (1980): 14–21.

43. This move lies also at the heart of the *Theological-Political Treatise,* which articulates as one of its central concerns not only its radical critique of institutionalized religion but also the attempt to break grounds for a secularized yet thoroughly spiritual form of modern religiosity.

44. Cf. Hodge, "The Parable in *Nathan,*" 14.

45. In terms of its hermeneutic aspects this dramatic intervention is discussed in Robert S. Leventhal, "The Parable as Performance: Interpretation, Cultural Transmission, and Political Strategy in Lessing's *Nathan der Weise,*" *German Quarterly* 61 (1987): 502–27. As far I can see, Cassirer is the only critic speaking of the "ring narrative" (*Ringerzählung*) rather than a "ring parable" as the convention in Lessing literature has come to call it. See Cassirer, "Die Idee der Religion bei Lessing und Mendelssohn," 38.

46. L 5, 381.

47. Aamir Mufti has directed my attention to the fact that Saladin does not so much come to represent Islam but the state power and interests of the emerging modern nation-state. See Mufti, "Secularism and Minority: Elements of a Critique," *Social Text* 45 (1995): 75–96.

48. Heller, "Paduan Coins"; Newman, "The Parable of the Three Rings"; Atkins, "Die Ringparabel in Lessing's *Nathan der Weise*"; Demetz, "Lessings 'Nathan der Weise'"; and Shell, "What Is Truth?" 161 n. 15.

49. Rüdiger Zymner, "'Der Stein war ein Opal . . .': Eine versteckte Kunst-Apotheose in Lessings morgenländischer 'Ringparabel'?" *Lessing Yearbook* 24 (1992): 77–96. Opals could, however be cheaply faked. The production of "foil-backs" and "nacre-backs" creates a superficially similar appearance by inserting a foil as a kind of mirror's tain into a piece of glass cut to look like an opal. But even today it is impossible due to the intricate color pattern to produce identical opals synthetically. I owe this information to Neil H. G. Garrioch. On the symbolic connotations of the opal see Morton Nirenberg, "The Opal: Lessing's Ring Re-Examined," *Modern Language Notes* 85 (1970): 686–96.

50. See, e.g., Newman, "The Parable of the Three Rings," 7. For a more recent example that illustrates the widespread negligence of this detail see Schneiders's otherwise crisp and precise survey *Das Zeitalter der Aufklärung,* 109.

51. Koebner's "*Nathan der Weise:* Ein polemisches Stück?" calls attention to the fact that the rules in the ring story change from a traditional legalism to a new order that awards succession to the most beloved son, thus following the principle of individuality rather than that of traditionalism. Astutely, Koebner observes that the case in point with the father of three sons presents a new situation, for it is no longer love that distiguishes the sons but obedience. It is thus

due to this obedience that the father cannot help but "love" them all the same. This, however, is no longer authentic love but rather the expression of the disappointment over the sons' formalism (ibid., 152–53). The passage "All three of whom were duly dutiful, / All three of whom in consequence he needs / Must love alike" (M 232) ("Die alle ihm gleich gehorsam waren, / Die alle drei er folglich gleich zu lieben / Sich nich entbrechen konnte") (act III, scene 7; L 2, 277) is indeed so carefully worded that it seems to allude to Spinoza's view that obedience is what defines institutionalized religion. Obedience without genuine love is, then, the ring story seems to imply, the low point to which religion has fallen: unloving, doctrinary subjection that, of course, is so paralyzing for the father that he needs to change the rules of the game. On love and obedience with regard to God cf. TTP, chapter 16, 490; Y 16.8.3 and Spinoza's annotation 34.

52. This, of course, is the key argument of the *Theological-Political Treatise*'s separation of theology from philosophy.

53. See Michael Böhler, "Lessings 'Nathan der Weise' als Spiel vom Grunde," *Lessing Yearbook* 3 (1971): 128–50. For Kant's recasting of the truth concept see Goetschel, *Constituting Critique.*

54. I owe the clarification in this paragraph to a discussion with Nils Roemer. In addition, it needs to be kept in mind that the *Education* is conceived as a thought experiment to play through the Augustinian idea of a philosophy of history in three stages as outlined in Augustine's *Civitas Dei* bk. 10, chapter 14. Cf. the preceeding chapter and Augustine, *Concerning the City of God*, 392.

55. See William James, *Pragmatism: A New Name for Some Old Ways of Thinking and The Meaning of Truth: A Sequel to Pragmatism* (Cambridge: Harvard University Press, 1975), 105, where James gives a German version of Lessing's epigram.

56. I would like to thank David Suchoff for providing this translation.

57. L 1, 23.

58. James, *Pragmatism,* 105.

59. Peirce, *Selected Writings,* 183.

60. Ibid., 124, 192, 204; cf. 183. For pragmaticism as a word so ugly it is safe from kidnapping see 186 and 123.

61. James, *Pragmatism,* 28, 30.

62. Ibid., 32.

63. Ibid., 34.

64. Ibid., 104; cf. James, *The Meaning of Truth,* section IX, "The Meaning of the Word Truth," ibid., 283.

65. Wucherpfennig has been the first one to point out the pragmatic turn the play stages: "Daß der Pragmatismus an die Stelle der Wahrheit das stets vorläufige Zeichen setzt, das reflektiert Nathan am Bild der Münze" ("Nathan, der weise Händler," 63 n. 8). The term "pragmatisch" to describe some moments in *Nathan* is applied by Ralf Simon, "Nathans Argumentationsverfahren: Konsequenzen der Fiktionalisierung von Theorie in Lessings Drama *Nathan der Weise,*"

Deutsche Vierteljahrsschrift 45 (1991): 609–35. But Simon reduces Nathan's argumentative praxis to a theory of consensus and does not follow up the philosophical implications of the role of pragmatism. Neither Wucherpfennig nor Simon engage in a discussion of pragmatism. Hodge, "The Parable in *Nathan,*" speaks of "Nathan's pragmatic humanism" (16) and calls him a "pragmatic idealist" (19). For a survey on the use of the term "pragmatic" see Gudrun Kühne-Bertram, "Aspekte der Geschichte und der Bedeutungen des Begriffs 'pragmatisch' in den philosophischen Wissenschaften des ausgehenden 18. und des 19. Jahrhunderts," *Archiv für Begriffsgeschichte* 27 (1983): 158–86.

66. Ludwig Stein, *Philosophical Currents of the Present Day,* trans. Shishirkumar Maitra (Calcutta: The University of Calcutta, 1918), vol. 1, 44–100, quote on 47; Ludwig Stein, "Die neupositivistische Bewegung (Der 'Pragmatismus' von William James)," in *Philosophische Strömungen der Gegenwart* (Stuttgart: Ferdinand Enke, 1908), 33–75, quote on 35. This chapter is basically identical with Stein's article "Versuch einer Geschichte des Terminus 'Pragmatismus,'" *Archiv für systematische Philosophie,* n.s., 14 (1908): 143–88.

67. Richard Rorty, *Consequences of Pragmatism* (Minneapolis: University of Minnesota Press, 1982), introduction and 162.

68. Richard Rorty, *Contingency, Irony, and Solidarity* (Cambridge: Cambridge University Press, 1989).

69. Ibid., xv.

70. Richard Rorty, *Hoffnung statt Erkenntnis: Eine Einführung in die pragmatische Philosophie* (Vienna: Passagen, 1994), 80.

71. Letter of 9 January 1771, Lessing, *Briefe,* 11.2:145.

72. James, *Pragmatism,* 30.

73. E4P18 Schol.

74. E4P20; CW 557.

75. E4P40; CW 570.

76. Y 16.5.14.

77. TTP, chapter 16, 474.

CHAPTER 17. HEINE'S DIS/ENCHANTMENT OF HEGEL'S HISTORY OF PHILOSOPHY

1. Heine cut this epithet in later editions, cf. Heinrich Heine, *Historisch-kritische Ausgabe,* ed. Manfred Windfuhr, vol. 6, ed. Jost Hermand (Hamburg: Hoffmann und Campe, 1973), 736 (critical text with the variant to the first edition of Nordseereise for page 157, 11 which Heine deleted in later editions). For Hess see Shlomo Avineri, *Moses Hess: Prophet of Communism and Zionism* (New York: New York University Press, 1985); Freud, *Der Witz und seine Beziehung zum Unbewussten, Studien Ausgabe,* 4:75.

2. Few studies that address the role of philosophy in Heine avoid mistaking him for a Hegelian, and most of them display a rather crude understanding of Hegel and philosophy at that. Rudolf Malter, "Heine und Kant," *Heine*

Jahrbuch 18 (1979): 35–64, is a welcome exception. Malter paints a differentiated picture of the precise use of the representation of Kant in Heine's narrative as the critical countermove to de Staël's presentation of Kant.

3. R 276; B 3, 604.

4. Theodor Mundt quoted in Martin Bollacher, "Aufgeklärter Pantheismus: Die Deutung der Geschichte in Heines Schrift *On the History of Religion and Philosophy in Germany*," in *Heinrich Heine: Artistik und Engagement*, ed. Wolfgang Kuttenkeuler (Stuttgart: Metzler, 1977), 144–86, quote on 150.

5. Wolfgang Wieland, "Heinrich Heine und die Philosophie," in *Heinrich Heine*, Wege der Forschung vol. 289, ed. Helmut Koopmann (Darmstadt: Wissenschaftliche Buchgesellschaft, 1975), 133–55, 154. Wieland claims that this is also how Heine saw himself.

6. Ibid., 141; Malter, "Heine und Kant," 35.

7. Wolfgang Harich, "Heinrich Heine und das Schulgeheimnis der deutschen Philosophie," in Heinrich Heine, *On the History of Religion and Philosophy in Germany*, ed. Wolfgang Harich (Frankfurt: Insel, 1966), 7–52, speaks, for instance, without blinking, of the "eigentümliche Synthese von Hegel, Goethe und Saint-Simon" (42); see also Manfred Windfuhr, "Heine und Hegel: Rezeption und Produktion," in *Internationaler Heine-Kongreß 1972*, ed. Manfred Windfuhr (Hamburg: Hoffmann und Campe, 1975), 261–80. Eduard Krüger, *Heine und Hegel: Dichtung, Philosophie, und Politik bei Heine* (Kronberg Ts.: Scriptor, 1977), seems, when comparing Heine with Hegel, free of any doubts concerning the grounds on which such a comparison could proceed. Unburdened by any reflection on the constitutive difference that informs Heine's writing as distinct deflection of Hegel, Krüger reads the countercurrent at work in Heine's rewriting of Hegel as another form of Hegelian discourse rather than its interruption. Helmut Motekat, "Hegel and Heine," in *A Hegel Symposium*, ed. D. C. Travis (Austin: University of Texas, 1962), 65–79, presents a rather skimpy view. For a bibliography on Heine and Hegel see Jean Pierre Lefebvre, *Der gute Trommler: Heines Beziehung zu Hegel*, trans. Peter Schöttler (Hamburg: Hoffmann und Campe, 1986), 207. Dolf Sternberger, *Heinrich Heine und die Abschaffung der Sünde* (Hamburg: Claassen, 1972), argues in his chapter "Absage an die Adresse Hegels" that the role of Hegel for Heine should not be overestimated. For his critique of Harich see 385 n. 57. For pantheism as the vantage point of Heine's critique of Hegel see esp. Bollacher, "Aufgeklärter Pantheismus."

8. J. P. Stern, *Re-interpretations: Seven Studies in Nineteenth-Century German Literature* (New York: Basic Books, 1964), doubts Heine's philosophical competence and views the whole as a joke that coincidentally hits a gold mine (209), although he acknowledges that "the prose in which this serious joke is told amounts to an enormous liberation" (216).

9. Bollacher, "Aufgeklärter Pantheismus," 176.

10. Wieland, "Heine und die Philosophie," 140.

11. Ibid., 137.

12. For an exception see Herwig Friedl, “Heinrich Heine und Friedrich Nietzsche,” in *Heinrich Heine im Spannungsfeld von Literatur und Wissenschaft,* ed. Wilhelm Gössmann und Manfred Windfuhr, Symposium anlässlich der Benennung der Universität Düsseldorf nach Heinrich Heine (N.p.: Hobbing, 1990), 195–214, 209ff.

13. In privileging such a reading, the potential of Spinoza’s critical reworking of the question of sensualism and spiritualism, whose dichotomy is rendered obsolete by his philosophy of nature, receives its effective silencing. The specific political thrust of Heine’s project of disenchantment is likewise suppressed. While Heine’s Spinoza offers a promising solution to that impasse of such bipolar and restrictedly metaphysical argumentation, the crucial role of Spinoza’s philosophy seems to have largely gone unrecognized. Heine’s subtle ironies, shifts, and turns have distracted those critics who just follow the “plot” line of Heine’s comic description of the progress of history, for Heine leaves no doubt that, taken all together, the discourse of sensualism and spiritualism has become as obsolete as all the other spider webs of metaphysics. If Ritchie Robertson, *Heine* (London: Halban, 1988), 36–49, identifies “two tracks” in Heine’s presentation of history, one of the “rationalist” philosophers and one of the “pantheists,” he simply repeats the conventional lineage that Heine sets out to challenge, undermine, and implode. J. P. Stern stands as representative for the attitude of those critics who downplay the significance of Spinoza for Heine: “Like Goethe, Heine is content to take from Spinoza’s teaching the catchword *Deus sive natura,* or, as he puts it, the identification of God with the world” (*Re-interpretations,* 214).

14. For an exception see Jean-Pierre Lefebvre’s incisive study “Heine, Hegel, et Spinoza,” *Cahiers Spinoza* 4 (1982–83): 211–29, which demonstrates the interventionist aspect of Heine’s Spinoza interpretation that takes a perceptively oppositional stand against Hegel’s narrative.

15. *Hegel’s Lectures on the History of Philosophy,* trans. E. S. Haldane and F. H. Simson. (1896; London: Routledge and Kegan Paul; New York: Humanities Press, 1963), 252.

16. Georg Wilhelm Friedrich Hegel, *Lectures on the History of Philosophy: The Lectures of 1825–1826,* vol. 3, ed. R. F. Brown, trans. R. F. Brown and J. M. Stewart with the assistance of H. S. Harris (Berkeley: University of California Press, 1990), 151.

17. Georg Wilhelm Friedrich Hegel, *Vorlesungen über die Geschichte der Philosophie 3, Werke,* vol. 20 (Frankfurt: Suhrkamp, 1986), 158.

18. *Lexikon der Philosophie,* founded by Heinrich Schmidt and continued by Georgi Schischkoff (Stuttgart: Kröner, 1974).

19. R 242; B 3, 561.

20. Lefebvre, “Heine, Hegel, et Spinoza,” speaks of Heine’s “sympathie profonde” (226) and enthusiasm (224) toward Spinoza’s philosophy.

21. Goethe, *Dichtung und Wahrheit,* bk. 16, in *Sämtliche Werke,* 10:730ff.

22. Avineri, *Moses Hess.* See also Avineri’s discussion of the role Spinoza

played in the thought of Hess and his generation, cf. esp. chapter 2, 21ff.; see also the opinionated Michel Espagne, "Heinrich Heine und Moses Heß," in *Heinrich Heine, 1797–1856: Schriften aus dem Karl-Marx-Haus* 26 (Trier: Karl-Marx-Haus, 1981), 80–97, 93. Untrammeled by any sense of irony, Espagne takes Heine's witticism that Judaism is not a religion but an ailment literally, concluding that the "return" to Judaism was simply caused by Heine's illness (90).

23. One of the rare occasions when the second book is actually conceded any importance is in E. M. Butler's study *The Saint-Simonian Religion in Germany: A Study of the Young German Movement* (New York: Fertig, 1968), 148–49: "This, from our point of view, is the nucleus of the book, for in these pages Heine joined forces with the Saint-Simonians in demanding the 'rehabilitation of the flesh'; and he did this in language which puts their prosaic eloquence completely into the shade. His pantheism however, based on the pantheism of Spinoza, is rather different from theirs." For a categorical rejection of Spinoza by the Saint-Simonists see 149 and 152. Butler, however, still detects traces of Saint-Simonism in Heine where Spinoza seems the philosophically more convincing source, e.g., when she states that Heine owed "the original revelation of the possibility of a harmony between senses and spirit" to the Saint-Simonist (154), a thought that lies at the very core of Spinozist thought. Jeffrey L. Sammons has pronounced a justified caveat for the assessment of the role of the Saint-Simonists in Heine's development: "His pantheistic ideas also antedate his acquaintance with the doctrine [of Saint-Simonism]; they appear to be the consequence of filtering his experience of philosophy through a modernized reception of Spinoza, another of his inheritances from Goethe." Sammons, *Heinrich Heine: A Modern Biography* (Princeton: Princeton University Press, 1979), 161. Although Heine was associated with the Saint-Simonists in his early years in Paris, he preferred to be remembered as a Spinozist. See the 1838 description of Heine expounding Spinoza's philosophy published in *Europa,* a journal edited by his friend August Lewald, reprinted in Michael Werner, ed., *Begegnungen mit Heine: Berichte der Zeitgenossen* (Hamburg: Hoffmann und Campe, 1973), 1:352–53. In his entry on Heine in *Biographie universelle,* Saint-René Taillandier takes issue with Heine's "boundless admiration" for Spinoza. "Son admiration pour Spinosa [*sic*] était sans bornes. C'est au nom du spinosisme et des théories hégéliennes qu'il a passé sa vie à persifler toutes les religions établies"; see *Biographie universelle,* 19:54–58, quote on 58.

24. Hegel, *Hegel's Lectures,* trans. Haldane and Simson, 252.

25. Hegel, *Vorlesungen über die Geschichte der Philosophie,* 157–58.

26. Heine, *Historisch-kritische Ausgabe,* 6, 736 (critical text with the variant to the first edition of Nordseereise for page 157, 11, which Heine deleted in later editions). For this passage see also Hermann Levin Goldschmidt, "Heine und Freud," in Goldschmidt, *"Der Rest bleibt," Aufsätze zum Judentum, Werke,* vol. 4, (Passagen: Vienna, 1997), 197–209. The passage as a whole deserves attention because it testifies to Heine's early acquaintance with the critical implications of Spinoza's political philosophy that Hegel's account passes over: "unless

one assumes, [like my fellow non-believer Spinoza,] that what cannot preserve itself also has no right to exist"—Heine speaks here of the doomed Hannover aristocracy but implies this to be true for the ancien régime as a whole (B 2, 232 line 4).

27. R, 244; B 3, 563; the French version: Heine, *Historisch-kritische Ausgabe,* 8.1, 296.

28. Hermann Cohen, "Heinrich Heine und das Judentum," in *Jüdische Schriften,* ed. Bruno Strauß (Berlin: Schwetschke, 1924), 2:2–44.

29. Cohen's essay dates from 1867, when the twenty-five-year-old had not yet developed the anti-Spinozist affect that became the trademark of the later Cohen. As Franz Rosenzweig has pointed out, the age that produced Cohen himself would itself not have been possible without Spinoza. Rosenzweig, "Über den Vortrag Hermann Cohens 'Das Verhältnis Spinozas zum Judentum,'" in *Zweistromland: Kleinere Schriften zu Glauben und Denken, Gesammelte Schriften,* ed. Reinhold Mayer and Annemarie Mayer (Dordrecht: Nijhoff, 1984), 3:165–67.

30. R 266; B 3, 590–91.

31. For a reclaiming of Spinoza as both representing the inner spirit of Judaism and the champion of modern philosophy see Immanuel Wolf's [Wohlwill] programmatic essay "Ueber den Begriff einer Wissenschaft des Judenthums," *Zeitschrift für die Wissenschaft des Judenthums* 1 (1823): 1–24, 14.

32. See Heine's comment that he did not return to Judaism, since he had never left it. Michael Werner, *Begegnungen mit Heine,* 2:155. For Leopold Zunz's insistence that Heine never left Judaism see his letter to Heine's first biographer, Adolf Strodtmann. Ismar Elbogen, "Briefe um Heinrich Heine: Adolf Strodtmanns Anfrage an Leopold Zunz," *Zeitschrift für die Geschichte der Juden in Deutschland* 8 (1938): 40–51, 44 (this article was never published, but a copy of the galley exists in the Ismar Elbogen collection at the Leo Baeck Institute in New York).

33. Heinz Pepperle, "Heinrich Heine als Philosoph," in *Heinrich Heine: Ästhetisch-politische Profile,* ed. Gerhard Höhn (Frankfurt: Suhrkamp, 1991), 155–75, like most critics, sees at the end of Heine's life a revoking of his pantheism. His contextualization of Heine with Cieskowski and Hess (169) deserves attention. It is no coincidence that they all used Spinoza as a corrective stand against a Hegelian view of philosophy of history.

CHAPTER 18. TRADITION AS INNOVATION IN HEINE'S "JEHUDA BEN HALEVY"

1. Heinrich Heine, *The Prose and Poetical Works,* vol. 2, trans. Charles Godfrey Leland (New York: Croscup and Sterling, [1920]), 387.

2. Heine, *Ludwig Börne: Eine Denkschrift,* B 4, 18.

3. Reinhart Koselleck, *Futures Past: On the Semantics of Historical Time,* trans. Keith Tribe (Cambridge, Mass: MIT Press, 1985), 267–88.

4. Hal Draper, *The Complete Poems of Heinrich Heine: A Modern English Version* (Boston: Suhrkamp/Insel, 1982), 655. I refer to this edition as HD.

5. Hartmut Kircher, *Heinrich Heine und das Judentum* (Bonn: Bouvier, 1973), 270, calls this a "poetic paraphrase," and Alberto Destro follows him in the commentary of the *Historisch-kritische Gesamtausgabe der Werke,* calling this passage a "fast wörtliche Übernahme aus dem Psalm 137, 5–6." But Heine follows here word for word the psalmist, just not in the Luther translation but most likely in the version he had heard from his friend Moses Moser. Heine's rendering of Psalm 137 goes "backwards" with the order of verse 6.1 followed by verse 5.2 and 5.1. For Moser see Heine's letters to Moser from 9 January 1824 and 23 April 1826, Heinrich Heine, *Säkularausgabe, Band 20, Briefe 1815–1831* (Berlin and Paris: Akademie-Verlag and Editions du CNRS, 1970), 133 and 240.

6. See Heine's letter to Moser of 23 April 1826: "I remember, the psalm 'we sat by the rivers of Babylon' was then your special strength and you recited it so beautifully, so wonderfully, so touchingly, that I still might cry today, and not just about the psalm" ("Ich erinnere mich, der Psalm 'wir saßen an den Flüssen Babels' war damals Deine Force, und Du rezitirtest ihn so schön, so herrlich, so rührend, daß ich jetzt noch weinen möchte, und nicht bloß über den Psalm" [*Briefe,* 240]).

7. Draper's "phantom figures" does not quite render the empowering moment *Traumgestalten* connotes of figures produced by the creative aspect of imagination.

8. Leopold Zunz, *Die gottesdienstlichen Vorträge der Juden historisch entwickelt,* appeared first in 1832 (rpt. 2nd ed., Hildesheim: Olms, 1966). According to Zunz, the modern sermon develops out of the interpretative Hagada (341–42).

9. "Law and freedom are to the body politic what head and heart are to the individual human being: The head and the law must lay down the hard and fast rules; freedom and the warm heart apply those rules, and make exceptions."

10. See ibid., 316–42, esp. 61ff., 324, 334, 341. For a brief discussion of Heine's new assessment of the Hagadic tradition see Maren R. Niehoff, "Heine und die jüdische Tradition," in *"Ich Narr des Glücks": Heinrich Heine, 1797–1856, Bilder einer Ausstellung,* ed. Joseph A. Kruse (Stuttgart: Metzler, 1997), 318–24. For Zunz see Niehoff, "Zunz's Concept of Haggadah as an Expression of Jewish Spirituality," *Year Book of the Leo Baeck Institute* 43 (1998): 3–24. While Niehoff stresses the differences between Zunz and Heine, Heine's abundant use of botanic imagery with its floral metaphors of lush and uninhibited growth seems to point to Zunz as possible source of inspiration. For Zunz as the source for Heine's distinction between Halacha and Hagada see also Israel Tabak, *Judaic Lore in Heine* (Baltimore: Johns Hopkins University Press, 1948), 17.

11. Semiramis, the mythic founder of Babylon, invites a number of associations. Her name suggests that the history of Jewish exile represents the inspiring source for the creativity of Jewish tradition.

12. Heine might have followed here an interesting lead in Lessing's *Education of Humanity* where Lessing points out that the Hebrews did not recognize the more profound meaning of the Bible until they came in contact with Persian culture in the Babylonian exile.

13. Jehuda Ha-Levi, *Sefer Hakusari, Das Buch Kusari,* trans. and ed. David Cassel, 5th ed. (Berlin: Louis Lamm, 1922), 1:64–65, 47.

14. Mark H. Gelber, "Heinrich Heine und das Judentum: Gestern und heute," in *Heinrich Heine und das Judentum,* ed. Peter Grab (Augsburg: Presse-Druck, 1994), 8–13, 130.

15. While self-referentiality is certainly present in abundance, memory is more than merely a stage for self-representation, as Wolfgang Preisendanz would have it. On the contrary, Heine's self-referentiality becomes a site for rewriting history as counterhistorical critique. See Preisendanz, "Memoria als Dimension lyrischer Selbstpräsentation in Heines Jehuda Ben Halevy," in *Memoria: Vergessen und Erinnern,* ed. Anselm Haverkamp and Renate Lachmann, Poetik und Hermeneutik 15 (Munich: Wilhelm Fink, 1993), 338–48, 348.

16. Ruth Wolf, "Versuch über Heines 'Jehuda ben Halevy,'" *Heine Jahrbuch* 18 (1979): 84–98, 92, points out that the Greek forms of Darius's box reflect Heine's former Hellenism.

17. For a discussion of the schlemiel in Heine see Hannah Arendt, "The Jew as Pariah: A Hidden Tradition," in *The Jew as Pariah: Jewish Identity and Politics in the Modern Age,* ed. Ron H. Feldman (New York: Grove, 1978), 67–90; Tabak, *Judaic Lore in Heine,* 151ff.; Hartmut Steinecke, "'Wir stammen von Schlemihl': Jüdische Dichter-Bilder in Heines Spätwerk von Jehuda ben Halevy bis Rabbi Faibisch," in *Aufklärung und Skepsis: Internationaler Heine-Kongress,* ed. Joseph Kruse, Bernd Witte, and Karin Füllner (Stuttgart: Metzler, 1999), 303–21; Roger F. Cook, *By the Rivers of Babylon: Heinrich Heine's Late Songs and Reflections* (Detroit: Wayne State University Press, 1998), 330–39.

18. In his English translation, Hal Draper renders Heine's *Schlemihl* as *Schlemihl.* But rendering *schlemiel* as *Schlemihl* compromises Heine's reclaiming of Chamisso's Schlemihl as a Jewish schlemiel. Draper thus overwrites the e with the German h without attending to the sensitive double meaning of *Schlemihl* as the name of a German novella's character and the name for a jinxed person. Arendt and Tabak curiously follow the German spelling with h, while usual English usage spells *schlemiel.* The problematic h in the English translation stands out—like Hitzig's H—as the sign of assimilation's absorption that clashes with the whole critical impulse of the poem.

19. In his translation Robertson has skipped a whole section, B 3, 611–27, including this key passage crucial for Heine's Spinoza reception.

BIBLIOGRAPHY

BARUCH DE SPINOZA

The Collected Works of Spinoza. Vol. 1. Ed. and trans. Edwin Curley. Princeton: Princeton University Press, 1985.

Lebensbeschreibungen und Dokumente. Ed. Manfred Walther. Hamburg: Felix Meiner, 1998.

The Letters. Trans. Samuel Shirley. Indianapolis: Hackett, 1995.

Political Treatise. Trans Samuel Shirley. Introduction and notes by Steven Barbone and Lee Rice. Indianapolis: Hackett, 2000.

Politischer Traktat/Tractatus politicus. Trans. and ed. Wolfgang Bartuschat. Hamburg: Meiner, 1994.

Theologico-Political Treatise. Trans. Martin D. Yaffe. Focus Philosophical Library. Newburyport, Mass.: Pullins, 2004.

Tractatus de intellectus emendatione and Ethics. Ed. A. Koyré. Paris: Vrin, 1979.

Tractatus theologico-politicus/Theologisch-Politischer Traktat. Ed. Günter Gawlick and Friedrich Niewöhner. Darmstadt: Wissenschaftliche Buchgesellschaft, 1979.

MOSES MENDELSSOHN

Gesammelte Schriften. Jubiläumsausgabe. In association with Fritz Bamberger, Haim Borodianksi, Simon Rawidowicz, Bruno Strauss, and Leo Strauß, initiated by Ismar Elbogen, Julius Guttmann, and Eugen Mittwoch, continued by Alexander Altmann in association with Haim Bar-Dayan, Eva J. Engel, Leo

Strauß, and Werner Weinberg. Berlin, 1929–32; Breslau, 1938; Stuttgart–Bad Cannstatt: Friedrich Frommann-Günther Holzboog, 1974–98.

Jerusalem, or On Religious Power and Judaism. Trans. Allan Arkush. Intro. and commentary by Alexander Altmann. Hanover, N.H.: University Press of New England, 1983.

Phaedon; or, the Death of Socrates. Trans. Charles Cullen. London: J. Cooper, 1789.

Philosophical Writings. Ed. and trans. Daniel O. Dahlstrom. Cambridge: Cambridge University Press, 1997.

GOTTHOLD EPHRAIM LESSING

Briefe. Ed. Helmuth Kiesel. 3 vols. Frankfurt: Deutscher Klassiker Verlag, 1987–94.

Nathan the Wise, Minna von Barnhelm, and Other Plays and Writings. Trans. Bayard Quincy Mortan et al., ed. Peter Demetz. New York: Continuum, 1991.

Sämtliche Schriften. Vol. 5. 3rd ed. Ed. Karl Lachmann and Franz Muncker. Stuttgart: Göschen, 1890.

Werke. Ed. Herbert G. Göpfert. Munich: Hanser, 1979.

HEINRICH HEINE

The Complete Poems of Heinrich Heine: A Modern English Version. Trans. Hal Draper. Boston: Suhrkamp/Insel, 1982.

Historisch-kritische Ausgabe. Ed. Manfred Windfuhr. Vol. 6, ed. Jost Hermand. Hamburg: Hoffmann und Campe, 1973.

On the History of Religion and Philosophy in Germany. Heinrich Heine. *Selected Prose*. Trans. and ed. Ritchie Robertson. London: Penguin, 1993.

The Prose and Poetical Works. Vol. 2. Trans. Charles Godfrey Leland. New York: Croscup and Sterling, [1920].

Säkularausgabe. Band 20. Briefe 1815–1831. Berlin: Akademie-Verlag and Paris: Editions du CNRS, 1970.

Sämtliche Schriften. Ed. Klaus Briegleb. 2nd ed. Munich: Hanser, 1975–1985; Munich: Deutscher Taschenbuchverlag, 1997.

LITERATURE ON SPINOZA

Alexander, Bernhard. "Spinoza und die Psychoanalyse." *Chronicon Spinozanum* 5 (1927): 96–103. Rpt. in *Almanach für das Jahr 1928*. Vienna: Internationaler Psychoanalytischer Verlag, 1928.

Allison, Henry E. *Benedict de Spinoza: An Introduction*. New Haven: Yale University Press, 1987.

Althusser, Louis. "The Only Materialist Tradition." In *The New Spinoza*, ed. Montag and Stolze, 3–19. Minneapolis: University of Minnesota Press, 1998.

———. "Sur Spinoza." In *Éléments d'autocritique,* 65–83. Paris: Hachette, 1974.

Balibar, Etienne. "L'institution de la vérité: Hobbes et Spinoza." In *Hobbes and Spinoza: Science and Politics,* ed. Daniela Bostrenghi, 3–22. Naples: Bibliopolis, 1992.

———. "A Note on 'Consciousness/Conscience' in the *Ethics.*" *Studia Spinozana* 8 (1992): 37–53.

———. "Potentia multitudinis, quae una veluti mente ducitur." In *Ethik, Recht, und Politik bei Spinoza,* ed. Marcel Senn and Manfred Walther, 105–37. Zürich: Schulthess, 2001.

———. *Spinoza et la politique.* Paris: Presses universitaires de France, 1985.

———. "Spinoza, the Anti-Orwell: The Fear of the Masses." In *Masses, Classes, Ideas: Studies on Politics and Philosophy before and after Marx,* 3–37. New York: Routledge, 1994.

Bernard, Walter. "Psychotherapeutic Principles in Spinoza's *Ethics.*" In *Speculum Spinozanum, 1677–1977,* ed. Siegfried Hessing, 63–80. London and Boston: Henley and Routledge & Kegan Paul, 1977.

Bertman, M., H. De Dijn, and Manfred Walther, eds. *Spinoza and Hobbes. Studia Spinozana* 3 (1987).

Bertrand, Michèle. "Spinoza et la psychanalyse." *Studia Spinozana* 8 (1992): 171–90.

Bickel, Lothar. "Über Beziehungen zwischen der Psychoanalyse und einer dynamischen Psychologie" (1931). In *Spinoza in neuer Sicht,* ed. Leo Sonntag and Heinz Stolte, 145–68. Meisenheim am Glan: Anton Hain, 1977.

Brown, Norman O. "Philosophy and Prophecy: Spinoza's Hermeneutics." *Political Theory* 14 (1986): 195–213.

Brykman, Geneviève. *La judéité de Spinoza.* Paris: Vrin, 1972.

Burbage, Frank, and Nathalie Chouchan. "Freud et Spinoza: La question de la transformation et le devenir actif du sujet." In *Spinoza au XXe siècle,* ed. Olivier Bloch, 527–48. Paris: Presses universitaires de France, 1993.

Cahan, Jean Axelrad. "Spinoza's Theory of Immanence Reconsidered." *Journal of Jewish Thought and Philosophy* 5 (1995–96): 81–98.

Cohen, Hermann. "Spinoza über Staat und Religion, Judentum und Christentum." In *Jüdische Schriften,* ed. Bruno Strauss, 3: 290–372. Berlin: Schwetschke, 1924.

Curley, Edwin. *Behind the Geometrical Method: A Reading of Spinoza's "Ethics."* Princeton: Princeton University Press, 1988.

Curley, Edwin, Albert Heinekamp, and Manfred Walther, eds. *Spinoza and Leibniz. Studia Spinozana* 6 (1990).

Dascal, Marcelo. "Spinoza and Leibniz: Language and Cognition." *Studia Spinozana* 6 (1990): 103–45.

Deleuze, Gilles. *Spinoza et le problème de l'expression.* Paris: Les Éditions de Minuit, 1968.

———. "Spinoza and the Three 'Ethics'." In *The New Spinoza,* ed. Montag and Stolze, 21–34. Minneapolis: University of Minnesota Press, 1997.

Delf, Hanna, Julius H. Schoeps, and Manfred Walther, eds. *Spinoza in der europäischen Geistesgeschichte*. Berlin: Hentrich, 1994.

Den Uyl, Douglas J. "Sociality and Social Contract: A Spinozistic Perspective." *Studia Spinozana* 1 (1985): 19–51.

Dilthey, Wilhelm. "Die Autonomie des Denkens, der konstruktive Rationalismus und der pantheistische Monismus nach ihrem Zusammenhang im 17. Jahrhundert." *Gesammelte Schriften*, vol. 2. Leipzig and Berlin: Teubner, 1914.

Dobbs-Weinstein, Idit. "Rereading the *Tractatus theologico-politicus* in Light of Benjamin's 'Theologico-Political Fragment.'" In *Piety, Peace, and the Freedom to Philosophize*, ed. Paul Bagley, 67–89. Dordrecht: Kluwer, 1999.

Donner, Herbert. "Prophetie und Propheten in Spinozas Theologisch-politischem Traktat." In *Theologie und Wirklichkeit: Festschrift für Wolfgang Trillhaas*, ed. Hans Walter Schütte and Friedrich Wintzer, 31–50. Göttingen: Vandenhoeck & Ruprecht, 1974.

Eckstein, Walter. "Rousseau and Spinoza: Their Political Theories and Their Conception of Ethical Freedom." *Journal of the History of Ideas* 5 (1944): 259–91.

Faur, José. "Spinoza and the Secularization of Western Society." In *In the Shadow of History: Jews and Conversos at the Dawn of Modernity*, 142–75. Albany: State University of New York Press, 1992.

Field, Eduard. "Spinoza the Jew." *Modern Judaism* 9 (1989): 101–19.

Franck, Isaac. "Spinoza's Onslaught on Judaism." *Judaism* 28 (1979): 177–93.

———. "Was Spinoza a 'Jewish' Philosopher?" *Judaism* 28 (1979): 345–52.

Friedman, Georges. *Leibniz et Spinoza*. Paris: Gallimard, 1962.

Garrett, Don. "Truth, Method, and Correspondence in Spinoza and Leibniz." *Studia Spinozana* 6 (1990): 13–43.

Gatens, Moira. *Imaginary Bodies: Ethics, Power, and Corporeality*. London: Routledge, 1996.

Gatens, Moira, and Genevieve Lloyd. *Collective Imaginings: Spinoza, Past and Present*. London: Routledge, 1999.

Giancotti, Emilia. "The Birth of Modern Materialism in Hobbes and Spinoza." In *The New Spinoza*, ed. Montag and Stolze, 49–63. Minneapolis: University of Minnesota Press, 1997.

Giovanni, George di. "The First Twenty Years of Critique: The Spinoza Connection." In *The Cambridge Companion to Kant*, ed. Paul Guyer, 417–48. Cambridge: Cambridge University Press, 1992.

Goetschel, Willi. "Spinozas Modernität: Kritische Aspekte seiner politischen Theorie." In *Ethik, Recht, und Politik bei Spinoza*, ed. Marcel Senn and Manfred Walther, 209–24. Zurich: Schulthess, 2001.

Haddad-Chamakh, Fatma. *Philosophie systématique et système de philosophie politique chez Spinoza*. Tunis: Université de Tunis, 1980.

Harris, Errol E. "Method and Metaphysics in Spinoza." *Studia Spinozana* 2 (1986): 129–50.

Haserot, Francis S. "Spinoza and the Status of Universals." In *Studies in Spinoza: Critical and Interpretive Essays,* ed. S. Paul Kashap, 43–67. Berkeley: University of California Press, 1972.

Heerich, Thomas. *Transformation des Politikkonzepts von Hobbes zu Spinoza: Das Problem der Souveränität.* Würzburg: Königshausen & Neumann, 2001.

Israel, Jonathan I. *Radical Enlightenment: Philosophy and the Making of Modernity, 1650–1750.* Oxford: Oxford University Press, 2001.

Jacobs, Wilhelm G. "Spinozas *Theologisch-Politischer Traktat* und das Problem der Geschichte." In *Tradition und Innovation: XIII Deutscher Kongreß für Philosophie,* ed. Wolfgang Kluxen, 82–89. Hamburg: Meiner, 1985.

Kashap, S. Paul, ed. *Studies in Spinoza: Critical and Interpretive Essays.* Berkeley: University of California Press, 1972.

Lang, Berel. "The Politics of Interpretation: Spinoza's Modernist Turn." In *The Anatomy of Philosophical Style,* 217–43. Oxford: Basil Blackwell, 1990.

Levene, Nancy. "Ethics and Interpretation, or How to Study Spinoza's *Tractatus Theologico-Politicus* without Strauss." *Journal of Jewish Thought and Philosophy* 10 (2000): 57–110.

Levinas, Emmanuel. "The Spinoza Case." In *Difficult Freedom: Essays on Judaism,* trans. Séan Hand. London: Athlone Press, 1990.

Lloyd, Genevieve. *Part of Nature: Self-Knowledge in Spinoza's "Ethics."* Ithaca: Cornell University Press, 1994.

Macherey, Pierre. "The Problem of the Attributes." In *The New Spinoza,* ed. Montag and Stolze, 65–95. Minneapolis: University of Minnesota Press, 1997.

Matheron, Alexandre. *Individu et communauté chez Spinoza.* Paris: Minuit, 1969.

———. "The Theoretical Function of Democracy in Spinoza and Hobbes." In *The New Spinoza,* ed. Montag and Stolze, 207–17. Minneapolis: University of Minnesota Press, 1997.

Montag, Warren. *Bodies, Masses, Power: Spinoza and His Contemporaries.* London: Verso, 1999.

Montag, Warren, and Ted Stolze, eds. *The New Spinoza.* Minneapolis: University of Minnesota Press, 1997.

Moreau, Pierre-François. "Fortune and the Theory of History." In *The New Spinoza,* ed. Montag and Stolze, 97–106. Minneapolis: University of Minnesota Press, 1997.

———. *Spinoza.* Paris: Seuil, 1975.

———. *Spinoza: L'expérience et l'éternité.* Paris: Presses universitaires de France, 1994.

Morrison, James C. "Spinoza and History." In *The Philosophy of Baruch Spinoza,* ed. Richard Kennington, 173–95. Washington, D.C.: Catholic University of America Press, 1980.

Mugnier-Pollet, Lucien. *La philosophie politique de Spinoza.* Paris: Vrin, 1976.

Nadler, Steven. *Spinoza: A Life.* Cambridge: Cambridge University Press, 1999.

———. *Spinoza's Heresy: Immortality and the Jewish Mind.* Oxford: Clarendon Press, 2001.

Negri, Antonio. "*Reliqua Desiderantur:* A Conjecture for a Definition of the Concept of Democracy in the Final Spinoza." In *The New Spinoza,* ed. Montag and Stolze, 219–47. Minneapolis: University of Minnesota Press, 1997.

———. *The Savage Anomaly: The Power of Spinoza's Metaphysics and Politics.* Trans. Michael Hardt. Minneapolis: University of Minnesota Press, 1991.

Ogilvie, Bertrand. "Spinoza dans la psychanalyse." In *Spinoza au XXe siècle,* ed. Olivier Bloch, 549–75. Paris: Presses universitaires de France, 1993.

Osier, Jean-Pierre. "L'herméneutique de Spinoza et de Hobbes." *Studia Spinozana* 3 (1987): 319–47.

Otto, Rüdiger. *Studien zur Spinozarezeption in Deutschland im 18. Jahrhundert.* Frankfurt: Lang, 1994.

Pines, Shlomo. "Spinoza's *Tractatus Theologico-Politicus* and the Jewish Philosophical Tradition." In *Jewish Thought in the Seventeenth Century,* ed. Isadore Twersky and Bernard Septimus, 499–521. Cambridge: Harvard University Center for Jewish Studies, Harvard University Press, 1987.

Polka, Brayton. "Spinoza's Concept of Biblical Interpretation." *Journal of Jewish Thought and Philosophy* 2 (1992): 19–44.

Préposiet, Jean. *Spinoza et la liberté des hommes.* Paris: Gallimard, 1967.

Ravven, Heidi M. and Lenn E. Goodman, eds. *Jewish Themes in Spinoza's Philosophy.* Albany: University Press of New York State, 2002.

Roudinesco, Elisabeth. "Lacan et Spinoza: Essai d'interpretation (1916–1964)." In *Spinoza au XXe siècle,* ed. Olivier Bloch, 577–88. Paris: Presses universitaires de France, 1993.

Savan, David. "Spinoza and Language." In *Studies in Spinoza: Critical and Interpretive Essays,* ed. S. Paul Kashap, 236–48. Berkeley: University of California Press, 1972.

Schlenke, Hubertus. *Vermeer, mit Spinoza gesehen.* Berlin: Mann, 1998.

Schmidt-Biggemann, Wilhelm, ed. *Baruch de Spinoza, 1677–1977: Werk und Wirkung.* Ausstellungskataloge der Herzog August Bibliothek, vol. 142. Wolfenbüttel, 1977.

Scholem, Gershom. Introduction to Abraham Cohen Herrera, *Das Buch Pforte des Himmels,* 7–67. Frankfurt: Suhrkamp, 1974.

———. "Die Wachtersche Kontroverse über den Spinozismus unf ihre Folgen." In *Spinoza in der Frühzeit seiner religiösen Wirkung,* ed. Karlfried Gründer and Wilhelm Schmidt-Biggemann, 15–25. Wolfenbütteler Studien, vol. 12. Heidelberg: Lambert Schneider, 1984.

Schröder, Winfried. "Pantheismus." In *Historisches Wörterbuch der Philosophie,* 7: 59–63. Basel: Schwabe, 1989.

———. *Spinoza in der deutschen Frühaufklärung.* Würzburg: Epistemata, 1987.

Shmueli, Efraim. "The Geometrical Method, Personal Caution, and the Ideal of Tolerance." In *Spinoza: New Perspectives,* ed. Robert W. Shahan and J. I. Biro, 197–215. Norman: University of Oklahoma Press, 1978.

Simon, Ernst. "Zu Hermann Cohens Spinoza-Auffassung." In *Brücken: Gesammelte Aufsätze,* 205–14. Heidelberg: Lambert Schneider, 1965.

Smith, Steven B. "How Jewish Was Spinoza?" In *Piety, Peace, and the Freedom to Philosophize,* ed. Paul J. Bagley, 191–208. Dordrecht: Kluwer, 1999.

———. *Spinoza, Liberalism, and the Question of Jewish Identity.* New Haven: Yale University Press, 1997.

Stein, Ludwig. *Leibniz und Spinoza: Ein Beitrag zur Entwicklungsgeschichte der Leibnizischen Philosophie.* Berlin, 1890.

Strauss, Leo. *Spinoza's Critique of Religion.* Trans. E. M. Sinclair. New York: Schocken, 1965.

Tosel, André. *Du Matérialisme de Spinoza.* Paris: Kimé, 1994.

———. "La théorie de la pratique et la fonction de l'opinion publique dans la philosophie politique de Spinoza." *Studia Spinozana* 1 (1985): 183–208.

Ueno, Osamu. "Mentis oculi ipsae demonstrationes: Jouissance et démonstration dans l'Éthique de Spinoza." In *Spinoza: Puissance et Ontologie,* ed. Myriam Revault D'Allonnes, 73–84. Paris: Kimé, 1994.

Vernière, Paul. *Spinoza et la pensée française avant la Révolution.* 2nd ed. Paris: Presses universitaires de France, 1982.

Walther, Manfred. "Biblische Hermeneutik und/oder theologische Politik bei Hobbes und Spinoza: Historische Studie zur Theorie der Ausdifferenzierung von Religion und Politik in der Neuzeit." In *Hobbes e Spinoza,* ed. Daniela Bostrenghi, 623–69. Naples: Bibliopolis, 1992.

———. "Institution, Imagination, und Freiheit bei Spinoza: Eine kritische Theorie politischer Institutionen." In *Politische Institutionen im gesellschaftlichen Umbruch: Ideengeschichtliche Beiträge zur Theorie politischer Institutionen,* ed. Gerhard Göhler, Kurt Lenk, Herfried Münkler, and Manfred Walther, 246–75. Opladen: Westdeutscher Verlag, 1990.

———. *Metaphysik als Anti-Theologie: Die Philosophie Spinozas im Zusammenhang der religionsphilosophischen Problematik.* Hamburg: Meiner, 1971.

———. "Politik, Moralität, und Freiheit in der Philosophie Spinozas." In *Selbstbehauptung und Anerkennung: Spinoza, Kant, Fichte, Hegel,* ed. Helmut Girndt, 7–23. St. Augustin: Academia, 1990.

———. "Spinoza als Kritiker der Neuzeit?" *Philosophische Rundschau* 28 (1981): 274–300.

———. "Spinozas Kritik der Wunder—ein Wunder der Kritik? Die historisch-kritische Methode als Konsequenz des reformatorischen Schriftprinzips." *Zeitschrift für Theologie und Kirche* 88 (1991): 68–80.

———. "Spinozas Philosophie der Freiheit—eine 'jüdische Philosophie'?" *Edith Stein Jahrbuch* 3 (1997): 99–133.

———. "Spinoza und das Problem einer jüdischen Philosophie." In *Die philosophische Aktualität der jüdischen Tradition,* ed. Werner Stegmaier, 281–330. Frankfurt: Suhrkamp, 2000.

———. "Spinozismus ille Spinoza oder wie Spinoza zum 'Klassiker' wurde: Zur Etikettierungs-, Rezeptions-, und Wirkungsgeschichte Spinozas im europäischen Vergleich." In *Beobachter und Lebenswelt. Studien zur Natur-, Geistes-, und Sozialwissenschaft,* ed. Helmut Reinalter, 183–238. Thaur: Thaur, 1996.

———. "Die Transformation des Naturrechts in der Rechtsphilosophie Spinozas." *Studia Spinozana* 1 (1985): 73–104.

Wartofsky, Marx. "Action and Passion: Spinoza's Construction of a Scientific Psychology." In *Spinoza: A Collection of Critical Essays*, ed. Marjorie Grene, 329–53. Notre Dame: University of Notre Dame Press, 1979.

Wiehl, Reiner. "Die Vernunft in der menschlichen Unvernunft: Das Problem der Rationalität in Spinozas Affektenlehre." In *Metaphysik und Erfahrung: Philosophische Essays*, 277–322. Frankfurt: Suhrkamp, 1996.

Wolfson, Harry Austryn. *From Philo to Spinoza: Two Studies in Religious Philosophy.* New York: Behrman, 1977.

———. *The Philosophy of Spinoza: Unfolding the Latent Processes of His Reasoning.* 1934. Cambridge: Harvard University Press, 1983.

Yovel, Yirmyahiu. *Spinoza and Other Heretics.* 2 vols. Princeton: Princeton University Press, 1989.

Zac, Sylvain. "État et nature chez Spinoza." In *Philosophie, théologie, politique dans l'oeuvre de Spinoza*, 117–43. Paris: Vrin, 1979.

LITERATURE ON MENDELSSOHN

Altmann, Alexander. *Moses Mendelssohn: A Biographical Study.* London and Tuscaloosa: Routledge & Kegan Paul and University of Alabama Press, 1973.

———. "Moses Mendelssohn's Concept of Judaism Reexamined." In *Von der mittelalterlichen zur modernen Aufklärung: Studien zur jüdischen Geistesgeschichte*, 234–48. Tübingen: Mohr, 1987.

———. *Moses Mendelssohns Frühschriften zur Metaphysik*. Tübingen: Mohr, 1969.

———. *Die trostvolle Aufklärung: Studien zur Metaphysik und politischen Theorie Moses Mendelssohns.* Stuttgart–Bad Cannstatt: Frommann-Holzboog, 1982.

Best, Otto F. "Einleitung." In Moses Mendelssohn, *Ästhetische Schriften in Auswahl*, 1–24. Darmstadt: Wissenschaftliche Buchgesellschaft, 1974.

Breuer, Edward. *The Limits of Enlightenment: Jews, Germans, and the Eighteenth-Century Study of Scripture.* Cambridge: Harvard University Press, 1996.

———. "Politics, Tradition, History: Rabbinic Judaism and the Eighteenth-Century Struggle for Civil Equality." *Harvard Theological Review* 85 (1992): 357–83.

Christ, Kurt. *Jacobi und Mendelssohn: Eine Analyse des Spinozastreits.* Würzburg: Königshausen & Neumann, 1988.

Eisen, Arnold. "Divine Legislation as 'Ceremonial Script': Mendelssohn on the Commandments." *Association for Jewish Studies Review* 15 (1990): 239–67.

———. *Rethinking Modern Judaism: Ritual, Commandment, Community.* Chicago: University of Chicago Press, 1998.

Goetschel, Willi. "Moses Mendelssohn und das Projekt der Aufklärung." *The Germanic Review* 71 (1996): 163–75.

———. "Neue Literatur zu Moses Mendelssohn." *Lessing Yearbook* 29 (1998): 199–208.

Goldschmidt, Hermann Levin. "Moses Mendelssohns geschichtliche Bedeutung." In *"Der Rest bleibt," Aufsätze zum Judentum. Werke,* 4: 165–79. Vienna: Passagen, 1997.

Guttmann, Julius. "Mendelssohns *Jerusalem* und Spinozas *Theologisch-Politischer Traktat.*" *48. Bericht der Hochschule für die Wissenschaft des Judentums,* 31–67. Berlin: 1931.

Hilfrich, Carola. *"Lebendige Schrift": Repräsentation und Idolatrie in Moses Mendelssohns Philosophie und Exegese des Judentums.* Munich: Wilhelm Fink, 2000.

Meyer, Herrmann M. Z. *Moses Mendelssohn-Bibliographie: Mit einigen Ergänzungen zur Geistesgeschichte des ausgehenden 18. Jahrhunderts.* Mit einer Einführung von Hans Herzfeld. Berlin: de Gruyter, 1965.

Michelsen, Peter. "Die Erregung des *Mitleid*s durch die Tragödie: Zu Lessings Ansichten über das Trauerspiel im Briefwechsel mit Mendelssohn und Nicolai." *Deutsche Vierteljahrsschrift* 40 (1966): 548–66.

Morgan, Michael L. *Dilemmas in Modern Jewish Thought: The Dialectics of Revelation and History.* Bloomington: Indiana University Press, 1992.

Nolte, Fred O. "Lessing's Correspondence with Mendelssohn and Nicolai, August 31, 1756 to May 14, 1757." *Harvard Studies and Notes in Philology and Literature* 13 (1931): 309–32.

Petsch, Robert. *Lessings Briefwechsel mit Mendelssohn und Nicolai über das Trauerspiel.* Leipzig: Dürr, 1910.

Ricken, Ulrich. "Sprachauffassung und geschichtliches Menschenbild der Aufklärung." In *Logos Semantikos: Studia Linguistica in honorem Eugenio Coseriu,* ed. Horst Geckeler et al., 1: 41–55. Madrid and Berlin: Gredos and de Gruyter, 1981.

Schillemeit, Jost. "Lessings und Mendelssohns Differenz: Zum Briefwechsel über das Trauerspiel (1756/57)." In *Digressionen: Wege zur Aufklärung: Festschrift für Peter Michelsen,* ed. Gotthardt Frühsorge, Klaus Manger, and Friedrich Strack, 79–92. Heidelberg: C. Winter, 1984.

Schulte-Sasse, Jochen, ed. Gotthold Ephraim Lessing, Moses Mendelssohn, and Friedrich Nicolai, *Briefwechsel über das Trauerspiel.* Munich: Winkler, 1972.

Sorkin, David. *Moses Mendelssohn and the Religious Enlightenment.* Berkeley: University of California Press, 1996.

Zac, Sylvain. *Spinoza en Allemagne: Mendelssohn, Lessing et Jacobi.* Paris: Méridiens Klincksieck, 1989.

LITERATURE ON LESSING

Allison, Henry E. *Lessing and the Enlightenment: His Philosophy of Religion and Its Relation to Eighteenth-Century Thought.* Ann Arbor: University of Michigan Press, 1966.

———. "Lessing's Conception of Revelation as Education." *Studies in Eighteenth Century Culture* 4 (1975): 183–93.

———. "Lessing's Spinozistic Exercises." In *Humanität und Dialog: Lessing und Mendelssohn in neuer Sicht,* ed. Ehrhard Bahr, Edward P. Harris, and Laurence G. Lyon, 223–33. Detroit and Munich: Wayne State University Press and edition text + kritik, 1982.

Altmann, Alexander. "Lessing und Jacobi: Das Gespräch über den Spinozismus." In *Die trostvolle Aufklärung: Studien zur Metaphysik und politischen Theorie Moses Mendelssohns,* 50–83. Stuttgart–Bad Cannstatt: Frommann-Holzboog, 1982.

Atkins, Stuart. "Die Ringparabel in Lessings *Nathan der Weise.*" In *Lessings "Nathan der Weise,"* ed. Klaus Bohnen, 155–67. Darmstadt: Wissenschaftliche Buchgesellschaft, 1984.

Bauer, Roger. "Spinoza-Reminiszenzen in Lessings 'Nathan der Weise'?" In *Festschrift für Herbert Kolb,* ed. Klaus Matzel and Hans-Gert Roloff, 1–20. Bern: Peter Lang, 1989.

———. "Du 'Tractatus Theologico-Politicus' à 'Nathan der Weise.'" *Comparatistica* 5 (1993): 55–74.

Bodek, Arnold. "Warum ist Nathan ein Jude? Stimmen aus der Lessing-Literatur." In *Lessing-Mendelssohn-Gedenkbuch,* ed. Deutsch-Israelitischer Gemeindebund Leipzig, 350–76. Leipzig, 1879.

Böhler, Michael. "Lessings 'Nathan der Weise' als Spiel vom Grunde." *Lessing Yearbook* 3 (1971): 128–50.

Bohnen, Klaus. *Geist und Buchstabe: Zum Prinzip des kritischen Verfahrens in Lessings literarästhetischen und theologischen Schriften.* Cologne: Böhlau, 1974.

———, ed. *Lessings "Nathan der Weise."* Darmstadt: Wissenschaftliche Buchgesellschaft, 1984.

Bollacher, Martin. *Der junge Goethe: Studien zur Geschichte des Spinozismus in der Epoche des Sturms und Drangs.* Tübingen: Niemeyer, 1969.

———. *Lessing, Vernunft und Geschichte: Untersuchungen zum Problem religiöser Aufklärung in den Spätschriften.* Tübingen: Niemeyer, 1978.

Brodsky, Claudia. "Lessing and the Drama of the Theory of Tragedy." *Modern Language Notes* 98 (1983): 426–53.

Brodsky Lacour, Claudia. "'Is That Helen?' Contemporary Pictorialism, Lessing, and Kant." *Comparative Literature* 45 (1993): 230–57.

Calhoun, Craig, ed. *Habermas and the Public Sphere.* Cambridge: MIT Press, 1992.

Cassirer, Ernst. "Die Idee der Religion bei Lessing und Mendelssohn." In *Festgabe zum zehnjährigen Bestehen der Akademie für die Wissenschaften des Judentums, 1919–1929,* 22–41. Berlin: Akademie Verlag, 1929.

Danzel, Th. W. *Gotthold Ephraim Lessing, sein Leben und sein Werk.* Vol. 2.2 completed by G. E. Guhrauer based on Danzel's manuscripts. Leipzig: Dyk, 1854.

Demetz, Peter. "Lessings 'Nathan der Weise': Wirklichkeiten und Wirklichkeit." In *Lessings "Nathan der Weise,"* ed. Klaus Bohnen, 168–218. Darmstadt: Wissenschaftliche Buchgesellschaft, 1984.

Fick, Monika. *Lessing-Handbuch: Leben—Werk—Wirkung.* Stuttgart: Metzler, 2000.

Flajole, Edward S. "Lessing's Retrieval of Lost Truths." *PMLA* 74 (1959): 52–66.

Göbel, Helmut. "Die Bildlichkeit im 'Nathan.'" In *Lessings "Nathan der Weise,"* ed. Klaus Bohnen, 229–66. Darmstadt: Wissenschaftliche Buchgesellschaft, 1984.

Goetschel, Willi. Review of *Streitkultur: Strategien des Überzeugens im Werk Lessings,* ed. Wolfram Mauser and Günter Saße. Tübingen: Max Niemeyer, 1993. *Lessing Yearbook* 26 (1994): 145–50.

———. "Gotthold Ephraim Lessing." In *Encyclopedia of the Essay,* ed. Tracy Chevalier, 476–78. London: Fitzroy Dearborn, 1997.

———. "Lessing and the Jews." In *A Companion to Lessing,* ed. Barbara Fischer and Thomas Fox. Rochester, N.Y.: Camden House, forthcoming.

Goldschmidt, Hermann Levin. "Von der Toleranz zur Dialogik—Lessings und Mendelssohns Herausforderung zum christlich-jüdischen Gespräch." In *Aus den Quellen des Judentums: Aufsätze zur Philosophie. Werke,* 5: 145–56. Vienna: Passagen, 2000.

Guthke, Karl S. "Lessing und das Judentum. Rezeption. Dramatik und Kritik. Krypto-Spinozismus." In *Judentum im Zeitalter der Aufklärung: Wolfenbütteler Studien zur Aufklärung.* Vol. 4. Ed. Günter Schulz. Wolfenbüttel: Jacobi, 1977.

Heftrich, Eckhard. *Lessings Aufklärung.* Frankfurt: Klostermann, 1978.

Heller, Peter. "Paduan Coins: Concerning Lessing's Parable of the Three Rings." *Lessing Yearbook* 5 (1973): 163–71.

Hernadi, Paul. "Nathan der Bürger: Lessings Mythos vom aufgeklärten Kaufmann." In *Lessings "Nathan der Weise,"* ed. Klaus Bohnen, 341–49. Darmstadt: Wissenschaftliche Buchgesellschaft, 1984.

Hodge, James L. "The Parable in *Nathan* as a Gambit." *The Germanic Review* 55 (1980): 14–21.

Hoops, Johannes. "Lessings Verhältnis zu Spinoza." *Archiv für das Studium der neueren Sprachen und Litteraturen* 86 (1891): 1–28.

Jaspers, Karl. *Die grossen Philosophen: Nachlass.* Ed. Hans Saner. Munich: R. Piper, 1981.

Kahn, Ludwig. "The Changing Image of the Jew: Nathan the Wise and Shylock." In *Identity and Ethos: A Festschrift for Sol Liptzin on the Occasion of His Eighty-fifth Birthday,* ed. Mark H. Gelber, 235–52. New York: Peter Lang, 1986.

Koebner, Thomas. "*Nathan der Weise:* Ein polemisches Stück?" In *Interpretationen: Lessings Dramen,* 138–207. Stuttgart: Reclam, 1987.

Kommerell, Max. *Lessing und Aristoteles: Untersuchungen über die Theorie der Tragödie.* 3rd ed. Frankfurt: Klostermann, 1960.

Kowalik, Jill Anne. "*Nathan der Weise* as Lessing's Work of Mourning." *Lessing Yearbook* 21 (1989): 1–17.

Kühne-Bertram, Gudrun. "Aspekte der Geschichte und der Bedeutungen des Begriffs "pragmatisch" in den philosophischen Wissenschaften des ausgehenden 18. und des 19. Jahrhunderts." *Archiv für Begriffsgeschichte* 27 (1983): 158–86.

Lehrer, Mark. "Lessing's Economic Comedy." *Seminar* 20 (1984): 79–94.

Leventhal, Robert S. "The Parable as Performance: Interpretation, Cultural Transmission, and Political Strategy in Lessing's *Nathan der Weise*." *German Quarterly* 61 (1987): 502–27.

Maschler, Chaninah. "On the Wisdom of Nathan." *Interpretation* 15 (1987): 347–65.

McCarthy, John. *Crossing Boundaries: A Theory and History of Essay Writing in German, 1680–1815*. Philadelphia: University of Philadelphia Press, 1989.

———. "'Das sicherste Kennzeichen einer gesunden, nervösen Staatsverfassung': Lessing und die Pressefreiheit." In *Lessing und die Toleranz,* ed. Peter Freimark, Franklin Kopitzsch, and Helga Slessarev, 225–44. Detroit and Munich: Wayne State University Press and edition text und kritik, 1986.

Michelsen, Peter. "Die 'wahren Taten' der Freimaurer: Lessings 'Ernst und Falk.'" In *Der unruhige Bürger: Studien zu Lessing und zur Literatur des 18. Jahrhunderts,* 137–59. Würzburg: Königshausen & Neumann, 1990.

Modlinger, Samuel. *Lessing's Verdienste um das Judenthum*. Frankfurt: Selbstverlag, 1869.

Mufti, Aamir. "Secularism and Minority: Elements of a Critique." *Social Text* 45 (1995): 75–96.

Newman, Jay. "The Parable of the Three Rings in *Nathan der Weise*." *Mosaic* 12 (1978–79): 1–8.

Nirenberg, Morton. "The Opal: Lessing's Ring Re-Examined." *Modern Language Notes* 85 (1970): 686–96.

Nisbet, H. B. "Zur Funktion des Geheimnisses in Lessings *Ernst und Falk*." In *Lessing und die Toleranz,* ed. Peter Freimark, Franklin Kopitzsch, and Helga Slessarev, 291–309. Detroit and Munich: Wayne State University Press and edition text und kritik, 1986.

Pätzold, Detlev. "Lessing und Spinoza: Zum Beginn des Pantheismus-Streits in der deutschen Literatur des 18. Jahrhunderts." In *Aufklärung-Gesellschaft-Kritik: Studien zur Philosophie der Aufklärung,* ed. Manfred Buhr and Wolfgang Förster, 298–355. Berlin: Akademie-Verlag, 1985.

———. *Spinoza—Aufklärung—Idealismus: Die Substanz der Moderne*. Frankfurt: Peter Lang, 1995.

Quapp, Erwin. *Lessings Theologie statt Jacobis "Spinozismus": Eine Interpretation der "Erziehung des Menschengeschlechts" auf Grundlage der Formel "hen ego kai pan."* Bern: Peter Lang, 1992.

Rosenzweig, Franz. "Lessing's Nathan." In *Zweistromland: Kleinere Schriften zu Glauben und Denken. Gesammelte Schriften,* 3: 449–53. Dordrecht; Boston: Martinus Nijhoff, 1984.

Schings, Hans-Jürgen. *Der mitleidigste Mensch ist der beste Mensch: Poetik des Mitleids von Lessing bis Büchner.* Munich: Beck, 1980.

Schlütter, Hans-Jürgen. "'. . . als ob die Wahrheit Münze wäre': Zu *Nathan der Weise* III, 6." *Lessing Yearbook* 10 (1978): 65–74.

Schmoldt, Hans. *Der Spinozastreit.* Würzburg: Triltsch, 1938.

Schneider, Heinrich. "Lessing und die Freimaurer." In *Lessing: Zwölf biographische Studien,* 166–97. Bern: Francke, 1951.

Schneiders, Werner. *Hoffnung auf Vernunft: Aufklärungsphilosophie in Deutschland.* Hamburg: Meiner, 1990.

———. *Das Zeitalter der Aufklärung.* Munich: C. H. Beck, 1997.

Seeba, Hinrich C. *Die Liebe zur Sache: Öffentliches und privates Interesse in Lessings Dramen.* Untersuchungen zur deutschen Literaturgeschichte, vol. 9. Tübingen: Niemeyer, 1973.

Shell, Marc. "'What Is Truth?' Lessing's Numismatics and Heidegger's Alchemy." In *Money, Language, and Thought: Literary and Philosophical Economies from the Medieval to the Modern Era.* Berkeley: University of California Press, 1982.

Simon, Ralf. "Nathans Argumentationsverfahren: Konsequenzen der Fiktionalisierung von Theorie in Lessings Drama *Nathan der Weise.*" *Deutsche Vierteljahrsschrift* 45 (1991): 609–35.

Slessarev, Helga. "Nathan der Weise und Adam Smith." In *Nation und Gelehrtenrepublik: Lessing im europäischen Zusammenhang,* ed. Wilfried Barner and Albert Reh, 248–56. Detroit and München: Wayne State University Press and edition + kritik, 1984.

Stiening, Gideon. "'Werden Sie lieber ganz sein Freund': Zur Bedeutung von Lessings Spinoza-Rezeption." In *Spinoza im Deutschland des 18. Jahrhunderts: Zur Erinnerung an Hans-Christian Lucas (1942–1997),* ed. Eva Schürmann, Norbert Waszek, and Frank Weinrich, 193–220. Stuttgart–Bad Cannstadt: Frommann-Holzboog, 2002.

Stockum, Th. C. van. *Spinoza—Jacobi—Lessing: Ein Beitrag zur Geschichte der deutschen Literatur und Philosophie im 18. Jahrhundert.* Groningen: P. Noordhoff, 1916.

Strohschneiders-Kohrs, Ingrid. *Vernunft als Weisheit: Studien zum späten Lessing.* Tübingen: Niemeyer, 1991.

Thielicke, Helmut. *Vernunft und Offenbarung.* Studien zur Religionsphilosophie Lessings. Gütersloh: Bertelsmann, 1936.

Timm, Hermann. *Gott und die Freiheit: Studien zur Religionsphilosophie der Goethezeit.* Vol. 1, *Die Spinozarenaissance,* 106–28. Frankfurt: Klostermann, 1974.

Wellbery, David. *Lessing's "Laocoon": Semiotics and Aesthetics in the Age of Reason.* Cambridge: Cambridge University Press, 1984.

Werner, Hans-Georg. "Zum Verhältnis zwischen 'öffentlicher' und 'privater' Sphäre im dichterischen Weltbild Lessings." In *Humanität und Dialog: Lessing und Mendelssohn in neuer Sicht,* ed. Ehrhard Bahr, Edward P. Harris, and Lawrence G. Lyon, 83–102. Detroit and Munich: Wayne State University Press and edition text und kritik, 1982.

Wessels, Hans-Friedrich. *Lessings "Nathan der Weise": Seine Wirkungsgeschichte bis zum Ende der Goethezeit.* Königstein: Athenäum, 1979.

Wild, Henrik de. *Tradition und Neubeginn: Lessings Orientierung an der europäischen Tradition.* Rodopi: Amsterdam, 1986.

Wucherpfennig, Wolf. "Nathan, der weise Händler." *Jahrbuch für Internationale Germanistik* 8.4. Akten des VI. Internationalen Germanistenkongresses. Basel 1980. Ed. H. Rupp and H.-G. Roloff, 57–64. Bern: Peter Lang, 1980.

Zymner, Rüdiger. "'Der Stein war ein Opal . . .': Eine versteckte Kunst-Apotheose in Lessings morgenländischer 'Ringparabel'?" *Lessing Yearbook* 24 (1992): 77–96.

LITERATURE ON HEINE

Adorno, Theodor W. "Heine the Wound." In *Notes to Literature,* trans. Shierry Weber Nicholsen, 1: 80–85. New York: Columbia University Press, 1991.

Arendt, Hannah. "The Jew as Pariah: A Hidden Tradition." In *The Jew as Pariah: Jewish Identity and Politics in the Modern Age,* ed. Ron H. Feldman, 67–90. New York: Grove, 1978.

Avineri, Shlomo. *Moses Hess: Prophet of Communism and Zionism.* New York: New York University Press, 1985.

Bollacher, Martin. "Aufgeklärter Pantheismus: Die Deutung der Geschichte in Heines Schrift *On the History of Religion and Philosophy in Germany.*" In *Heinrich Heine: Artistik und Engagement,* ed. Wolfgang Kuttenkeuler, 144–86. Stuttgart: Metzler, 1977.

Butler, E. M. *The Saint-Simonian Religion in Germany: A Study of the Young German Movement.* New York: Fertig, 1968.

Cohen, Hermann. "Heinrich Heine und das Judentum." In *Jüdische Schriften,* ed. Bruno Strauss, 2: 2–44. Berlin: Schwetschke, 1924.

Cook, Roger F. *By the Rivers of Babylon: Heinrich Heine's Late Songs and Reflections.* Detroit: Wayne State University Press, 1998.

Elbogen, Ismar. "Briefe um Heinrich Heine: Adolf Strodtmanns Anfrage an Leopold Zunz." *Zeitschrift für die Geschichte der Juden in Deutschland* 8 (1938): 40–51.

Espagne, Michel. "Heinrich Heine und Moses Heß." In *Heinrich Heine, 1797–1856: Schriften aus dem Karl-Marx-Haus 26,* 80–97. Trier: Karl-Marx-Haus, 1981.

Friedl, Herwig. "Heinrich Heine und Friedrich Nietzsche." In *Heinrich Heine im Spannungsfeld von Literatur und Wissenschaft,* ed. Wilhelm Gössmann and Manfred Windfuhr, 195–214. Symposium anlässlich der Benennung der Universität Düsseldorf nach Heinrich Heine. N.p.: Hobbing, 1990.

Gelber, Mark H. "Heinrich Heine und das Judentum: Gestern und heute." In *Heinrich Heine und das Judentum,* ed. Peter Grab, 8–13. Augsburg: Presse-Druck, 1994.

Goldschmidt, Hermann Levin. "Heine und Freud." In *"Der Rest bleibt": Aufsätze zum Judentum. Werke,* 4: 197–209. Passagen: Vienna, 1997.

Harich, Wolfgang. "Heinrich Heine und das Schulgeheimnis der deutschen Philosophie." In Heinrich Heine, *On the History of Religion and Philosophy in Germany,* ed. Wolfgang Harich, 7–52. Frankfurt: Insel, 1966.

Kircher, Hartmut. *Heinrich Heine und das Judentum.* Bonn: Bouvier, 1973.

Krüger, Eduard. *Heine und Hegel: Dichtung, Philosophie und Politik bei Heine.* Kronberg Ts.: Scriptor, 1977.

Lefebvre, Jean Pierre. *Der gute Trommler: Heines Beziehung zu Hegel.* Trans. Peter Schöttler. Hamburg: Hoffmann und Campe, 1986.

———. "Heine, Hegel et Spinoza." *Cahiers Spinoza* 4 (1982–83): 211–29.

Malter, Rudolf. "Heine und Kant." *Heine Jahrbuch* 18 (1979): 35–64.

Motekat, Helmut. "Hegel and Heine." In *A Hegel Symposium,* ed. D. C. Travis, 65–79. Austin: University of Texas, 1962.

Niehoff, Maren R. "Heine und die jüdische Tradition." In *"Ich Narr des Glücks" Heinrich Heine, 1797–1856: Bilder einer Ausstellung,* ed. Joseph A. Kruse, 318–24. Stuttgart: Metzler, 1997.

———. "Zunz's Concept of Haggadah as an Expression of Jewish Spirituality." *Year Book of the Leo Baeck Institute* 43 (1998): 3–24.

Pepperle, Heinz. "Heinrich Heine als Philosoph." In *Heinrich Heine: Ästhetisch-politische Profile,* ed. Gerhard Höhn, 155–75. Frankfurt: Suhrkamp, 1991.

Preisendanz, Wolfgang. "Memoria als Dimension lyrischer Selbstpräsentation in Heines Jehuda Ben Halevy." In *Memoria: Vergessen und Erinnern,* ed. Anselm Haverkamp and Renate Lachmann, 338–48. Poetik und Hermeneutik, vol. 15. Munich: Wilhelm Fink, 1993.

Robertson, Ritchie. *Heine.* London: Halban, 1988.

Sammons, Jeffrey L. *Heinrich Heine: A Modern Biography.* Princeton: Princeton University Press, 1979.

Steinecke, Hartmut. "'Wir stammen von Schlemihl': Jüdische Dichter-Bilder in Heines Spätwerk von Jehuda ben Halevy bis Rabbi Faibisch." *Aufklärung und Skepsis: Internationaler Heine-Kongress,* ed. Joseph Kruse, Bernd Witte, and Karin Füllner, 303–21. Stuttgart: Metzler, 1999.

Stern, J. P. *Re-interpretations: Seven Studies in Nineteenth-Century German Literature.* New York: Basic Books, 1964.

Sternberger, Dolf. *Heinrich Heine und die Abschaffung der Sünde.* Hamburg: Claassen, 1972.

Tabak, Israel. *Judaic Lore in Heine.* Baltimore: Johns Hopkins University Press, 1948.

Taillandier, Saint-René. "Heine (Henri)." In *Biographie universelle ancienne et moderne,* ed. Louis-Gabriel Michaud, 19: 54–58. Paris: Delagrave, n.d.

Werner, Michael, ed. *Begegnungen mit Heine: Berichte der Zeitgenossen.* Vol. 2. Hamburg: Hoffmann und Campe, 1973.

Wieland, Wolfgang. "Heinrich Heine und die Philosophie." In *Heinrich Heine,* ed. Helmut Koopmann, 133–55. Wege der Forschung, vol. 289. Darmstadt: Wissenschaftliche Buchgesellschaft, 1975.

Windfuhr, Manfred. "Heine und Hegel: Rezeption und Produktion." In *Internationaler Heine-Kongreß 1972*, ed. Manfred Windfuhr, 261–80. Hamburg: Hoffmann und Campe, 1975.

Wolf, Ruth. "Versuch über Heines 'Jehuda ben Halevy.'" *Heine Jahrbuch* 18 (1979): 84–98.

GENERAL LITERATURE

Aarsleff, Hans. "The Tradition of Condillac: The Problem of the Origin of Language in the Eighteenth Century and the Debate in the Berlin Academy before Herder." In *From Locke to Saussure: Essays on the Study of Language and Intellectual History*, 146–209. London: Athlohe and University of Minnesota Press, 1982.

Althusser, Louis, and Étienne Balibar. *Reading Capital.* Trans. Ben Brewster. 2nd ed. London: Verso, 1983.

Asemissen, Hermann Ulrich. *Die Malkunst: Aspekte eines Berufsbildes.* Frankfurt: Fischer, 1988.

Assmann, Jan. *Moses the Egyptian: The Memory of Egypt in Western Monotheism.* Cambridge: Harvard University Press, 1997.

Augustine, St. *Concerning the City of God against the Pagans.* Trans. Henry Bettenson. Penguin: London, 1984.

Bein, Alex. *Die Judenfrage: Biographie eines Weltproblems.* Stuttgart: Deutsche Verlagsanstalt, 1980.

Beiser, Frederick C. *The Fate of Reason: German Philosophy from Kant to Fichte.* Cambridge: Harvard University Press, 1987.

Bloch, Olivier. *Le matérialisme.* Paris: Presses universitaires de France, 1985.

Blumenberg, Hans. "Selbsterhaltung und Beharrung: Zur Konstitution der neuzeitlichen Rationalität." In *Subjektivität und Selbsterhaltung: Beiträge zur Diagnose der Moderne*, ed. Hans Ebeling, 144–297. Frankfurt: Suhrkamp, 1976.

Breuer, Mordechai, and Michael Graetz. *Deutsch-Jüdische Geschichte in der Neuzeit.* Vol. 1, *1600–1780*. Munich: Beck, 1996.

Brodsky Lacour, Claudia. *Lines of Thought: Discourse, Architectonics, and the Origin of Modern Philosophy.* Durham, N.C.: Duke University Press, 1996.

Buber, Martin. *On the Bible: Eighteen Studies*, ed. Nahum N. Glatzer. New York: Schocken, 1968.

Cassirer, Ernst. *Das Erkenntnisproblem in der Philosophie und Wissenschaft der neueren Zeit.* Rpt. 3rd ed. 1922. Vol. 2. Darmstadt: Wissenschaftliche Buchgesellschaft, 1974.

———. *Die Philosophie der Aufklärung.* 3rd ed. Tübingen: Mohr, 1973.

Cohen, Hermann. "Ein Bekenntnis in der Judenfrage." In *Der Berliner Antisemitismusstreit*, ed. Walter Boehlich, 124–49. Frankfurt: Insel, 1965.

———. *Religion of Reason Out of the Sources of Judaism.* Trans. Simon Kaplan. Atlanta: Scholars, 1995.

Condillac, Etienne Bonnot de. *An Essay on the Origin of Human Knowledge.* Trans. Thomas Nugent. London: J. Nourse, 1756. Rpt. New York: AMS Press, 1974.

Ebeling, Hans, ed. *Subjektivität und Selbsterhaltung: Beiträge zur Diagnose der Moderne.* Frankfurt: Suhrkamp, 1976.

Freud, Sigmund. *Studienausgabe.* Frankfurt: Fischer, 1969–75.

Funkenstein, Amos. *Perceptions of Jewish History.* Los Angeles: University of California Press, 1993.

Gay, Peter. *The Enlightenment: An Interpretation: The Rise of Modern Paganism.* New York: Knopf, 1966.

Goethe, Johann Wolfgang von. *Sämtliche Werke,* ed. Ernst Beutler. Zurich and Munich: Artemis and Deutscher Taschenbuch Verlag, 1977.

Goetschel, Willi. *Constituting Critique: Kant's Writing as Critical Praxis.* Durham, N.C.: Duke University Press, 1994.

———. "The Differential Character of Traditions." *Telos* 95 (1993): 161–70.

———. "'Jüdische Philosophie'—ein Querverweis." *Babylon* 14–15 (1994–95): 119–32.

———. "Kritik und Frieden: Zur literarischen Strategie der Schrift 'Zum Ewigen Frieden.'" In *Proceedings of the Eighth International Kant Congress,* ed. Hoke Robinson, 2: 821–27. Milwaukee: Marquette University Press, 1995.

———. "Models of Difference and Alterity: Moses Mendelssohn, Hermann Cohen, Franz Rosenzweig, Martin Buber, and Hermann Levin Goldschmidt." In *The German-Jewish Dilemma: From Enlightenment to Shoa,* ed. Edward Timms and Andrea Hammel, 25–38. Lewiston, N.Y.: Edwin Mellen Press, 1999.

Goldschmidt, Hermann Levin. "Stoa Heute." In *Aus den Quellen des Judentums: Aufsätze zur Philosophie. Werke,* 5: 21–83. Vienna: Passagen, 2000.

———. *Das Vermächtnis des deutschen Judentums. Werke,* vol. 2. Vienna: Passagen, 1994.

Goodman, Dena. "Public Sphere and Private Life: Toward a Synthesis of Current Historiographical Approaches to the Old Regime." *History and Theory* 31 (1992): 1–20.

Habermas, Jürgen. *The Structural Transformation of the Public Sphere: An Inquiry into a Category of Bourgeois Society.* Trans. Thomas Burger with the assistance of Frederick Lawrence. 1962. Cambridge: MIT Press, 1989.

Ha-Levi, Jehuda. *Sefer Hakusari, Das Buch Kusari.* 5th ed. Trans. and ed. David Cassel. Berlin: Louis Lamm, 1922.

Hegel, Georg Wilhelm Friedrich. *Hegel's Lectures on the History of Philosophy.* Trans. E. S. Haldane and F. H. Simson. 1896. Rpt. London: Routledge and Kegan Paul and New York: Humanities Press, 1963.

———. *Lectures on the History of Philosophy: The Lectures of 1825–1826,* vol. 3, ed. R. F. Brown, trans. R. F. Brown and J. M. Stewart with the assistance of H. S. Harris. Berkeley: University of California Press, 1990.

———. *Vorlesungen über die Geschichte der Philosophie 3. Werke,* vol. 20. Frankfurt: Suhrkamp, 1986.

Henrich, Dieter. "The Basic Structure of Modern Philosophy." *Cultural Hermeneutics* 2 (1974): 1–18.

Hobbes, Thomas. *Leviathan*. Ed. C. B. Macpherson. Harmondsworth: Penguin, 1968.

———. *On the Citizen*. Trans. Richard Tuck and Michael Silverthorne. Cambridge and New York: Cambridge University Press, 1998.

Husserl, Edmund. *Die Krisis der europäischen Wissenschaften und die transzendentale Phänomenologie*. Hamburg: Meiner, 1977.

Jacobi, Friedrich Heinrich. *Schriften zum Spinozastreit*. Ed. Klaus Hammacher and Irmgard-Maria Piske. Friedrich Heinrich Jacobi. *Werke. Gesamtausgabe*. Vol. 1. Hamburg and Stuttgart: Meiner and Frommann-Holzboog, 1998.

James, William. *Pragmatism: A New Name for Some Old Ways of Thinking and The Meaning of Truth: A Sequel to Pragmatism*. Cambridge: Harvard University Press, 1975.

Kant, Immanuel. *Anthropology from a Pragmatic Point of View*. Trans. Mary J. Gregor. The Hague: Martinus Nijhoff, 1974.

———. *Briefwechsel*. Ed. Otto Schöndörffer and Rudolf Malter. Hamburg: Felix Meiner, 1986.

———. *Foundations of the Metaphysics of Morals*. Trans. Lewis White Beck. New York: Macmillan, 1990.

———. *The Metaphysics of Morals*. Trans. Mary Gregor. Cambridge: Cambridge University Press, 1996.

———. *Werke*. Ed. Wilhelm Weischedel. Frankfurt: Insel/Suhrkamp, 1964.

Kondylis, Panajotis. *Die Aufklärung im Rahmen des neuzeitlichen Rationalismus*. Munich: Deutscher Taschenbuchverlag, 1986.

Koselleck, Reinhart. *Critique and Crisis: Enlightenment and the Pathogenesis of Modern Society*. 1959. Cambridge: MIT Press, 1988.

———. *Futures Past: On the Semantics of Historical Time*. Trans. Keith Tribe. Cambridge, Mass.: MIT Press, 1985.

Lange, Frederick Albert. *The History of Materialism and Criticism of Its Present Importance*. Trans. Ernest Chester Thomas. New York: Humanities Press, 1950.

La Vopa, Anthony J. "Conceiving a Public: Ideas and Society in Eighteenth-Century Europe." *Journal of Modern History* 64 (1992): 79–116.

Lexikon der Philosophie. Founded by Heinrich Schmidt and continued by Georgi Schischkoff. Stuttgart: Kröner, 1974.

Macpherson, C. B. *The Political Theory of Possessive Individualism: Hobbes to Locke*. Oxford: Oxford University Press, 1962.

Malter, Rudolf, ed. *Immanuel Kant in Rede und Gespräch*. Hamburg: Meiner, 1990.

Manheim Ernst. *Aufklärung und öffentliche Meinung: Studien zur Soziologie der Öffentlichkeit im 18. Jahrhundert*. Ed. Norbert Schindler. 1930. Stuttgart–Bad Cannstatt: Frommann-Holzboog, 1979.

Müller, Johannes. *Handbuch der Physiologie des Menschen*. Coblenz: Hölscher, 1834–40.

O'Neill, Onora. *Constructions of Reason: Explorations of Kant's Practical Philosophy.* Cambridge: Cambridge University Press, 1989.

Peirce, Charles S. *Selected Writings.* Ed. Philip P. Wiener. New York: Dover, 1966.

Reimarus, Hermann Samuel. *Apologie oder Schutzschrift für die vernünftigen Verehrer Gottes.* Ed. Gerhard Alexander. Frankfurt: Suhrkamp, 1972.

Römer, Nils. *Tradition und Akkulturation: Zum Sprachwandel der Juden in Deutschland zur Zeit der Haskalah.* Münster: Waxmann, 1995.

Rorty, Richard. *Consequences of Pragmatism.* Minneapolis: University of Minnesota Press, 1982.

———. *Contingency, Irony, and Solidarity.* Cambridge: Cambridge University Press, 1989.

———. *Hoffnung statt Erkenntnis: Eine Einführung in die pragmatische Philosophie.* Vienna: Passagen, 1994.

Rosenzweig, Franz. "Einleitung." In Hermann Cohen, *Jüdische Schriften,* ed. Bruno Strauss, 1: xiii–lxix. Berlin: Schwetschke, 1924.

———. "Über den Vortrag Hermann Cohens 'Das Verhältnis Spinozas zum Judentum.'" In *Zweistromland: Kleinere Schriften zu Glauben und Denken: Gesammelte Schriften,* ed. Reinhold Mayer and Annemarie Mayer, 3: 165–67. Dordrecht: Nijhoff, 1984.

Rousseau, Jean-Jacques. *Discourse on the Origin of Inequality.* In *The Basic Writings.* Trans. Donald A. Cress, 25–109. Indianapolis and Cambridge: Hackett, 1987.

Saine, Thomas P. *The Problem of Being Modern, or The German Pursuit of Enlightenment from Leibniz to the French Revolution.* Detroit: Wayne State University Press, 1997.

Scheler, Max. *Gesammelte Werke.* Vol. 9. Ed. Manfred S. Frings. Bern: Francke, 1976.

Schmidt, James, ed. *What Is Enlightenment? Eighteenth-Century Answers and Twentieth-Century Questions.* Berkeley: University of California Press, 1996.

Schmitt, Carl. *Roman Catholicism and Political Form.* Trans. G. L. Ulmen. 1923. Westport, Conn.: Greenwood, 1996.

Scholem, Gershom. "Revelation and Tradition as Religious Categories in Judaism." In *The Messianic Idea in Judaism,* 282–303. New York: Schocken, 1995.

Schulte-Sasse, Jochen. "Einleitung: Kritisch-rationale und literarische Öffentlichkeit." In *Aufklärung und literarische Öffentlichkeit,* ed. Christa Bürger and Peter Bürger, 12–38. Frankfurt: Suhrkamp, 1980.

———. "Das Konzept bürgerlich-literarischer Öffentlichkeit und die historischen Gründe seines Zerfalls." In *Aufklärung und literarische Öffentlichkeit,* ed. Christa Bürger and Peter Bürger, 83–115. Frankfurt: Suhrkamp, 1980.

Simmel, Georg. *The Sociology of Georg Simmel.* Ed. Kurt Wolff. Glencoe, Ill.: Free Press, 1950.

Smith, Adam. *An Inquiry into the Nature and Causes of the Wealth of Nations.* Ed. Edwin Cannan. Chicago: University of Chicago Press, 1976.

Spaemann, Robert. "Bürgerliche Ethik und nichtteleologische Ontologie." In *Subjektivität und Selbsterhaltung: Beiträge zur Diagnose der Moderne,* ed. Hans Ebeling, 76–96. Frankfurt: Suhrkamp, 1976.

Stein, Ludwig. "Die neupositivistische Bewegung (Der 'Pragmatismus' von William James)." In *Philosophische Strömungen der Gegenwart,* 33–75. Stuttgart: Ferdinand Enke, 1908.

———. "The Neo-Positivistic Movement." In *Philosophical Currents of the Present Day,* trans. Shishirkumar Maitra, 1: 44–150. Calcutta: The University of Calcutta, 1918.

———. "Versuch einer Geschichte des Terminus 'Pragmatismus.'" *Archiv für systematische Philosophie,* n.s., 14 (1908): 143–88.

Stern, Selma. *Der preussische Staat und die Juden.* Tübingen: J. C. B. Mohr (Paul Siebeck), 1971.

Vallée, Gérard, ed. *The Spinoza Conversations between Lessing and Jacobi.* Lanham, Md.: University Press of America, 1988.

Weinrib, Ernest J. "Publicness and Private Law." In *Proceedings of the Eighth International Kant Congress,* ed. Hoke Robinson, 1: 191–201. Milwaukee: Marquette University Press, 1995.

Wicki-Vogt, Maja. *Simone Weil: Eine Logik des Absurden.* Bern: Haupt, 1983.

Wolf [Wohlwill], Immanuel. "Ueber den Begriff einer Wissenschaft des Judenthums." *Zeitschrift für die Wissenschaft des Judenthums* 1 (1823): 1–24.

Wolff, Christian. *Rede über die praktische Philosophie der Chinesen.* Hamburg: Meiner, 1985.

Zunz, Leopold. *Die gottesdienstlichen Vorträge der Juden historisch entwickelt.* Rpt. 2nd ed. Hildesheim: Olms, 1966.

INDEX